The Quest for Authenticity

The Thought of Reb Simhah Bunim

THE QUEST FOR AUTHENTICITY

THE THOUGHT OF REB SIMHAH BUNIM

MICHAEL ROSEN

URIM PUBLICATIONS
Jerusalem • New York

The Quest for Authenticity: The Thought of Reb Simhah Bunim

by Michael Rosen

Copyright © 2008 by Michael Rosen

All rights reserved. No part of this book may be used or reproduced in any manner whatsoever without written permission from the copyright owner, except in the case of brief quotations embodied in reviews and articles.

Printed at Hemed Press, Israel. First Edition.

ISBN-13: 978-965-524-003-0

ISBN-10: 965-524-003-7

Urim Publications

P.O. Box 52287, Jerusalem 91521 Israel

Lambda Publishers Inc.

3709 13th Avenue Brooklyn, New York 11218 U.S.A.

Tel: 718-972-5449 Fax: 718-972-6307, mh@ejudaica.com

www.UrimPublications.com

CONTENTS

ADDENDA

This woodcut picture of R. Simhah Bunim of Przysucha, which was in the Berson collection near Warsaw, was commissioned by Berko and Tamar Bergson of Warsaw, c. 1824. The artist depicted both Hasidic rebbes of Poland, R. Simhah Bunim of Przysucha and R. Meir ha-Levi of Apta, when they were in Warsaw. The image was confirmed by elderly Hasidim who had known R. Simhah Bunim.

From Rabinowitz, Zvi Meir. "R. Bunim," *Sinai* 82 (1978): 82–86.

PREFACE

WHEN I FIRST BEGAN this book, I was aware of the dangers of romanticization, of projecting my own agenda onto the Przysucha (pronounced Pe-shis-kha) school of Hasidism. As a result, I tried to give the quotations their own voice rather than mine, even though I knew that I could only understand Przysucha Hasidism within a radius of my own experience. The initial result was a book that was almost inaccessible even to the most devoted.

I wanted to write a book of interest to the academic; but more importantly, I wanted to bring Przysucha Hasidism to the attention of the world. I hope that I have achieved both aims with this book. The academic can skip the first chapter and a half, while I hope that lay readers will be so captivated that they will continue to learn the Torah of Przysucha. The reward will be theirs.

מודה אני לפניך או״א ששמת חלקי מיושבי בית מדרש פרשיסחאי.

I wish to express my gratitude to Professor Moshe Idel for his guidance and to Peter Burns, who has engaged and accompanied me throughout the many stages of this book. I wish to thank Elisha Mallard, whose depth and literary gifts have added so much. May God continue to smile upon him. I wish to thank Jonathan Chipman, Bettyrose Nelson, and my dear wife Gilla, who copy-edited the manuscript. I would like to thank my family for having put up with the fact that during the last few years, whenever someone gave a *devar Torah* on Friday night, I invariably added, "Yes, but R. Bunim says...."

Last year, I had occasion to visit the Hebrew University library. There was an important quote in the name of the Yehudi in a book called *Bikkurei Aviv* by R. Bunim's pupil, R. Yaacov Aryeh of Radzymin, that I had to check. I found the quote in the book, which had been published in London in 1947. I looked in the back for an index to see whether there were other relevant quotes. There was no index. Instead, I found a list of donors who had made the publication possible. The first name mentioned was that of my late father, Kopul Rosen.

LINEAGE OF THE PSHISKHA SCHOOL

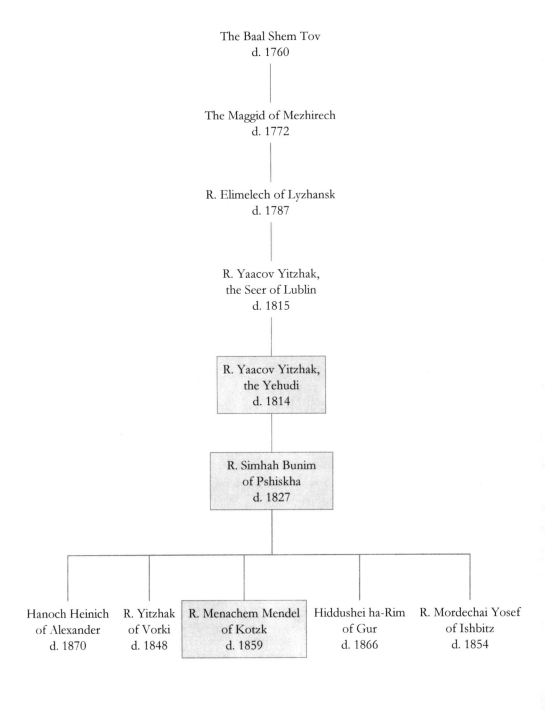

The Baal Shem Tov
d. 1760

The Maggid of Mezhirech
d. 1772

R. Elimelech of Lyzhansk
d. 1787

R. Yaacov Yitzhak,
the Seer of Lublin
d. 1815

R. Yaacov Yitzhak,
the Yehudi
d. 1814

R. Simhah Bunim
of Pshiskha
d. 1827

Hanoch Heinich
of Alexander
d. 1870

R. Yitzhak
of Vorki
d. 1848

R. Menachem Mendel
of Kotzk
d. 1859

Hiddushei ha-Rim
of Gur
d. 1866

R. Mordechai Yosef
of Ishbitz
d. 1854

PART I

INTRODUCTION

Religion itself, no matter how profound and sublime it may be, is, in the last analysis, only a vessel intended to contain the absolute – the vestment so to speak, of the absolute. And it is necessary to know how to distinguish the sacred treasure from the vessel which contains it; otherwise one risks falling into idolatry.

But men do not know how, or rather, do not wish, to make this distinction. Idols are to them – why one does not know – nearer, more comprehensible, than God.

Lev Shestov (Russian religious philosopher, 1866–1938)

The Essential Themes of Przysucha

AT THE BEGINNING of the nineteenth century (circa 1822), at a wedding in Ustilug (Austila), Poland, an attempt was made by the majority of the hasidic leaders of Poland and all of the hasidic leaders of Galicia to excommunicate a hasidic movement called *Przysucha* (Yiddish: *Pshiskha*, pronounced Pe-shis-kha).

The main hasidic dignitary at the wedding was Avraham Yehoshua Heschel, the rebbe of Apta. During the course of the festivities, a public debate was held in which the protagonists appealed to him to decide whether to outlaw Przysucha or not. The following vignette was related by one of those who wanted to see Przysucha excommunicated.

A certain person who was a hasid of the holy rebbe of Apta gave testimony that… his rebbe had given him as a talisman (lit., *segula*) a silken belt (i.e., a *gartel*) white as snow that he should wear continuously. And near his house there dwelt a neighbor who was a hasid of Przysucha, who used to come to his house and greatly mocked the talisman. And once, when nobody was around, the neighbor came and took the belt and smeared it all over with black paint, and afterwards was full of mirth… And many other opponents brought similar examples as to how the glory of the zaddikim of the generation was demeaned in the eyes of the hasidim of Przysucha; and that their teacher had definitely taught them thus, for only his way was the way of truth.[1]

What is being reflected here is not a one-time event but rather an attitude of non-conformity designed to provoke. But why?

At this time "there developed a new type of hasid – the sharp young man – who left his wife and family"[2] and found his way to Przysucha. There, spending weeks or months on end with R. Simhah Bunim, engrossed in the study of Torah and the hasidic way, he was able to come in contact with that aspect of himself without which life is not life. R. Bunim believed that within every Jew there was the assurance of a "treasure," dependent solely upon the capacity of each individual to dig and uncover it for himself.

This was nothing short of a revolution – completely within the framework of traditional Judaism, yet uncompromisingly aimed against the complacency into which the hasidic establishment had sunk. Hasidism as a movement was inaugurated by men of spirit, charismatic leaders who shared many traits similar to those found in the romantic movement emerging at roughly the same period[3] throughout Western Europe: **a respect for strong emotions, spontaneity, imagination and creativity, freedom from classical constraint in expression, and an out-and-out rebellion against social convention.** But within the span of a mere three generations, Hasidism had begun to resemble the rigid, fixed approach against which it had so recently fought to liberate itself. This was the moment for Eastern European Jewry to rediscover its soul.

---

[1] *Meir Einei ha-Golah*, §151; cf. §§141, 150.

[2] Aaron Ze'ev Aescoly, *Hasidut be-Folin,* edited by D. Assaf (Jerusalem: 1999), 80, has the additional phrase "without saying goodbye." But see Mordecai Wilensky, *Hasidim u-mitnaggedim* (Jerusalem: 1970), 2:357, who quotes Joseph Levenstein's letter to Dubnow stating that this is exactly what R. Bunim tells his hasidim not to do.

[3] See below, Addendum E.

During the second half of the eighteenth century, Hasidism slowly began making its way from its origins in the Ukraine into Poland as the students of R. Dov Baer, the Maggid of Miedzyrcz (Mezeritch; 1704–1774), began to infiltrate Galicia and Poland. But it only succeeded in reaching the level of a mass movement in Poland by the end of the eighteenth century due for the most part to the inspirational leadership of R. Jacob Isaac, the *Hozeh* (Seer) of Lublin (1740–1815). The Seer was a pupil of R. Elimelech of Lyzhansk,[4] who had broken with his teacher during the latter's lifetime and set up his own hasidic court in Lublin.[5] [6] After R. Elimelech died, the Seer was to become the dominant force in Polish Hasidism for the next thirty years.

The Seer was a spiritual leader of great charismatic influence, teaching humility and love for all those who comprised the nation of Israel, able to attract scholars and lay people alike. One of these scholars was a man who, curiously, bore the same name as the Seer, Jacob Isaac, and who was given the colloquial title of "The Yehudi" ("The Jew": Jacob Isaac ben Asher, 1766–1814) – possibly to prevent him from being called by the same name as his rebbe.[7] The Yehudi was a scholar of rare Talmudic acumen[8] who came to the conclusion that Talmudic wisdom alone was insufficient to bring one into a relationship with one's Creator. However, he eventually left the court of the Seer at Lublin.

The Yehudi was the Seer's favorite disciple and, as the Seer became preoccupied with the responsibilities of a mass movement he began directing

---

[4] On R. Elimelech of Lyzhansk, see Rivka Schatz-Uffenheimer, "The Doctrine of the *Zaddiq* in R. Elimelekh of Lyzhansk" (Hebrew). *Molad* 18 (144 [n.s. 45]) (1960): 365–378.

[5] Rachel Elior, "Between *Yesh* and *Ayin*: The Doctrine of the Zaddik in the Works of Jacob Isaac, the Seer of Lublin." In *Jewish History: Essays in Honor of Chimen Abramsky* (London: 1988), 393–455; idem. "Between Fear and Love" (Hebrew), *Tarbiz* (1993):62–63. Bracha Zak, "Studies in the Teachings of the Hozeh of Lublin" (Hebrew). In *Hasidut be-Polin*, edited by I. Bartal, R. Elior and C. Shmeruk. Jerusalem: 1994, 219–239.

[6] See *Tiferet Shlomoh: R. Shlomoh mi-Radomsk* 1803–1866 par. Vayelekh, 281. "As is well known regarding the man of God... R. Elimelech that in his old age he was so holy that he could no longer speak to those who gathered around him."

[7] See Yizhak Alfasi, *Ha-Hozeh mi-Lublin* (Jerusalem: Mossad ha-Rav Kook, 1969), 90, for various interpretations of this name.

[8] His father was "a scion of a distinguished rabbinic family."

newly-arrived young scholars visiting Lublin into the care of the Yehudi.[9] But this situation could not last long. The Yehudi was unable to endure the trappings of a mass movement, the low level into which the study of Torah had fallen, and the cult of miracle cures and wonder-working which had swept to the fore. The Yehudi was an intellectual and spiritual aristocrat[10] who felt (as has been wistfully observed by others) that

> Those I pray with, I cannot talk to.
> And those I talk to, I cannot pray with.

The Yehudi found the atmosphere in Lublin suffocating. He had to have a group that could pray and grow together in the service of God. The Yehudi was forced, compelled by his own sense of integrity, to leave Lublin for Przysucha, and there, with a number of the Seer's most influential students, including R. Simhah Bunim, he founded the School of Przysucha – hence his appellation, the "Rabbi of Przysucha." The Yehudi taught that one was obligated to purify one's inner motivations, whether in the service of God or in regard to one's fellow human being, and that one could not approach the service of God without first understanding who one really was. The Yehudi became infamous for "postponing the time of prayer," for waiting and preparing himself until he reached *et razon*, a fitting moment to commune with the Divine.[11] Only once he had made contact with himself, only once he was able to hear the voice within, could he come in contact with that which was different from himself.

The Yehudi wanted to do something that was totally new to Polish Hasidism: to unite the two worlds of **Talmud Torah** (traditional Talmudic learning) and of **tefillah** (prayer) – "the two wings of the bird." He also taught that it was forbidden to extinguish the light of one's own inner world to conform to the charisma of a zaddik. Just as intellectual acumen requires independent judgment and a sense of autonomy, so too – he argued – in matters of emotion and spirit one could only make contact if one were truly present, if one took responsibility for oneself, even at the moment of encounter with the zaddik. These qualities of **autonomy** and **purity of**

---

[9] *Niflaot ha-Rebbe*, 32, §54: "He (the Seer) only came to this world for someone whose name was the same as his."
[10] The Yehudi was known for his exceptional piety. See chapter 2.
[11] See chapter 10.

motive would bring Przysucha into direct conflict with the hasidic establishment.

In Przysucha, one found a type of *talmid hakham,* a Torah scholar-intellectual who was unafraid of individual thought and refused to be alienated from the demands of the spirit. Among the hasidim at this time, it was common to see a young hasid on his way to the zaddik of his choosing to spend sabbaths and festivals. There he would lose himself in the splendor and holiness of the zaddik and be enveloped in joy, *simhah,* with his fellow hasidim. In Przysucha, by contrast, one came not to lose oneself but to find one's own particular path – to find that style of service peculiar to one's own individual personality, within which one could constantly change and develop. The hasid of Przysucha would often remain for weeks or even months in order to integrate the teachings of his teacher (R. Bunim), and to leave with his sense of what he had learned for himself. Undoubtedly, learning continued, or perhaps only began, after one had left Przysucha. "Reality lies far away, before us, behind us. There is only one way to it and each of us will have to tread that way."[12]

During the lifetime of the Yehudi few attempts were brought to oppose Przysucha, largely due to the high regard with which he was held within the hasidic world, his Talmudic learning, and the purity of his bearing, which silenced any significant attacks.[13] But by the time R. Bunim assumed the helm of Przysucha, in the early nineteenth century, it had become a movement unto itself within Hasidism, and began to bear the brunt of concerted attacks by the hasidic establishment, culminating in a series of attempts by the vast majority of the hasidic leadership to excommunicate it.

As a generalization, one can say that the opponents of Hasidism, the *mitnaggedim,* stressed the learning of Torah as the main aspect of Divine service, while Hasidism stressed the value of "the service of the heart" as the main vehicle for achieving intimacy with God. Przysucha was that rare entity, a movement that put equal stress on both.

Przysucha must therefore be understood as a group of radical intellectual pietists seeking rejuvenation within Hasidism. It would go on to develop the future leaders of nineteenth-century Polish Hasidism; the rebbes of Warka (Vorki), Kotzk, Gur, Alexander and Izbica were all disciples of R. Simhah

---

[12] Lev Shestov, *Job's Balances.* Ohio University Press: Athens, Ohio, 141.
[13] *Tiferet ha-Yehudi,* 142 §2; cf. *Meir Einei ha-Golah,* §70.

Bunim. His teachings and personal path were to leave a mark on Polish hasidim that would prove indelible.

Przysucha began with the Yehudi (1766–1814), was continued after his death by his disciple R. Simhah Bunim (1765–1827), and was led in the third generation by R. Menahem Mendel of Kotzk (1787–1859).

But what was it about Przysucha that made it so challenging to the hasidic establishment? What was so unsettling in its program? The answer is simple: Przysucha had, directly or indirectly, declared an internal war upon the hasidic leadership of its time. It simply refused to accept anything that smelled of falseness and self-deception, be it the honor due to a zaddik or a particular religious practice. In short, Przysucha equated pretension and self-deceit with idol worship.

Menahem Mendel of Kotzk was known to proclaim that "anyone who does a command (*mitzvah*) whose ego is involved is like one who worships idols. For there is no difference between someone who worships idols and someone who worships himself."[14] Przysucha believed that a person needed to engage in struggle with his ego: to develop a kind of **psychology of Divine service,** in order to ferret out those motivations, whether the desire for honor or the urge to conformity, which place a veil between a human being and his Creator. One would need to "dig and uncover" the treasures of the real self that are hidden in the darkness of the ego.

The following incident is brought to illustrate that a person cannot always soar above or transcend his lower nature (his *yezer hara'*); but is rather forced to confront it.

> When R. Shemayah the Elder lay on his deathbed, his fellow Kotzk disciples asked him: "Shemayah, what about the *yezer hara'* (the evil inclination)? Does it still trouble a man even now?"
>
> "What a question," muttered R. Shemayah with his eyes half-closed. "Don't you all see how the *yezer hara'* is standing here at the head of the bed whispering in my ear; 'R. Shemayah, say "Shema' Yisrael" in a loud voice and draw out the word "ehad"?'"
>
> R. Shemayah continued; "I recognized him, the thief – I know his intention. He is trying to seduce me to say 'Shema' Yisrael' in order

---

[14] B. Mintz, in *Ketuvim* 52, 127; Z.M. Rabinowitz, "The Yehudi," 92; *Siah Sarfei Kodesh,* I:25, §121; *Hashavah le-Tovah; Likkutim,* 88–89.

that after my death you will say that R. Shemayah left this world in a pure state, on the word 'ehad.'"[15]

R. Shemayah calls the *yezer hara'* "that thief." "That thief," standing at the head of his deathbed, "seducing" him to re-enact the story of the death of Rabbi Akiva and to die a beautiful death in the presence of his comrades while they praised the beauties of his service of God. "He died the death of a zaddik," they would say.

But every death is a private affair. If R. Shemayah had given in to the promptings of the *yezer hara* and said the *Shema'* in a loud voice with his last life's strength, no one would have been present at the death of this man – neither the man going to meet his Maker nor the friends gathered about his deathbed – for they would all be acting out a script already written, giving praise to a legend, rather than standing in the mystery of the passing of a dear friend. It seems that the *yetzer hara'* is continually attempting to create a substitute, a sleight of hand, as it were, substituting the *kelipah* for the *pri*, the shell for the fruit, the appearance for the reality itself. But, in addition, R. Shemayah knew that he must not play to the gallery. At the most vulnerable moment of his life, suspended between heaven and earth, his requiem had to be sung alone, between God and himself, and no other. To have died while acting out a role or an image – to have participated in a communal ritual of death – is not to have died, but to have been already dead.

Przysucha was notably uncompromising in its opposition to the inauthentic performance of *mitzvot* (commandments) in that they could rob a man of his kiss with the Divine. As the Russian poetess Anna Ahkmatova said about the man who lives and writes his verse like an *apparatchik*, who leaves little of significance behind: "There the sheets have not been rumpled, there poetry has not spent the night." True, often all that we are left with from an experience is a *reshimu*, the memory of an impression, but robbed of this *reshimu* and its memory, how can we find our way? What are we without experiences that strip us bare? What happens to us when we begin to accept

---

[15] A popular version of a well-known story. See *Itturei Torah,* ed. A.Y. Greenberg, 1:80–81 (Tel Aviv: 1972), *Parshat Noah; Fun Unser Alter Oitzer,* ed. B. Yeushson (USA: 1957), par. Va-ethanan, 217. In these sources it is R. Wolfe of Strikov who asks this question of an elderly Kotzker hasid, R. Yisrael, and receives this response. See *Hashavah le-Tovah,* 130.

and honor reflections of the thing, and reject or ignore the thing itself? "Reflections of clouds and trees are not clouds and trees."

Przysucha was all too aware of the traps of extreme individualism, well marked out in romantic narcissism, and maintained itself as a movement which at all times operated within the context of religious Judaism. But *self-honesty was an essential prerequisite* that could in no way be overlooked. It was the first step to developing one's reality.

The Yehudi used to teach the following *midrash*:

> R. Shimon ben Gamaliel said, "Nobody honored their parents more than I, and yet I found that Esau did. Because when I served my father I would wear dirty clothes, and when I went outside I would get rid of the dirty clothes and dress in fine clothes. But Esau didn't behave like this: he would serve his father (at all times) in his best clothes.

The Yehudi asks, "Why couldn't R. Shimon ben Gamaliel wear fine clothes while serving his father, as Esau did?" He answers,

> Clothes are also a means of projecting an image. Esau serving his father in his best clothes is a way of saying that he projected a positive image of himself to his father... [The Rabbis say that] he would ask his father how one tithes hay and salt. And though he deceived his father [with his supposed piety], ultimately Isaac would not have wanted to have been deceived; to the contrary, he would have preferred to have seen his son's faults in order to correct them. Nevertheless, for a moment, Isaac enjoyed tranquility, imagining that his son was behaving correctly.
>
> It is regarding this (approach of Esau) that R. Shimon ben Gamaliel said, "I am unable to honor my father like Esau." He was not prepared to hide his faults from his father. On the contrary, he wears his dirty clothes. That is to say, he will reveal his reality to his father, his character faults, warts and all. And though his father would ultimately approve of such an approach because it allows him to correct the character failings of his son and to show him the Godly path, nevertheless, for the moment his father was upset.

Therefore (says the Yehudi), R. Shimon ben Gamliel could not honor his father as Esau did.[16]

The Yehudi's answer encapsulates the attitude of Przysucha toward behavior in the world. The Yehudi held that a relationship, be it with oneself, with another human being, or with God, is impossible without personal truthfulness, and that he was willing to pay a painful price for such a relationship. Although in the technical sense Esau kept the fifth commandment better than R. Shimon ben Gamaliel did, the Yehudi wasn't prepared to play that game.

The question arises: if the Yehudi identifies with R. Shimon ben Gamliel, who then is Esau? The inescapable conclusion is that Esau stands for any person – leader or private individual, hasid or not – who chooses to play to the crowd at the expense of his own inner integrity. It thus becomes clear why the entire hasidic establishment of Galicia and half that of Central Poland saw Przysucha as such a threat. Przysucha had simply raised the spiritual stakes too high or returned them to where they always should have been.

How then can human beings serve God? The Yehudi was known to say that "The seal of God is truth." But can one really be truthful with God or even with oneself? Can one ever know if the path one is following is true or false? As the Psalmist writes, "Deep calls unto deep" or, to cite the Jungian response some three thousand years later, "The process of achieving conscious individuality is the process of individuation, which leads one to the realization that one's name is written in heaven."[17]

In order to do this, a person must be willing to discover who he truly is, to take off the lid. Everything is put under scrutiny to catch a glimpse of ego or ulterior motive – anything that might be impure, anything that might erect a barrier between God and His servant. Truth has been redirected from a description of God to **a clarity of self-perception** for an individual person. When R. Bunim says that "if man purifies himself, he will recognize God from within the Torah," he is assuming that God, Torah and Truth, are all aligned, and that a person has the capability of making the connection, provided he is **authentic**.

---

[16] *Niflaot ha-Yehudi*, 52; *Orhot Haim*, 40.

[17] Edward Edinger, *Ego and Archetype: Individuation and the Religious Function of the Psyche* (New York, 1972). See also *Siah Sarfei Kodesh*, I:55, §258.

In various sources, we read that when a young hasid would find his way to Przysucha, R. Bunim would begin his education by telling him the following well-known story:

> R. Bunim used to tell every young man who came to him [the zaddik] for the first time... the story of R. Isaac [son of] R. Yekelish from Cracow. R. Isaac repeatedly dreamed that he should journey to Prague and that there, near the courtyard of the king, underneath the bridge, dig in the ground, find a great treasure and become rich. He journeyed to Prague, and when he came there, went directly to the bridge next to the King's courtyard. But soldiers were standing there, guarding it day and night, and he was afraid to dig in the ground to search for the treasure. But he was distressed, for how could he return home with nothing after working so hard to make the long journey? So every day he approached the bridge, going here and there.... The captain of the guard, standing there, seeing a Jew coming every day going around the bridge, called him and softly asked what he was looking for and for whom he was waiting for these last few days. He (R. Isaac) told him the whole story. The captain began to laugh and said, "Who believes dreams? I dreamt that I should journey to Cracow, and there find somebody called R. Isaac, (son of) R. Yekelish, and that if I dig there, in the home of the Jew, I'll find a great treasure under his stove. But do you think I give any credence to dreams?"... When R. Isaac (son of) R. Yekelish heard the captain's words, he understood that the purpose of his coming was to hear these words and to know that the treasure wasn't here, but in his home, and that he had to dig and search for the treasure in his own house, and there he would find it. He returned home, searched, found the treasure in his house under the stove, and became rich.

Similarly, every young man who comes to a zaddik and a rebbe must realize that the treasure is not to be found with the rebbe, but in his (own) house, and that when he journeys to his home, there he must search and dig, according to his capacity; and "If you make the effort, you will find – believe that." "For the matter is very close to you, in your mouth and in your heart to do." Literally next to you.[18]

What is the import of this story? Surely, that a person must know that the truth lies within one's own self. A person must not search for it by imitating another, however pious, but rather by going inside his inner being. By the term authenticity we mean, therefore, the process by which "the treasure" is revealed within the person. It is not a sanction for self-indulgence, but rather a process of refinement which reveals one's soul – it is like tracing the footprints of the Divine in one's being. A person tends to try to bribe God with his religious behavior. His piety can be motivated by what others think or say. But to be authentic begins with awareness of one's weakness and frailty and to strive to eliminate base motives in the service of God.

From an educational point of view, this story of R. Bunim is highly significant, for he is saying that in the service of God, a person has no alternative but to be true to himself.

The above values were a recipe for collision with the Polish hasidic establishment – and it was not long in coming. In 1822, at a gathering of the leaders of Polish Hasidism at the wedding in Austila with which we opened this chapter, the battle against Przysucha was launched and lost. Przysucha emerged victorious and went on to greater heights and extremes, irrevocably changing Polish Hasidism.

ॐ ॐ

There have been various misunderstandings of the nature of Przysucha and Kotzk. Gershom Scholem sees the ideas of Kotzk as unique and wonders what their connection to Hasidism is. In his opinion, "there occurred a revival of rabbinic learning, chiefly under the influence of the Rabbi of Kotzk.... Rabbi Mendel of Kotzk began to inveigh against the extravagant sentiments." Scholem thinks that Kotzk is "a phenomenon whose utter

---

[18] See *Ma'amarei Simhah*, no. 30; Buber, *Tales of the Hasidim, Later Masters,* trans. O. Marx (New York, 1964), 245, which includes all sort of additions. See also *Kol Mevaser,* 2:263; *Sefat Emet Likkutim,* par. Vayigash. For various nuances in the use of this parable, see Aviezer Cohen, "On Writing and Absence of Writing in the School of Przysucha" (Hebrew), *Dimui.*

uniqueness in the history of Jewish mysticism is highly thought-provoking and has been overlooked."[19]

But, as we shall see, Scholem is wrong. Kotzk was indeed a continuation of Przysucha. The revival of rabbinic learning did not begin with R. Mendel of Kotzk, and Kotzk can only be understood in the context of Przysucha.

Martin Buber[20] questions whether one can talk about the Yehudi, R. Bunim, and Menachem Mendel as a unit and whether there was a logical development from the Yehudi to R. Bunim.

To be sure, there were changes and developments between the Yehudi and R. Bunim and the Kotzker.[21] Had R. Bunim been the same as the Yehudi, he would have been an imitation of his mentor and a denial of everything that Przysucha stood for! While their ideas developed over time,

---

[19] G. Scholem, *Major Trends in Jewish Mysticism*. New York: 1967, 345.

[20] In correspondence between Scholem and Buber; Scholem writes (*The Letters of Martin Buber: A Life of Dialogue*, edited by N.N. Glatzer and P. Mendes-Flohr. New York: Schocken, 1991, §249. Munich, October 15, 1921):

Kotzk, a phenomenon whose utter uniqueness in the history of Jewish mysticism is highly thought-provoking and has been overlooked.... The teachings that the Rabbi of Kotzk put forth are likewise not to be found in any Kabbalistic book.... The Przysucha and the Kotzker have after all declared bankruptcy of their own accord, and none of them belongs to the classical period.

To which Buber responds (Happenheim, October 19, 1921, §251):

But has the theory developed equally logically from the Yehudi to Bunim to the Rabbi of Kotzk? In fact, can we even speak (with the teaching in mind) of "Kotzk" or even of Przysucha-Kotzk as a unit?... Kotzk theoretically is closer to Habad than people imagine, and is just as far from the psychological, sometimes quite sceptical (but not at all libertine) approach of the "wise Bunim" as he is from the literally "baptist" messianism of the Yehudi.... The connection is not basically a theoretical one, and not positive in nature. At the same time, there is this methodological and stylistic similarity, which makes differentiation more difficult.

We would disagree with both Scholem and Buber. Of course it all depends how one understands the term "unit." There are similar ideas, concepts and values that are clearly traceable in all three of these personalities, representing a paradigm shift in the hasidic world. Clearly, values are refracted through personality, and clearly these three personalities have their own characteristics and emphasis. In Przysucha the basic shared values are mediated through the personal authenticity of each teacher.

[21] See chapter 11. In another light, Alan Brill seeks the source of R. Bunim's ideas in the influence of urbanization during the first half of the nineteenth century in Poland. For a critique of those who explain the emergence of religious movements as being based on maladjustment or readjustment, see Mary Douglas, *Natural Symbols* (London: Routledge, 1996; second edition, 5–7).

each remained true to the unchanging basic principles. Nevertheless, the ideas of Przysucha, in toto, differ from those of the rest of the hasidic world and can be recognized as such. And though each individual idea of Przysucha was not necessarily original – that is to say, there might have been an existing precedent within Hasidism – taken together they form a package which in any other form of Hasidism might be part of a larger picture, but in Przysucha is the picture itself.

Przysucha was not a fringe group of radical pietists of marginal influence. To the contrary, archival evidence and reports of the local authorities reveal its expansion and jostling for domination in the Polish hasidic world. Glenn Dynner shows how R. Bunim's influence extended far beyond Przysucha.[22] In the town of Zelechov, a major hasidic stronghold, a police report divided the hasidim into two hostile groups: followers of R. Jacob Simon Deutch, and those of R. Bunim. Complaints were registered by the Parczew police chief in 1823 against Przysucha hasidim. One can gauge the influence of R. Bunim from the following report in 1824, which states: "Every district except Augustov is more or less infected with them and the city of Przysucha, in the Sandomierz district, is their main abode."[23]

We have no written works by these three generations of Przysucha. There is no primary work per se, not by the Yehudi, not by R. Bunim nor by the Kotzker. In the case of R. Bunim there are two extant works by people who knew him personally. The first, *Kol Simhah*, was written by R. Zusha of Plozk (Breslau, 1859), a disciple of R. Bunim. But this work was severely criticized by his contemporaries as being totally inadequate. The other major source is a work entitled *Ramatayim Zofim*, compiled by R. Shmuel of Sieniawa (Warsaw, 1882), which is a collection of teachings that he heard from a variety of teachers. Moreover, even such noted disciples of R. Bunim as R.

---

[22] Glenn Dynner, "Men of Silk: The Hasidic Conquest of Polish Jewry, 1754–1830." Unpublished Ph.D. diss., Brandeis University, 2002, 78–80. I am immensely indebted to Dr. Dynner, whose work I have quoted at length. (This work was recently published in book form with the title *Men of Silk: The Hasidic Conquest of Polish Jewish Society*, New York: Oxford Univeristy Press, 2006.)

[23] Dynner, 63. Archival evidence (Warsaw, vol. 1871) concerning the governmental enquiries into religions (1823–1824), described Przysucha "as being the main center of the Hasidim."

Yitzhak Meir Alter (Rottenberg) of Ger and R. Hanoch Heinich of Alexander did not write the works published in their names (*Meir Einei ha-Golah; Hiddushei ha-Rim* or *Hashavah le-Tovah*). Later compilations such as *Simhat Israel,* with its three sections, *Or Simhah, Ma'amarei Simhah* and *Torat Simhah,* were published in Piotrkow 1910, and the compendium *Siah Sarfei Kodesh* (Lodz-Piotrkow) was published in 1923–1924.What this means is that *we must not give too much credence to any one source. Rather, we need to build our thesis on the basis of multiple quotations from different sources in order to begin to paint the contours,* an approximation of this movement. [24]

Toward the end of his life Menahem Mendel went into semi-seclusion for some twenty years. With his death in 1859, Przysucha ceased to exist as a movement. One can see an immediate retrogression of values even among those nearest to him.[25] Przysucha became absorbed into general Hasidism and its radicalism was blunted. For three generations, though, it had blazed a trail of God-consciousness – a paradigm for those who wanted then, and want now, a Judaism which is both analytical and spiritual.

"Blessed is the flame that was extinguished but inflamed the hearts."[26]

---

[24] For an in-depth analysis and use of the secondary sources, see Addendum A.

[25] See below, Chapter 12.

* Throughout this book, my translation of the Hebrew has often suffered by my attempt to be true to the original text.

[26] Hanna Szenes (1921–1944), "Blessed Is the Match"

THE HOLY REBELLION

This righteous person [the Yehudi] wanted to bring, from above
to below, a new approach; to infuse the hearts of the Jewish
people as to how to serve God with Torah and prayer together.
And that had never been [done before] in the world.

Uri (the Saraf) of Strelisk

From Lublin to Przysucha

HASIDISM BEGAN WITH R. Israel Baal Shem Tov,[1] affectionately known as
the Besht, who was one of those souls who succeeded in breaking through
and touching the heavens, and even more surprisingly, in bringing back a
taste of that with which he came into contact. The Baal Shem Tov was not
the only one to serve God, but all agree that he was something special and
that he had touched the secret of how "to see and to be seen."

But what was the "circle of the Baal Shem Tov?" And what was their
cause? They were people who came to show that God was to be served with
heart and with joy. They were "souls on fire" – God-intoxicated people –
who felt a sense of God's life energy in everything. Hasidism came, not to
add one iota to the words of God, but to inflame God's people with a new
joy and thanksgiving and to cause them to feel seen by their Creator.

---

[1] A.J. Heschel, *The Circle of the Baal Shem Tov* (Chicago: University of Chicago Press,
1985); Moshe Rosman, *Founder of Hasidism: A Quest for the Historical Baal Shem Tov*
(Berkeley: University of California Press, 1996); idem., "Meidzyboz and Rabbi Israel
Baal Shem Tov," in *Essential Papers on Hasidism: Origins to Present,* ed. G.D. Hundert
(New York: NYU Press, 1991), 209–225.

At his death (1760), R. Israel (Baal Shem Tov) left, if not a closely knit group, then at least a highly admiring and deeply convinced inner circle of disciples, surrounded by an outer fringe of former leaders of other hasidic groups who adhered to him while dissenting from his views to some extent, and a broad base of devout in the townships and villages of southeast Poland-Lithuania.[2]

It was only with the Maggid of Mezeritch that Hasidism graduated to the rank of a movement. Hasidism originated amidst the Carpathian Mountains of the Ukraine, the birthplace of the Baal Shem Tov, and gradually, with the disciples of the Maggid, began to spread through the townships and villages of Volhynia, Belorussia, Galicia and Lithuania, until it finally made its way into central Poland. Thus, it was only with the third generation of its adherents that Hasidism slowly emerged in the heartland of eastern European Jewry, central Poland, and it was only under the influence of the Seer, in the town of Lublin and its environs, that Hasidism reached the level of a mass movement in Poland. [3]

After R. Shmelke's death,[4] Jacob Isaac Halevi Horowitz[5] (later known as the Seer of Lublin), became the student of R. Elimelech of Lyzhansk,[6] by

---

[2] *Encyclopaedia Judaica*, VII: 1392.

[3] The following has been said about the emergence of Hasidism in Poland:
Hasidism in Poland is generally reckoned to have begun with the activities of R. Samuel Shmelke Horowitz and R. Elimelech of Lyzhansk. R. Samuel Shmelke (1726–1778), a disciple of the Maggid of Mezhirech, taught in Sieniawa, in the district of Lwow in Galicia, from the beginning of the 1760s to the first third of the 1770s. R. Elimelech settled in Lyzhansk, in Galicia, in the early 1770s and set up a Hasidic "court" there, which functioned until his death in 1787.
(Rachel Elior, "Between *Yesh* and *Ayin:* The Doctrine of the Zaddik in the Works of Jacob Isaac, the Seer of Lublin." In *Jewish History: Essays in Honor of Chimen Abramsky* [London: 1988], 393–455.)

[4] Among R. Shmelke's disciples were R. Levi Isaac of Berdichev, R. Israel of Kozienice (Koznitz) and R. Jacob Isaac, the Seer of Lublin. On R. Samuel Shmelke, see Ignacy Schiper, *Przyczynki do dziejow chasydyzmu w Polsce,* s.v. R. Samuel Shmelke (later of Nikolsberg). While still in Sieniawa, near the end of 1772, he wrote a letter to the Brody Kahal in response to their anti-hasidic ban earlier that year: "The Letter of the Rabbi Samuel Shmelke Horowitz, Rabbi of Nikolsberg, to the Brody Kahal," in Wilensky, *Hasidim u-mitnaggedim,* I:85.

[5] Rachel Elior, cited above, ch 1, n. 5.

[6] On R. Elimelech of Lyzhansk, see Rivka Schatz-Uffenheimer, "The Doctrine of the *Zaddiq* in R. Elimelekh of Lyzhansk," cited above, ch. 1, n. 4.

whom he was greatly valued. But over the course of time, relations between the two men chilled and became complicated. There is a phenomenon, especially in Polish Hasidism, that certain destinies cannot be played out under the auspices of another looming figure. At a certain point, one needs and comes to demand one's own domain. When R. Elimelech died the Seer became the dominant force in Polish Hasidism for the next thirty years.

> In those days Lublin was a city full of scribes and scholars great in Torah and in the fear (of Heaven). But all of them were *mitnaggedim* and they had not stepped in the path of Hasidism; and one who went on such a path was regarded as strange, for they didn't understand that a hasid could also serve God with all his heart. They imagined that hasidim transgress the law of Moses and Judaism and don't behave in accordance with the *Shulhan Arukh. Even though there were hasidim of R. Elimelech to be found in those days, they were only one in a town or two in a family.* And when they heard in Lublin that close to their town a breach had been made, and someone (the Seer) had settled there who behaved in the manner of a hasid and was drawing near to him people who were sitting at his table and learning with him, so that they too should behave like him, they became very angry.[7]

Interestingly enough, hasidic tradition is quite open and did not hide the fact that initially its success in Poland was quite modest. Thus, the situation of Hasidism in Warsaw during the lifetime of the Maggid (d. 1772) left something to be desired.

> At the time of the Maggid of Mezerich (Miedzyrzicz)... there were hardly any hasidim in Warsaw even though it had a sizeable Jewish community. Hasidim relate that once R. Moishe Leib of Sassov spent some time in Warsaw on a matter involving "redeeming captives." After having succeeded in getting them released (it was close to the Sabbath)... he decided to journey outside the town and not remain in Warsaw. When he was asked why he was in such a hurry, he replied that he was frightened to remain in Warsaw.

---

[7] *Eser Orot,* 90.

When the Maggid of Kozienice first came to the Maggid of Mezeritch, he asked him from what town he came. He replied "From Kosienice, which is ten miles from Warsaw." The Maggid smiled [upon hearing] that ten miles from Warsaw there were people saying "Keter."[8]

But if, in the time of the Maggid, saying "Keter" in Poland was a modest gain, within a generation, by the end of the eighteenth century, the situation had changed dramatically. Dynner says the following:[9]

By the beginning of the nineteenth century, according to the memoirist Abraham Gottlober, "the hand of Hasidism had already attacked in Volhyn, Podolia, and all the land of Poland and Russia, apart from the district of Lithuania, until one could not dare to publicly oppose them..."[10]

Before the close of the eighteenth century, Hasidism was well entrenched in Warsaw and other parts of the region. Writing in the capital in 1797, Jacques Calmanson warns that the zaddikim "stand to become despots if the Government fails to consider the means to thwart their spread immediately...."[11] [12]

This complete change seems to have taken place within some twenty years. So reports the Polish maskil, an eventual convert to Christianity, Jacques Calmanson, whose tract on Jewish reform published in Warsaw, 1797 (two years after the final partition)

---

[8] *Meir Einei ha-Golah*, 2:80 §1. "Keter" is the introductory word of the doxology according to the Ari, which became typical of the Hasidic rite. On the specific denunciation of inserting the *Keter* prayer, see R. Abraham Katzenellenbogen's letter to R. Levi Yitzhak from 1784, in Wilensky 1.128.

[9] Glenn Dynner, "Men of Silk: The Hasidic Conquest of Polish Jewry, 1754–1830." Ph.D. diss., Brandeis University: 2002, 14.

[10] Abraham Gottlober. *Zikhronot u-Masa'ot* (Jerusalem: Mossad Bialik, 1976), I:63, refers to a time preceding the death of R. Levi Isaac of Berdyczew (d. 1809).

[11] Jacques Calmanson. *Uwagi nad niniejszym stanem Zydow Polskich y ich wydoskonaleniem* (Warsaw: 1797), 18–19.

[12] Instead of yielding to bans against hasidic liturgical innovation and his mystical methods for determining Jewish law, R. Yisrael of Kozienice threatened the Kahal and demanded that they beg his forgiveness in the synagogue. Re Kozcenice, see Dynner, 64–73.

contains the following: "This particular sect is only known to Polish Jewry, and only appeared twenty years ago..."[13]

† ‡

But what is clear from a variety of different sources is that, by the end of the eighteenth century, the dominant personality in Polish Hasidism was the Seer of Lublin, R. Jacob Isaac ha-Levi Horowitz (1745–1815). What is it that drew both scholars and lay people to the Seer?

Many people are unable to recognize greatness. But for others, the experience can be disconcerting. They realize where they really stand, their false self-image is taken away, and they are able to come into contact with that true good which stands ever above them and within. Even those living in direct contact with greatness are often at a loss to understand and articulate just what it is that makes up the special character of such an individual – and this is as it should be. All one knows, all that one is left with, is the awareness that one has touched something that defies explanation or easy categories of perception. He or she stands without, but provokes us to the very core of our being. It is as if one were to gaze upon a person who lives in contact with that still small voice within themselves. If the observer is sensitive, he feels himself stripped naked, impoverished, and begins to search within himself for that same still, small, sacred voice of his or her own.

The Seer of Lublin succeeded as no other zaddik had before him, as attested to by friend and foe alike, by both Jewish and Gentile sources.[14] What was the secret of his near-dominance of the hasidic world? More specifically, what was it that the Yehudi found so attractive about the Seer? There is no doubt that in terms of Talmudic knowledge, the Yehudi far surpassed him.[15] What then was the Yehudi looking for, and what did he

---

[13] See above, Calmanson. While his observations about Hasidism in Poland are reliable, those about Hasidism outside Poland clearly are not.

[14] See Addendum B. See also Wilensky, *Hasidim u-mitnaggedim*, II: 356; *Niflaot Ha-Rebbe*, 53 (118), Dynner, 14–15.

[15] For examples of the Yehudi explaining the teaching of the Seer, see *Niflaot ha-Yehudi*, 17, 76.
The Gaon, R. Baruch Fränkel-Teomim, once asked the Yehudi why he spent time with the Rebbe of Lublin: Wasn't he (the Yehudi) able to learn Torah better than the Rebbe? What then did he learn from him? The Yehudi replied: "I learned from

find? The Yehudi was looking for that quality not necessarily provided by knowledge of Torah alone – namely, God-consciousness. In the eyes of the Yehudi, the Seer was a man who lived in the presence of God and walked humbly before Him, "knowing Him in all thy ways."

The story of the Seer begins in Lublin, where Hasidism began to take root and spread with a seemingly endless vigor. And perhaps it is safe to say that in this age, in Poland, all roads led to Lublin. All religious movements – and perhaps this is an indication of their vibrancy and health – pass through periods of change in which they are challenged to draw upon all that is available to them within their tradition. If we want to understand the Yehudi, we first need to appreciate the world of the Seer and to come close to his light, for it was from his court and from much of his teachings that Przysucha would be born.

In a work written after the Seer's death, *Or le-Shamayim* by R. Meir of Apta, who inherited his mantle of leadership, the Seer is quoted on virtually every other page. What emerges from these quotations is a clear picture of a man with whom the Yehudi would have felt enraptured. The Seer believed that the closer one came to a realization of one's Creator, the more it aroused a deep sense of one's own insignificance. This sense of insignificance (*ayin*) was therefore born of intimacy. It was the result of someone who had sensed the enormity of what might be beyond the veil. It came as a gift to one who was engaged with the Source of all life, and its consequence for the Seer was a demand to respond.[16]

Above all, the Seer was known to be a man of truth, aware of his weaknesses, of which he spoke freely from morning to evening to all who would listen. Only someone extremely secure in a relationship, in this case with God, can bare himself so completely before another – and not before

---

my Rebbe that when I lie down to sleep, I immediately fall asleep" (*Niflaot ha-Yehudi*, 65). To date, there is no comprehensive biographical work on the Seer of Lublin. Such a work would have to deal with the psychological issues that, consciously or unconsciously, were a part of his relationship with the Yehudi.

16 Thus, in *Or le-Shamayim*: "Only one who has the quality of *ayin* ("nothingness") and only seeks the greatness of God, and (does not act) at all for his own benefit, only he will benefit from the light." – 77; "A man has to arouse within himself the quality of nothingness and to be humble in his own eyes" – 82; "It is important before God that man recognize his own unworthiness" – 117; "Jacob asked that he should have the quality of nothingness... and through this feel the greatness of the Creator, blessed be He" – 25.

that person alone, but before all those who care to look and hear. A religious person allows such confessions in order to remove the dross of human frailty and to provide space for a stronger bond. There was no masochism in the Seer. He simply unveiled the chamber of his heart in order to know the Divine more intimately. R. Bunim once told the following story:

> Rabbi Azriel Horowitz, the Rabbi of Lublin, would distress the Rebbe of Lublin (the Seer) with all sorts of questions. Specifically, (he would ask him) why he leads and draws others after him, seeing that he knows that he is not a rebbe. To this question he replied "What can I do?" So the Rabbi told him that the following Sabbath he should publicly proclaim this fact (i.e., that he is not a rebbe) so that they could all go on their way. And so he did. With a broken heart, he apologized for his limitation.... And his words of humility enraptured everybody, so that they became even more devoted. Later on, when they met, the Seer told (the Rabbi) that he had done what the Rabbi had asked him to do, and that it hadn't helped. So the Rabbi said, "Tell them about your greatness, that you are one of the truly righteous..." To which the Rebbe (the Seer) replied, "True, I am not a Rebbe, but neither am I a liar. How then can I say about myself that I am a righteous person – the opposite of the truth?"[17]

The following is reported in a hasidic source:

> I heard from the holy mouth... of the Seer of Lublin... in his exceedingly great humility and with a broken heart the following about himself: "Woe to the generation of which I am the leader."[18]

Hasidic tradition has recorded the following:

> A pupil of his once heard him say... "There is no one in this world worse than I. Even if an angel of the Lord said that I was righteous,

---

[17] *Ramatayim Zofim* (A.Z.) 24.22.

[18] *Mishmeret Itamar;* par. Ki Tisa (*Niflaot ha-Rebbe,* 55, §129). In the same genre we have a tradition that says the following: "I heard from the Rabbi of Lublin... that he said: 'I am one who recognizes his Creator and yet rebels against Him....'" – *Ramatayim Zofim,* 23.18. For further sources on humility in the thought of the Seer, see *Niflaot ha-Rebbe,* 95, n. 331; *Or Hokhmah,* 9, n. 38; and *Sefat Emet,* par. Vayishlach, 5634, quoting the Seer to the effect that even humility is a Divine gift.

I would not believe him. And even if the Almighty Himself would say that I am righteous, I would only believe Him for that moment and not more, for one can easily slip into hell."[19]

There is no end to the depths of the man who is truly humble, or of the treasures that lie at his disposal. Perhaps it is for this reason that the Seer managed to draw so many promising disciples to his court – in fact, nearly all those who were to become the leaders of Polish Hasidism. With the Seer, one could not help but feel that one was in the presence of someone with a secret, the secret of how precious it is to stand before the Divine.

For the Seer, it was the quality of "nothingness" which allowed the kiss of intimacy with the Divine. Compare this was a famous exchange between R. Bunim and the Yehudi:

> R. Simhah Bunim once asked the Yehudi, "The ultimate goal is for a person to know that one is nothing (*ayin*). But what sort of goal is it to know that one is nothing, when in fact one is indeed nothing?" And our teacher replied, "The seal of God is truth, and if man really knows that he is nothing then he is attached to the truth, and therefore attached to God whose seal is truth. And that is the ultimate goal: to be attached to the truth."[20]

But from other sources, it seems that R. Bunim asked this question of the Seer, and it is the Seer who replies,

> For via this (knowing that one's service is nothing) one is attached to truth.[21]

It should not surprise us that hasidic tradition attributes this exchange both to the Yehudi and the Seer, for it was the agenda of both. The sense of "nothingness" was their existential reality, born of their awe of being in His presence, and its corollary is a personal purifying process towards being truthful about oneself.

---

[19] *Heikhal ha-Berakhah,* par. Ki Tisa, 276.

[20] *Niflaot ha-Yehudi,* 60.

[21] *Siah Sarfei Kodesh,* 5:22, no. 8. See *Hashavah le-Tovah, Likutim,* 121: "The seal of God is truth, and if a person thinks that he has attained something himself, that is false." The same source relates, "R. Bunim once apologized to the Rebbe of Lublin that he is nothing. And he replied, 'That is very good.'"

The Seer urged continual renewal in the service of God. Thus,

> One who walks in the darkness and in lowliness before Him... and imagines that he has not achieved or accomplished anything and that he has to begin anew....[22]
>
> I heard (from the Seer), who said in the name of the Rabbi... of Berditchev... that a man is obligated to arouse within himself the quality of "*ayin*," to be lowly in his own eyes, and to continually add to this, day by day.[23]

Reading these comments, one could almost believe that it was the Yehudi talking. The motto, nay, the battle cry of the Yehudi, was his call for continual renewal, starting afresh to reach a point of utter simplicity. With true humility there are no limits to the levels to which a person can ascend.

> I once heard from... the Yehudi that if a person who is serving God sees within himself that today is just like yesterday, and that he serves God in exactly the same fashion as he did the day before, he should know indeed that he has fallen from his original level; his mere repetition in his service today detracts and diminishes the value of his service from the day before, for a person is always in the aspect of becoming, and not standing.[24]

Unless a person is in a continual dynamic of growth, he runs the risk of losing all he has worked towards in the past. For the Seer, **one can only begin to be truthful through humility and spiritual renewal** and therefore that quality is paramount. He once said that

> He loves the wicked person who knows that he is wicked more than the righteous person who knows that he is righteous. When the holy Rabbi of Przysucha asked him why this was so, he answered that the wicked person who knows that he is wicked cleaves to the truth — and God is truth, and He is called Truth. But the righteous person

---

[22] *Or le-Shamayim*, 206, 19.

[23] Ibid., 82.

[24] *Beit Yaakov, Shabbat Hol ha-Moed Sukkot*, 91b. On the Yehudi's desire for renewal, see *Siftei Tzaddik*, par. *Vayera*, 59; *Aron Edut, Zer Zahav*, par. Nitzavim, 40; *Sefat Emet*, par. Bamidbar, 5639; *Birkhat Tov*, par. Vayehi, 142; *Siah Sarfei Kodesh*, 5:42; *Tiferet ha-Yehudi*, 174, n. 89.

who knows that he is righteous most definitely is not, "for there is no righteous in the land…"; all the more so one who feels that he is righteous – clearly is not… he is connected to falsehood, and falsehood is the enemy of God. Therefore He hates him.[25]

Yet if there was one person whose constant refrain was the quest for truth, who continually stressed that God's seal is truth and that therefore there can be no sham or pretense if one wants to be in communion with God – such a person was the Yehudi.

The Yehudi (Jacob Isaac ben Asher) was born in 1766. He came from a non-hasidic rabbinic family, which traced its ancestry back to the brother of the Taz (R. Yitzhak Ha-Levi). Though hasidic leaders are usually described in hagiographic language, it is generally agreed that the Yehudi was quite exceptional. There is even a tradition that R. Akiva Eiger said of him "Who can comprehend the mind of the holy Yehudi?"[26] But even if we assume that this was somewhat exaggerated, we know that, already as a young man, the Yehudi was acknowledged by all as an outstanding rabbinical scholar. He was someone who was prodigious in the very field that earned the ultimate accolade, i.e., intellectual acumen in the study of Talmud. But for the Yehudi rabbinical scholarship alone was inadequate.[27] For him the study of Torah alone did not necessarily lead to perfection, and for that he turned to the spirituality of the Seer.

The Seer exercised enormous influence on those who came into contact with him.[28] But as he became more and more successful, he found it necessary to delegate the authority for dealing with young scholars to the Yehudi.[29]

The Seer succeeded as no one before him had done in arousing the souls of the Jewish people. But almost as suddenly as they awoke they fell back into slumber – so dependent had they become on the great man. His beloved student, the Yehudi of Przysucha, was unable to bear the low spiritual level to which Judaism had sunk. Thus was born the quarrel between Lublin and Przysucha – between a great and inexhaustible love for

---

25 *Niflaot ha-Rebbe.* 54 (124), *Ramatayim Zofim* 5.60, *Torat Simah* 298.

26 *Nifla'ot ha-Yehudi*, 68 §8. *Keter ha-Yehudi*, introduction.

27 *Nifla'ot ha-Yehudi*, 75–76.

28 See the bemoaning of this fact by R. David Makov in Wilensky, ibid., 2:15, 356.

29 *Tiferet ha-Yehudi*, 154 §21.

the entire nation of Israel and an unwillingness to sacrifice the least of them, as represented by Lublin, and the desire to awaken and to inflame the Jewish people so that each individual would be inspired to seek and serve his Heavenly Father from the very essence of his own personality, as represented by Przysucha. Had the heavens ever seen such a thing, such wrestling "for the sake of Heaven"?

The Yehudi left Lublin but always protested that he had not left the Seer. In fact, he kept on returning to the Seer. There is a heart-rending source in which the Seer declares his belief in the purity of the Yehudi but entreats him to stop coming to Lublin since he, the Seer, cannot stand the tension generated by the Yehudi's opponents. However, the Yehudi replied, "The majority of my wisdom came from him, from the Rebbe of Lublin, and therefore on no account can I accept his advice and stop journeying to my teacher and master."[30]

If the Yehudi kept returning to the Seer, why did he leave in the first place? If they had such a symbiotic relationship, if they had so much in common, what was the problem?

The problem was the following, and it was an unbridgeable chasm: The Seer understood the role of the zaddik as being one that was limited to the select few, those who are metaphysically different from the rest of humanity. But the "call of the Yehudi" was to anyone who could respond. For the Yehudi it was as impossible to imagine that one could enter the Kingdom of Heaven on the coattails of a zaddik as to imagine that one could learn a page of Talmud vicariously through the learning of another *talmid hakham*. The idea was simply absurd.

In order to understand the Seer, one needs to understand the entire kabbalistic system that underlay his philosophy. Outrageous as it may sound, the Seer believed that any deficiency in the physical welfare of the Jewish people caused a rupture between God and His *Shekhinah*. It was the role of the zaddik to repair this rupture. And he did this, from the depth of his humility, by interceding and beseeching God to bring goodness down to the Jewish people. For the Seer, "nothingness" is the entrée to repairing both the Heavenly world and this earthly one. The Jewish people are "the limbs of

---

[30] *Tiferet ha-Yehudi*, 177, n. 95. See also *Zekhuta de-Avraham, Nahalei Emunah*, 17.

the Almighty"[31] and "in their distress, so is He distressed." The *Shekhinah* cries out to the zaddik to be healed and reunited.[32]

The Seer stressed intoxication with God – "drunk, but not with wine." A person must cleave continually to his Creator[33] and his ecstasy must be joined to life within this world.

> "For in all their distress, He is in distress." **And if [the zaddik] chooses [the path of] affliction, Heaven forbid, he causes distress on high.** But the quality of choosing good for himself in this world is with the intention that there should not be any distress on high.[34]

There we have the inner philosophy of the Seer. By bringing benefits into this world, the zaddik benefits the celestial world – for the sake of the *Shekhinah*.

This provides the philosophical base for the "Levi Yitzhak of Berditchev" type of unqualified love for the Jewish people which is so appealing in the thought of the Seer, and which the Yehudi would have found so attractive. But throughout the three generations of Przysucha no kabbalistic concept is used, no kabbalastic terms are mentioned, and thus, anything having to do with repairing or influencing God simply falls away.[35] Humility is the gateway to a person's rendezvous with the Divine, not a method of trying to influence it.

With such a kabbalistic understanding of the role of the zaddik, we can understand another major difference between Lublin and Przysucha; in Lublin the credentials of the zaddik were related to his ability to perform the miraculous. R. Meir of Apta makes the following telling statement in the name of R. Hayyim Vital:

---

[31] *Or le-Shamayim*, 186.

[32] Ibid., 6. On the very first page, on the sentence (Isaiah 63:9) "*bechol zaratam lo zar,*" the Seer gives meaning to both the *keri* and the *ketiv*. Because "in all their distress He is in distress" (**lo** with a *vav*), the zaddik beseeches God to remove distress from the Jewish people, thus removing distress from Himself (**lo** with an *aleph*). See *Ramatayim Zofim* 6.23: "As the Rebbe of Lublin says... prayer is for the sake of the Shekhinah."

[33] *Or le-Shamayim*, 197.

[34] *Or le-Shamayim*, 226, also 32, 55, 113. On serving God through richness see *Or le-Shamayim* 109, *Niflaot ha-Rebbe*, 94, n. 322.

[35] See below, Chapter 4.

As for the statement "Don't be involved in the esoteric," this applies to earlier generations. But in the last generation [i.e., in our time], on the contrary, the esoteric and involvement in the mysteries has a great impact on people.[36]

Indeed the zaddik's very ability to break the laws of nature revealed both his and God's greatness.[37] But Przysucha looked at the world from a profoundly different perspective. For them, the world was not full of holy sparks, the world was not an unreal mirage, and the goal was "not to realize the ideal, but to idealize the real."

In Lublin, the Yehudi found heaven on earth. For him, the Seer was personally thrilling, and Przysucha always acknowledged the greatness of the Seer. R. Yaacov Aryeh of Radzymin, a pupil of R. Bunim, says

> that he heard from the Yehudi that we walk on a more elevated level than the Rebbe of Lublin, but whatever point we reached, he (the Seer) is the Rebbe.[38]

But for the community there was a price to be paid for the Seer's belief in zaddikism: the only absolute demand placed on the hasid in Lublin was total and utter allegiance to the zaddik. Time and again the Seer explained that the greater the belief of the hasid in the zaddik, the more the zaddik was empowered to affect God.[39] The claim on the hasid was therefore not one of personal improvement, or purity of motive, but one of allegiance. Individuals might be inspired by the Seer, but this was not the raison d'etre of Lublin. Individual redemption was not the goal.[40] The Yehudi found the atmosphere in Lublin insufferable. He maintained that he never left the Seer. But despite his protestations, there was an ideological difference between the

---

[36] *Or le-Shamayim,* 181.

[37] Ibid., 120, 30.

[38] See *Bikkurei Aviv,* Introduction, 6.

[39] *Or le-Shamayim,* 92, 110, 127.

[40] On personal redemption in Hasidism, see M. Faierstein in *Hasidism Reappraised* (1996); Moshe Idel, in *Messianic Mystics* (New Haven: Yale University Press, 1998), Chapter 7, "Hasidism: Mystical Messianism and Mystical Redemption," 236, mentions Scholem's claim "that the question of private or individual redemption is a totally modern dilemma and does not exist in the Jewish tradition before 1750. If it does exist afterwards, it is still a debatable issue." Idel shows that this view is mistaken and points out its antecedents within traditional medieval mysticism.

two of them; while the Seer used his gift to repair the celestial world, the Yehudi used his gift to repair the terrestrial one.

Whereas in Przysucha the leader acknowledged the right of the hasid to draw from the wells of his own authenticity, even if his conclusion was different from that of his teacher, in Lublin the hierarchical structure meant that there was only one-way traffic from above to below, and that autonomy from the zaddik was not a possibility.

Przysucha stood in the breach between the mystic and the person uninterested or unable to believe in his ability to approach the Divine. Przysucha brought down and raised up. It demanded that a human being learn to listen to himself, to hear and receive the blessings of heaven. In Przysucha the challenge was this: How could one serve without seeking, and how could one seek without believing that one would eventually make contact? Human beings could be described as "broken cisterns that hold no water," but a vessel created by God without the capacity of holding a blessing was inconceivable.

In Przysucha, the drama of becoming human was squarely focused on the individual and not on the zaddik. And a person, if not the author of his destiny, was surely required to stand in attendance to all that his destiny would have to say to him.

In Przysucha, the zaddik as teacher was essentially *a living paradigm*, albeit also a charismatic personality, who endeavored to help the student fulfill his own potential. Under no circumstance was the disciple under any obligation to abrogate his own personality or responsibility to the zaddik. On the contrary, the role of the teacher was to help the disciple develop his own sense of judgment and discrimination, to develop his own sense of autonomy. Those students who were unable to accept responsibility for themselves were not fit to be part of Przysucha.

The Yehudi was unable to abide the low level to which Hasidism had fallen. Learning, the study of Torah, had fallen into such a pitiable state as to be untenable (an indication of a lack of ability to think for oneself), and spirituality was to be found solely in relation to the Seer. The Yehudi was seeking a radical rejuvenation within Hasidism, from top to bottom, one in which the essential demand was on the individual. He was averse to all externalities and to the trappings of a mass movement. Thus, to the end of his days the Yehudi focused his efforts on arousing each person to become what he could be. The Yehudi could feel the draw of the Seer as an outstanding religious personality. But he also saw the potential damage in the philosophy of the Seer – that of vicarious redemption.

The Yehudi's program was focused on creating a new form of Hasidism, designated for the learned, those who would engage in Torah study as a way of life. In some ways it was similar to the early Habad strain of Hasidism of White Russia, but lacking the latter's characteristic of kabbalistic and theological abstraction.

The Seer was able to accept, and in a certain manner even to praise, the behavior of the Yehudi[41] because he was able to see the root cause of his action, which arose out of a sincere desire to serve God. However, the Seer's disciples, as well as those in the wider hasidic world, were unable to behave with such depth of vision and tolerance. At every possible opportunity they criticized the behavior of the Yehudi and his disciples, seeing in him a threat to the system of their rebbe, and an unsettling of the established order.[42]

The Yehudi was known for his exceptional piety, as was acknowledged even by his critics.[43] R. Bunim was simply amazed that a human being could so transform himself as the Yehudi had done.[44] For him, the Yehudi was the living paradigm of what a human being could become. It may well be that because he was such an exceptional person,[45] no attempt was made to ostracize Przysucha during the Yehudi's lifetime. But although the Yehudi was drawn to the Seer and saw him as his rebbe, his Talmudic learning, his intellect, did not allow him to follow the crowd. The values he sought were different from what was happening in the court of the Seer. Przysucha must therefore be seen in the context of the success of the Seer of Lublin. His very success brought about a major reason why the Yehudi had to leave him.

Unlike Przysucha, Lublin believed in and stressed simple and wholehearted faith in God and in the zaddikim themselves. There is a great deal of beauty in this simplicity, but it presumes that one is already perfect or

---

[41] Z.M. Rabinowitz, *Mi-Lublin le-Przysucha*, 281–282. The Seer would send those bright young men who came to Lublin to the Yehudi. See *Tiferet ha-Yehudi*, 154 n. 21; Aescoly, *Hasidut be-Folin*, 55.

[42] The Yehudi was relentlessly persecuted by some of the pupils of the Seer for having "left." *Niflaot ha-Yehudi, Mikhtevei Te'udah*, 15–16; 55. See Aescoly, *Hasidut be-Folin*, ed. David Assaf, (Jerusalem: 1999), 55, 45.

[43] Based on *Tiferet ha-Yehudi*, 142 §2.

[44] *Tiferet ha-Yehudi*, 151 §13.

[45] *Tiferet ha-Yehudi*, §142. Cf. *Meir Einei ha-Golah*, 70.

that one knows one's level, and that one is unable or does not need to learn through doing and seeking. "Simple faith" is a kind of sleep, well guarded by social constraints of behavior. The seeker is hard pressed to work, not only against his own limitations, but also against the group's perceptions of what is deemed dangerous, but is, in truth, for the sake of Heaven. One begins to see a kind of utopian ideology developing within the system of belief in the zaddikim, the fear of otherness, a dependence on rules of behavior, a need to explain everything in terms of the group, and the beginnings of complete dependence on a leader figure. The relation between solitude and solidarity is always a subject of acute interest, and the moment one or the other begins to dominate, or one begins to silence essential questions, an alarm needs to be sounded.

But it was not only the relationship between the hasid and the Seer that Przysucha questioned, but also the individual's relationship with God Himself. There is a distinct difference between the one who approaches with bowed head, coming again and again in the same position, and the one who seeks his Heavenly Father face to face, so to speak, and is conscious not only of the gift, but also of the giver and the purpose for which the gift has been given.

The Seer clothed and fed his hasidim, sustained them by his radiance, but was unable to make them autonomous and, in a strange way, perhaps no one suffered from this more than he did. As a consequence of being unable to demand more of his students, they were also unable to ask more of him.

Perhaps the perception of the Seer exacted a heavy price on himself, and arguably on the people as well, so dependent were they upon him. The Lyzhansk-Lublin definition of the zaddik was of someone on a separate metaphysical plane, with whom all Jewish souls were interwoven and dependent as a root-soul. The role of the zaddik was to redeem the masses and, if he was successful, to create a mass movement. All this the Seer had done as had no one else before him in the history of Hasidism – but there was a price to be paid, including a personal one. The Seer said:

> In my youth, I had a desire to write a book on the order Kodshim. But afterwards with all of my immense communal responsibilities...

not only could I not write a commentary, I even find it difficult (to learn it) myself, for I have no time to study in depth.[46]

As we shall see, there was a profound ambivalence in Przysucha regarding a mass movement (i.e., if the crowd is too big). This is conveyed in the following parable told by R. Menachem Mendel of Kotzk:

There was once a Jew who, having lost his snuffbox, came across a ram.

> The sacred ram was pacing the earth, and the tips of his black horns touched the stars. When he heard the old Jew lamenting, he leaned down to him and said, "Cut a piece from my horns, whatever you need to make a new snuffbox." The old Jew did this, made a new snuffbox, and filled it with tobacco. Then he went to the house of study and offered everyone a pinch. They sniffed and sniffed, and everyone who sniffed it cried, "Oh, what wonderful tobacco! It must be because of the box. Oh, what a wonderful box! Wherever did you get it?" So the old man told them about the good sacred ram. And one after the other they went out on the street and looked for the sacred ram. The sacred ram was pacing the earth and the tips of his black horns touched the stars. One after another they went up to him and begged permission to cut off a bit of his horns. Time after time the sacred ram leaned down to grant the request. Box after box was made and filled with tobacco. The fame of the boxes spread far and wide. Every step he took, the sacred ram met someone who asked for a piece of his horns. **Now the sacred ram still paces the earth – but he has no horns.**[47]

What sort of man tells such a parable unless it be someone who experiences the tension between "giving" and "being"? The image of the ram pacing the earth while the tips of his horns touch the stars is reminiscent of Jacob's ladder "that was rooted on the earth, yet whose head reached the heavens." And just as the ladder might well be a metaphor for a human

---

[46] An approbation to the work *Zon Kedoshim*; see Yitzhak Alfasi, *Ha-Hozeh mi-Lublin*, 178.

[47] *Or ha-Ganuz*, M. Buber (Heb: 443–445); *Tales of the Hasidim: Later Masters* (Eng), 288–289. I have changed the word "goat" to "ram." A. Bick, *Yesod ha-emunot be-Hassidut, Gilayon ha-dor* on Hasidut. New York: Tammuz: 1945.

being, so is the sacred ram a metaphor for the zaddik. For Przysucha, to combine both is to be a Jew – with "solitude for company."

In Poland, the Seer developed Hasidism into a mass movement. But a mass movement must, by definition, appeal to a lower common denominator both intellectually and spiritually, and often brings out the weakest elements in its ideology. His very success planted the seeds of its own superficiality.

Lublin and Przysucha symbolize a clash of models of leadership. Lublin might well have argued that any meritocracy, be it a Lithuanian one of Talmudic scholarship, a hasidic one of personal piety, or a combination of both (i.e., Przysucha), excludes the majority of the Jewish people. Lublin represents the achievement of the Seer in giving the Jews of Poland a sense of access to sanctity.[48]

There are hints within hasidic tradition that the Seer recognized that the approach of the Yehudi was a more elevated one than his own. R. Yaacov Aryeh of Radzymin, a disciple of R. Bunim, related:

> The Rebbe of Lublin said that the truth is that the path of the Yehudi is higher than ours, but what can we do, for it (our path) was created by R. Elimelech.[49]

R. Mordechai of Chernobyl (who came from a very different hasidic tradition) is reported as saying:

> In this world the Rebbe of Lublin is the Rebbe of all and has achieved more, but in the higher world the Yehudi achieved a more elevated level.[50] [51]

---

[48] See Zak ("Studies," op. cit., chap. 1, n. 6), who argues that the Hozeh consciously developed a charismatic leadership based on the total allegiance of the devotee to the zaddik (229); the zaddik was capable, nay, obligated, to intervene and influence the Divine for the material benefits of his community (232); and that the function of prayer was essentially for earthly needs (233). The Seer's understanding of the role of the zaddik is to be seen within the context of his teacher R. Elimelech of Lyzhansk. The latter is reported to have said that he had annulled the "pre-messianic pangs" (*Toldot Adam*, par. Ekev, 63; par. Ki Tetze, 68).

[49] *Bikkurei Aviv*, Introduction.

[50] *Ramatayim Zofim*, 22.65; *Niflaot ha-Yehudi*, 22; *Magdil Yeshuot Malko*, 10 n. 3. See also what R. Naftali of Ropshitz – an opponent of the Yehudi – said in admiration about him (*Niflaot ha-Yehudi*, 19).

But Lublin might well have argued that the world of Przysucha left the majority of the Jewish people out in the cold. Not everyone was capable of such independence. R. Meir of Apta said explicitly,

> For there are those who do not have the strength for self-sacrifice in practice other than by connecting to zaddikim. And that is what is meant by "every Jew has a portion in the world to come." That is to say, that they have a portion in the world to come by connecting with zaddikim, but not by themselves alone.[52]

This tension in leadership roles is reflected in the difference between the original school of Habad and modern-day Lubavitch. The founder, Rabbi Shneur Zalman of Liady, formulated a series of enactments designed specifically to restrict and limit access of his devotees to himself. A hasid could only come to R. Shneur Zalman under certain conditions, at specific times. Moreover, he demanded that he not be disturbed by hasidim asking him questions about their personal, material welfare that any local rabbi was as competent to answer as he. These enactments, known as *Takkanot Liozna (Lyozna)*,[53] are in complete contrast with that of modern day Lubavitch, which enjoys the "success" of a mass movement – like Lublin. The Seer was prepared to sacrifice himself in order to bring Hasidism to as many people as possible. R. Shneur Zalman was not, nor were the Yehudi, R. Bunim, or the Kotzker.

With all of the Yehudi's genuine admiration for the Seer, the values that the Yehudi sought were different from those taught in the court of the Seer. What later became known as Przysucha was simply a different world from Lyzhansk and Lublin. Przysucha was a form of Hasidism unlike any other form known until then. In fact, some scholars doubt that Przysucha can even be called Hasidism.

---

[51] However, Przysucha admired the Seer. See *Niflaot ha-Rebbe*, 82 (240): "Hiddushei ha-Rim said... he was called the Rebbe by all the generations, for he is Rebbe until the Messiah." See also what R. Bunim said about the Seer, ibid., 90 (303). See also *Tiferet ha-Yehudi*, 146, no. 7, for R. Mordechai of Chernobyl's evaluation of the Seer and the Yehudi.

[52] *Or le-Shamayim*, par. Vaera, 71.

[53] D.Z. Hillman, *Iggerot Ba'al ha-Tanya u-venei doro* (Jerusalem: 1953); idem., *Sefer ha-Toldot: R. Shneur Zalman mi-Liady*, chap. 5, 67–77.

Over and beyond everything else, Przysucha demanded truthfulness; that the individual be true to himself – a process that took place through the mind and through piety. For only then could one be true to one's God. This was a demand with no compromise, which continued for three generations – inaugurated by the Yehudi, through R. Bunim, to the Kotzker.

A BIOGRAPHICAL SKETCH
OF R. SIMHAH BUNIM

"He spoke with passion and with such an inner confidence that
he believed that he had the capability to bring all the deniers back
to the fold."

Yitzhak Miesis

A Biographical Sketch

HASIDIC TRADITION RELATES that when R. Bunim first came to Lublin, the
Seer was very complimentary to him and said:

"My dear Bunim, hold yourself fast to me and you will receive the Holy
Spirit from the celestial world and the whole world will run before you."[1]

And if ultimately R. Bunim broke with the Seer, at least the prognosis
turned out to be true. For R. Bunim was the dominant hasidic personality of
his day in Poland.

ॐ ∾

R. Simhah Bunim (Bonhardt) was born in Vodislav, Poland circa 1766.[2] His
father, R. Zvi, was a well-known *darshan* (preacher), whose collected
sermons, *Eretz Zvi,* bears an approbation from the famous R. Yehezkel
Landau of Prague, the *Noda' be-Yehudah*. R. Zvi was born in Germany; his

---

[1] *Ramatayim Zofim*, chap. 18, n. 63.
[2] Yehuda Menachem Boem, *R. Bunim* (Bnei Berak: 1997), 25; Rabinowitz, "From
Lublin to Przysucha," 294, mentions two other possible dates: 1765 and 1767.

dress, manners and mother tongue were German,[3] and he was well-traveled. He placed particular emphasis on clear intellectual understanding of the text. In the introduction to his book *Eretz Zvi*, he states:

> I haven't brought in this book any astute hermeneutics; rather, as is my way, I have straightened what was crooked on the basis of the literal meaning of the text and what is compatible with it, in such a way that human intelligence will agree with and vouch for it.[4]

R. Zvi was interested in medieval Jewish philosophy.[5] [6] Thus, many of the rationalist elements we shall later identify in the thought of R. Bunim are already to be found in his father, who might be called a traditional rational pietist.

Thus R. Bunim grew up in a house of learning (his mother's family traced its ancestry to R. Joel Sirkis, the *Bach*), one marked by awareness of the larger world within the German cultural orbit.[7] (German was the key to secular culture; few, if any books on secular disciplines were available in Hebrew). Unlike most "hagiographical" (or larger than life) accounts, which describe the origins of various zaddikim, R. Bunim was not[8] a child prodigy

---

[3] Boem, 26. Regarding R. Zvi Hirsch son of Judah Leib, the Maggid from Vaidislov (Wlodzyslow), see S.Y. Glicksburg, *Ha-Derashah be-Yisrael* (Tel Aviv: 1940). R. Zvi wrote two works: *Eretz Zvi* (Prague: 1786) and *Asarah le-Meah* (Berlin: 1796).

[4] *Asarah le-Meah*, 3–4.

[5] In *Eretz Zvi*, he quotes, among others, Ben Sira, Bahya ibn Paquda's *Hovot ha-Levavot*, Maimonides, Nahmanides, Ibn Ezra, Radak, Albo, Abrabanel, Moses Alshekh, and the *Shelah* (R. Isaiah Horowitz's *Shenei Luhot ha-Berit*). The very first issue discussed in this work is Maimonides's negative approach to miracles (with which R. Zvi identifies). He talks about God as "the source of intelligence." R. Zvi is concerned with issues of personal piety such as humility, service of God without an ulterior motive, equanimity, and a sense of being true to who one really is. R. Bunim occasionally quotes his father. See *Kol Simhah*, par. Vayetze, 34 and *Siah Sarfei Kodesh* 1.12, n. 27; *Torat Simah*, n. 64. R. Zvi is also concerned with *peshat*. He uses the parable as an educational methodology (a hallmark of R. Bunim).

[6] Unlike his son, he also frequently quotes the Zohar, the Ari (R. Yitzhak Luria), and R. Hayyim Vital.

[7] Rabinowitz, "From Lublin to Przysucha," 295. R. Bunim spoke German, Polish and Romanian. See *Keter Kehunnah*, 127.

[8] *Ramatayim Zofim*, chap. 18.59. Rabinowitz, "R. Bunim," 13–14, argues the opposite (as does Aescoly in *Hasidut be-Folin*, 74). Ultimately, the source in *Ramatayim Zofim* is

(an *ilui*). At an early age he was sent to Hungary to the Yeshiva of R. Yirmiya, who was a friend of his father's.[9] After learning in the yeshiva for about ten years,[10] R. Bunim went into business, and was involved in financial matters until at least 1812.[11] R. Bunim married Rebeccah, the daughter of R. Moshe Auvergir-Kogov. They had one son, Avram Moshe, and two daughters.

R. Bunim worked in various businesses. He was a bookkeeper for the Konsumpcja in the town of Siedlice;[12] he journeyed to the fair in Danzig as part of the timber business;[13] and worked for Tamril,[14] wife of Berke

---

self-contradictory and the second part may have been added as part of Hasidic hagiography.

[9] There were no yeshivot in Poland at the time, so there is no major significance to R. Bunim being sent to a yeshiva in Hungary. However, Boem, 36, n. 14, does attach some significance to this decision on the part of R. Bunim's father. There is a dispute between Boem and Rabinowitz as to whether R. Bunim studied in the yeshiva of R. Mordechai Banitt (and was deeply influenced by him). *Ramatayim Zofim* (chap. 18, n. 59) says so explicitly. Rabinowitz attributes to R. Banitt a profound influence on R. Bunim. But Boem points out, inter alia, that there is no mention whatsoever of R. Bunim by R. Banitt, a point that he argues in detail (35). Rabinowitz ("R. Bunim," 14), by contrast, suggests that R. Bunim's inclination to medieval Jewish philosophy and his knowledge of languages came from R. Banitt but, as mentioned above, this seems to have come from his father. R. Jeremiah of Mättersdorff, a native of Poland and author of *Moda'ah Rabba* (Lemberg, 1798), was invited to head the yeshiva in Mättersdorff in 1770. He presided over the yeshiva for twenty-eight years, and he also gave an approbation to R. Bunim's father's book *Eretz Zvi*.

[10] Boem, 37.

[11] Boem, 707. See G. Dynner, "Men of Silk: The Hasidic Conquest of Polish Jewry, 1754–1830," Ph.D. diss. (Brandeis: 2002), 321–322, who says, "He appears to have been influenced to undertake worldly pursuits by his brother-in-law, a medical doctor named Joshua Leib Beneliowski." Cf. Z.M. Rabinowitz, "Sources and Documents for the History of Polish Hasidism" (Hebrew), *Sinai* 82 (1978): 85. Rabinowitz finds mention of this brother-in-law in the appendix to R. Simhah Bunim's father's book, *Asarah le-Meah* (Berlin, 1801). The reference was deleted in subsequent additions.

[12] *Siah Sarfei Kodesh* 4, 15:6. This is verified in a contract signed by R. Bunim (Dynner 241), according to *Siah Sarfei Kodesh he-Hadash*, 4.170, n. 21. He was a bookkeeper for R. Yekil Fachter of Przysucha.

[13] *Or Simhah*, §§40, 63.

[14] Boem, p. 61. See Aescoly, *Hasidut be-Folin*, D. Assaf (ed.), (Jerusalem, 1999), 75. "This Tamril, the archetype of the assimilated (Jews) in Poland. It would appear that

Bergson (son of Shmuel Zeditkover, one of the heads of the council of Warsaw), which took him regularly to Leipzig.[15] R. Bunim was widely traveled.[16] He eventually settled and became an apothecary,[17] opening a shop in Przysucha. To qualify as an apothecary, R. Bunim would have to have been proficient in German (his mother tongue), Latin, and the secular requirements of the profession.[18] On the whole, R. Bunim seems to have had his ups and downs in his business activities.[19] [20]

---

her support for the hasidim and their zaddikim was a type of hobby for the wealthy." This is a scurrilous remark. Dynner gives a full biography of the Bergson family; its founder Shmuel Zbytkower (133–138, which was probably the source for Aescoly's remark); his son Berek Sonnenberg-Bergson (138–150) and his wife Tamril (150–159).

[15] On all this see Rabinowitz, "R. Bunim," 17–18; *Siah Sarfei Kodesh he-Hadash*, 4.164–183 §§2, 11, 12, 21; *Siah Sarfei Kodesh*, 1.33, n. 160. On the role of Leipzig in Jewish affairs, Dynner says (121): "The acceleration of Jewish involvement in international trade in the eighteenth century is reflected in the records of the Leipzig trade fairs. In 1775, 413 Polish merchants attending the Leipzig fairs were Jewish, compared with 68 non-Jews. By 1796, 791 were Jewish, while the number of non-Jewish merchants from Poland had declined to 60." R. Simhah Bunim supervised the floating of timber to Danzig, as well as its sale, an activity that began during Berek's lifetime (*Siah Sarfei Kodesh*, 2. 15.24).

[16] Apropos of this, R. Bunim said of himself that his soul was from the tribe of Zevulun. *Siah Sarfei Kodesh*, 1.26, n. 123; *Siah Sarfei Kodesh he-Hadash*, 4.181, n. 65.

[17] This is disputed by Dynner, 155, n. 199, who believes such a statement to be doubtful because Jews could not obtain pharmaceutical licenses in Galicia until 1832, five years after R. Simhah Bunim's death. See A. Eisenbach, *The Emancipation of the Jews in Poland, 1780–1870* (Oxford, 1991), 204. But other traditions suggest that it was the Russian government that later decided to forbid Jews from being chemists and it was this that led R. Bunim to sell his shop. See *Torat Simhah*, n. 284; *Keter Kehunnah*, 127, n. 4; Boem 79; J. Fox, *Rabbi Menachem Mendel of Kotzk* (Jerusalem, 1967), 35.

[18] See Rabinowitz, "Sources and Documents" (op. cit., n. 10), 82–86. R. Bunim was known as a doctor of medicine: Rabinowitz maintains that when he became rebbe he closed his chemist shop in Przysucha and soon thereafter he became blind; see n. 19. Boem (p. 597) disputes both assertions. R. Bunim ceased to be a chemist because the Russian government forbade Jews from practicing that profession. Nor does he think that R. Bunim became blind immediately, but only later on (and even then it is not clear if this was total or partial). R. Bunim was presumably an autodidact (Aescoly, 75).

[19] Regarding R. Bunim's financial affairs see *Siah Sarfei Kodesh*, 2:15, n. 24; *Siah Sarfei Kodesh he-Hadash*, 4:171, n. 24; *Or Simhah*, n. 56. Already by 1793, we find R. Bunim in Przysucha: *Siah Sarfei Kodesh*, 1:58.

While in the West, R. Bunim visited the theatre and played chess and cards with assimilated Jews.[21] He was fully conversant with the culture of the age.[22] R. Bunim never denied any of these activities (however we might explain his motives). To the contrary, he argued that it was these very experiences that gave him insights into human nature.[23] Nor did he change out of his western dress[24] when he returned to Poland. Hasidic tradition was aware of this exceptional behavior and expressed this in its own fashion. His disciple, the Hiddushei ha-Rim, said of R. Bunim:

> My teacher, R. Bunim, would enter places as a trial (i.e., despite the danger); something the tannaim and amoraim would not do.[25]

Although R. Bunim was later vilified[26] because of these activities,[27] [28] he never forsook his concern for assimilated Western Jewry.[29] Many stories reflect his efforts to maintain contact with wayward assimilated Jews and, during his leadership, he continued to send his disciples to make contact with them.[30] Whereas the Yehudi accepted the validity of this type of work,[31]

---

[20] *Siah Sarfei Kodesh*, 4.15, n. 6.

[21] *Torat Simhah*, n. 284; *Siah Sarfei Kodesh he-Hadash*, 4. 167 ns. 13, 18, 20, 22; *Siah Sarfei Kodesh* 1.48, n. 225; 122, n. 629; *Or Simhah*, n. 63; *Siah Sarfei Kodesh he-Hadash*, par. *Ekev*, 1. 125; *Siah Sarfei Kodesh*, 4.15, n. 7; 5.58.

[22] When R. Bunim had to rescue a wayward young man from a brothel, he was prepared to do that as well. *Or Simhah*, n. 42; see also *Siah Sarfei Kodesh he-Hadash*, 4.170, n. 20.

[23] See Chap. 11.

[24] *Ramatayim Zofim*, chap. 18, n. 63. In spite of his western dress, R. Bunim was accepted as such by the Seer: *Or Simhah*, n. 57, and of course by the Yehudi, *Siah Sarfei Kodesh*, 2.10, n. 5.

[25] *Or Simhah*, n. 12.

[26] Regarding R. Bunim's possible projection of his own situation onto Joseph, see Chap. 7 and, e.g., *Siah Sarfei Kodesh*, 2:85, n. 285.

[27] *Ramatayim Zofim*, 18, n. 62; *Or Simhah*, n. 58.

[28] See below, Chap. 11.

[29] Of course it was these very qualities that enabled R. Bunim to defend the hasidic world when it was under attack from the reformers and from the Russian government. R. Bunim was chosen to represent the Hasidic world on behalf of Polish Hasidism in dealing with the Russian and Polish governments. See Addendum D.

[30] Boem, 453–467.

R. Bunim was proactively engaged with it[32] and philosophically committed to this contact even after he became a rebbe.[33]

An early biographical sketch of R. Bunim appears in the work *Keter Kehunnah*, published some forty years after his death, in 1866. *Keter Kehunnah,* written by Alexander Zederbaum, editor of the first Hebrew weekly, *Ha-Melitz,*[34] was essentially an anti-hasidic work.[35] As a maskil (a proponent of the Enlightenment [Haskalah]), Zederbaum clearly had his own agenda, which he projects onto R. Bunim – and, in some cases, he is factually incorrect.[36] But notwithstanding these reservations, an impression of R. Bunim can be gained from this work.

> A great man,[37] erudite in Talmud, in religious literature and in Jewish science. An expert chemist who knew something about medicine, but more about natural science... he also knew German, Polish, Latin; a diligent man. R. Bunim had seen a lot in his youth; he had mixed amongst different groups as a result of his contractual dealings with the government and the army commanders during the Polish wars.[38] Only in old age,[39] when he had lost his wealth, was he forced to stay at home in his own town, the place where the zaddik, Yaakov Yitzhak (named the Yid [i.e., the Yehudi]) had hung his sign.

---

[31] Regarding the Yehudi's connection with assimilated Jews, see *Siah Sarfei Kodesh,* Additions, n. 54, *Tiferet ha-Yehudi* 174, n. 86; *Meir Einei ha-Golah,* n. 153; Rabinowitz, "The Yehudi," 140, n. 18.

[32] *Or Simhah,* n. 23; *Siah Sarfei Kodesh,* 3.136, n. 514; Boem 458; *Siah Sarfei Kodesh,* 1:54, n. 256.; *Torat Simhah,* n. 64; *Siah Sarfei Kodesh,* 1:122, n. 629 and 48, n. 225.

[33] *Siah Sarfei Kodesh,* 3:136 n. 514; 4:15 n. 7; *Siah Sarfei Kodesh he-Hadash,* 4:173, n. 38; 180, n. 58; *Or Simhah,* n. 22; *Torat Simhah,* n. 101.

[34] Published in Odessa, 1866.

[35] *Encyclopaedia Judaica,* 16:965.

[36] For example, Zederbaum says that R. Bunim only came to Przysucha in his old age. But we have testimony that R. Bunim was in Przysucha in 1793, when he was twenty-seven years old. Is it possible that Zederbaum was misled because, as a Maskil, he couldn't imagine how such a worldly person could get involved in Hasidism unless of course he was an old man and couldn't do anything else. See also Weissenfeld's note of a factual mistake in *Keter Kehunnah* in his "Exchange of Letters," 80.

[37] *Keter Kehunnah,* 127.

[38] See *Ramatayim Zofim,* chap. 30, n. 89.

[39] See above, note 36.

He drew near to him... and when the zaddik was close to death he appointed R. Bunim his successor.[40]

How was a person who spent so much time in the West, whose mother tongue was German rather than Yiddish, who dressed as a Western person, had a secular profession (and practiced as an apothecary in Przysucha) that involved him in secular culture, who had visited the theatre (all of which was indeed acknowledged and held against him) – how was such a person able to become one of the most prominent figures in the history of Polish Hasidism? To appreciate the significance of all this one need only recall what R. Shneur Zalman – the founder of Lubavitch – said about Napoleon (and in his wake, the Enlightenment):

> If Napoleon wins, the Jewish people will be more wealthy... but their hearts will become distant and separated from their Father in Heaven; and if Alexander our master wins, though the Jewish people will be poorer... their hearts will be closer and joined to their Father in Heaven.[41]

R. Shneur Zalman expressed his opposition to the openness of the western world. Yet here was R. Bunim, whose close acquaintance with Western culture did not detract from his religiosity. There were no contemporary hasidic leaders in Eastern Europe who had a secular profession, hardly any that spoke any language other than Yiddish, and no one was conversant with Western culture. Yet it is R. Bunim who became the dominant hasidic figure in Poland. R. Bunim contained a number of worlds within himself. He balanced the realms of enlightenment and tradition in a way that detracted from neither, but rather inspired both. He was able to combine religious integrity and enthusiasm in a manner that in no way hindered originality or soundness of thought. Ultimately, this pronounced disparity from the traditional narrative of the Jewish zaddik stands as a testament to the religious personality of R. Bunim. Whatever the

---

[40] This contradicts other information which indicates that following the death of each of the three major leaders of Przysucha, it was not clear who was going to be the successor. Nor is there any indication that any one of them was appointed by the departing leader to take over his mantle.

[41] See Addendum D.

elements needed to explain this phenomenon, it surely attests to the power of his personality.

⇛ ⇚

When R. Bunim first came to Lublin he is reported to have said:

> He (the Seer) said Torah on the Sabbath night, and he (R. Bunim) said he didn't understand a word that the rebbe z"l said. **But one thing I well knew: namely, that the higher world – the world to come – was here in this world with this rebbe."**[42]

Yet despite the enormous reverence and personal intimacy that R. Bunim enjoyed with the Seer, he was one of the main advocates, if not the principal one, for the Yehudi's break with the Seer. And whereas the Yehudi maintained that he never broke with the Seer, his rebbe,[43] R. Bunim most certainly did[44] – a point later held against him by his opponents.[45] But what

---

[42] *Ramatayim Zofim* 18.63.

[43] *Tiferet ha-Yehudi* 177, n. 95 (the source is heartrending). The Seer drew an analogy between his own rupture with his teacher R. Elimelech and that between himself and the Yehudi. R. Bunim accepted what the Seer said to the Yehudi and said, "If you would listen to me, my advice to you would be to accept the advice of the rebbe of Lublin and no longer journey to him.... Do not journey to Lublin any longer." However, the Yehudi poignantly replied that the Seer was able to leave R. Elimelech because the Seer was also a disciple of the Maggid. But as for himself, "The majority of my wisdom came from him, from the rebbe of Lublin, and therefore on no account can I accept his advice and stop journeying to my teacher and master." According to Aescoly (64): "The Yehudi's separation was the most significant political incident in the heritage of Hasidism. The Yehudi became a leader, holding court while yet in Lublin."

[44] *Or Simhah*, n. 34.

[45] On the relationship between R. Bunim and the Seer, see *Ramatayim Zofim*, Chap. 17, §52; *Niflaot ha-Rebbe* 90, n. 303. *Bet Yaakov* (Introduction, p. 16), and *Dor Yesharim* 20 (i.e., the Izbica and Radzin tradition), emphasize the intimacy between R. Bunim and the Seer – to the extent that the Seer, rather than the Yehudi, is pictured as the major influence on R. Bunim. The Seer "gave him (R. Bunim) the secrets of the Torah." I suspect that what is being reflected here is an attempt to place the Izbicer (and by extension R. Bunim) in the direct line of Lublin–Lyzhansk and Mezeritch. Boem, 370, is critical of the way R. Gershon Henokh tried to project his grandfather. There is clearly an agenda, but one that runs counter to the philosophy of R. Bunim. Many of the issues that concern the Izbicer (e.g., theology

is most striking is that R. Bunim was able to reconcile his profound disagreement with the Seer as a zaddik and yet maintain that the Seer "had brought the higher world into this world."[46]

It was R. Bunim who developed Przysucha into a movement, not just in articulating its philosophy, but also organizationally. It was through R. Bunim's efforts that centers were created throughout Poland that held allegiance to Przysucha.[47] What might have to some extent been intuitive in the mind of the Yehudi (because of his personality) was now clearly articulated by his disciple, R. Bunim. Though the "great rebellion" had started with the Yehudi,[48] war was not declared on[49] Przysucha during the time of his leadership. This may have been due to the Yehudi's outstanding combination of Talmudic excellence and personal piety. But it also may be due to the fact that the movement, which during the Yehudi's time had been relatively muted and limited to a few, was now competing for dominance over the heart of Polish Hasidism.

There is a certain tendency among supporters of a hasidic movement to deflect radicalism from the zaddik to his hasidim. The argument most typically invoked is that the disciples failed to understand their master[50] – the politician would argue that he was misquoted. Thus friction is ascribed to misunderstanding or failure of some other sort. While it is true that some of R. Bunim's disciples had difficulty in keeping up with the master[51] (he was clearly too profound and complex for some of them[52]), the essential

---

and Kabbalah) are more akin to the Seer, and have little significance in the thought of R. Bunim.

[46] *Ramatayim Zofim*, chap. 18, n. 63.

[47] See Aescoly, 73–74. Dynner, on the basis of Polish archival material, says (64) "Continued hasidic prominence in Zelechow up to 1823 is verified in a police report from that year, which divides Hasidim into two adversarial groups: adherents of the Rabbi Simon Deutsch and those of the Rabbi of Przysucha, R. Simhah Bunim."

[48] Aescoly, ibid., 55–66. See Rabinowitz, *The Yehudi,* 116, based on *Siah Sarfei Kodesh,* 5, p. 74, for the antagonistic reaction of the Seer's pupils.

[49] Aescoly, ibid., 55.

[50] E.g. Aescoly, 53.

[51] *Or Simhah,* n. 23.

[52] This is certainly true of the Yehudi's children. What is so fascinating about Przysucha is that not only is there no inheritance, no dynasty, but one gets the impression that their children do not appreciate the complexity of their fathers. The case of the Yehudi's third son, R. Nehemiah Yehiel of Bihova, who became an

radicalism of Przysucha – its cardinal values and everything that followed from them – were clearly developed under the leadership of R. Bunim, although they had been initiated by the Yehudi. Despite the vitriolic accusations leveled against R. Bunim, he never backtracked, apologized, or compromised. His moral compass remained steadfast.[53] R. Bunim knew that the values he was espousing implied a declaration of war against the normative hasidic world of his time and that, inevitably, war would be declared against him. But R. Bunim's creed was authentic and he was not going to retreat. The soul of Polish Hasidism was at stake, and R. Bunim was prepared to fight for it.

There is a form of human greatness which is reflected in the fact that different people find a resonance in the personality of a great man. It is as if people find themselves in some aspect of him. R. Bunim was a multi-faceted personality, attracting around his table a variety of religious knights. Thus R. Yaacov Aryeh of Radzymin (the longest-lived pupil of R. Bunim) is proudly described by his grandson as being famous for his miracles.[54] Hiddushei ha-Rim, an outstanding Talmudic scholar, was impressed by R. Yisrael of Ruzhin; so was R. Yitzhak of Vorki.[55] The Isbitzer was a theologian immersed in Kabbalah and issues of determinism. All the above was alien to the world of Menachem Mendel of Kotzk.[56] Yet all saw themselves as pupils of R. Bunim and believed him to be their rebbe. Clearly they found a personal resonance in this man. They identified with him but translated his teachings through the prism of their different personalities. When R. Bunim died, his pupils divided into two groups. There were the firebrands, who were attracted to Menachem Mendel; but there were the other pupils of a

---

adherent of R. Yisrael of Ruzhin, is instructive. If there is a form of Hasidism as distant from Przysucha as can be imagined, it is Ruzhin. Ruzhin is a Ukrainian Hasidism that essentially serves the uneducated. Cf. D. Assaf, "The Spread of Hasidism: On R. Nehemiah Yehiel of Bihova, son of 'The Holy Jew'" (Hebrew). *Mehqarim be-tarbut yehudit likhvod Chone Shmeruk* (Jerusalem: 1993), 269–298., and ibid., 289, n. 74, for R. Yisrael of Ruzhin's positive attitude towards the Yehudi. In the case of R. Bunim's son, Avram Moshe, cf. Boem, 458; *Siah Sarfei Kodesh*, 1:54, n. 256.

[53] See Chapter 11.

[54] *Bikkurei Aviv*, Introduction, p. 5.

[55] *Meir Einei ha-Golah*, nos. 371–379; *Ohel Yitzhak* 269.

[56] *Emet ve-Emunah*, n. 863.

softer mien, such as Rabbi Yitzhak of Vorki, who followed R. Bunim's son Avram Moshe. Yet they are all contained within the essence of R. Bunim.

R. Bunim's Self-Doubt

There are sources that suggest that R. Bunim had self-doubt, possibly due to the slings and arrows of criticism, a sense that his audience wasn't capable of understanding him, or that, due to his associations with the outside world, he wasn't completely accepted.

> I heard from him (R. Bunim), z"l, of something that once happened while on a journey close to Warsaw. And this is what he said: I knew that I had to tell about a certain incident, but it was something secular and I knew that it would be seen as a great joke if I told the story. My evil inclination said that I shouldn't tell the story for I would lose the world **and they would no longer regard me as a rebbe.**[57]

R. Bunim's intellectual isolation and expected misinterpretation by his audience are to a certain extent reminiscent of the observation that, "you know what a secret is; a secret is that which you can say openly, to an entire audience of people and it still remains a secret, hidden." One risks a sense of self-betrayal and inadequacy at the moment when one reveals new wisdom and yet if one were to lower the "plane of regard" one would risk losing the very essence of what one is trying to elucidate.

> The Rabbi of Plonsk wrote to me the following. Once, R. Bunim was crying… and he said, "Do you know why I am crying? Come and I'll tell you about an incident. When I was with the holy R. Ephraim of Sedilkov (the author of *Degel Mahaneh Ephraim*), he said that there is no wise man in the world except me and one other who

---

[57] *Ramatayim Zofim*, Chap. 30, n. 88. For further sources on R. Bunim's self-doubt, cf. *Yekhabed Av*, 31 (*Torat ha-Yehudi*, 321, n. 37); *Siah Sarfei Kodesh* 4:45, n. 38, *Or Simhah*, n. 57.

dwells in a certain village; and at this moment that person has just become an apostate."[58]

What does it mean for someone to say of himself (or to repeat what someone else said about him) that there are only two wise people in the world, and the other has just become an apostate? It sounds as though R. Bunim felt insecure as to how far he could go, and what might happen to him if he went too far;[59] he is sensitive to what society could tolerate. R. Bunim lives within the paradox that truth often brings one into dissonance with one's community. Once the teacher accepts that he has to accept and practice the options that "common consciousness" lays before him, he becomes a lost man who has died before his body dies, or is at the very least asleep.

A similar sense of aloneness comes through from the following passage:

> Once he said the following Torah (on the verse) "and they called his name Esau" – everybody called him so. For the use of the term "calling" is a matter of extension (hamshakhah). **For everyone is drawn to falsity, but not everyone understands truth."[60]**

Truth always comes as a revelation of human personality. One is forced to engage; it is insufficient to merely comment, assess, agree or disagree; one is compelled to stand eye to eye.

Based on such a clear sense of dissonance, what motivates a person to maintain his cause, when he essentially knows that in many ways he is fighting a losing battle? Where does a person find his inspiration within such an insoluble state of affairs? Where is the ground beneath his feet? One is essentially leading one's hasidim to *"ayin,"* to the place of questions and not answers, and each soul responds differently to the encounter. It is understandable that one might feel abandoned or that perhaps one is doing more harm than good.

---

[58] *Or Simhah*, n. 28.

[59] *Siah Sarfei Kodesh*, 1:49, n. 230; *Hashavah le-Tovah*, 165; *Or Simhah*, n. 28. The sequel lends itself to this interpretation. R. Bunim explains how he investigated the reason why this second person became an apostate. He explains that this person was well known to the nobility for his wisdom and that they used to come with their heretical books and argue with him until he was eventually drawn after them.

[60] *Or Simhah*, n. 58.

R. Bunim considers the wise man so recently turned to apostacy, identifies with him, asking, what is the difference between me and that man? "There but for the grace of God go I." Perhaps the difference is the acceptance, however difficult, of one's limitations, and hearing a voice that says, "Day draws near, another one, do what you can."

R. Bunim's self-disparagement might also have been due to his personal humility. R. Bunim, like the Seer, is reported to have said: "And I myself am no rebbe."[61] But is R. Bunim's expressed self-doubt anything more than the expression of a great man who, because of his greatness, is aware of his limitations? Or is it the expression of an outsider? There are two types of people who can say, "I am no rebbe." It might be said by someone who indeed is not a rebbe; or it may be said by someone who, because of his depth, realizes what a rebbe could be, the supreme example being Moses. If so, R. Bunim's self-disparagement becomes something entirely different, an expression of strength rather than of weakness, made by someone who has a deep-seated sense of identity.

> I heard in the name of the holy R. Bunim about the Midrash that the Almighty showed Adam each generation and its leaders... and he asked why God showed the generation before its leaders. And he said that if God had first shown Adam the leader, then Adam would have said, "How could Simhah Bunim have been a leader?..."[62]

What is confirmed by this Midrash is R. Bunim's deep awareness of his inadequacies, while at the same time his deep self-confidence, much like the Seer. It seems that R. Bunim's self-disparagement speaks to an ability to acknowledge contradictions and the awareness of his abilities and inadequacies.

R. Bunim clearly felt the vitriolic language of his antagonists. One hears in the following the voice of someone who is describing his own situation:

> On the sentence "they shall curse, but You shall bless" he is reported as saying, "One who has enemies who curse him is blessed

---

[61] *Ramatayim Zofim*, Chapter 3, n. 20.
[62] *Ma'amarei Simhah*, n. 81.

by God... for if he didn't have enemies, he would not receive the blessings."[63] [64]

One of the "blessings" that R. Bunim is referring to here is the kind of self-knowledge which comes about as the consequence of standing face to face in equanimity before one's enemies. He was not above criticism, which in many cases had more than a side of truth, and yet there was a value that overrode it. R. Bunim's vulnerability made it possible for him to accept this self-knowledge. Even more remarkable, is that R. Bunim's vulnerability seems to have in no way undermined his own sense of himself nor that of his movement.

಄ ಬ

The following words exquisitely express the dialectic between R. Bunim's perception of his own significance and his awareness of the "world" around him:

> R. Bunim once said, were it not for the fact that I am afraid of the world (i.e., what people might say) I would blow the Shofar on Rosh ha-Shanah that falls on the Sabbath. For the rabbinic Court of the Rif used to blow the Shofar on Rosh ha-Shanah that fell on the Sabbath, and my group is as important and great as they were.[65]

Here one sees R. Bunim with the awareness of his own greatness, but he is nonetheless aware that he is operating within a context and that it is prudent to choose one's battles wisely, to know where they will have the greatest possible significance.

One might add that at least seven or eight times in the work *Kol Simhah*, R. Bunim is quoted as saying, "It is impossible to explain it further," which

---

[63] *Kol Simhah* nos, Psalms, 114, and see also the sequel, "so that even if he is not worthy of blessings himself...," *Torat Simhah*, n. 149.

[64] See *Hashavah le-Tovah*, par. Korah, 54; *Torat Simhah*, §327, where R. Bunim notes that Moses has been accused of the very thing which he is not. One wonders whether R. Bunim might also have been thinking of himself. See also *Torat Simhah*, n. 57.

[65] *Kol Mevaser*, 3:45, n. 37.

may suggest a certain sensitivity to what people are incapable of understanding.[66]

Yet with all this circumspection, R. Bunim is not a torn soul. One does not find within him the Herculean clash between soul and body. To the contrary, R. Bunim is convivial, but his *joie de vivre* should in no way be taken as indicating a lack of spirituality. Just as obscurity should not be confused with profundity, so angst does not necessarily indicate depth, nor its lack superficiality. There is something almost perverse in the assumption that a harmonious soul indicates a certain shallowness. R. Bunim proposes a philosophy of groundedness, an aversion to *frumkeit*, a wisdom of "living in the world," an intensity born not of a sequestered asceticism but rather of serving the Creator very much in this world.

In R. Bunim's thought, the thrust is not on repairing the Godhead, uniting the *Shekhinah* with its source, or penetrating the secrets of the Divine,[67] but rather with trying to penetrate the human psyche. The issues in the world of Przysucha are those of self-reflection, the quest for purity of motive with the concomitant danger of depression.[68] The litmus test for this is the willingness to engage in preparation – and what underpins these issues is an awareness of human personality, and the desire for that personality to be integrated. Though there is nothing fundamentally original in these ideas, it is the thrust or emphasis they are given that marks Przysucha as being different from most other forms of Hasidism.[69]

---

[66] *Bereshit,* 9; *Vayetze,* 32; *Shemot,* 55; *Vaera,* 58; *Mishpatim,* 73; *Shelah Lekha,* 87; *Va-ethanan,* 107; *Tehillim,* 114. The seventh quote appears in the first edition (Breslau: 1859), which was reprinted on the basis of manuscripts with "additions" by R. Aaron Walden (1903; repnt. Jerusalem: 1997). See also *Torat Simhah,* §148.

[67] See below, Chap. 4.

[68] See below, Chap. 8.

[69] Habad may also talk about the *middot* of man, but there it is all subsumed within the structure of kabbalah. This is virtually nonexistent in Przysucha; the difference between the two is like that between theology and its impact on humanity, and psychoanalysis. See below, Chap. 4.

R. Bunim was rebbe for some twelve years (1815–1827). There are contradictory traditions as to precisely when R. Bunim went blind (as well as to whether he was totally blind or only partially so). It is also not clear whether this hardship occurred toward the end of his life[70] or soon after he became rebbe.[71] But, here was a man who had experienced a rich life who now found himself blind. Perhaps, this physical impediment facilitated a process of going inwards – and of drawing on his own inner world in order to understand other people. This capability became more finely attuned and was combined with R. Bunim's understanding of himself to produce the supreme teacher – one who had an inner light.

R. Bunim was once asked why he didn't go to doctors to cure him of his blindness. He replied, "I can see all I need to see."[72][73] Harold Bloom says of the blind Milton:

> He yearns, most movingly, for the visible, but he does not need it, and its absence became one of the greatest of his astonishing panoply of strengths.

About Blake (a contemporary of the Yehudi), Bloom says:

> … He wants us to see… but how we see and even at times what we see, will depend upon the self-purging of our own eyes.[74]

Przysucha could not have said it better. As Susan Sontag wrote in a letter to Borges,

> Your modesty was part of the sureness of your presence.… The serenity and the transcendence of self that you found are to me exemplary. You showed that it is not necessary to be unhappy, even while one is clear-eyed and undeluded about how terrible everything

---

[70] Boem, 597–602; so too P. Sadeh, "*Ish be-ḥeder sagur*," 35. So *Keter Kehunnah*, 128.

[71] Rabinowitz, *Mekorot u-Teudot be-Hasidut Polin*, 85 §19. See also *Nifla'ot Ha-Yehudi*, 68, §7.

[72] *Or Simḥah*, §§38, 106.

[73] See *Sefer Alexander*, 31: "When R. Bunim's eyes were no longer able to see he said 'Legally I don't see a thing; but practically I see millions of people born like cats, living like cats, and dying like cats."

[74] Harold Bloom, "The Ringers in the Tower." In *Studies in Romantic Tradition* 40, 38. In his opinion, by appealing to the holy light to shine inward, Milton created English Romanticism.

is. Somewhere you said that a writer – delicately you added: all persons – must think that whatever happens to him or her is a resource. (You were speaking of your blindness.)[75]

ॐ ॐ

One of the questions that naturally presents itself is this: To what extent were R. Bunim's ideas influenced by his family background, his German mother tongue and, more important, to what extent did his experience of and exposure to the culture of the West influence those ideas? It has been argued[76] that the sense of self is rooted in the social dislocation of modernity, in changes in living conditions. Thus, Przysucha ought to be seen in the context of the sweeping changes brought about in Congress Poland by urbanization and immigration, leading to an internalization of religion, a striving for personal purity, an individualistic concept of the relationship between man and God. Modernity causes sensitivity towards the individual self[77] leading to an anthropocentric turning away from the metaphysical and diminishing discussion of the nature of God – all of which are indeed characteristics of Przysucha. This approach might be called the sociology of dislocation. It describes the movement from the country to the town, creating the fertile ground for modernity in which the self becomes central.

An alternative approach is to talk about the influences of the Zeitgeist (the spirit of the age). Gershon Hundert[78] and others have drawn attention to the similarities between Hasidism and other eighteenth century spiritual movements such as pietism, quietism, and others. He describes the appearance of a similar Geist at a similar Zeit and says that perhaps "religious individualism characterizes an unexplained eighteenth-century Zeitgeist that applied to Hasidism and other contemporary movements."

---

[75] Susan Sontag, *Where the Stress Falls.* Vintage, Great Britain 2003, p. 112.

[76] A. Brill, *Thinking of God: The Mysticism of Rabbi Zadok of Lublin* (New York: Yeshiva University Press, 2002), 365–367.

[77] On the birth of the modern self, see C. Taylor, *Sources of the Self: The Making of the Modern Identity* (Cambridge, MA: 1989).

[78] "The Contexts." In *Essential Papers on Hasidism Origins to Present,* edited by G.D. Hundert (New York, 1991); cf. R. Schatz-Uffenheimer, *Hasidism as Mysticism: Quietistic Elements in Eighteenth-Century Hasidic Thought* (Hebrew: Jerusalem: 1988; English: Jerusalem–Princeton: 1993), esp. Chapter 1.

However, it is clear from the two works written by R. Bunim's father that, as a traditional pietist, R. Zvi drew on medieval Jewish philosophy and its rationalism. This frame of reference was then brought by R. Bunim[79] into contact with Hasidism[80] – specifically with the personality of the Yehudi. Our claim is that the essential themes of Przysucha were created by the Yehudi. There are no sources we know of to indicate that the Yehudi was influenced by the outside or that he had a conscious sense of dislocation. The societal framework may have sharpened the issues for R. Bunim rather than created them.[81] Yet the ideas of R. Bunim have a certain independence of the social milieu – a certain quality of eternity; for they are found throughout the ages. His background and the influence of his age are felt in the emphases given to certain ideas and values.

At times, we make a great effort, in an attempt to "explain" the nature of greatness. We imagine that if we lay him, R. Bunim, on the couch, we might come to some causal explanation of how he came to be who he was; as if somehow the facts (for example it is argued that it was his brother-in-law who persuaded him to develop a secular profession[82]) can explain the mystery of his religious greatness. But, as Rabindranath Tagore said, "By plucking the petals one does not gather the beauty of the rose." This is not to deny the value of a historical approach. On the contrary, the quest for authenticity means to breathe organically the rhythm of one's age. It may even be seen as an expression of belief in Divine providence – that is, that God created each person at a certain moment in history, **not to imitate another age or its way of thinking**. Indeed, it was the Seer who is reported to have commented on the verse "And they the judges shall judge the people at all times – they shall evaluate the law according to the time and the period."[83]

---

[79] On R. Zvi's attitude toward Hasidism see *Siah Sarfei Kodesh* 1:57, n. 265, but see also *Or Simhah,* n. 35 and *Niflaot ha-Rebbe* 84, n. 260.

[80] Boem, 85–114.

[81] There are similarities between the ways of thinking of R. Bunim and of what is known as Romanticism. See Addendum E.

[82] See note 11 above.

[83] *Or le-Shamayim,* Behukotai, 140.

One final point must be mentioned. What motivates a person who has t
the "west" to go "east"? In other words, why would an intellectual
sophisticate like R. Bunim leave the world of modernity and go to Eastern
Europe? It would appear that then as now, modernity, for all its benefits,
cannot supply food for the soul. Its quest is not for sanctity; its concern is
not how a human being can bring himself to stand before God – but this
was R. Bunim's goal.

PART II

The Seminal Ideas of Przysucha as reflected in
the Thought of R. Simhah Bunim

TORAH AND THEOLOGY

"From the Torah we can come to all the levels that previously
could be achieved via the revelation of the Shekhinah."

The Yehudi

Torah

IN THE PHILOSOPHY of the *mitnaggedim,* someone who studied the rabbinical
texts of the Torah was a partner with God in creation. R. Hayyim of
Volozhin – the leading disciple of the Gaon of Vilna, a contemporary of the
Yehudi – expressed this value in the following way:

> One who is occupied with the holy Torah completes the intention of
> God when He created the world. [God's intention in creating the
> world] was only that the Jewish people should occupy themselves
> with Torah.[1]

The revolution of Hasidism was to stress the service of the heart as the
primary value; hence, it no longer placed such emphasis on the traditional
value of learning.[2]

Przysucha was a reaction to a type of Hasidism that had, in Poland,
become a mass movement – which by definition, appeals to a lower

---

[1] *Nefesh ha-Hayyim,* Gate Four, Chapter 13 (Vilna: 1824).

[2] G. Scholem, *Major Trends in Jewish Mysticism* (New York: 1967), 335. "Its founder
had evolved a new form of religious consciousness in which rabbinical learning,
whatever its intrinsic significance, played no essential part." On the tension between
Torah study and mysticism in the Maggid see Rivka Schatz-Uffenheimer, "Hasidism
and Mysticism: Contemplative Prayer in Hasidism" (Hebrew). In *Studies in Mysticism
and Religion Presented to Gershom G. Scholem* (Jerusalem: 1967), Chapter 14.

common denominator. It was Przysucha that reasserted the value of learning Torah as a primary value also in Hasidism. Like Habad, it demanded that the would-be hasid become a scholar (*talmid hakham*) as well as a spiritual seeker.

Where, for Przysucha, did the study of Torah stand in the pantheon of Jewish values? And how, was its view of Torah study perceived by hasidic contemporaries? The following is quoted in the name of the Saraf, R. Uri of Strelisk (d. 1826), a contemporary of the Yehudi:

> This righteous person (the Yehudi) wanted to bring, from above to below, a new approach; to infuse the hearts of the Jewish people as to how to serve God with Torah and prayer together. And that had never been (done before) in the world.[3]

For R. Uri of Strelisk, a hasidic master of no small significance, the Jewish world was divided into two: those who followed the classic rabbinic path of the study of Talmud, as contrasted with the new world of hasidic piety. To fuse both was seen by him as something totally original.

The phrase "a new approach" (*derekh hadash*) is significant, for it suggests that, already during the Yehudi's lifetime, his contemporaries recognized that what he stood for was not limited to himself alone, but was in fact an approach which could challenge the culture of hasidism throughout Poland.

The next generation clearly saw the uniqueness of the Yehudi's approach. *Hiddushei ha-Rim* says the following:

> The holy Yehudi merited (to have) two senses: the sense of the revealed Torah and the sense of Hasidism. And neither hurt the other.[4]

For the Yehudi, Talmudic study and piety were inseparable. We therefore find him making statements such as:

> Gemara with Tosafot purify the mind.[5]

---

[3] *Imrei Kodesh ha-Shalem,* §68. In addition, the phrase "from above to below" (which describes God's Torah rather than man's prayer) might suggest that what was so new was the reintroduction of "learning" into the hasidic world.

[4] End of *Meir Einei ha-Golah,* §71.

[5] *Tiferet ha-Yehudi,* 161 §29. The Yehudi's challenge was aimed at the heart of Hasidism. If Hasidism in Poland (following the Ukrainian model popularized by the

Via Torah, one can achieve all previous levels… even revelation.[6]

If a person has no mikveh, then he should learn gemara instead.[7]

When the Yehudi says, "Learning *gemara* and *Tosafot* is preparation for prayer," he is being polemical. These are not merely clever aphorisms; rather, they express values that strike at the heart of Hasidism. To equate *gemara* with the *mikveh* is to equate learning with piety, and thereby to reassert the role of learning within the repertoire of the hasidic world. When the Yehudi says that though one might fall to the depths, Torah has the power to cleanse one, he is basically throwing down the gauntlet to the world of Hasidism. Not only piety and prayer, but Torah, can redeem one.

R. Bunim continued the process initiated by the Yehudi in asserting the seminal value of Torah. To R. Bunim, Torah meant studying the classic Rabbinic literature and all that flowed from it.

> R. Bunim once said that he would not go to Hell, for anyone who had a special way of behaving and had never broken it would not be taken into Hell. His special custom of behavior was that he studied Gemara every day[8]; and in the celestial world, he would choose to learn Shas with the Amsterdam edition.[9]

Even if we assume that this statement is exaggerated, it still serves our purpose, for what is being expressed is a value that was identified with R. Bunim or, alternatively, an image that R. Bunim projected. Translated, it meant that the best insurance policy against going to Hell was to learn Talmud.[10]

Commenting on the gemara in *Berakhot* …[11]

Seer) had legitimized the simple faith of the uneducated, to be on par with that of the scholar, then the Yehudi was undermining that cardinal of faith.

[6] *Niflaot Hadashot, Seder Hayom*, 66.

[7] *Mikhtevei Torah*, Letter 60; *Kedushat ha-Yehudi* 257.3.

[8] See also *Emet ve-Emunah*, §853 in the name of the Kotzker.

[9] *Or Simhah*, §73.

[10] R. Bunim had a fixed time each day for studying *Tanna de-Bei Eliyahu* (*Ramatayim Zofim*, Ch. 1, §34); he also studied *Hoshen Mishpat* (*Ramatayim Zofim*, Ch. 3, §2). *Kol Simhah* has a wide range of commentaries on rabbinical topics.

[11] *b. Berakhot* 5b.

If he examined himself (as to why he was suffering) and did not find a sufficient reason, he should attribute it to his not studying Torah enough,

R. Bunim asks:

How can one say "he did not find" if indeed he had not learned enough? To which R. Bunim replied that "not studying Torah enough" is not the reason for his suffering, but the reason why he can't explain why he is suffering.[12]

Learning Gemara meant that the Torah study would provide insight into one's weaknesses. If one learned more, one would realize that "at every step, one had not fulfilled one's obligation to God."[13] Torah is thus the gateway to self-analysis: someone who is not engaged in the world of learning has simply alienated himself from a primary mechanism for self-understanding.[14] [15] [16]

For R. Bunim the Torah is the source of all life:[17]

All the life force of creation comes from the ten (primordial) words of the Torah... For through the Torah the whole world is renewed;

---

[12] *Siah Sarfei Kodesh*, vol. 1:32 §155; *Ramatayim Zofim* (AZ), Ch. 16, §27; Levinger, "Authentic Statements by the Rebbe of Kotzk" (Hebrew), *Tarbiz* 55 (1986): §32.

[13] *Torat Simhah*, §7; see, however, *Siah Sarfei Kodesh*, 5: 63, where this interpretation is mentioned in the name of the Yehudi; R. Bunim, by contrast, gives a more insightful understanding. See Ch. 8 below.

[14] See *Ma'amarei Simhah*, §55: "A *segulah* (a propitious act) for livelihood is to get up every night and to learn Torah."

[15] R. Bunim said that after the destruction of the Temple, everything in the world had become sullied. Only Torah retained its pristine purity. In addition, the supremacy of Torah led R. Bunim to disparage ritual somewhat. See *Siah Sarfei Kodesh*, 3:5, §4. Cf. *Siah Sarfei Kodesh*, 5:44, where Menachem Mendel of Kotzk is quoted as saying: "If he doesn't learn Torah, he won't know how to look for sin."

[16] "The Gemara explains [the phrase] "This is the burnt sacrifice (olah)" to mean that one who learns the laws of the burnt sacrifice is as if he actually offered up a burnt sacrifice. To which R. Bunim added that when someone would come to Aaron to offer up a sacrifice, Aaron would say to him, 'Why are you bringing a sacrifice? It would be better to learn.'" *Siah Sarfei Kodesh*, 1:9, §5; *Siah Sarfei Kodesh he-Hadash*, par. Tzav, 90.

[17] *Torat Simhah*, §174.

especially after the Torah was given all creation was rejuvenated through the strength of the Torah.[18]

But for R. Bunim, Torah meant something wider than Rabbinic learning. Already in Rabbinic literature and in the Zohar we find that the Torah was construed as a conceptual entity with a real existence, identified as Wisdom.[19] But if the Torah is identified with Wisdom, then by the same token Wisdom is identified with Torah.

> Everything was made with Wisdom – that is to say with the Torah – as is written in the Midrash at the beginning of Genesis.... And that is what is meant by the phrase "you made **all** in wisdom" – *that is to say, the Torah.*[20]

The Yehudi, as well, was unwilling to limit Torah to Talmud study alone,[21] but saw Wisdom as something that could be learned from looking inside oneself and then observing the outside world.

> Once the Yehudi went for a walk with his pupil R. Peretz and saw birds flying and animals pasturing, and all the while chirping and making a noise. R. Peretz said to the Yehudi, "I would really like to understand their chirping and their language." The Yehudi replied, "When you really understand the words that you speak, then you will be able to understand the words that they speak."[22]

---

[18] *Torat Simhah*, §166.

[19] *Gen. Rab.* 1.1; cf. G. Scholem, *On the Kabbalah and its Symbolism* (New York: 1969), 47.

[20] *Torat Simhah*, §148; cf. *Ramatayim Zofim*, Ch. 2, §28.

[21] For the Yehudi, the intellect is not limited to a narrow definition of Torah. Just as prayer cannot be limited alone to the narrow definition of a ritual act, so service of God via the mind is an entire state of being. For the Yehudi, studying Torah extends to using one's intellect in general. Moreover, according to the Yehudi, only after one begins to understand oneself, by means of intellect and introspection, can one begin to understand the world around oneself. But the Yehudi's challenge went further (and was recognized as such by his combatants). The Yehudi not only believed that learning Torah was the basis for the service of God, but he also believed in the use of the intellect per se. For the Yehudi, the intellect should be applied to everyday life. The Yehudi did not challenge the value of Torah; on the contrary, the Yehudi dealt extensively with scholars of the Talmud.

[22] *Tiferet ha-Yehudi*, 152, §15 (a free translation).

Human behavior provides the possibility for engagement so as to deepen one's religiosity, through the prism of gleaning wisdom from all creation.[23] For R. Bunim, two things followed from this: first, that wisdom was to be learned from everyone and from everything; second, that wisdom meant being analytical. This suggests that wisdom meant, not only how one looked at the world but, more important, how one looked at oneself.

> ... there is a person who has reached the quality that he learns from everyone. Even from the speech of ordinary people talking about worldly matters, he finds some allusion to wisdom, how to serve God.[24]

Humanity's task is to relate to the everyday, physical world. For R. Bunim, the world is not filled with divine sparks, nor is it a world from which humanity must extricate itself. The world is what it is and humanity's role is to see it for what it is. Similarly, mundane and profane conversations are not to be construed as veiled allusions to mystical secrets that can only be reclaimed through a Lurianic combination of letters or *yihudim*. The mundane, physical world is real; how one relates to it is in the hands of human beings.

According to this perception, the world is not something to be shunned. The ordinary day-to-day living of simple people becomes an opportunity for the service of God. This applies to Jews and Gentiles alike.

> R. Bunim said that if a person truly wants something he could learn this quality even from non-Jews. For example, we see that when non-Jewish people want the state run in a certain way that is for the benefit of the state, according to their understanding, they pay no heed to their own selves. They endanger themselves and fight wars until they conquer all according to their will.[25]

It is clear from this last example that R. Bunim is not translating the mundane into something of mystical significance, but merely evaluating "the

---

[23] R. Bunim justified his own behavior in the West on the basis that it gave him insight into human behavior. See Ch. 11, below.
[24] *Kol Simhah*, par. Vayetze, 35.
[25] *Siah Sarfei Kodesh*, 5: 43; *Siah Sarfei Kodesh he-Hadash*, 3: 133 §93; see also *Emet ve-Emunah*, §811.

everyday needs of the state" for what they are. R. Bunim looks at the Polish nationalism of his time and observes, even in admiration, the passion and commitment of its non-Jewish adherents to a greater good. And so it follows, just as the nationalist has passion, so must a Jew have passion in the service of God. There are values to be learned from the non-Jewish world.

For R. Bunim being analytical was a must. He said that "affliction of the mind is worse than the affliction of the body."[26] In Przysucha, the focus of intellectual interest moved away from works on mysticism towards medieval Jewish philosophy.[27] Typically, R. Bunim is interested in *"peshat"* – the literal meaning of the text. 'For peshat is the essential secret, and the text cannot be taken away from its literal meaning."[28]

In Przysucha the use of the mind is a supreme value:

> Anyone who has the courage to draw near to the Holy has to weigh his path in the scales of intelligence and knowledge – even his good deeds, whose intention is wholehearted.... Indeed, a Jew who cleaves to God and His Torah is able to penetrate with his mind and his intelligence everything that is fitting for him.[29] [30]

Menahem Mendel of Kotzk asked R. Bunim why God didn't give the Torah immediately after the Exodus. He replied:

> (The Jewish people) were sick – that is to say, they didn't recognize their sickness, that they had been truly blemished by their servitude in Egypt, a place of impurity. Therefore, God made them wait three months in order for their mind to be settled....[31]

---

[26] *Siah Sarfei Kodesh*, 2:17, §32.

[27] See Ch. 11.

[28] *Ramatayim Zofim*, Ch. 1, §1. On Bunim's concern with *peshat,* see *Ramatayim Zofim,* Ch. 18, §54; Ch. 29, §80; *Hashavah le-Tovah,* par. Zachor, 29; *Siah Sarfei Kodesh,* 5: 105, §8; *Kol Simhah,* par. Noah, 13; *Hiddushei ha-Rim,* par. Ki Tetze, 244. This is very much like his father.

[29] *Kol Simhah,* par. Vayakhel, 78; see also *Torat ha-Yehudi,* 21 §3.

[30] Menahem Mendel of Kotzk maintained that one had to "love mind with all one's heart and soul... and that it was forbidden to have compassion on someone who had no mind." He said, "For you rejected knowledge and I reject... for there are hasidim who stumble in this...." *Ramatayim Zofim,* Ch. 1, §127; *Ramatayim Zofim* (AZ), Ch. 14, §9.

[31] *Ohel Torah,* par. Yitro, 36.

Someone who doesn't use his mind is sick. The following is said in the name of Hiddushei ha-Rim:

> When I first came to Kotzk, our teacher called me and said, "Come and I'll tell you what a hasid is. A hasid asks himself: Why?"[32]

Mind is the prerequisite to introspection and self-analysis, as is succinctly expressed by the following statement: "R. Bunim once said: It is possible for a person to be pious and to be an idiot."[33]

Through this emphasis on analysis, a revolution was created in Polish Hasidism. As a result, the crème de la crème of intellectual Polish hasidic Jewry gravitated towards Przysucha.[34] This movement instigated the intellectual rejuvenation of Polish Hasidism by reasserting the value of "learning" and the use of the intellect in general (a process that started with the Yehudi)[35] was now flourishing. R. Bunim was not only a magnet drawing many hasidic scholars in Poland, but Przysucha now challenged the dominance of the existing hasidic establishment.[36]

There is, however, an ideological underpinning to R. Bunim's world-view which, as we shall see later,[37] has enormous significance in regard to his attitude towards human nature. Both the Yehudi and R. Bunim believed that once one had made contact with one's own inner truth, one would thereafter somehow be aware of the truth of the Divine design within nature.[38]

For R. Bunim, there is not just an equation between Torah and wisdom (and truth); there is also an alignment between Torah and the order of things in nature. R. Bunim's philosophy runs something like this: once a *talmid hakham* learns to look inside himself and to behave with truthfulness (i.e., wisdom), he begins to see the same aspects outside himself in nature. Nature herself is aligned with Torah.[39]

---

[32] *Amud ha-Emet*, 101.

[33] *Ma'amarei Simhah*, 28. See *Siah Sarfei Kodesh*, 1:52, §244. Because our mind is in exile, the things we ask from God are banal.

[34] *Meir Einei ha-Golah*, §§66–67.

[35] Unlike Levinger, who claims that this phenomenon started with Kotzk.

[36] Aescoly, *Hasidut be-Folin*, ed. Assaf, 70.

[37] See Chap. 7, below.

[38] The source seems to be the Maharal, *Netivot Olam*, 1.

[39] On all this see below, Chap. 7.

R. Zadok ha-Kohen of Lublin mentions in the name of R. Bunim the idea that God's name, *SH-D-Y,* conveys the idea that it is *sufficient* for human beings to recognize the Divine from the world that He created.[40]

The corollary is that the scholar, who has developed his own inner world, can see Torah in everything and develop Torah. In Przysucha, human beings become Torah by aligning themselves with their own truthfulness and the natural order.

The natural order of things, the way the world should be run, is according to the Torah. The Torah is "the order of the world and all the world should function according to the Torah, for as the Torah decrees, so it is."[41]

> ... However, after He completed the Torah for them, all order of things is permanently according to the order of the Torah.[42]
>
> That via the Torah... we can comprehend the Divine, His Unity, and how He is concerned with all existence... The Holy One blessed be He is written in the Torah and man can comprehend the work of God by becoming absorbed in Torah.[43]

God has, as it were, left His footsteps in nature, and via wisdom (i.e., Torah in its fullest sense), human beings can retrace those footsteps to uncover the Divine. It is this alignment of nature (i.e., the natural order of things) with Torah that allows scholars (who know himself) to develop and expand the Torah. In a sense, human beings are God's partners in Torah.

> The children of Issachar... understood (with their minds) the appropriate place and the appropriate time, what to do and what not to do; to attune the law – everything in its place.[44]

Torah is therefore not something imposed on human beings against their own innate nature. On the contrary, it is because the natural order of the world is aligned with Torah that man, by purity and awareness of his real self, can become the vehicle of God's Torah.

---

[40] R. Zadok ha-Kohen, *Peri* Zaddik, par. Vaera, 19 (10), §3.

[41] *Kol Simhah,* par. Matot, 100.

[42] *Hiddushei ha-Rim,* par. Ki Tavo, 250; Torat Simhah, §183.

[43] *Kol Simhah,* par. Bamidbar, 84. For mind as a value per se, see *Ramatayim Zofim,* Ch. 5 n. 127 in the name of Menahem Mendel.

[44] *Kol Simhah,* par. Vayakhel, 78.

The values of Przysucha are perhaps encapsulated in the following quotation attributed to the Yehudi. On the phrase, "and all we have left is this Torah," he said:

> Since He left us the Torah, we have everything. For from the Torah we can come to all the levels that previously could be achieved via the revelation of the Shekhinah.[45] [46]

Here speaks the authentic voice of the Talmudic scholar – namely, that which in the past required revelation now requires the intellectual study of the Torah.

According to the work *Ohel Yitzhak*, R. Bunim encouraged those of his pupils who were capable of doing so to make an original contribution when learning Torah (*le-haddesh*).

> Once R. Bunim went on a journey with his top pupils and he said that each one should say something original (*hiddush*) in Jewish law, and that anyone who did not would be fined – and everyone did. But our teacher R. Yitzhak from Vorki said that he had never learned in order to be original... and he pleaded with him (R. Bunim). And R. Bunim said that, on this occasion he would have compassion, but he should accept upon himself to say something original (in the future).[47]

This approach of being creative (*le-haddesh*) fits in well with a profile of Przysucha that demands that one brings one's personality to the text; that mind cannot be limited just to understanding a traditional interpretation, but must also find its own resonance.[48] [49]

---

[45] *Niflaot Haddashot, Seder HaYom*, 66.

[46] For another source of the Yehudi's value of intellectual independence, see *Tiferet ha-Yehudi*, §5: "Good lineage can help someone a lot in the service of God so that when God hides His face, a person can make a great effort. So that what he achieves is by his own effort and not by that of his pedigree. For someone that eats what is not his, is embarrassed to look at it in the face." See also *Siah Sarfei Kodesh*, 3:143, §545.

[47] *Ohel Yitzhak*, p. 64, §164.

[48] See Addendum E.

[49] There are contradictory sources in the traditions of Przysucha as to where one was to draw one's religious inspiration (see Addendum A). Was it from Nature ("Lift up your eyes and see who created all this"; Isaiah 40:26) – if you like, the

The Limitations of Torah

But despite the supreme value of learning Torah and of the use of the mind, Przysucha is fundamentally Hasidic in the sense that it believed that although one who learned was connected to Torah, this was not exactly the same thing as being directly connected to God.[50]

> ... someone who is occupied with Torah and mitzvot is joined to Torah by his action; and even though through this he is attached to God, nevertheless, his action and his attachment is through the Torah.[51] [52]

In other words, learning Torah is an intermediary, a medium, which in and of itself is insufficient to create the *homo religiosus*; or, in more prosaic language, to get one "inside."[53]

What would lead someone acknowledged by all to be a supreme scholar, someone steeped in Talmudic learning, to be drawn to Hasidism? Why would someone perceived as outstanding in the very Jewish field that gave one the ultimate accolade – i.e., intellectual acumen in the field of the Talmud – feel that all this was somehow inadequate? Fortunately, we have a source which reveals the Yehudi's answer to this question:

---

world of nature? Or was it from the Exodus – i.e., revelation? Though these traditions cannot be used to confirm who said what, their common denominator is that the disciple (be it R. Bunim or the Kotzker) thought that religious inspiration was to be drawn primarily from an awareness of God's hand in nature and not from revelation, but the master (whether the Yehudi or R. Bunim, in his turn) corrects the disciple and declares that for the Jew it should be the Exodus. The difference between the two positions is essentially whether religious inspiration is out there in nature or inside, within human beings. The teacher of Przysucha affirmed that the drama of religious experience takes place within human beings – in their recreation of the revelation of the Exodus within themselves. But it is of major significance that the pupil of Przysucha thought that religious inspiration was to be drawn essentially from observing nature.

[50] Compare *Siah Sarfei Kodesh*, 5:44 in the name of R. Menahem Mendel of Kotzk: "A hasid has fear and awe of God; a *mitnagged* has fear of the *Shulhan Arukh*."

[51] *Kol Simhah*, par. Matot, 101.

[52] This is not exactly the same as the Tanya.

[53] Compare Maimonides's critique of Rabbinical learning alone in his *Guide for the Perplexed* 3.51.

When the holy R. Hanoch Heinikh from Alexander was thirteen years old, he was taken as a bridegroom by R. Yekil Factor (who lived in Przysucha). While the engagement ceremony (tennaim) was being arranged he asked his father-in-law to ask our holy master (the Yehudi) to examine him (in Talmud). Our master asked him a question and R. Hanoch was unable to answer him immediately. Some time later, when he had regained his composure and thought deeply, he replied to his question.

Our master (the Yehudi) pinched his cheeks and said to him, "When I was thirteen years old I could say greater (ideas) than this; and when I reached the age of eighteen I had achieved greatness in Torah. But I saw that from Torah alone a person cannot come to perfection... but there is a God of heaven and earth who rules over the world, and from this comes the goal of perfection."[54]

The Yehudi in no sense rejected Talmudic learning. His teachers may have suspected him of such laxity, but their fears were allayed.[55] To feel the need to integrate intellect with one's being is not to reject the intellectual pursuit of Talmudic learning. In fact, it could be said that the Yehudi's efforts were only appropriate for those who were scholars. Time and again, the Yehudi emphasized that Talmudic learning is crucial.

And yet, he is saying that Talmudic learning alone is inadequate. Medieval thought might have emphasized right thinking, but the Yehudi emphasizes right being.

This sense of the inadequacy of Torah study alone, or at least of pursuing such learning without an accompanying sense of devotion to God, is of course one of the criticisms originally made by the hasidim about the *mitnaggedim*. It is reflected in a barbed comment reportedly made by the Yehudi.

Of what value is all the intellectual casuistry (*pilpulim*) without an accompanying sense of awe of God?[56]

It wasn't just the obvious reservation that with an intellectual mastery of Talmud there came ego and pride.[57] It was also a sense that "learning" alone

---

[54] *Niflaot ha-Yehudi*, 75–76.
[55] *Tiferet ha-Yehudi*, 142, §2. This was not true of others: see *Torat Simhah*, §308.
[56] *Hemdat Zvi*, par. Miketz, 184 (*Torat ha-Yehudi*, 196, §8).

was inadequate to the challenge of the age; that "learning" was bankrupt and unable to respond to the needs of the Jewish people. There are various traditions of R. Bunim meeting R. Akiva Eiger, the great Torah luminary of his age. In all the versions of this story, what comes across is R. Bunim's respect for R. Akiva Eiger combined with a strong sense of critique of his traditional learning alone.

> R. Bunim told that once he travelled to a spa and on his return he was in Posen, with the Gaon R. Akiva Eiger, z"l, and he went to his special room. And R. Bunim asked R. Akiva Eiger a question: "Posen is a place of scholars, and Torah protects both when one is engaged (in study) and when one is not. How come the town of Posen is not protected (from assimilation)?" And he didn't answer him a word. And our teacher said, "I'll tell you the answer. Before the pre-messianic stage, learning the revealed Torah was sufficient; but today, in the pre-messianic stage, the revealed Torah is insufficient. One needs something hidden in the innermost part of one's heart."[58]

By the word "hidden" (nistar), R. Bunim is not referring to some mystical teaching. The operative phrase is "the innermost part of the heart." In face of the onslaught of the Enlightenment, learning Talmud alone is simply inadequate. Judaism has to touch a person's heart. For R. Bunim, learning could only take one so far:

> With regard to the first section of Shema' it is written "and you shall repeat them (ve-shinantam; lit., sharpen them) to your children." But in the second section (it says) "And you shall teach them." That is to say, in the second section ("And it shall come to pass"), which is a matter of accepting the commandments, (the term) "teaching" is

---

[57] In Siah Sarfei Kodesh, 1:12, §27, R. Bunim quotes his father thus: "Behold, there are people who, when they learn a page of Gemara, become full of pride, saying: I've learnt a lot; his stomach is full of Torah." See Likkutim Haddashim, 23–24 (Boem, Kol Mevaser, 2:180), "Passion helps even when Torah cannot."

[58] Hashavah le-Tovah, 121–122; Or Simhah §15; Siah Sarfei Kodesh, 1:118, §616; Siah Sarfei Kodesh, 3:89, §295; see also A. Ovadia, "R. Akiva Eiger" (Hebrew), Sinai 1 (1938): 545. On R. Bunim's visit to R. Akiva Eiger, see M. Vitz, Ateret Paz 87 (Kalish: 1938), 64. See M. Wilensky, Hasidim u-mitnaggedim, vol 1, 335–348, for a letter critical of hasidism forged in R. Akiva Eiger's name.

applicable. But in the first section of the Shema' which is a matter of accepting the yoke of Heaven, (the term) "teaching" is not applicable, but rather "to sharpen" – a double-edged sword, so that the yoke of the Kingdom of Heaven enters into one.[59]

One can teach something, but it remains external. What R. Bunim seeks is to touch the real, touch the essence. That is why we find R. Bunim talking about repenting before one learns Torah.

A man has to do repentance before learning Torah,[60] or purify himself before learning Torah.[61] [62]

One who has not purified oneself before studying is in danger of learning for the wrong reasons. Learning that is not done in order to bring the student closer to God is likely to foster ego and conceit. As Mahler, a modern scholar,[63] writes:

An echo of the holy war waged by the Ba'al Shem Tov's disciple, R. Jacob Joseph of Polonnoye, against the conceited scholars is discernible in the sarcastic sayings of R. Mendel of Kock which express his deep contempt for scholars of this type: "They go about with ugliness in their hearts and fondle their bellies with a few pages of Gemara."[64] He defined the difference between a Hasid and a Mitnagged in a similar vein: "A hasid fears God and a *mitnagged* fears the *Shulhan Arukh*."[65] The main goal in studying the Torah is to learn a proper way of life, and only then does it become the study of Torah for its own sake: the very meaning of the word Torah – R. Mendel expounded in etymological terms – is "that it instructs

---

[59] *Siah Sarfei Kodesh,* 3:58, §169.

[60] *Siah Sarfei Kodesh,* 1:20, §95; *Siah Sarfei Kodesh he-Hadash,* 3:23.

[61] *Ramatayim Zofim,* Ch. 17, §4.

[62] There is a parallel here, on some level, with R. Israel Salanter and the Musar Movement. Cf. E. Etkes, *R. Israel Salanter and the Beginnings of the Musar Movement* (Hebrew: Jerusalem, 1984; English: Philadelphia, 1993).

[63] R. Mahler, *Hasidism and the Jewish Enlightenment: Their Confrontation in Galicia and Poland in the First Half of the Nineteenth Century,* trans. E. Orenstein (Philadelphia, 1985), 287–288.

[64] *Siah Sarfei Kodesh,* 1:67, §322.

[65] *Emet ve-Emunah,* §645.

man." The Rabbi of Kock asked of an eminent scholar who had told him he had studied Shas to the end: "To what end?"[66] [67]

In other words, one might have learned a text, but has the text been integrated into one's being?

The following heartrending story is told in the name of R. Yitzhak of Vorki (a disciple of R. Bunim).

> Once a great scholar who had sat cloistered learning Torah with effort for thirty years came from Lithuania. When the reputation of the greatness of R. Yitzhak spread in the world, he (the Lithuanian) decided that he would journey to him (R. Yitzhak). And when he came to him, he (R. Yitzhak) asked him "you are a scholar and you have learned many years, do you know what God is saying?" He (the Lithuanian) did not understand the intention (of R. Yitzhak) and he replied, "God says to lay tefillin, to pray and to learn Torah." But he laughed at this and said that he (the Lithuanian) didn't understand what he was asking of him. And he went away greatly depressed. And so it would happen that whenever he came to him, he didn't say a word but asked him again "Do you still not know what God is saying?" And he didn't know what to reply. And he (R. Yitzhak) didn't want to speak about anything else. And he (the Lithuanian) remained for several weeks but didn't succeed in learning anything from him (R. Yitzhak). So he decided to journey home and went to receive permission. And he (R. Yitzhak) asked him again: "Why are you journeying home, since you don't know what God is saying?" And he began to cry with a bitter soul and said: "Rebbe, I came to you to be able to know something." And he (R. Yitzhak) replied: "Thus God says: 'Even if a man hides in secret places' (Jeremiah 23:24) – that is, that he sits cloistered for thirty years learning Torah

---

[66] *Siah Sarfei Kodesh* 1:72, §364. see Mahler, *Hasidism and the Jewish Enlightenment*, 390, n. 316: "The wordplay hits home with greater force in the language of the conversation, Yiddish: The one who is asked said, 'I have learned (*oysgelernt*) the entire Shas,' to which R. Mendel replied, 'And what did the Shas teach you?,' employing the expression *oyslernen* in a second sense – to teach something perfectly, to teach the way of life." See also *Yemot Olam*, 157 (*Noam Siah*, 171).

[67] For additional sources that learning Torah is not simply a technical process, see *Siah Sarfei Kodesh*. 3:24, §7; 26, §22.

– nevertheless, 'I will not look at him.' That is to say: 'I can't stand him,' says God. That is to say, Scripture concludes that that is what God says." And when he heard this he was aghast and couldn't respond and became lifeless, for he had never heard anything like this. For he lived a long distance away and yet nevertheless the Rebbe knew all of this. But immediately he regained his composure and said: "Rebbe, I have one question to ask," and he said: "Ask." And he said: "What is the law when names torn from holy books fall on the floor? What should one do?" And he (R. Yitzhak) replied, "The law is that one should lift them up so that they should not be disgraced." And as soon as he heard that he threw himself – fully stretched – onto the floor and began to sob and cry with a bitter soul. "Rebbe, Rebbe, a basketful of books of Torah – Shas, Sifra, Sifrei, Tosefta – has fallen before you. All of them have fallen to the ground – and now, Rebbe, lift and raise them up so that they will not be disgraced, and elevate them to their holy source." And the Rebbe immediately took him under his hand and lifted him up and did him a great benefit.[68]

This story about R. Yitzhak and the Lithuanian scholar poignantly reflects the philosophy of Przysucha. A Torah scholar who has no relationship with God, who does not know what God is saying, is missing the point of learning Torah. He can fool himself that by shutting out the world he is dedicating himself to Torah. But he doesn't understand that one has to learn Torah in order to hear the cry in the street. Przysucha was a world that asked, "Why am I learning Torah?" "What does God want of me?" "Can I hear what God is saying to me?" What R. Bunim wanted, as did all three generations of Przysucha, was not a cognitive process alone. To undertake a voyage of personal truthfulness requires being self-critical, analytical, and asking oneself, "What does God say?" and not to hide behind what Kierkegaard called "technical wisdom." The Yehudi would make fun of the Galician Jews who "loved talking Torah."[69] By that he meant that Torah is not some interpretation, some clever resolution of conflicting texts. Torah

---

[68] *Ohel Yitzhak*, 126, §295. Instead of the sentence Jer. 23:24 being taken rhetorically, it is being understood as a statement of fact.

[69] *Zekhuta de-Avraham*, 41 (*Torat ha-Yehudi*, 19).

is something that touches one's essence. For Przysucha, Torah has to be something that changes and purifies the human being.

The Esoteric and Kabbalah

In order to appreciate the revolution in mentality created by Przysucha, it will be useful to begin with the specific question: what was Przysucha's attitude with regard to the kabbalah? Clearly, it is necessary to understand how kabbalah (i.e., the Zohar and the Ari) was perceived in the world of Polish Hasidism. At the turn of the nineteenth century kabbalah was part of the intellectual baggage of every literate Jew, whether he was a *hasid* or a *mitnagged*.[70] However, Hasidism emphasized kabbalah not just as a part of being an educated Jew but rather as the path to the service of the Divine.

> Those people who serve God, but without making any effort to recognize Him – the truth of His existence and His awesome greatness – such is not the quality of "inside." But those who make every effort to recognize and know Him... one who serves in such a way is on the inside of the inside; and such knowledge is the vessel, as it were, to understand the Most High, who unites all the sefirot.[71]

In Polish Hasidism, the Maggid of Kozienice[72] (a personal friend and supporter of the Yehudi) was an example of this confluence of Talmud and Zohar. However, the reality in Lublin was that scholars who came to Lublin were soon learning the Zohar rather than Talmud.[73]

One of the characteristics of Hasidism is the way it takes kabbalistic concepts and turns them into insights into human nature. There is a

---

[70] Zeev Gries, "The Hasidic Managing Editor as an Agent of Culture." In *Hasidism Reappraised* (London: 1997), 152, says: "The gulf between the intellectual worlds of Hasidim and *mitnaggedim* was not as wide as we might have imagined." And in note 39, he adds: "Another indication of this is the fact that Hayyim of Volozhin, the famous disciple of the Gaon of Vilna, and the eminent Hasidic leader, Levi Isaac of Berdichev, were able to give their approbations to the same books and have them published alongside each other."

[71] *Avodat Israel*, par. Naso, 137.

[72] Regarding the Maggid of Kozienice, cf. Rabinowitz, *From Lublin to Przysucha*, 180–187.

[73] *Torat Simhah*, §308; Aescoly, *Hasidut be-Folin*, 88.

magnificent statement by R. Shneur Zalman of Liady who explains the difference between kabbalah and Hasidism in the following way:

קבלה עשתה מא-להים אדם, והחסידות עשתה מהאדם א-להות.

> The Kabbalah made God into a human being, but Hasidism makes humanity into Divinity.[74]

Presumably, this means that kabbalah translated the Divine into human beings, but Hasidism translated the human being into the Divine. This is not so very different from Scholem's observations that "Hasidic writers are fond of reinterpreting the conceptual language of the kabbalah, which originally referred to the mysteries of the Godhead, in such a manner that it seems to concern the personal life of man and his relation to God."[75]

This sums up the paradigm shift from trying to comprehend the Divine, to personal mysticism. But if so, then Przysucha must be seen as the natural corollary of this approach. Przysucha, more than any other form of Hasidism, is *Torat Adam* (the Torah of humankind) – with no books (other than the Torah and the Rabbinical literature and what flows from it), no path (other than 613 commandments), just one's own personal path. Therefore anything that would interfere with this goal is to be softened or rejected. Kabbalah is muted, the miraculous is irrelevant. Scholem, unconsciously, provides an almost perfect definition of Przysucha when he says:

> It is by descending into the depths of his own self that man wanders through all the dimensions of the world; in his own self he lifts the barriers which separate one sphere from the other, in his own self... The distinctive feature of the new school is to be found in the fact that the secrets of the Divine realm are presented in the guise of mystical psychology.[76]

---

[74] A. Hen, *Sinai* 7 (238); Rabinowitz, *From Lublin to Przysucha*, 181.

[75] G. Scholem, *The Messianic Idea in Judaism* (New York: 1972), 236–237. Scholem says about the Maggid: "We find page after page in which he almost systematically takes up individual Kabbalistic concepts in order to explain their meaning as key-words for the personal life of the pious." Scholem says: "Not only have Kabbalistic concepts been inverted; but once the insight into human nature has been made, one's communion with the Divine is seen as the goal, then the structure which might have facilitated this [i.e., the Kabbalah] has been disregarded."

[76] G. Scholem, *Major Trends,* 341.

This is a perfect definition of Przysucha, so long as the phrase "mystical psychology" is now understood as service of God without kabbalah.

R. Bunim was no innocent. He consciously engaged in educational warfare. He sent the following question to R. Meir of Apta.

> "The Shema' can be read in any language." If so, what secret "intentions" should one have if one said the Shema' in Polish?...[77]

"Intentions" were an integral part of the kabbalistic rite, so that to ask what "secret intentions" one should have if one said the *Shema'* in Polish was to poke fun at the very essence of his opponents' philosophy. In a somewhat cynical mood perhaps, he said to his disciple:

> I'll tell you what Rebbe you should choose after me: anybody who can give a clear explanation of half a page of the Zohar – and it strikes you as peshat – you should choose as Rebbe."[78]

In a more strident manner he said of a famous kabbalist, "He doesn't understand kabbalah." He said:

> He doesn't know kabbalah just as one says he doesn't know a town – because he was never there. And that is what I meant when I said, "He doesn't know how to learn kabbalah" – because to learn kabbalah means that one can grasp enlightenment.[79]

The phrase "because he was never there" has major significance from an educational point of view. R. Bunim insists that one can only truly talk within the radius of one's experience. Otherwise, what one is saying is technical knowledge; something read or copied from another – not something that arises from within one's soul. Wisdom or true mystical knowledge is a reality of one's inner being, not an acquired technique.

The influence of the kabbalah in Przysucha is muted, in sharp contrast not only to the rest of Polish Hasidism, but to Habad as well. What is the significance of Przysucha's subdued relationship with Kabbalah? Kabbalah is a form of theology. It explains the design of the Creator: how He came to

---

[77] *Siah Sarfei Kodesh*, 3:7, §16.
[78] *Ramatayim Zofim*, Ch. 29, §80.
[79] *Ramatayim Zofim*, Ch. 30, §85.

create the world and the place of human beings in the Creation. Theology is by definition an attempt to explain the behavior of the Divine.

All this is simply not to be found in Przysucha (in these three generations). It rebounds with verve in the *Mei Shiloah* (by the Kotzker's younger contemporary, the Ishbitzer, who broke with him). The Ishbitzer is a theologian who deals with issues of determinism,[80] free will, and whether one can ever know the truth of God's intentions. But during the three generations of Przysucha, theology was not a central occupation (God, the revelation at Sinai, and personal providence were all assumed).

Hasidic literature might protest that R. Bunim studied the Zohar with Menahem Mendel every night;[81] that on the day he graduated as an apothecary, he went and bought the Zohar.[82] But the simple fact is that in all sources that report R. Bunim's insights into Torah, kabbalah and even its basic terminology are notably absent.

If the medium is the message, then we should note that in the work *Kol Simhah* (the first compilation of sayings attributed to R. Bunim) there is only one reference to the Ari.[83] This is in sharp contrast to the Hasidic world that existed immediately prior to Przysucha and immediately after the Kotzker. For example, the work known as *Hiddushei ha-Rim*, attributed to Yizhak Meir Rottenberg Alter or even *Neot Deshe* by the Kotzker's son-in-law, R. Avraham of Sochaczew,[84] are replete with quotations from the Ari and the Zohar.

---

[80] There are one or two examples of possible determinism in *Kol Simhah;* e.g. par. Vayeshev, 40, 42, dealing with Judah and Tamar (though R. Bunim is quoting a midrash), and in *Hiddushei ha-Rim,* par. Matot, 228. On determinism in the thought of R. Bunim, see A. Brill, "Grandeur and Humility." To some extent the greater the intimacy a person has with God, the more he senses that "it had to be this way." But determinism in R. Bunim is muted. In the Mei ha-Shiloah, who is a theologian, it abounds. It seems that kabbalah also facilitates archetypes. See A. Cohen, "Al ketivah ve-hoser ketivah le-vet Przysucha" (Hebrew). *Dimui* 5765 (2005).

[81] *Eser Niflaot*, §8 (Boem, *Kol Mevaser*, 2:188).

[82] *Ramatayim Zofim*, Ch. 18, §62. In *Siah Sarfei Kodesh*, 1:20, n. 93, R. Bunim quotes the Ari. See *To'afot Reem*, 32; *Torat Simhah*, §168 (=*Kol Mevaser*, 2: 282), where R. Bunim is quoted as saying, "All my greatness comes from the holy Zohar."

[83] *Kol Simhah*, par. Vayeshev, 42.

[84] A compilation from manuscripts, edited by A.Y. Bornstein, 1983. It is not clear how much these two works are a true reflection of these masters. Have they been edited? On the basis of these printed works, we can say that there is a clear retreat from the radicalism of Przysucha. See chapter 12.

The Zohar is quoted nineteen times in *Kol Simhah*, but only as an ancillary source, as a support – not as a primary text. It is used along the lines of "as it says in the Zohar." There is no substantive interpretation of the Zohar. Moreover, if the Zohar is quoted nineteen times, it should be noted that the Talmud is quoted sixty-six times. Kabbalistic and Lurianic terminology is virtually non-existent in *Kol Simhah*. One would be hard pressed to find even basic Kabbalistic terminology, which one would have expected to have passed into normative parlance. Even that is missing.[85]

The difference is qualitative rather than quantitative. It isn't just the paucity of quotation, but the nature and object of the interpretation, which reflects where R. Bunim's real interest lies. *Kol Simhah* is essentially a record of R. Bunim's commentary (i.e., a series of insights) on *Midrash*. Both of the works of R. Bunim written by his pupils (*Kol Simhah* and *Ramatayim Zofim*) are collections centered around Midrash. In *Kol Simhah* the Midrash is quoted seventy times; it is the cornerstone of the entire work.

The above observations regarding *Kol Simhah* are even truer with regards to the work *Ohel Torah* – a collection of interpretations attributed to Menahem Mendel of Kotzk.[86] In *Ohel Torah* the Ari is mentioned once; the Zohar only five times. It too is essentially a series of commentaries related to the text of the Midrash.

What we do find is a tremendous affinity of R. Bunim with the Maharal (of Prague).[87] In *Kol Simhah* there are likewise quotations from Maimonides,[88] Nahmanides, and Ibn Ezra – that is, from medieval Jewish philosophers.

---

[85] The term *kelipah* appears once (par. *Vayetze*, 32); *yihudim* is mentioned once (par. Yitro, 71, and once in brackets, 72). *nefesh, ruah, neshamah, hayah, yehidah* each appear twice in par. Vayera, 23, both times in brackets; *beri'ah, yetzirah, 'assiyah, atzilut* are mentioned once (par. Bereshit, 8), and that is more or less it. The paucity of kabbalistic language speaks volumes.

[86] The Zohar is quoted five times: in par. Kedoshim, 60; par. Emor, 62; par Balak, 74; par. Vaethanan, 82; par. Re'eh, 87. The Ari is mentioned in Passover, 53. This compilation was edited by R. Eliezer Zvi Zeligman in 1909 (reprinted Jerusalem: 1997). Though it is the first collection of teachings of Menahem Mendel, it includes material from other sources as well.

[87] *Ramatayim Zofim*, Ch. 18, §53. However, there is none of the Maharal's kabbalah in R. Bunim.

[88] On Maimonides' influence on Hasidism, see J. Dienstag, "*The Guide for the Perplexed* and *Sefer ha-Mada* in Hasidic Literature" (Hebrew). In *Sefer ha-Yovel likhevod Dr. Avraham Weiss* (New York: 1964), 323. Nahmanides is mentioned eight times in *Kol Simhah*. There are at least four places in which R. Bunim praises Ibn Ezra, e.g.,

It is possible that Przysucha saw Kabbalah as a diversion from the main issue – the human being. Kabbalah seemed to be a fertile ground for the breeding of the miraculous.

In Przysucha, miracles were looked down upon. It wasn't that one didn't believe that a zaddik could perform miracles; but rather that human beings – *qua* human beings – are the real miracle. One of the pithiest of epigrams is one often cited in the name of the Kotzker, who is believed to have said:

> I could revive the dead, but I have more difficulty in reviving the living.[89]

Similar statements, in one form or another, were said by all three generations of Przysucha.

The Yehudi would have related to the Zohar as he would have related to other Rabbinic works. It was part of his inherited canon, but, unlike the Seer, it held no special significance for him.[90] [91] [92]

Shem mi-Shmuel, par. Vayehi, 375 (*Kol Mevaser*, 2:243–244). See Naftali Ben Menahem, "The Relationship of the Leaders of Hasidism to Ibn Ezra," 107–111 (Hebrew), in *Sefer ha-Besht* (Jerusalem: Mossad ha-Rav Kook, 1960). See *Keter Kehunnah*, 128, for what might be described as the syllabus of studies in Przysucha.

[89] *Emet ve-Emunah*, §901. The same was said about R. Bunim; cf. *Or Simhah*, §11. See also *Emet ve-Emunah*, §217.

[90] Regarding the Yehudi and the Kabbalah, see *Siah Sarfei Kodesh*, 2: 112 §423; cf. *Nifla'ot ha-Yehudi*, 72; *Or Simhah*, 36 §99; *Siah Sarfei Kodesh he Hadash*, 4:171 §26; *Torat ha-Yehudi*, 100 §15.

For Przysucha, unlike Habad, piety was not anchored in theosophic speculation – in comprehending *emanation, contraction,* and the *sefirot*. If Habad maintained that *da'at* ("knowledge") had to pass into *middot* ("character"), they meant by "*da'at*" the knowledge of the kabbalah. But for Przysucha, "knowledge" meant understanding of oneself. For Przysucha, knowledge meant learning Talmud and the use of one's intellect to be introspective and self-analytical. The Yehudi didn't reject kabbalah; it simply wasn't his focus. Piety was not to be gained by learning a text or comprehending a body of knowledge; its source lay in oneself, in the psychology of self-understanding, and in the groundedness of how one related to the other. For Habad, the phrase "There is none other than He" demanded intellectual comprehension. The Yehudi, by contrast, asked the individual whether in his inner world – within his own human reality – the phrase was real. Real wisdom lay in one's inner depths.

[91] See *Niflaot ha-Yehudi* 91 *(Michtevei Teudah* 17) for an example of the Yehudi explaining an idea of the Seer based on the Zohar.

The following is reported about the Yehudi:

> In the year 1808 our holy teacher was in Lublin on the Fast of
> Esther. When he entered the bet midrash he saw the holy R. Zvi
> Hirsh of Zhidachov sitting, and people were gathered around him.
> He was speaking to them about high levels (*me-heikhalot u-madregot*).
> Our holy teacher turned round and said to him, "You are teaching
> about *madregot* (levels), but the Rebbe (the Seer) doesn't teach that."[93]

It is clear from these words that the concern with esotericism (at least
publicly) is something the Yehudi was opposed to, as was R. Bunim and,
even more so, R. Menahem Mendel of Kotzk.

When we say that there is no theology in Przysucha, we mean the following:
for Przysucha, trying to understand the Divine, trying to understand the
problem of evil, trying to answer any ultimate theological question, is a dead
end. All a person can do – and here one senses the groundedness of Polish
Hasidism – is to function in the domain of the human. Free will is assumed.
Responsibility is a given. There can be no abrogation of one's responsibility
to another – whether he is a zaddik or not. If Przysucha has a theology, it is
this: The human being has the ultimate responsibility to develop a sense of
being in the presence of the Divine and by so doing, he is fulfilling *imitatio
dei*.

Przysucha's lack of interest in kabbalah was born not only from an
opposition to esotericism. It was also the result of a paradigm shift: namely,
that truth – the imprint of the Divine – was within oneself, provided one

---

[92] For the Yehudi, learning Talmud (which was the gateway to wisdom for the
mitnagged) was on a par with immersing oneself in the mikveh (which was the
pathway to piety for the hasid), but both were insufficient to get one truly "inside."

[93] A book describing the emergence of the Habad School was entitled *Communicating
the Infinite*. An equivalent work regarding Przysucha might have been called
"Communicating the Finite." To talk about the Infinite presupposes some body of
knowledge, be it philosophical or esoteric. But though Przysucha would agree that
awareness of God's existence is the purpose of Judaism, trying to understand the
Creator and His cosmos is no longer the main thrust. If one can communicate
anything about God's existence, it is only via personal experience (N. Loewenthal,
Communicating the Infinite: The Emergence of the Habad School [Chicago, 1990].

first purified oneself. Torah, wisdom, nature, and the human being could all be aligned and be sensed within an individual. The emphasis is no longer outside but inside. If kabbalah had made the human being the fulcrum of the celestial worlds, then for Przysucha, the fulcrum is the human being alone without the celestial worlds.[94] The drama of religion is no longer to be found in the Infinite but in the finite. The drama of religious service now takes place in man – and very much in this world.[95] [96]

We have personal testimony of a hasid who learnt in Kotzk, who quotes Menahem Mendel as saying:

> Someone who learns Zohar and doesn't (sense) that he is divested of his corporality doesn't understand a word. And anyone who says that he knows is mistaken.

The hasid continues:

> During the lifetime of the holy Rabbi of Kotzk only exceptional people learnt Zohar.[97]

It would seem that learning Maimonides's *The Guide to the Perplexed* was just as normative in Kotzk as learning Zohar.[98]

There is a tradition that Menahem Mendel of Kotzk became very annoyed when he heard that people were visiting the graves of the zaddik*im*, in the cemetery of Lublin. He said:

> They are no longer there.[99]

---

[94] *Tiferet ha-Yehudi*, 171 §75. Cf. *Shem mi-Shmuel: Moadim*, 120b, in the name of the Kotzker.

[95] Regarding the ritual of *Tikkun Hatzot*, which was so much a part of sixteenth-century Safed mysticism (see M. Idel, *Messianic Mystics* [New Haven: 1998], 308–320) and part of the Hasidic-Kabbalistic oeuvre, Menahem Mendel is supposed to have explained that "for him, *Tikkun Hatzot* consisted in his saying '*Uvneh Yerushalayim*' during the recitation of *Birkat ha-Mazon* after the evening meal."

[96] Mahler, *Hasidism and the Jewish Enlightenment*, 289, quoting *Siah Sarfei Kodesh*.

[97] *Ginzei ha-hasidut: da'at Torah: der kvitel fun Kotzker Hasid: Yaacov Yitzhak (Zelig) of Valezlavek*. Jerusalem: 1967, 61.

[98] See chapter 11, notes 81 and 83.

[99] *Siah Sarfei Kodesh*, 3:118, §430. See also M. Orian, Sinai, vol. 47, 1960, 204, who quotes the Kotzker as saying, "I'm not a Jew who visits graves."

The Miraculous

In order to understand R. Bunim's attitude to miracles and the miraculous, one needs to appreciate the dominant attitude of Polish Hasidism to this subject in his day. In the world of Lublin, the zaddik's ability to perform miracles revealed not only God's glory, but the credentials of the zaddik himself. Nature veiled the Divine and the zaddik revealed the kingdom of heaven by breaking the laws of nature.

This was the context in which Przysucha proclaimed its aversion to the performance of miracles. In *Kol Simhah* we read:

> All the miracles performed by God were in order that all (creation) should recognize that He is the creator of everything... But such a recognition lasts only for the moment; for after the miracle has past, they didn't have that knowledge in practice, but only as a remembrance..."[100]

If a person has not prepared himself – if one isn't an appropriate "vessel" – then the impact of the miraculous is transient.

> The celestial inspiration came to them; at what was not yet their appropriate level. Therefore it could be that after it (the inspiration) finishes they would fall in a moment from all their levels.[101]

If the process is first initiated by a human being, then the affect of the miracle, of the inspiration, may endure. For the person has hewn himself from within, like a vessel, to receive in accordance with his preparation. But if the miraculous comes from outside a human being, not in accordance with his level, then it is likely that its impact will dissipate, and will have no lasting influence (if not worse).

R. Meir of Apta, the heir of the Seer, approved of miracles. He said:

> Abimelech was a wise Gentile, but he was immersed in nature and did not believe in Divine providence. And Abraham defeated (the

---

[100] *Kol Simhah*, par. Bamidbar, 84. The Kotzker also saw the impact of miracles as transient; cf. *Ohel Torah*, par. Yitro, 34; Psalms, 109.
[101] Kol Simhah, Yitro, 71.

five kings) and forced him to believe in Divine providence and not in nature.[102] [103]

R. Kalonymous of Cracow, another pupil of the Seer (and an opponent of the Yehudi), writes:

> The Almighty created all the worlds and their emanation in order that His Shekhinah should be revealed in the lower worlds... via the zaddik of the generation... healing a sick person, or a barren woman having a child, God is revealed clearly to all the people of his generation.[104]

The Yehudi saw the miraculous as a diversion from and irrelevant to the main work of a human being. In Przysucha, it wasn't a question of whether a zaddik could or could not perform miracles. It was rather that the greatness of human beings lay not in their being able to manipulate some cosmic force so much as being able to be human beings.

"To be a miracle worker is no big deal," said the Yehudi. "Anybody of standing can overturn heaven and earth. But to be a Jew – that's terribly difficult."[105]

There speaks someone who has touched his core. The human being is indeed the miracle. The greatness of being a human being is not in realizing an ideal, but in idealizing the real. The real is not some meta-rational force

---

[102] *Or le-Shamayim*, 30.

[103] The idea of the miraculous, specifically the role of the zaddik and his ability to influence the celestial worlds in order to bless the earthly, was propounded clearly by R. Elimelech of Lyzhansk. It was further developed by his pupil, the Seer. Rachel Elior, in "Between *Yesh* and *Ayin* – the Zaddik in the Works of Jacob Isaac the Seer of Lublin." In *Jewish History: Essays in Honor of Chimen Abramsky* (London: 1988), 412–413, says the following:

"The second criterion of charismatic authority is concerned with the earthly aspect of this illumination and its relation to the general good: it is the ability to influence the upper worlds and to perform miracles... and they [the Zaddikim] are also called angels of the Lord of hosts because thereby they perform miracles and wonders, for the Lord is with them.... The charismatic leader acquires his authority by proving his ability to perform miracles and recognition of this ability by his followers is a crucial test of his charisma. This recognition is unreservedly assured him when a sign or proof of a miraculous nature is given."

[104] *Maor va-Shemesh*, par. Miketz.

[105] *Siah Sarfei Kodesh*, 4:67, §17 (*Torat ha-Yehudi*, 238, §30). Cf. *Emet ve-Emunah*, §174.

that can produce physical "goodies." It is the ability to stand before God as a Jew. The everyday reality of being a human being is more fantastic than the miraculous.

The Yehudi was skeptical as to what could be achieved by the miraculous. He said that "if he thought that a revelation from Elijah would benefit the Jewish people, he would ask Elijah to reveal himself to them." He is also reported to have said:

> If he thought that he could help the Jews in the West with signs and wonders, he would journey to them and would show them miracles the like of which Moses showed in Egypt. But it is impossible to capture the heart of a Jewish person via signs and miracles.[106]

This is really throwing down the gauntlet. A cardinal tenet of Hasidism was that miracles and signs brought one closer to God. The Yehudi is saying that this belief is simply untrue.

R. Meir of Apta, who was so vitriolic toward R. Bunim, said bluntly:

> The righteous zaddik of a generation brings down Divine providence so that people do not believe in any external natural cause. For the righteous zaddik annuls nature and brings down effluence via non-natural ways.[107]

R. Bunim felt that "miracles" would not work for anybody intelligent. As we have seen, his teacher, the Yehudi, had already said the same thing. R. Bunim once said that "if he thought that by miracles he could get Israel to repent, he would move all the trees from Danzig to the streets of Przysucha."[108]

True, Piekarz argues that in *Kol Simhah* we find a few references to miracles performed by R. Bunim himself. But the point is not whether R. Bunim did or did not perform a miracle on occasion; the point is what significance he attributed to it.[109]

---

[106] *Siah Sarfei Kodesh*, n. 54 (addenda); *Torat ha-Yehudi*, 121, §5.

[107] *Or le-Shamayim*, par. Vayera, 30b.

[108] *Siah Sarfei Kodesh*, 1:57 §266.

[109] M. Piekarz, *Ideological Trends of Hasidism in Poland during the Interwar Period and the Holocaust* (Hebrew) (Jerusalem: 1990), 288, §25a, he quotes, e.g., *Simhat Yisrael, Or Simhah*, 13 §23; 15 §32; 19–20 §41; etc. Cf. *Siah Sarfei Kodesh he-Hadash*, 4:147, §76.

R. Bunim was opposed to miracles as a normative educational force. "R. Bunim wouldn't pay attention to miracles – not even his own."[110] He once said that he knew about everybody what they had done since their birth.

> But why don't I reveal this? Because it would achieve nothing. Just that people should know that I can work miracles and that I have the Holy Spirit? Everybody knows his or her ulterior motives and how to do repentance. But my role is to arouse people and to reveal that which is hidden from them – the weaknesses they do not think about.[111]

A person has their frame of reference, their filter by which they translate their experience and how they see reality. The role of the Rebbe is to "reveal that which is hidden from them." In other words, the challenge is to change human nature. To change a person in the natural world is the real miracle; not something supernatural or extra-terrestrial.

Echoing Maimonides,[112] R. Bunim thought that a Jew didn't need miracles to achieve faith.

> "And the Almighty will be for me as God" – that is to say, without miracles and wonders or changing nature I will have understanding. For a Jew doesn't need any of this; and as for what was in Egypt, that was for the Egyptians.[113]

The Egyptians were the ones who needed miracles to be convinced of God's power, but a Jew didn't and shouldn't need a change of nature to give him faith. Such language, used by R. Bunim, was articulate, pulled no punches, was challenging, and at times derogatory.

There seems to have been an even deeper philosophical layer to R. Bunim's antagonism to miracles. As we shall see,[114] both the Yehudi and R. Bunim believed that once one had made contact with one's own inner truth, one could then 'somehow' become aware of the truth of design created by

---

[110] *Ramatayim Zofim*, Ch. 31, §106. R. Bunim also made fun of "levels" (*madregot*): *Torat Simhah*, §295.

[111] *Ramatayim Zofim*, Ch. 3 §4; *Or Simhah*, §110.

[112] Maimonides' *Mishneh Torah, Yesodei ha-Torah*. See also the work by Bunim's father, *Eretz Zvi*, specifically the opening page.

[113] *Ramatayim Zofim* (AZ), Ch. 23 §16; *Torat Simhah*, 107 §234.

[114] See below, Chap. 7.

God in nature. Thus R. Bunim's opposition to miracles is a philosophical concept of enormous gravity. R. Bunim believes that Torah, too, was part of the natural world.

> It is well known that God created the world with the Torah. The Holy One, blessed be He, looked into the Torah and organized all existence. It follows, therefore, that the Torah is the norm [lit. *seder*] of all existence; and the norm of Torah is that the world should function via nature. Thus, all miracles and signs that are above nature are an exception to the order of Torah, and it is as if a person has committed a sin.[115]

It is difficult to overstate the significance of what R. Bunim is saying here. For R. Bunim, miracles are not simply an irrelevance; they are an affront to the design of the Almighty, who created the natural order of the world in harmony with Torah. Someone whose norm is the use of the miraculous is breaking the Divine design, is breaking Torah. We thus arrive at the conclusion that the normative use of the miraculous is sacrilegious.

> R. Bunim said regarding the sentence, "And God did not give you the heart to understand... until this day." [In spite of] all the miracles and wonders that God did with them, nevertheless, since they were not according to nature, they were only momentary. But

---

[115] *Kol Simhah*, par. Masei, 103. It is interesting to compare this view of R. Bunim with that of the *Shem mi-Shmuel* (the Kotzker's grandson) to see the change that took place in nineteenth-century Poland. R. Bunim argues that God works through nature when, unfortunately, He has to perform a miracle. But the *Shem mi-Shmuel* (Passover, 97) says:

"The function of the miracle is in order to cleave to God without the medium of Nature. For if the effluence would come via the medium of nature then the cleaving to God would be clothed in nature. So that when their success (the crossing of the Red Sea) was miraculous without the medium of nature, so the cleaving to God was without any medium."

According to the *Shem mi-Shmuel,* the function of the miracle is to break the laws of Nature – the greater the supernatural element, the better. One wonders what R. Bunim, living at the beginning of the nineteenth century, would have said about this spiritualization articulated at the end of the nineteenth century.

after He completed the Torah for them, so that everything functions according to the Torah, this became permanent for all times.[116] [117]

The equation is something like this: Nature functions according to a norm. The norm is fixed by Torah. Therefore, someone who breaks the norm of nature is breaking Torah.[118]

R. Bunim went even further. Taking aim, possibly, at some of his contemporaries, he said:

> Someone who has not reached perfection, even if he is a zaddik, requires a miracle in order to strengthen his righteousness even more. But someone who has reached perfection doesn't need miracles to be performed even from Heaven, for he himself does what is needed.[119]

In *Nifla'ot ha-Yehudi,* a story is told about the Yehudi who, of all people, became known for his miracles. Apparently he had received hospitality from someone who respected him, and when the time came to leave, the master of the inn asked the Yehudi to bless him. So he did. The Yehudi then entered his carriage and suddenly heard the innkeeper calling him to come and bless his daughter as well. The Yehudi was extremely irritated by this and told the innkeeper that, rather than him getting down from the carriage to bless the girl, she should come to him. So she did. What the Yehudi didn't know was that the girl had been ill for eleven years, lying on her sickbed, unable to move.[120]

The sophisticate from the West looks superciliously at a world that believed in miracles and asks the question, 'Did it really happen?" But there is a more important issue going on here. If, for the sake of argument, this event did not actually happen, then the story was made up. If it was made up, then the question arises: what was the purpose of this story? What is the author trying to tell us about the Yehudi? After all, the Yehudi is described

---

[116] *Torat Simhah,* §183; *Hiddushei ha-Rim,* par. Ki Tavo, 250.

[117] A similar idea appears in *Kol Simhah,* par. Bamidbar, 84.

[118] See *Ramatayim Zofim,* Ch. 9 §13: "After the giving of the Torah, it is forbidden to perform 'unifications' unless it is needed for a mitzvah. Otherwise it is like a sacrifice slaughtered outside the Temple (*shehutei hutz*)."

[119] *Kol Simhah,* par. Vayeshev, 38.

[120] *Nifla'ot ha-Yehudi,* 69.

as being extremely irritated by the innkeeper's request, *and as having no knowledge of the girl's situation.* Otherwise, he would have certainly descended from the carriage a second time. In other Hasidic circles, say for example in Chernobyl, or in Lubavitch in our generation, the story would have been told in terms of the Rebbe having the holy spirit (*ruah hakodesh*) and really knowing the situation of the girl. But it is clear from this story that the Yehudi did not know; he had no inkling of the situation, and became angry at what he deemed to be an unnecessary imposition on him. What value is being expressed here? If the story was invented, what was the purpose of its invention?

It clearly portrays the belief in zaddikism and the miraculous. For what is being conveyed is clearly miraculous, albeit something that happened indirectly. The story is telling us that the Yehudi became known as a miracle worker in spite of himself. He did not intend to perform a miracle and wasn't interested in doing so.

Przysucha, of course, believed that a righteous man could affect the world. But why should he want to spend his time doing so? To change oneself is much harder – and more worthwhile.

The following is told about the Kotzker, when he first came to the Seer as a young man:

> When he came (to Lublin) he bought himself a knife, and when he came before the Rebbe, he (the Seer) said to him, "You've come to me to buy a knife?" He (the Kotzker) replied, "I didn't come here to see the Holy Spirit; you won't capture me [i.e., make me your hasid] with such [behavior]."[121]

The impudence of the young man (who later in life is reported to have regretted his brashness) and the slap in the face of the Seer for thinking that he, Menahem Mendel, would be influenced by hocus-pocus, sum up the chasm that was to divide Lublin from Przysucha.

In *Keter Kehunnah* we find the following description by the *Maskil* Alexander Zederbaum:

> R. Bunim removed the veil of the miraculous and the supernatural. He led his troops of believers as a *moreh derekh,* to teach them how to

---

live. He did not extend his blessings to the sick and barren, nor did he receive redemption money whose amount corresponded to the secrets of practical Kabbalah. Rather, he gave his trustworthy advice to those who wanted his opinion on business matters, on which he was an expert. He also gave advice to the sick and childless and made them remedies from herbs and medicine from natural science. He did this free at his pleasure.[122]

In conclusion, the world of Lyzhansk and Lublin was one in which the miraculous proved the Divine – and nature merely interfered – and the zaddik, by contravening the laws of nature, revealed the Divine. In contrast, Przysucha proclaimed that nature itself revealed the Divine and that the veil of nature was not something to be removed, but was rather to be seen as the garment of the Creator.

The Messiah

There is a well-known Hasidic tradition that the Seer tried to bring the Messiah. Few incidents in Hasidic folklore have gripped the imagination as much as the attempts by the Hasidic leaders of Poland to intervene either on behalf of or against Napoleon, and the ramifications with regard to the coming of Messiah and the Redemption. Buber's romantic novel, *For the Sake of Heaven* (in Hebrew, *Gog and Magog*), which portrays this clash of hasidic titans, inspired a love for Hasidism in many. Aescoly went even further, and argued that it was this very issue of messianism that prompted the Yehudi's great rebellion against the Seer. But as Alfasi has shown, "notwithstanding all the beauty of this story, it has no historical truth."[123]

What was the Yehudi's attitude toward the coming of the Messiah? The Yehudi certainly never doubted the messianic coming, but would have felt that forcing God's hand was not man's responsibility.

---

[122] *Keter Kehunnah*, 128. This is in sharp contrast with the hasidic norm. See M. Idel, *Hasidism: Ecstasy and Magic* (Albany: Suny Press, 1995); A. Brill. "The Spiritual World of a Master of Awe… *Degel Mahaneh Ephraim*," *JSQ* 8:1 (2001): 31–35.

[123] See Addendum A. Cf. Rabinowitz, "The Yehudi," 121 §4: "One should not rely on these stories; they are purely the fruit of imagination."

With the greatest respect to those zaddikim who reveal the time of the Messiah, in truth it is a great secret and anyone who knows it cannot, under any circumstances, reveal it. And anyone who does reveal it — that is proof that he does not truly know it.[124]

The Yehudi fervently believed that the Messiah was close and that he was living in a period of the footsteps of the Messiah.[125] [126]

R. Bunim has a groundedness that in no way diminished his belief in the Messiah. He was neither naïve nor a messianic activist:

> He related that once the Yehudi and R. David of Lelov were in Lublin, and they spoke about redemption — about the statement in Tractate Sanhedrin that the coming of the Messiah is dependent on (the Jewish people) doing repentance. And when he (R. Bunim) heard this discussion, he went to the table on which a Humash (printed Pentateuch) was lying, in the presence of those sitting there, swore on that object that the Jewish people would not repent and that yet the redeemer would come.[127]

As revealing as these anecdotes are (especially in the way they project different perceptions of the Yehudi and R. Bunim), they have nothing in common with the theurgic (the attempt to influence God) thrust of attempting to hasten the coming of the Messiah.[128]

---

[124] *Ateret le-Rosh* Zaddik, 136.

[125] *Siftei* Zaddik, par. Bereshit, 17.

[126] *Siah Sarfei Kodesh*, 2:107, §398. "Our holy rabbi would discuss a great deal with his pupil, the holy Rabbi R. Simhah Bunim, matters concerning the coming of the Messiah. In one of these conversations he asked him, 'It is clear that the Messiah can come any moment; when do you think, according to your way, will be the coming of the Messiah?' The holy Rabbi R. Simhah Bunim answered him: 'I will go and sleep a little, and while slumbering, I will hear the cry of the Jewish people that the Messiah has come.' The holy Rabbi said to him, 'Excuse me, how can you go to sleep when we are in the footsteps of the Messiah?' R. Simhah Bunim moved his head in agreement that he was right." While the last part of the story is enigmatic, it clearly reflects their belief in the Messiah and possibly his imminence; but no more.

[127] *Ramatayim Zofim*, Ch. 22 §66.

[128] See *Ma'amarei Simhah*, §§61, 68, where there is an awareness that although confusion or doubt will reign prior to the messianic coming. However, an awareness of the Messiah is not the same as trying to hasten his coming.

The Yehudi would not have wished to have become involved in any mystical enterprise attempting to force God's hand.[129] For the Yehudi, the role of the Jew – even of a zaddik – is to be a Jew, to have a whole-hearted belief in the Messiah, but not to be involved in the esoteric; to him, such a mystical concern would be a diversion from the real challenge of life.

R. Bunim told the following:

> At the moment I feel within myself the ability to entreat and hasten the time of the coming of the King Messiah. But I imagine to myself how it will be: When the Messiah comes he will go to the heads of the generation, and all the great zaddikim will gather together to receive him. The eldest and most eminent of our time is the holy Rabbi of Apta, and there in his house all the rabbis and leaders of the Jewish people will meet and will all sit at a long table. And I will also have a place at the edge of the table.... And certainly, the Rabbi of Apta will ask the Messiah, "Who was it that worked to hasten the time to bring you?" And he will tell them the truth: that it was Bunim of Przysucha, who is sitting at the edge of the table. And this will be greatly annoying to the Rabbi of Apta. Therefore I desist from occupying myself with this so as not to cause any annoyance.[130]

Though these ironic words give us insight into R. Bunim's perception of himself, his capabilities, and his jocular sense of humor, they do not give any indication of a Messianic leaning that he might have had. Rather, they are essentially a tongue-in-cheek gibe against his opponents. It is reminiscent of the Yehudi's genre of critique.[131]

Another source says in the name of R. Bunim:

> The last [stage of] leadership until the Messiah starts from me.[132]

---

[129] The traditions of the Yehudi's involvement in hastening the coming of the Messiah (e.g., *Mikhtevei Te'udah*, 18) are contradictory and unreliable. It seems to me that to reduce the Yehudi's involvement in hastening the Messiah to an anecdote about how his wife was rude to his mother on Passover is to degrade the whole issue to a level of banality. See Addendum A.

[130] *Meir Einei ha-Golah*, §139.

[131] *Tiferet ha-Yehudi*, 145–146. See Ch. 5.

[132] *Siah Sarfei Kodesh, Likkutei Yonatan*, 4:39 §5.

But this statement also reflects his sense that Hasidism was in a state of crisis more than any premonition that the Messiah was around the corner.

What does all of the above add up to? It reflects the mind-set of Jewish leaders who believed, in total sincerity, in the coming of the Messiah and possibly that they were living in a pre-messianic era. But nowhere is there any suggestion that the Yehudi or R. Bunim were involved in attempts to hasten his coming. The coming of the Messiah is God's business. There is a fundamental difference between the longing for and man's preparation for the coming of the Messiah, and the activism of forcing God's hand. All a person can or should do is prepare himself.

This approach is reflected in the following quotation:

> Once Jacob David of Kozienice came to Kotzk... and the Kotzker asked him, "How is your Rebbe (i.e., the Rebbe of Lantshe)? I love him a lot. But why does he shout to God to send the Messiah? Rather, he should shout to Israel to repent."[133]

Przysucha is not involved in any theurgic act to influence the Divine. Rather their focus is on human beings to change themselves so that the Divine may respond.

Various streams of Hasidism have, at one time or another, thought that their leader was the Messiah. It would seem that theurgic Kabbalah provides a fertile territory for active messianism, if only for the fact that a person's actions are seen to affect the Divine, even to repair the Godhead. Such a philosophy has the potential to engage actively in hastening the coming of the Messiah.[134]

This could not have happened in Przysucha, and for two reasons. One is that there is no Kabbalah, no theosophy or theology in Przysucha. The traditions about the Yehudi participating or not in the bringing of the Messiah are based upon dubious historical foundation. Secondly – and this highlights the seminal difference between Przysucha and other hasidic movements – the former is too self-analytical, too self-critical, too grounded in this-worldly reality to imagine that anyone, however outstanding, could

---

[133] *Siah Sarfei Kodesh he-Hadash*, 1:68.
[134] On Lubavitch messianism, see M. Idel, *Messianic Mystics* (New Haven: 1998) 242–243; also 16.

have anything to do with bringing the Messiah. It's simply not part of their vocabulary.

ॐ ॐ

The character of Przysucha is highlighted by the events of the year 5600 (1840). According to the Zohar:

> In the six-hundredth year of the sixth millennium the gates of wisdom on high and the fountains of wisdom below will be opened, and the world will prepare itself to enter the seventh century, just as a person readies himself at sunset on Friday to enter the Sabbath.[135]

This Messianic expectancy not only had an impact on the Hasidic world, but also led to the major *aliyah* of the pupils of the Gaon of Vilna.[136] However, its impact on Kotzk was minimal. Here, too, it seems to us that there is a correlation between kabbalah and active messianism (whether in the Hasidic or Mitnaggedic world). The Rebbe of Ishbitz, who broke with his teacher Menahem Mendel and whose work, *Mei Shiloah,* is suffused with kabbalah, theology, and determinism, saw in this date a mystical allusion which allowed him to reveal his kabbalistic theology.[137] But in Kotzk and in Vorki[138] it left no real impact.

---

[135] Zohar *Vayera,* vol. 1, p. 117a.

[136] See Aryeh Morgenstern, "Messianic Expectations Prior to the Year 1840" (Hebrew), in Z. Baras, ed., *Meshihiyut ve-Eskhatologiah* (Jerusalem: 1983), 343–364.

[137] *Mei Shiloah,* 2: 5. On messianic leanings in Izbica, see S.Z. Shragai, *Be-ma'agelei ha-hasidut: Ishbitz ve-Razhin* (Jerusalem: 1973); Shaul Maggid, *Hasidism on the Margin: Reconciliation, Antinomianism and Messianism in Izbica and Radzin Hasidism* (Madison: University of Wisconsin Press, 2003).

[138] *Emet ve-Emunah,* §263. But cf. *Ramatayim Zofim,* Ch. 2. §14. Here *Hiddushei ha-Rim* typically gives significance to this date. See Chapter 12.

ZADDIK AND LEADERSHIP

Once the Yehudi was travelling with R. Bunim, and in the middle
of the journey the Yehudi saw somebody at a distance. He
jumped down from the carriage, went to him, and returned to his
carriage. R. Bunim asked him who that person was. And he
replied that he was someone deceased and he wanted a favor. R.
Bunim asked the Yehudi, "Did you do him a favor?" The Yehudi
replied, "No." When R. Bunim heard that, he said, "If so, you are
not my rebbe and I am not your disciple, since you left a deceased
person without doing him a favor." When the Yehudi heard R.
Bunim's words, he immediately jumped a second time from the
carriage, went to the deceased, and did him the favor and
performed for him a *tikkun* (a "fixing").

Siah Sarfei Kodesh

The Role of the Zaddik in Przysucha

THE SEER SAW HIS ROLE as zaddik as his very raison d'être – something we
know both from his students[1] and from what he himself wrote. Kabbalah
understands that at the moment of Creation a rupture took place in the
celestial world. The Seer understood that the *Shekhinah* is beseeching the
zaddik so that she may be reunited with God; to achieve this is the destiny of
the zaddik.[2] His philosophy of the zaddik is articulated in the works *Zot
Zikaron* and *Zikaron Zot*, written at an early stage in his career. He writes that

---

[1] See Chapter 2.
[2] *Or la-Shamayim,* 6, introduction. So e.g. *Likkutim Yekarim* 224, *Zavaat ha-Rivash* 73,
Meor Einayim 51a, *Noam Elimelech, Shemot* 33a.

the role of the zaddik is to affect God, in order to bring physical benefit down from Heaven into this world:

> Hold fast to a rebbe, who is called a father, and he will help you in every matter in which you have need. For he is attached to Him through the truth, which is God, and He will bless you.[3]

In other words, the zaddik intercedes with the Divine in order to improve the physical condition of the Jewish people. But why is he doing this? The answer is that by ensuring their physical welfare in this world, the zaddik heals the world on high.

The theological significance of this idea is that God and the Jewish people are inextricably intertwined in such a way that what happens to one affects the other.

> I heard from our Master and Teacher, Yaacov Yitzhak of Lublin, z"l… that there are two types of zaddikim. One whose whole desire is to serve God even through distress and poverty and other afflictions, since he despises the world. The second continually desires to do his Creator's will, and asks to receive blessings of "children, life and sustenance" in this world. The second is higher: "For in all their distress, He is in distress." And if (the zaddik) chooses (the path of) affliction, Heaven forbid, he causes distress on high. But the quality of choosing good for himself in this world – with the intention that there should be good on high – is higher than the first (approach)… so that there not be any distress on high.[4]

In this paradigm the role of the hasid is to strengthen the zaddik, which he does by his utter devotion and allegiance to him. The consequence is that anyone who is in unity with the zaddikim will himself enter into eternal life because he is bound up with them.[5]

There is no point in trying to emulate the zaddik, for he is metaphysically different from other human beings. The Seer writes:

> For the zaddik compares the Creator, blessed be He, to himself: in the same way as the Creator, blessed be He, decrees and performs,

---

[3] *Divrei Emet,* 46.

[4] *Or la-Shamayim,* 226.

[5] *Zot Zikaron,* 35.

so too does the zaddik decree and the Holy One, blessed be He, performs; and he can also annul the decrees of the Creator, blessed be He.[6]

There is therefore no claim on the hasid other than to be a devotee. This model of leadership provides access to holiness for everyone, but redemption is vicarious, one simply rides on the coattails of the zaddik.[7] [8]

The question is: how did the different concepts of Zaddikism translate themselves into the world of Przysucha? Regarding the radical position of Przysucha towards Zaddikism (and other issues), Mendel Piekarz (a contemporary scholar)[9] finds the views of Aescoly, Rabinowitz, and Heschel

---

[6] *Zot Zikaron,* 38.

[7] Gershom Scholem, *Major Trends in Jewish Mysticism* (New York: 1967), 342–343. "Nothing is further from the truth than the view which regards Zaddik*ism*, that is to say the unlimited religious authority of an individual in a community of believers, as foreign to the nature of Hasidism, and insists that one must distinguish between the 'pure' Hasidism of the Baal Shem and the 'depraved' Zaddikism of his followers and their followers. This simon-pure Hasidism never existed because anything like it could never have influenced more than a few people. The truth is that the later development of Zaddikism was already implicit in the very start of the hasidic movement...."

[8] However, Aescoly, *Hasidut be-Folin* 70, says: "The leader, the Rebbe, was one of a group in which the group acknowledged his greatness and accepted his authority. It was they who, as it were, chose him, that he should lead the community – while at the same time he remained a Rebbe colleague." M. Fairstein, *"All Is in the Hands of Heaven": The Teachings of Rabbi Mordechai Joseph Leiner of Izbica* (New York: 1989), 99, n. 7, says the following:

"In the first two generations of Hasidism, succession was from master to disciple. Gradually, this changed, and succession became dynastic, from father to son. By the early part of the nineteenth century the dynastic style of succession was becoming the dominant mode."

[9] Piekarz, *The Beginnings of Hasidism: Ideological Trends, Midrash and Mussar Literature* (Hebrew) (Jerusalem: 1978), Ch. 10, "Przysucha to Ger," 283–292. It would appear that immediately after the death of the Kotzker there was a change, if not a retreat, from the values of Przysucha, even among the closest associates of Menahem Mendel. An example of this is the use of the Zohar, the Lurianic writings, and other mystical works. During the three generations of Przysucha this was muted, but in the world of Hiddushei ha-Rim or in the work *Neot Deshe* (an edition based on manuscripts attributed to the Kotzker's son-in-law, R. Avraham of Sochaczew) all this abounds. These two figures are *lamdanim,* Talmudic scholars. The author of *Mei Shiloah* (a disciple of R. Bunim) was a theologian whose concerns are determinism

too romantic; he feels that they have all been somewhat hoodwinked. Piekarz does not find much difference between Przysucha and other streams in Hasidism, as all espouse the cardinal value of belief in zaddikim. Piekarz supports his argument with the following:[10]

> The Yehudi used to quote the Mishnah (Kelim 12:2), "Anything connected with something holy becomes holy." [R. Bunim] asked, "Is God so indulgent? How can it be that by [doing] something so easy, one attains the level of a zaddik who has never benefited from the world!?" And he [The Yehudi] replied that it is very difficult to be connected to a true zaddik. It is more difficult than being a zaddik oneself, and thus there is no "indulgence" on the part of God.[11]

In a different context, Piekarz criticized Scholem. The latter maintained that what distinguished Hasidism from former mystical traditions was that "Devekut is no longer an extreme ideal to be realized by some rare and sublime spirit. It is no longer the last rung on the ladder of ascent, as in Kabbalism, but the first."[12] Piekarz shows that *devekut* has a variety of meanings. On the higher level, there is a kind of *devekut* which is the domain of the spiritual elite (zaddikim, Torah scholars); but all that the community at large need to do is "join the hasidic fraternities and provide for the maintenance of the Zaddik so as to free him to devote himself to his social and religious mission."[13] That is to say, the masses of ordinary people function on a lower level of *devekut* through their connection to the zaddik. Hence, for Piekarz the originality of Hasidism lies in its socio-religious aspect, reflected through its belief in Zaddikism.

---

and free will (buttressed by esoteric works). On this retrogression immediately following the Kotzker, see Chapter 12.

[10] Piekarz, *The Beginnings of Hasidism*, 284–285.

[11] *Ramatayim Zofim*, Ch. 3 §34; and with variations in *Tiferet ha-Yehudi*, 145 §6; *Ramatayim Zofim*, Ch. 10 §20.

[12] M. Piekarz, "Hasidism as a Socio-Religious Movement: On the Evidence of 'Devekut.'" In *Hasidism Reappraised,* edited by A. Rapoport-Albert, 227 (London: 1996), quoted from Scholem, *The Messianic Idea*, 203–227, at 208.

[13] M. Piekarz, ibid., p. 237. On the idea that the role of the hasid is to strengthen the zaddik by his belief in him, see *Or le-Shamayim* 127, 92, 100.

But if Piekarz is right, if Przysucha believed in Zaddikism like every other group in Polish Hasidism (and that *devekut* essentially meant attachment to the Zaddik), then in the above story the Yehudi ought to have replied to R. Bunim, "You are right. It is easy. All one has to do is cleave to a zaddik." But what the Yehudi is saying is diametrically opposed to that. He does not say "All one has to do is…;" but rather "It is harder to attach oneself to a zaddik than to be a zaddik oneself." The Yehudi's statement contradicts Piekarz's understanding that, even for Przysucha, all a person had to do was to attach oneself to a zaddik (i.e., the lower level of *devekut*). The Yehudi is saying that to be attached (*davek*) to a zaddik is terribly difficult.

Moreover, the statement that it is more difficult to be connected to a true zaddik than to be a zaddik oneself is understood by Piekarz to equate the approach to Zaddikism in Przysucha with that of the rest of Hasidism. But it all depends what one understands by the belief in the zaddik. To what does the concept of Zaddikism obligate one or, more precisely, to what does it obligate a follower of Przysucha?

Scholem says the following about Zaddikism:

> All this demanded from the first, and particularly during the most creative and virile period of the movement, the existence of the zaddik or saint as the actual proof of the possibility of living up to the ideal…. He who has attained the highest degree of spiritual solitude, who is capable of being alone with God, is the true center of the community, because he has reached the stage at which true communion becomes possible."[14]

All spiritual movements, in all religions, acknowledge that a human being can attain a level of spirituality above the norm. The question is, what conclusion is one to draw from this? For Piekarz, the above statement by the Yehudi implies the absolute belief in the Master. But perhaps what's being said is a major psychological insight: as one draws close to a great person, one feels a sense of dissonance, because if one is on the level at which one is able to appreciate spiritual grandeur (i.e., "connected to purity"), then one realizes how life ought to be led. On the other hand, if one isn't on that level, if one doesn't have a sense of greatness, nor a sense of what one could

---

[14] Scholem, *Major Trends*, 343.

be oneself, then one has no difficulty in attuning oneself to the zaddik. It is easy, because the relationship is vicarious – and this is what the majority of hasidim want. But in Przysucha, one cannot yield personal responsibility to a zaddik or to anyone else.

In the book *Nifla'ot Hadashot* we find the following tradition that reflects how R. Bunim saw the relationship between rebbe and hasid. He said:

> When a Jew goes to the zaddik, his heart becomes broken within him, for he sees the difference between himself and the zaddik.[15]

This is what Przysucha meant by a zaddik. In the world of Przysucha, Zaddikism meant the service of human greatness that obligated the hasid himself to strive for greatness. It is in this context that one may understand the above words, "It is very difficult to be connected to a true zaddik – more difficult than being a zaddik oneself – and there is no 'indulgence' on the part of God."

A better source to buttress Piekarz's position is the following:

> Anyone who thinks in his heart that he does not need to be subservient to the zaddik, the foundation of the world, to make pilgrimage to him (*le-chatet raglav elav*) and thinks that he himself is righteous, is a wicked person.[16]

But what the Yehudi is criticizing here is the person who, because he is a prisoner of his own imagined righteousness, is unable to recognize greatness in the other. In our opinion, the Yehudi understands the concept of being a zaddik as describing an outstanding human being – outstanding in his combination of spirituality together with his human frailty. And to be aware of such a person, to be connected with him, is both thrilling and also terribly disconcerting. In the world of Przysucha, Zaddikism meant the awareness of another's human greatness; and it obligated the hasid, not so much to be subservient to the zaddik, as to become greater himself. *The engagement with greatness arouses an echo within oneself.* Przysucha might well have said that someone who has never been engaged with greatness it condemned to live in mediocrity.

---

[15] *Nifla'ot Haddashot* 22. The Kotzker said the same thing; see *Shem mi-Shmuel, Bereshit*, 1: 257b; *Emet ve-Emunah*, 249.

[16] *Nifla'ot ha-Yehudi*, 50b.

The devotee's admiration of the zaddik may well have been greater in the world of Przysucha than it was in some other types of Hasidism. But such service would not have been uncritical or an act of blind faith. Initially the hasid had to exercise his own intellectual autonomy when choosing a rebbe (in Przysucha the mantel of leadership never passed automatically, and most definitely never went from father to son).

The Yehudi said:

> When the Messiah comes, all the righteous will go to meet him – the leaders with their hasidim. But there will be those leaders to whom the Messiah will say, "Go away with your hasidim." Then the hasidim will come near and cry a great deal, saying: "O Messiah, how have we sinned? Did we not have faith that he (our rebbe) was a true zaddik? What is your criticism of us?" And the Messiah will reply, "Throughout a man's life he should pray to God that he merit to connect to a true zaddik, and God will not withhold good from those who are wholehearted. If you truly wanted to connect with a true zaddik, He would have enlightened your eyes in truth. Clearly, in truth, your desire was not genuine."[17]

The Yehudi demanded from every person the autonomy of making a true decision – if only one tried hard enough.

Piekarz's second argument is that the Yehudi's children espouse very different values from the ones held by their father with regards to zaddikism. Now, while it is true that the Yehudi's children were very different from their father, what does this difference prove? Children do not always understand their father's complexity or agree with him. David Assaf[18] has pointed out that Nechemya of Buchana (a son of the Yehudi) became a hasid of Ruzhin – a stream of Hasidism as far removed from Przysucha as

---

[17] *Tiferet ha-Yehudi*, 145–146.

[18] Assaf, "The Spread of Hasidism" (above, Ch. 3, n. 52): He maintains that all three children based their "leadership" on the performance of miracles (290–291); that R. Nehemia espoused miracles even though his Rebbe, R. Yisrael of Ruzhin, did not (291, n. 82); and that R. Yerahmiel took the diametrically opposite position to what one would call the philosophy of Przysucha (290). The same divergence, at least in tone, happened in the case of Avraham Moshe, the son of R. Bunim. According to S. Porush, *Sinai*, 47:9–10 (1960), 219, "R. Yerachmiel did not identify with his father's new way."

can be imagined. The children and some of the Przysucha hasidim found the behavior of the rebbe (whether that of the Yehudi or of R. Simhah Bunim) a little too radical.[19] But this is how it should be in Przysucha. The Rebbe is not leading by consensus, by responding to the needs of the hasidim, so much as demanding that they respond to the example that he sets.[20]

Piekarz's third argument is that in the world of Przysucha, there are two axes that function side by side: a concern for physical welfare and at the same time a deep reservation about vulgar Zaddikism (what one might call soft Zaddikism). Now, while it is true that both elements are found in Przysucha, the former is muted. One might draw an analogy to how one looks at miracles.[21] In Lyzhansk and Lublin they are seen as proof of Divine grace. In Przysucha, they are acknowledged but downplayed. The true grace lies in a person's ability to make contact with the Divine.

If Pickarz is right, one might ask, why was Przysucha perceived as being so revolutionary? And if it didn't challenge the authority of popular Zaddikism, why was Przysucha experienced as being so threatening? Why did the majority of hasidic leaders try to ostracize R. Bunim?

Przysucha did not believe in Zaddikism in the way Hasidism in general did. Furthermore, it was an implied critique of the Hasidic establishment which could not be ignored. How then was the concept of Zaddikism translated in the world of Przysucha? We have already quoted R. Bunim's sense of Divine presence when he first met the Seer of Lublin.

> And he (the Seer) said Torah on the Sabbath night, and he (R. Bunim) said of it, that he didn't understand a word the Rebbe z"l said. But one thing I well knew – namely, that the higher world, the World to Come, was here in this world with this rebbe.[22]

---

[19] See Avram Moshe's difficulty with his father in *Siah Sarfei Kodesh he-Hadash, Shemot,* 1: 63; *Or Simhah,* §29. As for his behavior when his father died – he could not bring himself to attend his father's funeral (*Or Simhah* §62) – it is all quite amazing. Regarding R. Yerahmiel's difficulty with his father, the Yehudi, cf. *Meir Einei ha-Golah,* §153.

[20] Regarding R. Bunim's idea that the leader should lead, even if the generation is on a lower level, see *Hiddushei ha-Rim,* Miketz, 108; Vayehi, 76; Hasidut, 353.

[21] Regarding miracles, see above, Chapter 4; but on this point too Piekarz would disagree.

[22] *Ramatayim Zofim,* Ch. 18 §63.

But as we have noted, this sense of holiness, of awe, did not prevent R. Bunim from being the main protagonist in getting the Yehudi (as well as himself) to break with the Seer.

There is an even more fascinating source that gives insight into the meaning of the rebbe-disciple relationship in Przysucha.

> Once the Yehudi was travelling with R. Bunim, and in the middle of the journey the Yehudi saw somebody at a distance. He jumped down from the carriage, went to him, and returned to his carriage. R. Bunim asked him who that person was. And he replied that he was someone deceased and he wanted a favor. R. Bunim asked the Yehudi, "Did you do him a favor?" The Yehudi replied, "No." When R. Bunim heard that, he said, "If so, you are not my rebbe and I am not your disciple, since you left a deceased person without doing him a favor." When the Yehudi heard R. Bunim's words, he immediately jumped a second time from the carriage, went to the deceased, and did him the favor and performed for him a tikkun (a "fixing").[23]

What are we to make of this amazing story? Either it is a tradition told by the Yehudi or by R. Bunim, or someone has made it up. But even if it is the latter, even if we assume that it is a fantasy of a later generation, that too expresses a value judgment. What value[24] is being expressed here by the author that typifies what a rebbe-disciple relationship meant to R. Bunim? Someone, consciously or not, is conveying to us that a rebbe-disciple relationship does not imply the abrogation of ethical judgment on the part of the disciple. This is not the dominant view of Hasidism in general.

The following story is told about R. Bunim in response to the "style of prayer" of one of his students:

> Our holy teacher, our master from Alexander (Hanoch Heinich), told that once when he visited R. Bunim, he recited the morning prayers in a house which was close to that of R. Bunim, and he prayed in a loud voice with a lot of movement [which was then the norm; however, this approach did not appeal to R. Bunim]. In the

---

[23] *Siah Sarfei Kodesh*, 2:10 §6.

[24] On a critique of a too rigid academic approach, see Addendum A.

middle of praying, R. Bunim came in. Immediately he stopped his noise and movement. But in a moment he settled his mind, saying: "Indeed, I am standing now before God, so why am I concerned at this moment with the rebbe?" He returned to his former style of praying loudly. After he concluded his prayers, the rebbe invited him to his house and said to him thus: "Heinich, today I enjoyed your praying."[25]

If this story can be relied upon, then it is a primary source related by the person to whom it happened. The story reflects what the future Rebbe (of Alexander) thought about the relationship between a zaddik and himself. What does it mean for Hanoch Heinich to have a rebbe? Clearly it doesn't mean that he is abdicating his own judgment, nor does it even mean that he will necessarily listen to his zaddik. Moreover, R. Bunim not only understands but approves of Hanoch Heinich's disregarding him because his behavior was authentic.

There is a tradition that when the Yehudi died, Menahem Mendel pondered as to who would be his rebbe, and the Yehudi came to him in a dream and told him not to worry, for he would continue to be his rebbe even after his death. To which the Kotzker is said to have replied, "I don't need a rebbe from that world. I need a rebbe from this world."[26]

In Przysucha, the ideological belief in zaddikism is present, but so too the need for a master of flesh and blood, present in one's earthly reality. The pupil challenges the "deceased" rebbe on his misjudgment, even though the teacher has now occupied the celestial realm.

It was impossible for someone who had absorbed the world of Przysucha to have a one-dimensional relationship with a zaddik: That which for the rest of Polish Hasidism was a sign of faith – namely, total reliance on the zaddik – was anathema to the world of Przysucha.

This revolution in thinking in Polish Hasidism began with the Yehudi. For the Yehudi, each person stands as an individual before God.

---

[25] Siah Sarfei Kodesh 5:21 §1; *Sefer Alexander*, 19. Cf. *Siftei* Zaddik*im, Emor, 21 (*Kol Mevaser* 3: 91).
[26] *Nifla'ot ha-Yehudi*, 79.

A pupil is obligated to help himself as much as possible... but if he does nothing but simply relies on the zaddik, then, unfortunately, the zaddik cannot help him.[27]

This view runs completely counter to the philosophy of R. Elimelech, and of the Seer, of R. Kalonymous Kalman, of R. Meir of Apta, and of the dominant philosophy of Polish Hasidism at the time. The Yehudi proclaimed that one could journey to zaddikim till kingdom come without achieving anything. Without doing the real work within oneself, the hasid, or devotee, was wasting his time.

> *What is to be gained by Hasidim without hasidut (piety)?...* For without that, their journey to zaddikim for periods of time adds nothing, and nothing will come of it.[28] [29]

The rebbe's relationship with the hasid was essentially that of a *moreh derekh*[30] – a living guide or paradigm. Responsibility could not be absolved. Moreover, anything that detracted from the individual's personal responsibility – be it the miraculous, the belief in salvation by another, or the external trappings of the zaddik's court – was to be shunned. In Przysucha, it was never so clear just who the next leader would be. However, which ever exceptional person assumed this role, he would essentially serve as a *moreh derekh*.[31] The zaddik, the rebbe, was a living example of what a human being could be. The hasid, the disciple, was encouraged to become what he could be by the example of his teacher. The teacher, through his achievement, signified that such a path existed and could be attained.

---

[27] *Toldot Adam*, eighth night of Hanukkah, 100.

[28] *Hiddushei ha-Rim,* Hasidut, 350.

[29] Describing the Seer, Elior says: "The dependence of the individual on his unifying with a zaddik was a decisive value.... This involved "the effective transfer of responsibilities for both spiritual and worldly affairs from the ordinary individuals to the zaddik." *See* R. Elior, "Between *Yesh* and *Ayin*: The Doctrine of the Zaddik in the Works of Jacob Isaac, the Seer of Lublin." In *Jewish History: Essays in Honor of Chimen Abramsky* (London: 1988), 403.

[30] According to Aescoly, "The Zaddik was essentially a teacher in the service of God in which he achieved a level of spiritual excellence" (Aescoly, 30).

[31] Ada Rapoport-Albert virulently disagrees with this assessment; so would Piekarz. But this term is used explicitly by Zederbaum, no lover of Hasidism, in *Keter Kehunnah,* 128.

Therefore the student should persevere, because there was a genuine reward to be achieved. But the effort and the reward were the disciple's, and if the disciple attempted to copy the teacher the reward could never be his.

The entire role of the zaddik in Przysucha was understood in such a way as not to create dependency. For dependency meant that the very quality on which everything hung – namely personal authenticity – was emasculated. For Przysucha, imitation, especially imitation of the zaddik, was the greatest sin. All a zaddik could do was to be a guide, a role model. By his very presence, by his own spiritual integrity, the student could find his own integrity as well. The function of the rebbe was to help people become themselves and to serve God in their truth. Vicarious redemption runs counter to the most basic values of Przysucha.

The following is a classic example of how R. Bunim saw his role as a leader.

> After the death of R. Uri of Strelisk (known as the Saraf), one of his disciples came to R. Bunim in order to join him. R. Bunim asked, "What was his (R. Uri's) main approach in his holy work to teach you the service of God and the paths of Hasidism?" His main approach (answered the hasid) was to implant in our hearts a sense of humility and lowliness. And his holy custom was that whoever came to him, whether he was an important rabbi or a wealthy person, he first had to take two big buckets and to fill them with water from the well in the marketplace, or do some demeaning work in public.
>
> R. Bunim... replied: "Let me tell you a story. It once happened that the king decreed that three people – two wise men and an idiot – were to be placed in a dark dungeon. Every day, food and utensils were lowered down to them. The thick darkness confused the mind of the idiot so that he couldn't understand what they were giving him. For example, he thought that the spoon was a plate and so on, and thus he didn't know to hold the cup to his mouth to eat and drink. Thus, each time, one of the wise men taught him, with signs, how to know what the utensils were, but it was necessary to teach him each time, because each time they were given different utensils. But the second wise man sat silently and didn't teach him anything. On one occasion the first wise man asked the second wise man,

'Why do you sit silently and not teach the idiot anything, so that I have to toil each time to learn with him? Why don't you teach him for once?' The second wise man replied: 'You are continually making an effort to learn with him, but there is no limit. For what will you do if tomorrow, they give him another utensil? Yet again you will have to teach him. And what will be if he knows how to use this, and does not know how to use that? I'm thinking and figuring out how to make a hole in the roof to let in light, so that then he will see everything."[32]

What is the meaning of this parable? Isn't the wise man who feeds the idiot every day more compassionate than the wise man who sits pondering? R. Bunim explains that, as kind as the first teacher is, the idiot is totally dependent upon him, so that the first wise man's efforts are misplaced and possibly misguided. For R. Bunim, education is not some sort of roadmap in which you can cover all the situations of a man's life: "For each time they would give him different utensils." The nature of education is to develop in the student the ability to be able to deal with situations that neither he nor the teacher has ever encountered.

The second wise man, who is totally engaged in thinking how to pierce the ceiling of the dungeon so that everybody can receive light, is not callous. On the contrary, he represents the rebbe/teacher whose focus is on how to make the pupil autonomous. Such a teacher is truly kind, unlike the one who makes the other dependent. This parable is therefore a critique of the type of charismatic leadership in which the disciple never achieves religious maturity. The prison is the world in which we live; the idiot doesn't know how to function; to pierce the ceiling is to bring "enlightenment" to the disciple. Everything, therefore, has to be concentrated on this goal.

The ending, "so that then he will see everything,"[33] suggests that light (i.e., insight) is not controlled by the person of the rebbe/teacher. Thus, this

---

[32] G. Rosenthal, *Hitgalut ha-Zaddikim*, ed. Nigal, 114–115; *Ma'amarei Simhah*, §43; *Or ha-Ganuz*, 409–410.

[33] R. Bunim's critique involves at least four areas:

(a) R. Uri presupposes that there is one approach: in this case, a menial task to instill humility.

(b) The approach is not individuated. It applies to all.

(c) The assumption is that the hasid will behave in the correct way even when he leaves his teacher.

is not an image of a hasid soaring on the wings of his rebbe so much as being inspired by the teacher to soar. The wise man facilitates light, but it is ultimately not refracted through the teacher. In the final analysis, the enlightenment one receives depends on who one is and on the ability to build oneself from within.

Moreover, because the light does not come down to the student through the person of the Rebbe (although it does come because of him), this suggests that there is no one path; for everyone receives the light depending on who they are. This is in contrast to R. Uri, who insisted that everyone "carry two buckets of water" – an approach without any individuation, in contrast to that of the light, which is received personally.[34]

R. Bunim's parable is a critique of R. Uri's entire approach to character building. It is possible for a teacher to demand a certain behavior (in this case, that even an important person must be prepared to engage in simple, humble tasks), but there is little guarantee or assurance that when he returns home he will have internalized the quality of humility so that it becomes part of him – for education, by definition, must be personal; it cannot be limited to a single approach.

(d) R. Uri imposes from without rather than drawing from within the hasid.

R. Bunim's concern, in contradistinction is to help the student develop as an individual in this world. No book, even a Divine one, can contain all the possible permutations of life. There is no substitute for life experience to help the pupil develop his character.

In addition, R. Bunim has reservations about nullifying the ego by doing some menial task. The dynamic suggested by R. Bunim is not the suppression of a bad quality but of the "increase of light" so that the context and significance of the bad quality changes.

Buber translates the ending of the story "that we can all see." If this is the original version, might it convey the idea that the teacher also benefits from the autonomy of the disciple? Whether or not this was R. Bunim's intention, he stands by the idea that the primary role of the Rebbe/Teacher is to get the other to be able to "eat" by themselves – that is, to empower the disciple so that he/she is autonomous.

[34] In R. Bunim's parable, the second wise man (R. Bunim himself) is made to appear somewhat callous ("the third prisoner sat silently and didn't pay attention to the idiot"). Why does R. Simhah Bunim represent himself in such a negative light? May this be parallel to the Yehudi's sense of the pain that he causes to his father by being too open? (see below, Ch. 6). In other words, Przysucha is saying that there is a price to be paid for authenticity – that not all is sweetness and that the quest for authenticity in the service of God is one that bears consequences.

In *Kol Simhah* R. Bunim says the following:

> Everybody needs a teacher to teach him both Torah and service, to learn the path in which light dwells; and a man should [follow that path] all the days of his life. But someone who has the quality of learning from everyone, even from simple people speaking about mundane matters, and who finds in them some wisdom that alludes to how to serve God – such a person does not need a master at all.[35]

The statement "does not need a master at all" could not have been made in any stream of Hasidism in Poland other than Przysucha. It assumes that someone who has developed to the extent that he can learn from life experience does not need a zaddik, a rebbe, or a master. And if R. Bunim felt that that was a rarefied level to be achieved only by a select few, he would have said so. To the contrary, he is painting a model of what every hasid should try to achieve.

In the work *Ohel Torah* the following is said:

> Many times a person learns Torah and the laws of the commandments and is involved in good qualities. And after all this he still doesn't know and doesn't understand how to behave or how to balance them.... For example, regarding the qualities of charity or humility.... But when he sees their performance by a zaddik or a pious person, then the performance of the commandment is clarified for him; what passion, desire, delight and beauty is found in it...[36]

The question that absorbs any good teacher, religious or not, is how to help the student internalize knowledge – that is, how to integrate it into one's personality. The answer given to this question in the world of Przysucha was that the zaddik accomplished this by his being and by his personal example.

The following is quoted in the name of the Kotzker's son in law, R. Avraham Sochaczew, the author of *Avnei Nezer:*

---

[35] *Kol Simhah,* Vayetze, 35.
[36] *Ohel Torah,* Aharei Mot, 59.

The true rebbe needs to open the heart of the person and bring him to a point where his qualities and comprehension will be aroused so that he can understand and influence others by himself.[37]

The real teacher – which is the seminal role of the zaddik – is concerned with making his disciple independent.

When a zaddik does the will of God, then the heart of Israel is aroused to draw near to him and to learn from his ways.[38]

The function of the zaddik is to set an example of what a human being can be: no more, but also no less.

Deliberately or not, this dialectic relationship with the rebbe (namely, the belief in zaddikim, but without abrogating autonomy) was created by the Yehudi himself. The Yehudi always protested that he had never broken with the Seer,[39] whom he regarded as his rebbe. He nevertheless created an alternative court during his own rebbe's lifetime. Hasidic tradition relates the following:[40]

In the last year of his life before Rosh Hashanah, our Holy Teacher (the Yehudi) told (the Seer) that, while learning the book Raziel ha-Malakh, he found it written that he must depart from this world immediately after Rosh Hashanah. The Rebbe (the Seer) replied, "Remain with us for Rosh Hashanah, for then you will live." But our Teacher didn't pay any attention to this, but took his leave from the Rebbe and journeyed home. During the journey home, he told the whole incident to his pupils and said the following, "Do you think the Rebbe was not telling the truth? Of course, he could have kept me alive; but he wanted to take my level away from me and I don't desire a life like that!"[41] [42]

---

[37] *Shem mi-Shmuel,* Passover Haggadah, 74.

[38] *Ohel Torah,* Tzav, 53.

[39] *Mikhtevei Te'udah,* 18–19; *Torat ha-Yehudi,* 282 §52; 284 §§67, 68.

[40] *Nifla'ot ha-Yehudi,* 86–87.

[41] Maybe this means that the Yehudi felt that by surrendering his level (i.e., his autonomy) he would have been totally subservient to the Seer.

[42] The symbiotic relationship between the Seer and the Yehudi is deserving of a study in its own right. This would need to involve some degree of psychological

We can never know if such an incident actually took place. But even if it did not, even if it was an invention, one must still ask: what value is being expressed in such an anecdote? Even if a later generation has created a hagiography, what does it tell us about how the Yehudi was seen and the values for which he stood?

This story encapsulates the dialectic. The Yehudi believed that the Seer was his zaddik, but at the same time he was not prepared to surrender his autonomy even to his rebbe, even in a case of life or death. The individual decides with his own intellect which rebbe to choose and to what extent to follow him, until it touches an area which is inviolate.

In describing the initial phase of Hasidism it has been noted that

> The Maggid of Mezhirech did not "inherit" the leadership of Hasidism as a result of a secret or controversial "nomination'" by the Besht; nor was he "elected'" to office by a majority of the Baal Shem Tov's disciples.... His accession to power was spontaneous, and it was based on his own charismatic personality, not on any formal rational procedures.... The status of the Maggid as the "heir" of the Besht was not that of a direct, immediate, and formally instituted successor but of an "heir" in the broadest sense of the word....[43]

This description is not far off the mark in describing Przysucha, in the fourth generation of Hasidism, as well. R. Bunim was "only one prominent personality amongst others" (there was, for example, R. Yitzhak of Vorki, a disciple of the Yehudi, who worked together with R. Bunim on communal matters but had his own center). The Yehudi did not nominate R. Bunim as his heir, "nor was he elected" – "it was based on his own charismatic personality." Thus, in a sense, the nature of the hierarchical structure in Przysucha was a reversion to the original relationship between the Besht and his inner circle.

---

analysis, including the fact that the Yehudi was greater in Torah than the Seer (see *Torat ha-Yehudi*, 282 §53; 284 §57).

[43] A. Rapoport-Albert, "Hasidism after 1772: Structure, Continuity and Change." In *Hasidism Reappraised*, edited by A. Rapoport-Albert (London: 1996), 92–93, 89; the analogy is only partially true.

It is interesting to note that in Przysucha they didn't talk that much about *Olam Haba* (the World to Come). Of course they believed in it, but it wasn't their focus. It would appear that this too is a consequence of a lack of emphasis on Zaddikism. Where Zaddikism is dominant, the hasid is aware that his entree to eternal bliss depends on the exceptional human being, the zaddik. But in Przyshcha, the emphasis was very much on how one behaves in this world – and what follows in the world to come, will come of its own accord.

Perhaps the final word on the subject should be given to *Hiddushei ha-Rim*, for there seems no reason, or ulterior motive, to doubt its authenticity.

> If the hasidim don't want, then the zaddikim can't help. For the main effort has to come from each person, to make an effort himself in Torah and commandments. The (biblical) verse itself warns "Do not trust in princes," the intention being to warn against even those whom the verse calls "a prince"... that is to say, the righteous of the generation. And regarding this it says "Do not trust in princes."... And in truth, in Przysucha he would (talk) a lot about this; that maybe it would have been better to abolish this type of leadership since the "world" relies too much on the zaddikim.[44] [45] [46] [47]

[44] *Meir Einei ha-Golah* 2:572; *Hiddushei ha-Rim*, Hasidut, 352, 356.

[45] The Hiddushei Ha-Rim disagreed. See Chapter 12.

[46] J.W. Weiss, *Iyyunim be-Hasidut Bretslav* (Jerusalem: 1974), 104, says the following: "No activity which he (the Maggid) attributes to the Zaddik is unique to the Zaddik. Those activities which are attributed to the Zaddik in the teachings of the Maggid are in fact the duty of every Jew. The only difference is that the Zaddik is certain to be more successful in carrying them out than anyone else. In other words: the Zaddik appears here as an ideal figure, the model for everyone's behavior. What the Zaddik does, anyone can and should do. The Maggid renounces in principle the unique religious status of the Zaddik." Rapoport-Albert, "God and the Zaddik as the Two Focal Points of Hasidic Worship." *History of Religions* 18:4 (1979): 318–319, demurs.

[47] For elements of Zaddikism in Przysucha see *Kol Simhah*, Noah, 12: "In every generation there is a Zaddik – the foundation of the world – who connects the celestial world with the lowly world."

Przysucha's Critique of Contemporary Hasidism

When the Yehudi observed the state of Hasidism in his time, he was appalled. The Yehudi was not an innocent party regarding the issue of leadership: how could he have been? Przysucha stands as a critique of the hasidic world, and that meant that it was the Yehudi who was leveling the accusation. Perhaps the most polemical statements of the Yehudi are those dealing with the hasidic establishment:

> I once heard a story about the Holy Yehudi; that he spent a night with his disciple R. Simhah Bunim. And the Yehudi didn't sleep but thought and groaned a lot. R. Simhah Bunim asked him why he was groaning and the Yehudi replied:
>
> "I thought (to myself): after Moses came the Judges, and after the Judges there came the Prophets, and afterwards the Men of the Great Assembly, and after them the *tannaim,* the *amoraim,* and the *poskim,* and afterwards those who reproved (the people) for the sake of heaven. And then that degenerated, and there were many reprovers for the sake of heaven. And then that degenerated, for there were many reprovers who were not genuine. And afterwards came the rebbes. And therefore I'm groaning, for I see that that too will degenerate – and what will the Jewish people do?"[48]

There could be no clearer expression of the state of Hasidism in the eyes of the Yehudi than his saying regarding the leadership of the rebbes of his time: "and they too will degenerate."

In the passage cited earlier in this chapter describing the meeting between the Messiah and the rebbes of his day, the Yehudi paints a graphic picture of the meeting between the Messiah and the hasidic establishment. Zaddikim will be surprised to find themselves rejected because they, the leaders, were a sham, and their followers were not independent or genuine enough to seek true leadership.[49]

It is not surprising that such an ideology would have aroused opposition. The disciples of the Yehudi would have understood completely what he

---

[48] *Likkutim Hadashim,* 56; *Kedushat ha-Yehudi,* 290.
[49] *Tiferet ha-Yehudi,* 145.

thought of the sorry state of Hasidism in his time. Pretence, sham, externals – but not the true, authentic quest.

It would be a travesty to imagine that these were isolated outbursts incongruous with the pietistic personality of the Yehudi, or that we should simply treat them as clever aphorisms. Once your primary value is authenticity, you cannot help but reject what you perceive as inimical to it.

> Someone who thinks he is a righteous man... is called a wicked person.[50]

The Yehudi referred to self-righteous people as "righteous charlatans."[51]

One can call this approach "iconoclastic" or say that it is an outsider's view. But these terms would have been irrelevant to the Yehudi, whose credentials both in the hasidic world and in terms of scholarship and personal piety were impeccable.[52] Therefore, what does it matter to Przysucha how it is viewed or even delegitimized by society? The issue is not whether one is legitimate in somebody else's eyes, but whether one has integrity before God and, as one can never know that, more importantly, in one's own eyes.

But these comments by the Yehudi are nothing in comparison to R. Bunim's sardonic irony and his acerbic barbs against those who behaved as if they were rebbes, but in reality were not.

> The Mishnah Peah (8:9) says, "He who is not lame nor blind and makes himself out as if he were, will became one of them before he dies." And R. Bunim asked "If so, is it right that someone who is not a rebbe and makes himself out as if he were should afterwards become a rebbe? The sinner benefits." He provided a parable: A wealthy man was on a journey, and he saw a poor drunk person lying by the wayside. He ordered his servants to put him in his carriage. When they came home, he ordered his servants to take the drunkard and place him in a nice room, wash him and shave him and dress him in a new tunic, put him in a nice bed and leave a priest's clothing next to him. And the master told his servants that when the drunkard woke up, they should immediately go to him and ask him,

---

[50] *Nifla'ot ha-Yehudi*, 50b.

[51] *Keter ha-Yehudi*, pt. 1, 37 §7.

[52] See *Meir Einei ha-Golah*, §70; *Tiferet ha-Yehudi*, 151 §13.

"Reverend Father, what would you like?" When the poor drunkard woke up and the servants behaved as their master had instructed them to do, the drunkard was exceedingly amazed, for he remembered that he was a poor despised person and here he was lying in a nice room with people calling him "Reverend Father," and the clothing of a priest was lying next to him. He was very confused and in doubt. Perhaps what he remembered of being a poor, despised person was just a dream, but he was really a priest. Alternatively, perhaps he really was a poor despised person and what was happening now – that the servants were giving him everything that he wanted and calling him "Reverend Father" – was only a dream. He decided to put it to the test, to see whether he was indeed a priest or merely dreaming. He (decided that he) would look in the books of the priests and see if he could understand them; (if so,) then in truth he was a priest and what he remembered about being a poor despised person was a dream. But if he didn't understand them, then what he remembered about being poor and despised was definitely true; and their now calling him a priest was the dream. So he tested himself, read the books, and saw that he didn't understand a word. Yet, nevertheless, they continued to address him as a priest. So he finally decided that indeed he was a priest – the proof being that he was being addressed as a priest. And as for the fact that he didn't understand what was written in the books of the priests: that simply proved that none of the priests understood what was written in them.

And the meaning of the parable is this. Someone who knows that he is not a rebbe, yet people call him a rebbe and he is in doubt as to whether indeed he is a rebbe: initially he tests himself by trying to learn the secrets of the Torah. Seeing that he can't understand them, yet nevertheless people call him a rebbe, he concludes that in truth he is a rebbe, and because he doesn't understand the secrets of the Torah he becomes a heretic saying that no zaddik understands anything.

And this is like (the Mishnah) "He who is not lame or blind but acts as if he were is punished by indeed becoming lame." Similarly here, initially he pretends that he is a rebbe and denies a little, but then the punishment is that he becomes a heretic and his punishment is great in the World to Come.[53]

There could not be a more biting satire of the ignorance and boorishness of the so-called rebbes of his day. This was not a one-time caustic comment. Far from it. R. Bunim said:

> Don't think that Esau appeared like a crude farmer. He was dressed in white and said Torah at the Third Meal.[54]

Of course the phrase "dressed in white and said Torah at the third meal" is taking direct aim at the zaddikim of his day. R. Bunim is saying, quite simply, that there are rebbes in his day who are Esau. This wasn't a slip of the tongue. It was consistent and portrayed exactly what R. Bunim, and therefore the world of his hasidim, thought about the state of Hasidism in general. In the recorded traditions about Przysucha it is noticeable that there are hardly any criticisms of the *mitnaggedim*. Criticism has become inverted – against the hasidic world. R. Yitzhak of Vorki (Warka), a disciple of R. Bunim, said something similar:

> Not everyone could tell the difference between Abraham and Balaam. For the wicked Balaam was a hypocrite and projected himself as a righteous person like Abraham....[55]

This is very typical of Przysucha. It takes some discernment to see beyond appearances and to appreciate the difference between the fake and the genuine article. The fake dresses up in the garb of piety, and one needs to look beyond the image. These statements reflect the existential state of not knowing. How can one differentiate between good and evil when, on the face of it, they both appear to be the same? This sort of insight reflects the difference between the way the medieval commentators portrayed Biblical characters and the approach of Przysucha. In the medieval world, there is utter clarity between good and evil. However, modern man is denied this

---

[53] *Ma'amarei Simhah*, §58. It seems noteworthy that Buber omits this piece from his selection of Hasidic tales. Maybe he found the ironic reference to priests politically incorrect.

[54] *Siah Sarfei Kodesh*, 3:6 §10.

[55] *Ohel Yitzhak*, 18 §34.

clarity.[56] The world of Przysucha is more circumspect. On the face of it, one cannot discern the true nature of Esau or of Balaam. It is only the discriminating eye that can see beyond the pose, the facade, to evaluate reality. Possibly, there may also be inherent in these statements (whether consciously or not) R. Bunim's own sense of how someone might have difficulty in differentiating between Przysucha and other hasidic groups. But basically R. Bunim is challenging us to differentiate between ignorant, incompetent leadership, or what masquerades as leadership, and the real thing.

Said R. Bunim: "Nowadays the world runs after rebbes, and that is a punishment."[57] When R. Bunim surveyed the hasidic world he felt, like the Yehudi, that it had all gone wrong. Surely he was not waxing nostalgic, but he seems to have wondered whether all structures had within them the very seeds of their own destruction.

Perhaps the whole approach needed to be changed.[58] His sardonic observation of Zaddikism is well-known:

> Rabbi Bunim told this story: When the Baal Shem Tov made the first hasidim, the Evil Urge was in great straits for, as he said to his followers, "Now the hasidim of the Baal Shem Tov will set the world ablaze with their holiness." But then he thought of a way out. He disguised himself, pretended to be someone else, and went to two hasidim who lived together in a certain town. "Your service is praiseworthy," he said to them, "but there ought to be at least ten of you, so that you can pray in a quorum." He fetched eight of his people and joined them to those two hasidim. And since they had no money to purchase a (Torah) scroll and other things they needed, he brought them a rich man – also one of his adherents – who provided them with whatever was necessary. He did the same everywhere. When he had finished he said to his followers: "Now

---

[56] Y. Gellman, *The Fear, the Trembling and the Fire.* Lanham, MD: University Press of America, 1994).

[57] *Siah Sarfei Kodesh,* 5: 22 §9. This tradition seems reliable, for it is brought by Hiddushei ha-Rim, who goes on to argue against his rebbe, R. Bunim, and to justify the value of the world running after rebbes. While one cannot rely on any one source, it is a little difficult to imagine from which world within Hasidism such a devastating *cri de coeur* could have emanated if not from R. Bunim himself.

[58] *Meir Einei ha-Golah,* vol 2. 572; *Hiddushei ha-Rim,* Hasidut, 352; cf. *Torat Simhah,* §5.

we no longer need be afraid of anything, for we have the majority, and that is what counts."[59]

R. Bunim seemed to have been almost disillusioned with his own world. Even though he attracted the cream of intellectual Hasidism, he wondered to his disciple Menachem Mendel whether the enterprise was justified, whether a small group of people could have achieved more,[60] and whether he should continue to be a rebbe at all.[61]

Dynasty

However we define the institution of zaddikim, a safety net against its degeneration is the avoidance of a hereditary dynasty. What helped prevent the institutionalization of zaddikim in Przysucha was the fact that, at each stage of transition, the mantle of leadership was always in doubt, with sometimes more than one candidate. But more important, the leadership never passed from father to son, even though the son might have set up "court." This was the case in the transition from the leadership of the Yehudi to that of R. Bunim,[62] and it was likewise true when it passed from R. Bunim to R. Menachem Mendel of Kotzk.[63]

According to Aescoly, R. Elimelech of Lyzhansk was the first to propound, from an ideological point of view, the idea of a dynasty: namely

---

[59] *Hashavah le-Tovah, Likkutei Shas*, 84; *Siah Sarfei Kodesh*, 3:44 §34. I have used Buber's translation.

[60] *Torat Simhah*, §345. See *Shem mi-Shmuel*, Haggadah, 74b, for the Kotzker's reservation on having too many people (cf. *Or ha-Ganuz*, 444). However, see Chapter 12 for the retrogression of Hiddushei ha-Rim.

[61] *Eser Nifla'ot*, §8. See also *Torat Emet, Shemot* (*Noam Siah*, 96) for R. Bunim's deep reservation about numbers of people.

[62] After the Yehudi's death his son R. Yerahmiel and R. Bunim both held court in the same town – i.e., Przysucha (*Meir Einei ha-Golah*, §86). When the Yehudi died it was not clear, for example, to Menahem Mendel that R. Bunim would be the next rebbe (Boem, 204, *Or Pnei Yitzhak*, §11), just as it wasn't clear to R. Yitzhak of Vorki (*Ohel Yitzhak*, §287) or to the future rebbe of Alexander (*Hashavah le-Tovah*, 157).

[63] See, e.g., *Siah Sarfei Kodesh he-Hadash*, 4:135, n. 24; *Meir Einei ha-Golah*, §§185–236. See *Meir Einei ha-Golah*, §§184–189 for the opposition to Menahem Mendel. *Or Simhah*, §100, says that the majority of R. Bunim's pupils followed Avram Moshe.

that the mantle of leadership ought to be inherited by the son from the father.[64] This is disputed by Dynner.[65] He argues that R. Elimelech (1717–1787) has been incorrectly described[66] as an advocate of hereditary succession. On the contrary, "R. Elimelech places the zaddik who is the son of a zaddik on a lower level than a self-made zaddik." R. Elimelech says:

> There are two types of zaddikim. There are zaddikim sanctified by their fathers who were holy and perfect and God-fearing and "the Torah returns to its lodgings," and there are zaddikim called "Nazirites" because they set themselves apart even though they are sons of common people. And these zaddikim [i.e., who are not sons of zaddikim] cannot quickly fall from their sacred rank, for they have nothing to rely on, and they stay humble and constantly watch themselves with open eyes. But the zaddikim who are sons of zaddikim, even if they are full of Torah and commandments, because of their fathers helping them, there can sometimes arise from that an element of self-aggrandizement, on the one hand, and loftiness, on the other [i.e., they become full of pride], and they quickly fall from their rank. And this is (the meaning of the verse) "Say to the priests the sons of Aaron" – this alludes to the zaddikim who are sons of zaddikim, who are called "priests, sons of Aaron," strictly warning them that they should not presume to think at all of the pedigree of their fathers… [but] must choose the best way for themselves."[67]

This well known teaching is corroborated by other passages.[68] The Seer also emphasizes merit. Two of R. Elimelech's sons succeeded him, but were not nearly as successful as was his disciple, R. Yaakov Isaac (the Seer of Lublin). The Seer's son, R. Yosele, held his own court, but his real successor

---

[64] Aescoly, 40.

[65] G. Dynner, "Men of Silk: The Hasidic Conquest of Polish Jewry, 1754–1830." Ph.D. diss., Brandeis University, 2002, 214.

[66] Ada Rapoport-Albert, "The Problem of Succession in the Hasidic Leadership, With Special Reference to the Circle of Nahman of Bratslav" (unpublished Ph.D. diss., University of London: 1970), 128–130.

[67] *Noam Elimelekh*, Emor, trans. by Shmuel Ettinger. "The Hasidic Movement" in *Essential Papers on Hasidism*, edited by G. Hundert, 240. New York: 1991.

[68] *Noam Elimeleh*, ed. G. Nigal (Jerusalem: 1978), Bamidbar, 104.

was his pupil, R. Meir of Apta (the antagonist of R. Bunim). Thus, whatever R. Elimelech or the Seer's real intentions were, their disciples, by and large, did not feel that they had to ally themselves with the master's children.[69] During the first quarter of the nineteenth century in Poland, "dynasty" had not yet taken hold in practice.[70]

It was R. Yehuda Leib of Zelechów, of Galicia, one of the Yehudi's antagonists, who articulates the intrinsic value of dynasty. He says:

> For a righteous person who establishes a son who is righteous, his service is not interrupted... for it is as if he didn't die and didn't depart from this world. For the power of the father is in the son. So that when the son performs a service, and it is accepted by God, it is as if the father himself is still performing his service without interruption.[71]

Dynner says: "On the issue of early hasidic succession, historians tend to share the misconception that Hasidism developed inexorably toward hereditary succession."[72]

He puts forward the following thesis:

> The zaddikim in Central Poland were seldom able to institute monarchic practices and dynastic forms of leadership which marked Ukrainian and Galician Hasidism. There are no reports of flamboyant, monarchic display by Polish zaddikim. Attempts to institute father-son succession were rarely successful. The application of Max Weber's theory of the "routinization of charisma" through dynastic institution, whereby charismatic leadership eventually succumbs to dynastic succession in order to obtain stability, simply does not hold true in Polish Hasidism until extremely late....[73]

---

[69] Jacob Isaac Halevi ("the Seer of Lublin"), *Divrei Emet* (New York: 1946), Hayyei Sarah, beginning, says "The generations of zaddikim, good deeds and disciples are considered spiritual sons" (Dynner, 226).

[70] R. Israel of Kozienice was the only Polish Zaddik of his day to institute a dynasty, bequeathing his leadership to his son, R. Moses.

[71] *Likkutei Maharil*, Vayera, fol. 4b.

[72] See Dynner, 202.

[73] Ibid., 32.

The Central Polish context helps explain this distinction. Polish Hasidism developed under constitutional regimes which were only absolutist in an indirect sense, excepting areas temporarily under Prussian or Austrian rule…. Individualism and meritocracy, which were outgrowths of the Polish experimentation with liberalism, also bore their mark. In contrast to the dynastic Hasidism of absolutist regimes, Polish Hasidism tended toward master-disciple succession. It was also characterized by a persistent cycle in which rebellious disciples appropriated part of their master's following during the latter's lifetime, only to be subjected to the same fate by their own star disciples.[74] [75]

In this respect, Przysucha reflects the same Polish characteristic. If dynastic succession was ever intended by any one of its three leaders, it never happened in reality.

Rabinowitz says:

After R. Bunim's death, there was a split amongst the hasidim. Some of them continued to journey to Przysucha, to his son Avraham Moshe. Numbered amongst his admirers was R. Yitzhak of Vorki, though the majority accepted the authority of Menahem Mendel of

---

[74] Ibid., 34; cf. 32, where he says: "The application of Max Weber's theory of the 'routinization of charisma' through dynastic institution, whereby charismatic leadership eventually succumbs to dynastic succession in order to obtain stability, simply does not hold true in Polish Hasidism until extremely late," and n. 92: "Several historians of Hasidism have applied Weber's rule to the movement." See Stephen Sharot, *Messianism, Mysticism, and Magic* (Chapel Hill, NC: 1982), 169–172; and Ada Rapoport-Albert, "Hasidism after 1772: Structural Continuity and Change" (op. cit.).

[75] Dynner says: "In the Ukraine and Galicia – parts of the former Polish Commonwealth now under direct reign of absolutism – zaddikim began to imitate their absolutist monarchs… but such a form of succession did not apply in Polish Hasidism until very late…. Polish zaddikim did not institute dynastic succession for the first half of the nineteenth century…. First, Central Poland lacked the monarchical model which prevailed in the Ukrainian, historic Lithuanian and Galician lands. After the partitions, Polish hasidim were confronted with a quasi-liberal, constitutional model of government and surrounded by a subjugated, demoralized nobility which was hardly worth imitating. Second, the conditions of the Duchy of Warsaw and the Congress Kingdom allowed a Jewish entrepreneurial class with unprecedented power and wealth to arise."

Kotzk, his outstanding disciple…. The Hasidim of Kotzk made fun of R. Simhah Bunim's son and said "What remains in Przysucha is hard drink, a harnessed carriage with four horses, a son of a zaddik, and a means of livelihood."[76] [77]

They were declaring that Przysucha was an attitude of mind. It was not limited to a particular person or place, and definitely not to a dynastic institutionalized Zaddikism.

In Przysucha, leadership was neither hereditary nor automatic, transition was always accompanied by hesitancy, doubt, alternatives. Even though both the Yehudi and R. Bunim[78] had children, they did not continue Przysucha. This fact flows from the value given to authenticity. It is also highlighted by the Yehudi's insistence that each person has to find a true rebbe, a rebbe that is true for them.

In Przysucha, not only is there no legacy or dynasty, but the children often do not understand their fathers, whether the Yehudi's or those of R. Bunim. The case of the Yehudi's third son, R. Nehemiah Yehiel of Bihova, is an instructive example: He became an adherent of R. Yisrael of Ruzhin who in terms of hasidic ideology is in another world when compared to Przysucha.[79]

In an article entitled "The Argument over the Inheritance of Habad," Rahel Elior states that there were three contenders for the succession after the death of R. Shneur Zalman.[80] She delineates three main areas of dissension:

- Who was fitting to fill the role of R. Shneur Zalman?
- Who had the authority to explain the Torah of the Baal ha-Tanya and to publish the remaining manuscripts?

---

[76] Rabinowitz, "R. Bunim," 43.

[77] Y. Gur Aryeh, *Kotzk* (Tel Aviv: 1936), 41.

[78] R. Avram Moshe tried to make a rapprochement with the Kotzker; see *Ramatayim Zofim*, Chap. 24, §71.
The Kotzker and R. Yitzhak of Vorki (who took over from Avram Moshe) got along well, even though their disciples did not (see *Ohel Yitzhak*, 35 §84; *Meir Einei ha-Golah*, §207).

[79] See Assaf, "The Spread of Hasidism" (above, Ch. 3, n. 52).

[80] R. Elior, "The Argument over the Heritage of Habad" (Hebrew), *Tarbiz* 49 (1980): 1–2, 167–187.

- How to explain the Habad service of God over and beyond that stated in the Tanya?

In fact, what Elior is describing is this: after the death of R. Shneur Zalman there was a corpus of work which, for Habad, had a degree of sanctity – a sort of canon. The second generation of Habad was in contention as to who was the rightful inheritor of the master's mantle and, of equal significance, who had the authority to develop this canon.

If one were to attempt to transpose the above discussion into the world of Przysucha, it would simply jar! When the Yehudi died it wasn't clear who would assume the role of leadership. The Kotzker certainly did not know who the next leader would be, nor did R. Yitzhak of Warka (Vorki).[81] R. Bunim himself was reluctant. The Yehudi hadn't nominated anyone.[82] But the real issue is this: it would not have occurred to them that their role was to develop a given corpus of work, a canon (and not only because they in fact didn't publish anything themselves). For Przysucha, each generation could only be inspired by its predecessor, not controlled by it. It was the ideals of the mentor, the way he behaved and looked at the world that he left for the next generation. But no one in Przysucha would argue about who had the right to explain something said or written by the previous generation, or to see their role as being the authoritative voice of interpretation of a previous generation.

For Przysucha, Torah was a continuous regenerative process in which each generation and each person was a critical part of this oral teaching. The emphasis was not on any one generation, or on any one person who had received revelation. There was no inheritance, neither dynastically nor spiritually (in the narrow sense). Rather, there was a master in each of the three generations who embodied certain ideas, and each disciple, as an individual, had to be inspired by the master to find his own personal path. What emerges from Elior's article is the attempt by Habad, following R. Shneur Zalman's death, to create an authoritative body of literature with an

---

[81] *Ohel Yitzhak*, §287. R. Yitzhak was a disciple of the Yehudi; when the Yehudi died, he journeyed with R. Moshe of Lelov to R. Mottele of Chernobyl to find a rebbe.

[82] Similarly, when R. Bunim died, it wasn't at all clear whether the mantle of leadership would pass to the Kotzker or to Hiddushei ha-Rim; see *Meir Einei ha-Golah*, §§185–200.

authoritative interpretation, to serve for future generations. In Przysucha there is an ambivalence about creating a movement, a fixed structure, let alone a body of sacred literature over and beyond the traditional one.

R. Menahem Mendel of Kotzk related that when the Yehudi died, R. Bunim approached him and said:

> The matter is closed; there's nothing to be done. The Rebbe is no longer. He left us the fear of Heaven. (But) the fear of heaven is no mere trifle (lit. "snuff-box"). Where the Rebbe's words are – that is where he is found.[83]

This statement highlights the difference and the similarity of Przysucha with other forms of Hasidism. In both, the relationship to the zaddik was of central importance. But whereas in other forms of Hasidism the zaddik's grave is holy and becomes a place of pilgrimage, in Przysucha his teachings remain the sole source of inspiration.

---

[83] *Hashavah le-Tovah*, 121.

THE QUEST FOR TRUTH
AND AUTHENTICITY

"In the service of God there are no rules, and this rule itself is no rule."

– The Yehudi

The Quest for Truth

SCHOLARS WHO HAVE WRITTEN about Przysucha have observed that certain salient characteristics make it completely different from any other form of Hasidism. They note the extreme quest for truth, the demand for sincerity, and the intolerance of and impatience with externals, etc. While all this is true, in a sense it misses the point. These are all significant elements in Przysucha, but the analysis could be compared to describing the "parts of the body" in an explicit and definitive manner, while losing focus on the specific function of the whole. How do the essential characteristics of Przysucha come together in a coherent, organic way?

All the major ideas of Przysucha were articulated by the Yehudi, R. Bunim and Menahem Mendel of Kotzsk, but since we have nothing written by these three masters, we can never be sure who said what.[1] Nevertheless, it is still possible to gradually form a character profile which explains how all these characteristics are integrated, and even though at times it is difficult to determine who said what, we can still maintain a certain degree of confidence as whether certain statements fit the general *Weltanschauung* of Przysucha.

---

[1] See Addendum A.

In my opinion, there is one seminal value from which all these characteristics ultimately flow, whether consciously or not: namely, the supreme value of **personal authenticity**.[2]

For the world of Przysucha, authenticity meant a process of truthfulness – to oneself and to one's Maker. Anyone and anything that helped in this process was considered holy, while anything that inhibited it was sacrilegious. I use the term "sacrilegious" because only by using such a loaded term can we begin to understand that Przysucha was not neutral (e.g., as has sometimes been argued, it was an innocent party that did not disturb anyone; that it was misunderstood by its hasidim and that its leaders were not to blame, etc.). Przysucha was at its core polemical and by way of definition opposed to anything and anyone who deviated from the path of truth.

To be authentic means to be truthful. In Przysucha, in order to be truthful one needed to be self-analytical, because only thus could one clarify the motive of one's own actions. Was one's religious behavior motivated by pride, by fear? Or was it in fact part of a process of attempting to be real? The enemy of truthfulness (especially in a religious context) was feigned piety; even appearing to do something for an external reason, was to be eradicated. Therefore, one needed to engage continually in self-analysis to understand why one was doing what one was doing. Was it because of public acclaim? Did one secretly want others to recognize one's piety? If so, it wasn't authentic. Przysucha prodded, examined, and tried to plumb the depths of personality, to purify motive. It could well be that one was genuinely oblivious to one's real motive. However, once one came to a state of authenticity, nothing else was important, and it didn't matter what anybody else thought. On the contrary, pure piety needed to be concealed for fear of being sullied by public recognition.

Perhaps the most penetrating analysis of motive is to be found in the name of the Kotzker. He explained that when Abraham asked his servant Eliezer to go and find a wife for his son Yitzhak, Eliezer was originally unaware of his ulterior motive (i.e., of wanting Yitzhak for his own

---

[2] Not the solipsism of the romantics, in which there is no reality outside oneself. Rather, we mean a sense of individuation, which is indeed to be found within one's personal soul, but which is seen as tracing, as it were, the foot-prints of the Divine. This sense of the Divine in oneself creates a demand on the human being to respond to God, but with his individuality.

daughter). It was only after experiencing the drama of being led by God that Eliezer was released from his ulterior motive. He was then able to be self-analytical and to acknowledge his prior subconscious desire not to succeed in his mission. In Przysucha truthfulness could only be achieved if one was genuine and sincere, aware that imitation was the kiss of death and that routine was death itself. In order to facilitate this process of truthfulness, a person had to be prepared, as it were, to remove the lid from his personality and to peer inside. Everything was placed under scrutiny.[3]

But analysis was only half of the drama. To be real required not only that one be self-analytical (the scholar), but also that one possess a whole series of other characteristics associated with the quest for piety (the *hasid*).

However, God-consciousness would not come about through intellect alone. The quest for the *mysterium tremendum* was beyond the intellect and beyond self-analysis.

The question which naturally asserts itself is: was everything challengeable? Did the quest for truth require that everything be put under the magnifying glass? The answer is no. There are certain concepts that are assumed, which create the structure for this quest. These are: the existence of God, His revelation at Sinai (written and oral), and personal providence. Nowhere are these concepts challenged. When the Yehudi states that the seal of God is truth, that is a given. The Yehudi requires that a person behave with truthfulness. Truth has been inverted, from being a description of God to becoming an educational approach for human beings.

Moreover, when R. Bunim says, "If man purifies himself, he will recognize God from within the Torah," he is assuming that God, Torah, and truth are all aligned; he is assuming that people have the capability of making the connection, and that this is part of the essence of a human being. Thus, for a person to embark on a path of truthfulness requires not only the analytical demand for self-criticism, but the spiritual acumen to recognize that there is a spark of the Divine within each person. Never before was there a movement in Hasidism which placed such emphasis on what we might call "religious psychology," all of which flowed inevitably from the centrality of personal authenticity.

---

[3] *Hiddushei ha-Rim;* Hayyei Sarah, 31. See *Ohel Torah,* Hayyei Sarah, 13; *Sefat Emet,* Hayyei Sarah 1872, 162. *Ohel Yitzhak*, 25, §57, brings the same idea in the name of R. Yitzhak of Vorki. Cf. *Emet ve-Emunah,* §477, *"Do not steal from yourself."*

It may be argued that none of Przysucha's ideas were original. Most, if not all, of Przysucha's essential credo had been expressed earlier, for example, by the Maharal of Prague or, interestingly enough, by the Seer himself (which is exactly why the Yehudi would have been so drawn to him). But the importance of their movement is not to be stressed by the originality of their ideas. While in other varieties of Hasidism these elements are part of a wider picture (and consequently their significance becomes muted), in Przysucha they were simply inviolable.

It may be that the psychological underpinning of this quest for authenticity was the sense that there is some essential core from which all else flows. Possibly, this is the context for understanding the following statement:

> The Yehudi said that he would give all of his portion in this world and the World to Come for one hairbreadth of Judaism (Yiddishkeit). For really, what is to be gained by having Hasidim without Hasidut (piety)? For the main thing is to plant deeply into the recesses of the heart – areas unknown to anyone else – the desire to serve God in truth. For only then does a hasid have a connection to the service of God. Without that, their journey to zaddikim for lengthy periods of time adds nothing and nothing will come of it.[4]

❧ ❧

The quest for authenticity can be expressed in both positive and negative ways. In the positive sense, it means, "I know who I am irrespective of how I am perceived by others" or even, perhaps, "I don't care how I am perceived by others."[5] In the negative sense, it means, "I am antagonistic to the whole apparatus which does not judge a man for what he really is." Przysucha's attitude was: "If a man knows who he is, he is not frightened of anyone." One who knows who he is will recognize the same quality in me, while one who does not will be unable to recognize my core qualities. All else is of secondary importance.

Authenticity means doing those things that "fit" the person who is doing them. As R. Bunim said:

---

[4] *Hiddushei ha-Rim, Hasidut,* 350.
[5] See, e.g., *Emet ve-Emunah,* §496.

138

> Also with regard to commandments, service and perfection, a person should clothe himself in something that is designated for himself.[6]

This necessitates knowing both who one is, and one's own capabilities and limitations.[7] [8]

Having a sense of who one is, of what is fitting to one's level, was critical, for otherwise one was likely to lose oneself in the world of illusion or hubris. Of course there is also a danger of resignation and passivity. But the world of Przysucha wasn't some sort of secular hedonism. Przysucha was theocentric, meaning that there was a demand made by God upon human beings to respond. The greater danger was that, in the world of piety and holiness, the evil inclination was dressed in white, and one could easily be fooled into thinking one was greater than one really was.

> Pharaoh thought he had achieved a certain level of the fear of God... for such is the way of fools. Once they achieve a little knowledge and awe, they think they have achieved a high level and don't realize how ignorant they are.[9]

To be real means to know who you are, one's limitations, as well as strengths. If authenticity means to touch some point of personal reality, then one's relationship with the commandments must be refracted through the prism of one's own soul.

---

[6] *Kol Simhah*, *Masei*, 103: "'I clothed myself in righteousness and it suited me' (Job 29.14). Also with regard to commandments, service and perfection, a person should clothe himself in something that is designated for him. And that is the meaning of [the word] 'and it fit me.'"

[7] See *Siah Sarfei Kodesh*, 1:55, §259, *Ma'amarei Simhah* 20 where the Seer is quoted as saying the same thing.

[8] R. Bunim said: 'Even though Eliezer was a great man, he knew himself – that he was a servant. And he didn't want to go outside the level that was his – a servant all his life. And this is a great wisdom for a man to know himself, his personality traits (*behinato ve-tzurato*), not to go out from them, but to follow the traits that are his." *Kol Simhah*, Hayyei Sarah, 27; *Torat Simhah*, §22.

[9] *Kol Simhah*, Vaera, 60.

> I heard in the name of the Yehudi that a man should choose two
> commandments from all the rest to which he is totally committed.[10]

This idea has long antecedents in Jewish thought.[11] The point here is that
it is part of a coherent philosophy, which flows from a first principle –
namely, the quest for authenticity. But it isn't just that one has one's own
path and one's own commandment. One must exercise one's autonomy in
choosing a zaddik as well. Said R. Bunim:

> May God open a man's eyes with intelligence to see which of the
> zaddikim he should cleave to – i.e., which one has the same root
> soul as he – and then he will find peace for his soul.[12]

This idea – namely, of having one's own path – is emphasized in
different ways time and again by R. Bunim:

> Rebbe said, "What is the straight path that a person should
> choose?... Whatever is honorable to the doer..." (Avot, Ch. 2).
> That is to say, that the soul of each individual has its own style in the
> service of God, in the performance of Torah and commandments,
> which he should not change.... Therefore he should not take a path
> that is not special or unique to him; even though he greatly admires
> the way of service of a [certain] righteous person and that way
> appeals to him more than his own – nevertheless, he should not
> move; a righteous person must hold fast to his path. And that is the
> proof that his path is true. And this is the sense of the above

---

[10] *Nifla'ot ha-Yehudi*, 59. *Keter Yehudi*, intro., 39, §14; *Torat ha-Yehudi*, 291, §2.

[11] The Baal Shem Tov had already made this point with his famous pun on the
word "*bishvili*" ("for me," "in my path") to mean that everybody has his own
individual path. In *Ohel Torah*, 4, we read: "Every man was created for a special
commandment which is his portion to correct with perfection. The way to evaluate,
to know what commandment he was created for, is through the sense of his
soul...." See also Scholem, "The Meaning of the Torah in Jewish Mysticism," in his
On the Kabbalah and Its Symbolism (New York: 1969), 32–86; M. Faierstein, "Personal
Redemption in Hasidism," in *Hasidism Reappraised*, edited by Ada Rapoport-Albert,
218–220 (London, 1996). And cf. M. Piekarz, *Ideological Trends of Hasidism in Poland
during the Interwar Period and the Holocaust* (Hebrew). Jerusalem: 1990, 45, who traces
its influence on Hasidism to R. Isaiah Horowitz. See Idel, *Hasidism: Between Ecstasy
and Magic* (Albany: 1995), Chap. 6, 201.

[12] *Torat Simhah*, §72.

mishnah – that he has a path for himself that is correct for him and by which he holds; nevertheless... he can praise and admire the path of his fellow zaddik....

Now understand this matter, for it is a major principle in the service of God not to be arrogant – [i.e., not to pretend to do] what is not one's [true] level – even in worldly matters.[13]

Someone who knows himself doesn't need to be anybody else. He can admire another without wanting to be that person – his job is to be himself. R. Bunim continues:

And that is what is meant by the statement: "A man is obligated to say: when will my actions reach the actions of my father?" (*Tanna de-Bei Eliyahu Rabbah*, 25) – that is to say, that there should be a connection [to his father's actions], but not that he should envy the righteous path of the Patriarchs of the world.[14]

And he said the following: If they were to ask me, How much would you pay to change your quality for that of Abraham our father so that he would be like you and you would be like him – I wouldn't give a dime, for what would God gain from it?"[15]

This piece is an educational manifesto by R. Bunim (which is also reminiscent of the famous statement by R. Zusha). The essence is that God created each person distinctive, not to be anybody other than themselves. Thus, it would add nothing to the glory of heaven were Bunim to "swap" with Abraham. Bunim's job is to be Bunim.[16]

---

[13] *Ramatayim Zofim*, Chap. 10, §17; *Kol Simhah*, Masei, 103; *Torat Simhah*, §289.

[14] I have translated the word *tzeruf* to mean "connection" on the basis of a parallel source in *Torat Simhah*, §241.

[15] I have translated according to the sense of the passage. Cf. *Hiddushei ha-Rim*, Vayeshev, 53 and *Ma'amarei Simhah*, §41.

[16] See *Siah Sarfei Kodesh he-Hadash*, 1:102. Even in the service of God, one's motive had to be pure. Why, when the princes brought an offering for the dedication of the Tabernacle, does the Torah mention that each one brought the same offering? Said R. Bunim: "The intention of each prince was not to offer the same offering that his friend had done the day before; rather, each one wanted to offer a new offering, from his own desire." Also *Torat Simhah*, §243. Reuven was the first person to do *teshuvah* for something he had done for the sake of heaven, namely wanting to save Joseph (see *Emet ve-Emunah*, §6).

Similarly, regarding the statement by the Rabbis, "A person should always say, 'When will my actions reach those of my fathers, Abraham, Isaac and Jacob?'", R. Bunim asked who on earth would be so idiotic as to imagine that his actions could be like those of the Patriarchs. R. Bunim's answer is that the point being made by the Rabbis is that a person can only hope to make a connection with his ancestors by his behavior, but not, Heaven forbid, to imagine that he could be on their level or wish to be the same as they.[17]

To imagine that one can reach the level of the Patriarchs is spiritual hubris. Furthermore, to wish to achieve their level is self-defeating. For in Przysucha there is no value in striving to achieve any level other that which one is capable of achieving.

> Mar Ukba said: "I am not as great as my father, for my father, after eating meat, would wait until the following day to eat cheese. But I only wait from one meal to the next" (Hullin 105a). R. Bunim asked, "In that case, why didn't Mar Ukba also wait until the following day like his father?" And he answered, "If a person wants to keep a stringency only because his father kept that stringency and he wants to do as his father did, he is not allowed to do so."[18]

R. Bunim is saying that in order to be authentic, traditional religious piety, custom, social norm, what is called "*frumkeit*"[19] are all to be rejected unless a person's behavior is true to himself. Even if one is learning Torah,[20] why is one learning Torah, and what are the dangers of, for example, ego when a person learns Torah? He is not saying, as some later generations would have it, that this approach is limited to the exceptional few. On the contrary, he is espousing this approach as an educational norm.[21] To be authentic meant, not only that religious piety had to be real, but that also the ideas, the Torah that one said, had to fit the person who was saying it.[22]

One can only know something or teach an idea within the radius of one's own experience. Otherwise, all one is doing is conveying "technical

---

[17] *Siah Sarfei Kodesh*, 1:9, §6.

[18] *Torat Simhah*, §48.

[19] *Siah Sarfei Kodesh*, 2:14, §17.

[20] *Kol Simhah, Beshalah*, 63.

[21] Boem, 524 §4.

[22] *Ramatayim Zofim*, Chap. 30, §85; *Torat Simhah*, §262.

wisdom." Few sayings project R. Bunim's emphasis on personal authenticity as well as the following:

> "And all the wells" (Gen 26:15): Behold, any path in the service of God must have an inner life force. For if it does not have an inner life force, it does not ascend. And the Philistines wanted to follow in the way of Abraham our father and behave as Abraham behaved. But they had no inner life force, and that is the blocking of this path.... Behold, every Jewish person who draws near to God has to dig by himself a well by which he can cleave to the Creator.[23]

Anyone who wants to serve with an inner life force has to find his own well of inspiration that is true for him; otherwise, he is a Philistine.[24] The goal is to be inside, to have experience of the thing itself, so that it becomes a part of who one is. Then knowledge becomes personally authentic.

This quest for truth reached its zenith in Kotzk. R. Menahem Mendel plumbed what we would nowadays call the subconscious. He said:

> When a man has ulterior motives, at that moment he doesn't realize it; and he imagines that he is being wholehearted. It is only afterwards, when he has extricated himself, that he can realize retroactively that he had an ulterior motive."[25]

Nothing in the world of motive could be more penetrating than that. The Rebbe of Kotzk demanded that one be analytical so that one's behavior would not be inconsistent. He once said:

> I don't know what they want of me. Throughout the week each one does whatever he wants to do; and when the holy Sabbath comes, each one clothes himself with garb of black silk, adorns himself with a black gartel and dons a shtreimel — and he is already engaged with

---

23 *Kol Simhah*, *Toldot*, 29–30. In *Siah Sarfei Kodesh*, 3: 128, §472. R. Bunim says this idea in the name of the Yehudi. Hiddushei ha-Rim had reservations about its applicability nowadays; see *Siah Sarfei Kodesh*, 3:48, §116. Later generations softened and spiritualized the radicalism of Przysucha; see *Sefat Emet, Toldot* 1873; *Shem mi-Shmuel Toldot* (1912), 265.

24 See *Siah Sarfei Kodesh he-Hadash*, 1, *Toldot*, 39; 1:11, §13.

25 *Hiddushei ha-Rim, Hayyei Sarah*, 31.

"Lekha Dodi." But I say: the way that he behaves during the week, so he behaves on the Sabbath.[26]

It was this point of truth that was ultimate for the Kotzker. He said:

The essential point of truth was only reached by the high priest at the moment that he stood in the Holy of Holies.[27]

Only the high priest of truth – the Kotzker himself – could have said that.

The Shem mi-Shmuel (the grandson of the Kotzker), is said to have asked his father, the Avnei Nezer (the son-in-law of the Kotzker), why Hiddushei ha-Rim and other outstanding scholars didn't move immediately to prevent the Rebbe of Izbica from breaking with the Kotzker and creating his own court. To this, his father replied that they weren't sure if their opposition was motivated by a pure motive or by jealousy.[28]

The following tradition epitomizes the abhorrence in Kotzk (but also in Przysucha generally) of imitation, and demands that self-definition not be dependent on the other.

If I am I because I am I, and you are you because you are you, then I am I and you are you. But if I am I because you are you, and you are you because I am I, then I am not I, and you are not you.[29] [30]

---

[26] *Hiddushei ha-Rim, Shabbat*, 308.

[27] *Shem mi-Shmuel*, 2:209b.

[28] S.Z. Shragai, "The Hasidism of the Baal Shem Tov According to Izbica-Radzin" (Hebrew). In *Sefer ha-Besht*, 166–167; cf. also quoting R. Pinchas Zelig Glicksman in his work *Tiferet Adam*, vol. 1, *Koltura* (Lodz, 1913).

[29] *Devarim Nehmadim*, quoted in *Emet me-Eretz Titzmah*, edited by M. Sheinfeld, 176 (Bnai Berak: 1994). Cf. R. Mahler, "Two Schools of Hasidism In Poland," in his *Hasidism and the Jewish Enlightenment*, 293; *Emet ve-Emunah*, §647, "Once our teacher said (the prayer) 'I give thanks before You' – 'Who is "I" and who is "before You"?' and he stopped and said nothing further."

[30] See in the name of R. Bunim, "'And you shall love the Lord your God with all your heart....' And not with the heart, or qualities, of another. For someone who serves God with the heart of another is like an idol worshiper." *Hasidim Mesaprim*, 1, §122.

Passion

Now it is all right to say that one must be authentic, but how is this to be achieved? I think that R. Bunim would have said that there are two essential components – the "two wings of a bird." The first is cognitive, and the second is affective. The first is the analytical search for the truth and the second is the heart, with its accompanying retinue of passion, sincerity, and purity of motive.

The source of authenticity lies within the heart.

> "And you shall seek from there… and find" (Deut 4:29). That is to say: all wisdom and analysis to comprehend God and His unity is called "there": that is to say, from somewhere else. But the real truth is literally in its place – that is to say, in his heart. For when a person properly purifies his character traits, he will find the Divine in his heart. And that is the "finding," for you should know that you don't need to inquire about God, to seek and search from anywhere, except in your heart and in your soul.[31]

There is a fundamental assumption in this quotation which informs Przysucha's search for authenticity. They assumed that man's heart, his inner core, is pure, and that it is the real source of connection with God.[32] They assume that Torah, wisdom, and intimacy with God are allied to the human being's hidden core.[33] R. Bunim said, on the verse, "If you seek it as silver, or search for it as a hidden treasure" (Prov 2:4).

> "Seeking" refers to human beings looking for something they never had; "searching" refers to something that has been lost, for which they search. The difference is that those who have lost something are greatly distressed and make an effort to find it, but when they find it their happiness is not that great because they already had the object before. In contradistinction, those who find something and who were not greatly distressed previously feel great happiness.

---

[31] *Kol Simhah*, Vaethanan, 107 (additions); cf. *Ramatayim Zofim*, chap. 5, §96; chap. 2, §84; *Siah Sarfei Kodesh he-Hadash*, 1:122. Cf. *Nifla'ot Hadashot*, 63, in the name of Menahem Mendel; *Emet ve-Emunah*, §485.

[32] *Ramatayim Zofim*, chap. 17 §47.

[33] See Chap. 7.

Therefore Scripture says about the service of God that one needs both – the great distress to make the effort to find something that one has lost, and afterwards, when one merits to find it, to be in a state of great happiness."[34]

R. Bunim's idea presupposes that the service of God is innate, natural to human beings. It is something he has or had in the past; it is not something external to him. If a person seeks hard enough, he will find God within himself. R. Bunim draws an analogy between the loss of a precious object and a person's sense of being distanced from the presence of the Divine. He calls upon us to believe that this quality lies within us and that it is natural for a person to be connected with God. With this understanding, one cay say that religion is not something imposed upon human beings from without, contrary to their own instincts, but rather the expression of their fundamental nature.

It is well known that whenever a student came to R. Bunim he would be told the story of R. Isaac of Cracow who journeyed to Prague in pursuit of a treasure only to be told by a non-Jew that the treasure lay at home – that is, within one's own heart.[35] In one version R. Bunim is quoted as saying: "Every Jew has a treasure in his heart, a hidden fortune; only he doesn't know it" – and only by being true to oneself can one reveal one's treasure.[36] R. Bunim said that the heart is the only faculty with which a person can sense the Holy Torah. For it is well known that a person feels through his senses, "but only the heart can sense the Holy Torah and its Godliness."[37] [38]

---

[34] *Torat Simhah*, §96; *Ramatayim Zofim* (AZ), chap. 14, §12.

[35] *Ma'amarei Simhah*, n. 30. Buber, in his *Tales of the Hasidim: The Later Masters*, 245, has all sorts of additions. Cf. *Sefat Emet Likkutim*, Vayigash; *Kol Mevaser*, 2:263. For various nuances in the use of this parable, see A. Cohen, "*Al ketivah ve-hoser ketivah le-Bet Przysucha*," *Dimui* (5765 [2005]).

[36] *Hiddushei ha-Rim*, 358, *Hasidut*.

[37] *Ramatayim Zofim*, chap. 11 §29.

[38] Another version continues: "Especially with regard to the secrets of the Torah (*sitrei Torah*), which are called the Torah of God, the sense is in his heart. Therefore he should not err." (*Torat Simhah*, §198). I am inclined to think that this is a later addition. R. Bunim in *Kol Simhah* does not use the phrase *Torat Elohim* to indicate *sitrei Torah*; nor in fact does he even use the term *sitrei Torah*.

Every human heart is unique. "Each person can only see by means of his own endeavor and his own understanding,"[39] and therefore every individual has a personal obligation to worship God in his own particular way, the source being the individual heart.[40] Nevertheless, one must be aware of the possibility of self-delusion, especially in the world of religious piety. In a pithy epigram, R. Bunim is reported to have said: "One's 'for the sake of Heaven" has to be for the sake of Heaven."[41]

But how is one to arouse the heart? The answer seems to be: through passion. Of course, it is almost superfluous to add that passion can be, and often is, superficial and dangerous, unless it is channeled and combined with introspection and preparation.

> "My soul thirsts for you... I have seen You in holiness" (Ps 42:3). R. Bunim explained: as "in accordance with King David's thirst, so was his seeing in holiness."[42]

Passion is the oxygen of the heart:

> Every zaddik has hidden in his heart the wrath of God; and through that wrath he is able to have compassion on people and bring them near to Torah. But as long as the wrath of God does not burn within his heart, it is difficult for him to do good for Israel.[43]
>
> I heard... from R. Simhah Bunim... that ever since the *yetzer* (inclination) of idol worship, which burned like fire, was annulled... the desire to serve God has cooled and there is not such a passion for holiness. For God made one in relation to the other.[44]

As has been mentioned, R. Bunim believed the value of passion was something that could be learned from the way the Gentiles felt in regard to their nationalism.[45] Once the Yehudi asked R. Bunim what he had learned

---

[39] Mahler, *Hasidism and the Jewish Enlightenment*, 297.

[40] *Ramatayim Zofim*, chap. 11, §29.

[41] *Siah Sarfei Kodesh*, 3:46, §102.

[42] *Torat Simhah*, §25.

[43] *Ma'amarei Simhah*, §19.

[44] *Ramatayim Zofim*, 2:66; *Torat Simhah*, §112. Cf., e.g., *Siah Sarfei Kodesh he-Hadash*, *Noah*, 18; *Meir Einei ha-Golah*, §138; Boem, 543.

[45] *Siah Sarfei Kodesh*, 5:43.

from his last trip to Danzig. R. Bunim replied that he heard the following epigram:

> To lose money is to lose nothing. To lose courage is to lose everything.[46] [47]

With a beautiful insight R. Bunim explains that even the passion of song can never fully express what man wants to say to God; and it is precisely that which cannot be expressed that is so precious in His eyes.

> R. Bunim explained the blessing, "God... who chooses songs of melody" – to mean that this refers to what is left over after the song – that the heart still longs to sing songs of praise in addition to what has already been said. And this is what God chooses most of all.[48]

R. Bunim is playing on the word "shirei" (songs). This word is superfluous, as the preceding word is "zimra," which also means song. He therefore explains "shira" as being associated with "shirayim," i.e., that which is left over. The idea is that emotion can be so passionate that even the pure art form of music cannot fully express itself.

Something that is real refuses to evaporate. It lingers and its intensity is best expressed in its silence. As the American composer Benjamin Boretz wrote, "In music, as in everything, the 'disappearing moment' of experience is the firmest reality." Why, asked R. Bunim, is the month after Tishrei called Marheshvan? "Because after Tishrei... the lips are still quivering (*merahashot*)."[49]

Przysucha believes that there is a litmus test for experience and passion: If the experience of the act lives on, then it is more likely to be genuine.

---

[46] *Shem mi-Shmuel, Yitro*, 268.

[47] With passion came will. "The main thing is the will." *Siah Sarfei Kodesh*, 4:15, §2; *Siah Sarfei Kodesh*, 2:85 §285: "The most important thing is the will."

[48] *Shem mi-Shmuel, Noah, Rosh Hodesh Marheshvan* (1920) 82a; *Hiddushei ha-Rim, Vayakhel*, 144 (cf. *Siah Sarfei Kodesh*, 1:11, §22; 3:57 §168; *Siah Sarfei Kodesh he-Hadash*, 1, Vayakhel, 89).

[49] *Imrei Emet*, Lublin, *Noah, The Third Meal (Kol Mevaser*, 3:56–57). The pun here is the associative meaning of *rahash*, meaning the fluttering and quivering of lips. Cf. *Hiddushei ha-Rim*, 269.

For an understanding that does not remain in a man until the next day has no endurance.[50]

This outlook runs counter to that espoused by other streams within Hasidism; there is an approach among them (possibly the dominant one) which extols spontaneity – the moment. Przysucha, with its circumspection as to what a person's motives and emotions really are, cannot agree. Spontaneity must have a context of preparation. Passion – yes; superficiality – no. Perhaps, one can draw an analogy with jazz music and improvisation. Improvisation is a take-off, a leap, within the structure of jazz. For Przysucha, the structure is the preparation for a *mitzvah* and improvisation, the beat of one's heart while the *mitzvah* is played out.[51]

R. Bunim said:

> When a person begins his service, heaven gives him enthusiasm and desire. If he's intelligent, he guards his path and doesn't leave it – then it will be good for his soul. But if he doesn't think, but throws himself into it with all his strength, not taking care that his desire should remain for a long time afterwards; then – as for his enthusiasm – "God gives and God takes away." He will remain empty as he was in the beginning.[52]

Unbridled enthusiasm, without thought of how to maintain it in the future, will evaporate. In Przysucha, one has to be apart from *and* a part of one's experience. Though the moment doesn't allow one to be self reflective (for otherwise one isn't immersed in the experience), nevertheless, Przysucha demands that a person evaluate himself in relation to the event.

The ability to combine passion with self-analysis is rare. On the whole, passion by its very nature operates as an emotional totality, usually committing the person to one uncompromising particular point of view, whereas the ability to be self-analytical comes with a certain hesitancy, and ability to see different aspects of the situation. Przysucha's demand for both

---

[50] *Sefat Emet*, Vayetze (1875), 235; *Bet Yisrael*, Vayishlah (1949); *Shem mi-Shmuel*, Vayetze (1915), 335.

[51] In one of the very few letters we have from R. Bunim, he said that "settling oneself (preparation) is more praiseworthy than eagerness *(zerizut)*." Rabinowitz, *From Lublin to Pryzsucha*, 294.

[52] *Kol Simhah*, 123.

is an expression of a type of Hasidism which must be expressed in a context of preparation, time and self analysis. It is an uneasy balance. Ultimately, R. Bunim is on the side of passion. For him, the very excess of generosity in building the *Tabernacle* is what created the intimacy between God and the Jewish people.[53]

Though the lingering of the experience – the whisper that remains afterwards – is the litmus test of whether what happened was in fact genuine, one should not dwell on it self-consciously. If there had been preparation, if the emotion was deep, then it will endure without one thinking, "Will I be able to carry it on into everyday life?" The afterglow is not self-conscious, but organic.

In the wake of passion comes sincerity.

> A person should not behave with deceit, saying that he is learning sincerely and in truth, whereas in reality this is not so, but it is only an image. Rather, a person should do everything for the sake of Heaven, without ulterior motive.[54]

The goal is to serve without self-interest, without ego, wholeheartedly, for the sake of Heaven.[55] All this was already taught by the Yehudi.

The Yehudi is reported as offering the following interpretation, which was typical of his approach.

> "Lot said, 'My brothers, please (*na*) do not do evil'" (Gen 19:7). The word *na* is used in the Torah to indicate something half-baked. Similarly, here too the word *na* means, "My brothers, do not be half-brothers."[56]

---

[53] *Hiddushei ha-Rim, Vayakhel*, 144.

[54] *Siah Sarfei Kodesh*, 1: 11, §13. On sincerity or insincerity, see also *Torat Simhah*, §§77, 120; *Ma'amarei Simhah*, §53.

[55] *Torat Simhah*, §§154, 350; *Ramatayim Zofim*, chap. 2 §112; chap. 12 §32. B. Mintz, in *Ketuvim* 52 (1927); *Hiddushei ha-Rim, Kohelet*, 276; *Hashavah le-Tovah*, 118, "service of God." "Hiddushei ha-Rim said in the name of the Yehudi: 'The Almighty has given a commitment (*shetar hov*) to the Jewish people that if they seek God they will find Him. But this is conditional on their being sincere.'" – *Nifla'ot ha-Yehudi*, 55.

[56] *Siah Sarfei Kodesh he-Hadash*, 1, Vayera, 31.

In other words, the Yehudi (like R. Bunim and the Kotzker) wants whole heartedness – total commitment, nothing half-baked.[57]

In a rather supercilious piece we read the following:

> A preacher in Germany expounded on the idea that God showed Moses a coin of fire. But why (he asked) not of metal? (The answer is that) man's giving of the coin must be with fire, with enthusiasm. And the Kotzker said: because they (in Germany) are particular about the commandment of hospitality, this Torah was revealed to him (the German preacher).[58]

A commandment must be done with passion; and the Kotzker could not imagine how this secret could have been discovered by someone living in the West unless by special merit for fulfilling the mitzvah of hospitality.

The following interpretation of Menahem Mendel seems to encapsulate Przysucha's idea that through passion one can express one's inner reality. The Biblical text ascribes the redemption of the Jewish people from Egypt to Moses's declaration that "God will surely visit you" (*pakod yifkod*). It is with this phrase that the Jewish people will believe the redeemer's credentials. In that case, asks the Kotzker, what is to prevent anyone from coming along and using that phrase? He answers, that the phrase "visit" (*pakod*) is an expression of intimacy and conveys the idea of yearning – "and this can only be done by the true redeemer, for he alone can so affect the heart of the Jewish people that they have yearnings for their Father in Heaven."[59]

A word is only an outward expression of an inner process. What brings about redemption? It is not the phrase (as if it were a password), but the ability of a human being to create transformation. That is the true sign of the redeemer.

The qualities of passion and sincerity are by themselves, of course, inadequate in the service of God: they need to be framed with the quality of

---

[57] There are various sources about R. Bunim and R. Akiva Eiger. It may not be irrelevant to note that the latter, in one of his letters, bemoaned the state of German Jewry. He wrote: "It is surprising in my eyes that, thank God, nearly everybody here [in Posen] fears God; but the fire [passion] does not burn inside them." Rabinowitz, "R. Bunim," 48, §14.

[58] *Hiddushei ha-Rim*, Shekalim, 116.

[59] *Emet ve-Emunah*, §354.

truth. If there is one quality associated with R. Menahem Mendel of Kotzk that is typical of Przysucha in general, it is the passion for truth.[60]

The Yehudi was uncompromising on the subject of truth:

> The seal of God is truth; and it is a seal that cannot be forged, for if one were to forge it, it could not be true.[61]
>
> The quality of truth has four hundred paths[62] until one comes to the quality of "There is none other than He."[63]
>
> Many love falsehood but few love truth. For one can love falsehood with truth, but truth cannot be loved with falsehood."[64]

If one says that God's seal – that is, that which typifies God – is truth, then anything fake cannot be God-like, by definition. A person is surrounded by falsehood, and must be ever vigilant to be sure that he is trying to be true. In other words, one cannot be true to God, in the sense of being honest to Him, if one is not true and honest towards oneself. The two relationships are totally interconnected.

We have already mentioned the Yehudi's interpretation of a Midrash in which he ironically explains that Esau kept the commandment of honoring one's parents better than R. Shimon ben Gamliel. This piece is so seminal that it merits a closer reading.

> R. Shimon ben Gamliel said, "Nobody honored their parents more than I, yet I found that Esau did. Because when I served my father I would wear dirty clothes, and when I went outside I would get rid of the dirty clothes and dress in fine clothes. But Esau didn't behave like that; he would serve his father [at all times] wearing his best clothes."

The Yehudi asks, 'Why couldn't R. Shimon ben Gamliel wear fine clothes while serving his father, as Esau did?" He answers,

---

[60] This quality of truth was one of the reasons that drew the Yehudi to the Seer. See chap. 2.

[61] *Siah Sarfei Kodesh*, 3:49, §124; cf. *Siah Sarfei Kodesh*, 1:53 §248, where this statement is quoted in R. Bunim's name. Note the editor's comment. Cf. *Hashavah le-Tovah*, *Hasidut*, 121, where the Seer teaches R. Bunim that the seal of God is truth.

[62] *Nifla'ot ha-Yehudi*, 60.

[63] *Vayakhel Shlomo* 15:2; *Torat ha-Yehudi*, 175 §5.

[64] *Hasidim Mesaprim* 3, §702 (*Torat ha-Yehudi*, 176, §6).

Clothes are also a means of projecting an image. By serving his father in his best clothes, Esau is saying, so to speak, that he (always) projected a positive image of himself to his father. (The Rabbis say that he would ask his father how one tithes hay and salt). And though he deceived his father (with his supposed piety), ultimately Isaac would not have wished to have been deceived but, to the contrary, would have preferred to have seen his son's faults in order to correct them. Nevertheless, for a moment, Isaac felt tranquility, imagining that his son was behaving correctly.

It is regarding this (approach of Esau) that R. Shimon ben Gamliel says that he is unable to honor his father like Esau. He is not prepared to hide his faults from his father. On the contrary, he will wear his dirty clothes. That is to say he will reveal his reality to his father, his character faults, warts and all. And though, ultimately, his father would approve of such an approach because it allows him to correct the character failings of his son and to show him the Godly path. Nevertheless, for a moment, his father was upset. Therefore, says the Yehudi, he (R. Shimon ben Gamliel) could not honor his father as Esau did."[65]

The Yehudi is by no means naive, and notably he pays attention to the pain that the approach of being open and of declaring one's character faults can cause to the other. Fulfilling one's individuality can easily lead to spiritual self-indulgence, albeit for the sake of heaven. Yet ultimately, without a striving for truth, one's very service of the Divine is of dubious value. It is clear from the way the Yehudi talks about the initial pain caused to the father that he senses this dialectic (the hurt of being too open to the other).[66] But without personal integrity, one's service of God is a sham.

It is important to note that what is reflected here is the laser light of the search for truth, which reached its zenith with R. Menahem Mendel of Kotzk. But this early source proves unequivocally that this quality starts with the very inception of Przysucha. It is not a later development. The first one

---

[65] *Orhot Hayyim*, 40; *Nifla'ot ha-Yehudi*, 52; *Torat ha-Yehudi*, 12.

[66] It seems to me that the word "father" has a double entendre, to include "Father in heaven." If one is not "truthful" with oneself and with one's biological father, then the inevitable slippery slope of being human is not to be "truthful," at least in one's own mind, to one's heavenly Father.

to see the quest for truth as seminal, without compromise – "You cannot forge truth" – in the world of Przysucha, was not the Kotzker, but the Yehudi (as learnt from the Seer).

R. Bunim was no less committed than his teacher:

> Once, after Rosh Hashanah… he said to everyone, "I am asking one thing from you; promise me that you will listen." And of course everybody replied that they would listen. He then requested that each one not say something false, but only the truth. And he said that to each one.[67]
>
> Once he spoke… about how falsehood was widespread amongst the masses … and he said the following, "If [the prohibition against] talking falsely were [perceived] as being as stringent as [that against] adultery, then the Redeemer would come."[68]

R. Bunim explained the following well-known Midrash which describes how God "consulted" before He created the human being.

> "Kindness said: Create man, etc. Truth said: do not create him, because he is full of lies…. Peace said: do not create him, because he is always quarreling. What did God do? He cast truth down to the earth, etc." And he [R. Bunim] asked: "But there still remains peace, which said 'Do not create.' But one can say that having thrown away truth, peace will be unable to argue, for if falsity is dominant, then those who quarrel appear to be friends, and there is no strife in the world.[69] [70]

In other words, peace can adjust to any situation so long as truth is not involved in the process. It is truth which does not allow peace to compromise or to sell its soul.

R. Bunim said "I could convert all the sinners in Israel, but only if (they behave) without lies or falsity."[71] He observed that the Torah, unlike the Rabbis, never made a "fence" around its words. The one exception was

[67] *Ramatayim Zofim* (AZ), chap. 29 §81; *Ma'amarei Simhah*, §84.
[68] *Siah Sarfei Kodesh*, 1:118 §617.
[69] *Siah Sarfei Kodesh*, 2:85–86 §286.
[70] This piece is almost identical with that found in the name of the Kotzker in *Ohel Torah, Bereshit*, 5.
[71] *Ma'amarei Simhah*, §§4, 69; *Siah Sarfei Kodesh*, 1:32 §156.

when dealing with falsity.[72] He would quote his master the Yehudi that the pursuit of justice must itself be done with justice and not with untruth.[73] The ends cannot justify the means in divine service.

This total lack of compromise with regard to purity of motive led to the rejection of a certain Rabbinical norm. The Rabbis always maintained that one should study Torah even if one does so with an ulterior motive. They believed that the "light" within the Torah would eventually bring a person to perform the commandment without an ulterior motive. Przysucha simply didn't accept that philosophy. Przysucha could not outwardly reject this Rabbinic principle, so it had to reinterpret it. As the Kotzker said regarding this matter:[74]

> If a person suspects that he is learning for an ulterior motive then he can strengthen himself in service. But if he really is learning for an ulterior motive, then it is not worth anything.[75]

That is, there is no justification for learning Torah with an ulterior motive. Rather, in the hands of the Kotzker, this can mean that a person should always be conscious that his supposedly pure motive is in fact full of dross, that his service of the Divine takes place within a context of human frailty. But this does not mean, heaven forbid, that one should learn in the first instance with an ulterior motive.

One cannot know for certain whether the Kotzker actually said this (the quotation comes from *Hashavah le-Tovah* where he says, "I heard from the Rebbe of Kotzk"). What we do know is that this is how later generations experienced the philosophy of Przysucha.

Said R. Bunim:

> The way of the false is to clothe themselves in the garb of truth and justice and to say "We are religious, we have never sinned." And their method is to search for proofs from the Torah to... justify themselves. But in truth it is wrong to do so, and anyone who does

---

[72] Exodus 23:7; *Torat Simhah*, §355; the word is *harhakah;* also *Torat Simhah*, §184.

[73] *Torat Simhah*, §329.

[74] B. Mintz, *Letters* (1927) vol. 52; Rabinowitz, "The Yehudi," 92; *Hashavah le-Tovah*, *Likkutim*, 88–89.

[75] *Siah Sarfei Kodesh*, 1:25 §121 where this idea is mentioned in the name of R. Bunim.

such a thing is an abomination to God. Rather, (one must) pursue, to find the strength and courage for words of righteousness and truth.[76]

Within the human context there is no such thing as perfection; every human being is a sinner. What is intolerable, is clothing oneself with a righteousness that is either disingenuous or an obvious lie, that if one analyzed afterward, would inevitably make itself apparent.

> In the name of R. Bunim... Throughout the year a man doesn't pay attention to praying properly. The exception is the Day of Atonement and the two days of the New Year. Then he stands to pray properly.... But his intention is only money, children, life and livelihood....[77]

Human frailty makes fools (if not liars) of us all.

There is always a sense of circumspection hovering in the world of Przysucha. The following insightful comment was expressed by R. Bunim.

> For all man's efforts and arousal, it could be that his experience is external (*me-hitzoniut*) to the heart; for the heart has many chambers. But that which comes down from heaven comes down to revive him – literally – as a living being.[78]

It is true that in Przysucha the religious drama takes place in the heart of man, but "the heart has many chambers." That is to say that man can never know whether his experience is genuine or not. With all his introspection, his emotion might still be "external." It is only when he makes contact with the Divine (when the Divine comes down and touches him) that he is brought into contact with his essential life force.[79]

---

[76] *Kol Simhah, Shoftim*, 109.

[77] *Torat Simhah*, §350. The interpretation is based on a pun on the verse Exod 21:21.

[78] *Ramatayim Zofim*, chap. 6 §28.

[79] *Hashavah le-Tovah, Mishpatim*, 25.

Purity of Motive

Like many pietistic movements, Przysucha focused on purity of motive. Human beings must learn to function within the framework of human frailty, prepared to ask themselves just how anyone could possibly stand with any integrity before the Divine. If they are not prepared to be conscious of their own weaknesses, if they do not prepare themselves internally, then whom are they fooling? Even if one can never be objective, there are myriad degrees of subjectivity, of bias, of prejudice, of self-interest. For Przysucha the process of being aware of God, in the Torah and in the world, was essentially not a cognitive one. The approach was not like that of some medieval philosopher or Kabbalist, who believed that by pondering and comprehending a body of knowledge one would achieve some understanding of God. What was crucial for Przysucha was to understand human beings.

It is interesting to note that the world of Przysucha, permeated by its emphasis on introspection, predates its Lithuanian counterpart – the Musar Movement[80] – by some two generations. However, though Przysucha is the Torah of the human being, and though the drama of religious service is seen to take place within the heart of the individual, this introspection was not allowed to become self-absorbing. For Przysucha, introspection is the entrée into the Divine presence, a methodology enabling one to serve with sincerity. No other movement in Hasidism tried so hard to explore and to purify motive. But introspection alone was insufficient. One first had to prepare oneself for holiness, and purity was the umbilical cord to God-consciousness.

---

[80] On the Musar Movement, see Kopul Rosen, *Rabbi Israel Salanter and the Musar Movement* (London: 1945); I. Etkes, *Rabbi Israel Salanter and the Beginnings of the Mussar Movement* (Hebrew). Jerusalem: 1982; English: Philadelphia, 1993. Some scholars maintain that Salanter was reacting to the onslaught of the Enlightenment. If so, then Pzysucha was different. For although R. Bunim thought that learning Torah alone was an insufficient defense against the Enlightenment in his day, this movement started earlier with the Yehudi. It is not at all clear to what extent the Yehudi was responding to outside factors (see Addendum E – Przysucha and Romanticism). Zvi Kurtzweil, "Rabbi Israel Salanter and Musar Movement," *Sinai* 23 (1960, 47/8): 102, maintains that the Musar Movement was essentially a response to Hasidism rather than to the Enlightenment.

> If a person purifies himself, then he will come to recognize the Divine from the Torah.[81]

This alignment of God and Torah is something that essentially takes place within a person's heart.

> A person must first cleanse his heart and mind for holiness, each one according to his level, according to his ability, so that his heart and mind are one and all his limbs and senses are literally as an offering....[82]

If the heart is purified, then it can see, then it can know – then knowledge can enter into the essence of a person,[83] into his *kishke*.[84] "Before a man learns Torah he has to repent."[85] And even repentance should not be motivated by a desire to be a righteous person (which is a form of self-interest), but rather by a sense of "bitterness" (i.e., dissatisfaction with one's own spiritual level), a sense that a human being cannot justify himself before God.[86]

One of the ways developed in Przysucha to help a person on this quest for personal purity was the idea of a Socratic core of would-be spiritual travelers whose function was to criticize, prod, and support the hasid in his quest. There was a camaraderie of would-be seekers of truth. The following is a description of what one might call "the reception committee" in Przysucha.

> The order was like this. In the outer room by which one entered into the inner sanctuary of R. Bunim, there sat a holy group of his pupils. And any hasid that came for the first time to the Rebbe was not allowed in before being examined seven-fold [to see] if he had the scent of the fear of God.[87]

---

81 *Ramatayim Zofim*, chap. 17 §47.
82 *Kol Simhah*, Terumah, 74–75.
83 *Hiddushei ha-Rim*, Bo, 93.
84 *Kol Simhah*, Psalms, 113.
85 *Siah Sarfei Kodesh*, 1:20 §95.
86 *Ramatayim Zofim*, chap. 15 §38.
87 *Or Simhah*, §18; cf. ibid., §23; *Nifla'ot ha-Yehudi*, 68 §7. This source may reflect R. Bunim's sense that things had gone too far.

This sort of treatment applied both to the initiate and to the inner group amongst themselves. Many are the stories told in Przysucha about how an apparently pious person was shown, after some revealing prank was played on him, to be motivated by ego or some other human weakness of which he might or might not have been aware. The purpose of this wasn't simply to sift out the negative. It was essentially a support system for the initiate to improve himself, and this was done by the critical love of his peers. Such behavior within this type of camaraderie was unintelligible to the outsider, but to the insider it was crucial.[88]

It seems to have been quite natural that, in a form of Hasidism based on the use of the intellect, on self-analysis, on individual authenticity, the devotee did not simply come for a brief visit to his Rebbe. Such an approach satisfied those streams of Hasidism based on the charisma of the zaddik, that believed in a vicarious redemption. But Przysucha developed a different educational norm. Its hasidim would leave their families for months to be with their rebbe. This gave them time to internalize his teachings. There developed a certain educational ambience which was less hierarchical – a rebbe who was a leader of a group. What the Yehudi and later R. Bunim were promoting was a Judaism which demanded a personal relationship between teacher and pupil.[89] [90] But such socio-economic insights, valuable as they may be, should not lead us to deny a religious movement its own integrity.

The devil (the *ba'al davar*) was more likely to be found in the world of religious piety than in any other. That is where one needed the critique of a support group. For the enemy was within. Those inside were most likely to recognize him:

---

[88] *Siah Sarfei Kodesh*, 1:27 §138; 3:10.

[89] It may be asked how a teacher's actions can be a model if he hides his qualities. The answer seems to be that the teacher reveals to his disciple what and when – and all this when the teacher feels that the student is ready.

[90] Some scholars explain the phenomenon of Przysucha within the context of the urbanization of Poland at the beginning of the nineteenth century, arguing that the hasidim of Przysucha were essentially middle class. A. Brill, "Grandeur and Humility in the Writings of R. Simhah Bunim of Przysucha." *Hazon Nahum* (New York: 1997), 444–446; Mahler, *Hasidim and the Jewish Enlightenment*, 272.

R. Bunim[91] said: "There are hasidim who think that they have attained some level of awe with an emotion of the heart and they think that is the entrée into holiness... You should know this is not so. You still have the devil (ba'al davar) and it could be that is the devil himself. For the devil(s) are not afraid, and they crawl[92] and tremble before God – and nevertheless it is the devil."[93] [94]

It was necessary to create a community that would identify the devil in its midst. A community of seekers of truth would help insure that all its members were devoted to purifying their motives. Nothing could be clearer than the following aphorism attributed to R. Bunim:

When a man looks inside himself and sees what he sees, it is very bitter for him. For the nature of humankind is to justify itself.[95]

Perhaps the essential idea is this: when a person first looks inside himself he senses the flaws of his own personality. But there comes a stage, if one is "successful" in the process, when one accepts what is inside, and then one comes to terms with one's inadequacies. As we shall see, R. Bunim was against morbidity, nor did he value angst.[96] However, there had to be introspection, and this is where the center of religious gravity lay for the world of Przysucha.

Intolerance of Routine and Externals

Inevitably, the quest for truth and purity of motive lent itself to intolerance of routine, for what was lifeless could not be true.

---

91 *Ramatayim Zofim*, chap. 3, §21.

92 The meaning here is somewhat ambiguous, perhaps deliberately so.

93 R. Bunim once said: "What is a pious person a hasid? One who is pious with his Creator and not pious with his fellow hasid in order to be a hasid, but just simply because of a recognition of his Maker and Creator" – *Torat Simhah*, §201. For other sources on purity of motive, see *Siah Sarfei Kodesh*, 1:51, §236.

94 See also *Siah Sarfei Kodesh*, 3:5 §1, where R. Bunim says that a hasid is one who doesn't fool himself.

95 *Ramatayim Zofim*, chap. 31, §95. *Emunat* Zaddikim, 82.

96 Alternatively, perhaps there is always some bitterness, because some of the "*baal davar*" is always there.

Concerning the Biblical verse (Deut. 12:4): "… Do not do so (*ken*) to the Lord your God," we are told that the Yehudi said something that became the byword of Przysucha for three generations: "Don't behave towards God in a lifeless manner (*keviut bli hayim*)."[97] A lifeless routine with no passion – simply saying "Yes" – is an insult to God and to one's own integrity. Said R. Bunim:

> This is a great praise to those who are knowledgeable – those who don't want to do the commandments out of routine, without reason, even though the essence of the matter might be good.[98]

For R. Bunim, the passion for truth inevitably led to an abhorrence of routine. Authenticity is not possible if one simply follows the commandments routinely. This is reinforced in R. Bunim's words:

> A Jew is not permitted to fix a path which he continuously follows. Rather, sometimes this way, sometimes that way. In order to change nature and routine.[99]

By this R. Bunim meant that one must constantly assesses one's nature and routine so that one does not fall into rote, but rather continually develops. This is more clearly articulated in the following quote:

> If keeping the Sabbath is simply a remembrance, namely that he remembers what he saw by his father; then even though he is called a Sabbath observer, he is not doing the will of God, for he is not thinking about that at all.[100]

Such a person is not remembering the Sabbath. He is remembering his father's remembering of the Sabbath. In order to fulfill God's will one must utilize the mind rather than simply repeat one's father's actions.

With an irony that strikes at the heart of traditional Jewish thinking, R. Bunim offers the following interpretation:

---

[97] *Mei Shiloah*, 2, *Beha'alotkha*, §29 (p. 57); R. Bunim made the same play on the word *ken* on Deuteronomy 18:14: see *Siah Sarfei Kodesh he-Hadash*, 1:130; *Siah Sarfei Kodesh*, 1.11 §15; as did Menahem Mendel, *Amud ha-Emet*, 46.

[98] *Kol Simhah*, Matot, 100.

[99] *Torat Simhah*, §251; *Siah Sarfei Kodesh*, 1:11 §15.

[100] *Torat Simhah*, §51; this quote is in brackets.

> Of what benefit is it if a person says all his life "You shall love the Lord your God" if he doesn't fulfill it? This is analogous to a teacher of small children dealing with a simpleton. He says to him, "Say 'aleph'" and the child responds, "Say aleph."[101]

But the quest for pure motive led not only to a rejection of routine, norm and tradition, but also led to a rejection of externals. This meant, firstly, those things external to oneself which are not pure.

> An idol is an image of that which is not real... and if one's service of God is done without the desired intention, it is a great abomination in the eyes of God, like the image used by an idol worshipper."[102]

Even those actions that man is commanded to do by Jewish tradition can become idolatrous if done with the wrong intentions. And, of course, this most definitely meant rejection of an external mien of piety, and of all appearances that are not genuine. During the debate at the famous wedding when Polish Hasidism tried to excommunicate R. Bunim, one of the arguments was[103] precisely that – Przysucha's contempt and ridicule for externals, such as a talisman, even when blessed by a zaddik.[104]

Of course, on this occasion the accusation was virulently denied. But one wonders: Even if R. Bunim didn't specifically promote such behavior, it flowed naturally from his philosophy. He was not an innocent. His was an educational approach. It became even more extreme in Kotzk, but it was already there in the very way in which Przysucha looked at the world.

Przysucha declared war on externals: Anything that interfered with human beings' ability to look at themselves for what they really are. The danger of externals, be they the accolades of society, acknowledgement by others, position, status, or clothes, is that they distract one from the primary

---

[101] *Torat Kohen, Likkutim,* 128.2 (*Noam Siah,* 341). The Kotzker said the same thing. *Ginzei ha-hasidut: da'at Torah – der kvitel fun Kotzker Hasid: Yaacov Yitzhak (Zelig) of Valezlavek,* p. 66, Jerusalem: 1967.

[102] *Ramatayim Zofim* (AZ), chap. 14, §7; *Siah Sarfei Kodesh,* 1:11, §13. The Kotzker, of course, said the same thing using different language. See *Siah Sarfei Kodesh he-Hadash,* 1, Toldot, 39; Vayetze, 43.

[103] See above, Chapter 1.

[104] *Meir Einei ha-Golah,* §151.

question, "Who am I?" For Przysucha the question is not, "How am I perceived by others?" but "How am I perceived by myself?"

In *Keter Kehunnah*, we read:

> They did away with any social niceties amongst themselves. Young and old, learned scholars and those just beginning, rich and poor – everybody was equal regardless of age and knowledge. The youngster greeted the elderly with the familiar singular "du" rather than "ihr." And if that was how they behaved with their own, imagine how they looked at others – elderly scholars, rabbis and householders.[105]

What is being described here, by someone who is no lover of Hasidism, is not a capricious rudeness but rather something closer to a Socratic camaraderie of seekers for truth that brooks no pretentiousness, neither in themselves nor in the other.

What might have started as a personal characteristic of the Yehudi, developed into a philosophy. He said:

> Just as publicity is not good for worldly matters, so it is not good for spiritual matters. To avert the evil eye and jealousy, it is better to hide a good quality or religious practice from someone who does not share it.[106]

The value of modesty is that it leaves one less vulnerable to the attraction of public acclaim and its negative impact upon the personality.

> The true service of God should be covered with modesty and secrecy. One should not long for public recognition and acclaim.[107]

The Yehudi once lamented that a colleague of his would live longer than he because the world had not recognized his friend's greatness. But since he, the Yehudi, was indeed recognized by the people, he would therefore would die young.[108]

---

[105] Alexander Zederbaum, *Keter Kehunnah* (1866), 128.
[106] *Mishmeret Itamar* (Warsaw: 1870), Toldot.
[107] Rabinowitz, "The Yehudi," 12, based on *Tiferet ha-Yehudi*, 189 §127.
[108] R. Aaron Marcus, *Der Hasidismus* (Hamburg a Elbe: S. Marcus, 1927), 304.

Personal temperament, the fear of jealousy, were all good reasons for the Yehudi to wish to conceal his personal piety. But all this was buttressed by a philosophy that the path of personal integrity meant behaving in a way that wouldn't be influenced by the outside. It had to flow from within and by itself. R. Bunim said it like this: "A person should hide his fear of Heaven."[109]

Fear of anything external also included the way one related to others. There was a conscious desire to hide one's religious behavior so that it would not be tainted by the approval of society. R. Bunim said:

> Modesty is very praiseworthy… for with the public performance of commandments one can come to pride.[110]
>
> Someone who fears heaven should hide his actions from the public.[111]
>
> He once said that a person who wants to be separate and alone so as to serve God in the middle of a remote wood, but has in his mind that perhaps someone knows about his separation – such a person is very unworthy.[112]

The greatest sin for a Kotzker hasid was to appear to be pious.

> What is the difference between the hasidim of Kotzk and other hasidim? The latter perform the commandments openly but commit transgressions in secret, while the Hasidim of Kotzk commit

---

[109] *Siah Sarfei Kodesh*, 1.11, §21.

[110] *Kol Simhah*, Vayera, 19; *Torat Simhah*, §228; see also *Kol Simhah*, Bo, 63, on pride while doing God's commandments. Cf. *Emet ve-Emunah*, §572, in praise of hiding one's religiosity even at the expense of being misunderstood. Brill, "Grandeur and Humility," 426, has the following note regarding hiding one's religiosity. "*Torat Simhah*, 194, 228; *Ramatayim Zofim*, 8a; *Milin Hadetin,* Korach; Shabbat Teshuva 80a. Bahye ibn Pakudah, *Hovot ha-Levavot, Sha'ar Yihud ha-ma'aseh*. Chap. 5 mentions this approach of hiding piety to avoid hubris and corruption from social pressures, but Bahye fears it will lead to laxness. The Sufi writer Sharafuddin Maner, in *The Hundred Letters* (trans., intro. and notes by P. Jackson [New York, 1980]), Letter §95 and passim, expresses both views of hiding and not hiding one's piety, and leaves the reader to decide which is better for his own situation.

[111] *Siah Sarfei Kodesh*, 1:11 §21; see also *Siah Sarfei Kodesh*, 2:84 §277.

[112] *Siah Sarfei Kodesh*, 1:54 §255; *Ma'amarei Simhah*, §27.

transgressions openly and perform the commandments secretly.[113, 114]

Fundamentally, the problem with externalities is that they detract from the internal (unless they are a manifestation of an inner process). If one's external behavior is ecstatic because of what is happening inside, that is one thing. But without the process starting from within, the external manifestation is probably shallow.

> Everybody was pushing to hear (the words of Hiddushei ha-Rim), and he said "What do you gain from this – everyone physically pushing? The main thing is that a person pushes his heart to be a good Jew. The Hasidism of Przysucha taught us that the main work is internal and one should not work on the external limbs.... Rather, the main thing is that this inner life force should extend to action. When a person does the work inside, his external limbs automatically become subservient."[115]

When one touches one's core, one becomes impervious to others. Said the Yehudi:

> If a person... does not think too much of himself, then he is not frightened of what others think of him.[116]

Przysucha was a group of radical pietists whose sense of the Divine meant that they felt that they had to go through a process of personal refinement so that ulterior motives, self-interest, and human dross would be reduced to a minimum. Abraham Joshua Heschel says:[117]

---

[113] M. Lipson, *Mi-Dor le-Dor*, Tel Aviv, 1929, n. 702.

[114] It is not incidental that we find a disciple of the Seer, R. Zevi Elimelech Shapira of Dynow (1783–1841) in one of his comments on the book *Sur me-Ra* criticizing at some length the followers of Hasidism who relax certain halakhic prohibitions in order to conceal their own piety from the public eye. Note 36 in his commentary on a book entitled *Sur me-Ra va-Aseh Tov* by R. Zevi Hirsch of Zhidachov (an opponent of the Yehudi).

[115] *Siah Sarfei Kodesh*, 3:46 §104; see chap. 10.

[116] *Tiferet ha-Yehudi*, 171 §76. *Emet ve-Emunah*, §133 quotes this in the name of Menahem Mendel.

[117] On personal redemption in Hasidism, see M. Faierstein, "Personal Redemption in Hasidism," in *Hasidism Reappraised* (op. cit.).

The most profound aspect of the Kotsker Rebbe's path was a striving for spiritual freedom. Spiritual freedom means: flattering no one, neither oneself nor the world; not being subservient to anyone, neither to the self nor to society.[118]

The quest for spiritual freedom manifested itself in Kotzk in a type of stoicism that disdained all expressions of vanity and disregarded social niceties.[119] But it all started with the Yehudi.

Perhaps more important is the circumspection expressed by R. Bunim when he said:

Only a hair's breadth separates the Garden of Eden and Gehinnom.[120]

---

[118] A.J. Heschel, *Kotsk: Ein Gerangel Far Emesdikeit*, 2 vols. (Tel Aviv, 1973), 523. Cf. also *Emet ve-Emunah*, §602.

[119] *Siah Sarfei Kodesh*, 3:10.

[120] *Hiddushei ha-Rim, Devarim*, 234 (*Zekhuta de-Avraham*).

TORAT HA-ADAM: HUMAN PSYCHOLOGY

> I thought of writing a book no longer than a quarter of a page and I would call it "man" and it would encompass the whole [essence] of man; but on further reflection I decided not to. [1]
>
> R. Bunim

As is known,[2] we have no written record by these three generations of Przysucha. But we do have the above tradition that R. Bunim intended to write a book.

Another version[3] reports that when R. Bunim was asked, "From which book does he say Torah [his teaching]?", he replied, "From the book of the generations of humanity" (Genesis 5:1).

Some people[4] have understood the phrase "the generations of humanity" as referring to R. Bunim's desire to write a commentary on the Book of Genesis. But this is too formalistic and misses the point. R. Bunim wanted to write a book about the human being, "about his essence,"[5] but he felt that ultimately this was impossible. In the same genre, there is a tradition that R. Bunim said:

---

[1] *Or Simhah,* §64; Rabinowitz, *Bunim,* 87, n. 1, cites this in the name of Menahem Mendel as well.

[2] See Addendum A.

[3] *Siah Sarfei Kodesh*, 2: 10 n. 4; Boem, 175; J. Fox, *Rabbi Menahem Mendel of Kotzk* (Hebrew) (Jerusalem: 1967), 14, has almost the identical quotation in the name of the Kotzker (Menaham Mendel).

[4] So the editor of the above citation in *Siah Sarfei Kodesh.*

[5] A quarter of a page doesn't sound like a very big book; certainly not a commentary. Clearly, the idea of a "book" shouldn't be taken too literally.

[E]veryone should make a book of himself; what a person does. Indeed he should be a book himself....[6] or, as R. Yitzhak of Vorki said: "Every Jew is a book."[7]

For a person to be a book means that each person has his own unique experiences from which he needs to learn the wisdom of life. In addition, any such work, written by a rebbe like himself, would ultimately be canonized and ritualized into a code of behavior. But essentially, R. Bunim concluded, just as oral law is more dynamic than written law, so similarly, real development is not to be found in a book. This is because there is no one path applicable to all. Each person can be helped, but no ultimate answers can be given. And as his teacher the Yehudi said, rather enigmatically:

In the service of God there are no rules, and this rule itself is no rule.[8]

If authenticity – in the sense of being true to oneself – is the seminal idea of the Yehudi, then it must follow that there can be no single path suitable for all, and no fixed means of service. The fact that a particular combination is correct in the service of the Divine for one person does not mean that it is right for another. The function of the rebbe is therefore to arouse in the disciple the qualities of which he is capable.

There is no escaping the trial and error of life. R. Bunim knew that his role was to facilitate[9] the hasid's becoming aware of his own individuality – within, of course, the halakhic context. *Torat Adam,* the book that R. Bunim wanted to write, therefore refers not to a commentary on Genesis but to life itself. R. Bunim wanted to write a book about life and realized, precisely because he was a supreme teacher, that the mission was, by definition, impossible.

There is no escaping the fact, that we have nothing written by the three masters of Przysucha. What inhibited them from writing? Was it just a

---

[6] *Yekhahen Pe'er,* par. Emor, 120.

[7] *Ohel Yitzhak,* 8 §8.

[8] *Tiferet ha-Yehudi,* 176, §93.

[9] On the story of R. Isaac R. Yekele of Cracow told by R. Bunim, cf. Chapter 1. This whole interpretation has been substantiated by A. Kohen, "Al ketivah ve-hoser ketivah le-Bet Przysucha" (Hebrew), *Dimui* (5765 [2005]).

historical quirk? It's not as if the hasidic zaddikim of Poland prior to the Yehudi, hadn't committed pen to paper. We have written works by R. Elimelech[10] and by the Maggid of Kozienice.[11] The Seer himself[12] was quite a prolific author. R. Meir of Apta,[13] R. Bunim's critic and the Seer's spiritual heir, wrote a book; while subsequent to Mordechai Joseph Leiner leaving Menahem Mendel of Kotzk in 1839, we have the *Mei Shiloah*.[14] Therefore, both before and after[15] these three generations of Przysucha the written word was an accepted genre in the world of Polish Hasidism. And yet we have nothing written by the Yehudi, R. Bunim, or Menahem Mendel of Kotzk themselves. And although we lack explicit evidence to substantiate such a claim, one is nevertheless inclined to believe that this was a deliberate choice – the result of an educational attitude which reflected the primacy of intimate human engagement between master and pupil, the magic of which cannot be committed to a book.

---

[10] R. Elimelekh of Lyzhansk, *No'am Elimelech,* ed. G. Nigal (Jerusalem, 1978). However, Zeev Gries, "The Hasidic Managing Editor as an Agent of Culture." In *Hasidism Reappraised* (London: 1997), 142, says that: "The living oral traditions of Hasidism must have played a more direct immediate and significant part in determining the nature of the Hasidic experience than did any of its written texts." On p. 147 he adds: "Early Hasidism did not consider the book an important tool for the dissemination of Hasidic ideas or the construction of a distinctive community ethos; both of these functions were performed primarily by the circulation of oral traditions."

[11] Israel b. Shabbetai Hapstein (Maggid of Kozienice), *Avodat Israel* (1842).

[12] On the writings of the Seer, see R. Elior, "The Doctrine of the Zaddik in the Works of Jacob Isaac, the Seer of Lublin." In *Jewish History: Essays in Honor of Chimen Abramsky* (London: 1988), 393–455; idem, "Between Fear and Love, in Depth" (Hebrew) (*Bein yira va-ahava, be-omek ve-gaven*). *Tarbiz* 62/1 (1993), 381–432; B. Zak, "Studies in the Teachings of the Hozeh of Lublin" (Hebrew), "*Iyun be-torato shel ha-Hozeh mi-Lublin.*" In *Hasidism in Poland*, 219–239.

[13] R. Meir of Apta wrote *Or le-Shamayim;* cf. Rabinowitz, "From Lublin to Przysucha," 370–388. R. Kalonymus Kalmish, another pupil of the Seer, wrote *Ma'or va-Shemesh.*

[14] The *Mei Shiloah* was published by the Ishbitzer's grandson, R. Gershon Henoch of Radzyn, in 1860.

[15] The Kotzker's son-in-law, R. Avraham of Sochaczew, also wrote *Neot Deshe.*

The next three chapters are an attempt to reconstruct R. Bunim's main lines of insight, how he looked at the individual in the world. For R. Bunim, Torah is not something imposed upon human beings against human nature; it is essentially the real nature of a person finding its expression. What sets R. Bunim apart from his contemporaries is his marked sense of "groundedness."[16] He was not an ascetic; nor did he wage war on the body, and he was tolerant in regard to human frailty. In brief, his approach was wholesome. For him, by looking inside oneself[17] one could discover the real truth of Torah, nature, and of oneself.

With the introduction of Hasidism, a paradigm shift takes place. Whereas, in kabbalah, the main thrust was to explore the mysteries of the Divine, Hasidism put its energies into the mysteries of being human. As has been observed,

> The whole energy and subtlety of emotion and thought... was turned about in the quest for the true substance of *ethico-religious conceptions* and for their *mystical glorification*. The true originality of Hasidic thought is to be found here and nowhere else...."[18]

Przysucha took this approach even further than normative Hasidism, since it wasn't involved in kabbalah. In this sense Buber was correct[19] in describing Hasidism as *"Kabbalah Turned Ethos,"* as long as we do not forget that we are dealing with an ethos with very specific terms of reference. Hasidism, and specifically Przysucha, was never antinomian.[20] It believed implicitly in God, Torah, and the Jewish people.[21] But within that narrative one had to seek out one's own personal redemption,[22] and for that one

---

[16] This concept of "groundedness" is discussed further on in Chapter 9.

[17] E.g., *Torat Simhah*, §108, 133.

[18] G. Scholem, *Major Trends in Jewish Mysticism* (New York: 1967), 343.

[19] Ibid., 342.

[20] The Ishbitzer might very well be turning in his grave if he could hear how, nowadays, his thought is being used by some as philosophical justification for their agenda. See Allan Nadler's review of Shaul Magid's *Hasidism on the Margin: Reconciliation, Antinomianism and Messianism in Izbica/Radzin Hasidism.* "Modern Jewish Philosophy and Religion." *The Jewish Quarterly Review* 96/2 (spring 2006): 276–282.

[21] G. Scholem, *On the Kabbalah and Its Symbolism* (New York: 1969), 47.

[22] On personal redemption in Hasidism, see M. Faierstein, "Personal Redemption in Hasidism," in Ada Rapoport-Albert (ed.), *Hasidism Reappraised* (London: 1996), 214–224.

needed a teacher – an example of spiritual excellence to liberate the resonance of life within – so that one uncovers one's own essential core.

ৰ্চ ৬৯

Noteworthy are R. Bunim's reservations in regard to teaching too many people; that the seeds of destruction, from an educational point of view, lay possibly within his very success.[23]

> I heard from [R. Bunim] that he said that when the crowd is too large on the Sabbath he finds it difficult to speak words of Torah. Because one needs a Torah for each individual and to include in the Torah each individual, so that each can receive what is for him.[24]

In another version,[25] R. Bunim expressed the judgment that only Moses was capable of saying Torah that was relevant and touched all the Jewish people.

When an exceptional teacher is speaking to a group of people, the individual experiences the master's insight as being directed specifically at him.[26] R. Bunim was sensitive to this experience. He was known for his exceptional use of parables as an educational method (possibly analogous to R. Nahman's stories). He felt that, on some level, he could create Torah that

---

[23] *Meir Einei ha-Golah*, §138. This reservation of R. Bunim about addressing too many people and those of the wrong sort is in stark contrast to the attitude of Hiddushei ha-Rim (*Siah Sarfei Kodesh*, 1:96, §526). On the increase in numbers when Hiddushei ha-Rim became Rebbe, cf. G. Dynner, "Men of Silk: The Hasidic Conquest of Polish Jewry, 1754–1830," Ph.D. diss., Brandeis University: 2002, 37, based upon archival evidence.

[24] *Ramatayim Zofim*, Chap. 5, §105; *Ma'amarei Simhah*, §88. See also *Torat Emet*, Shemot: "Numbers are likely to lead to arrogance."

[25] *Siah Sarfei Kodesh*, 1:11, §11; *Siah Sarfei Kodesh he-Hadash*, par. Devarim, 120.

[26] See Solomon Maimon's ironic piece, "On a Secret Society," in *Essential Papers on Hasidism: Origins to Present*, edited by Gershon D. Hundert (New York: 1991), §20. "What was even more extraordinary is that every one of the newcomers present believed that he had discovered, in that part of the sermon based upon his verse, something that had special relevance to the facts of his own spiritual life. We of course found this particularly astonishing." On the sense of uniqueness within multiple interpretations, see M. Idel, *Hasidism: Between Ecstasy and Magic* (Albany: 1995) 242, n. 19.

was experienced as a personal directive by those listening to him. In a more expanded version we read:

> He said that they judge above which person will be saved by a zaddik, and that healing will come to the souls via a [particular] zaddik and the Torah he says at the table. Just as a special doctor heals the body, so one who heals souls has to weigh his words even more – for they are more dangerous… and he said that it is difficult for him to say Torah when there is a big crowd. For then one has to weigh so that each person's pain is healed. Therefore it is difficult for a doctor to give one medicine for various sick people without causing harm, Heaven forbid, to one of them. On the contrary, there should be healing for each one of them. [27, 28]

The disciple's sense that, even in a crowd, the master is speaking directly to him is understood by R. Bunim as being born of the spiritual affinity that exists between them. From a psychological point of view, it is the disciple who finds himself in the master. Therefore the things that the master says are attuned to the personality of the disciple, because the disciple has chosen the master for whom he is ready. R. Bunim's greatness is that he knows his strength and his limitations. And if the crowd is too large he feels inadequate,[29] "for each individual to feel that he individually is included in Torah," for then Torah must relate to a lower common denominator. His sincere reservations about his capabilities and the awareness of his limitations in relation to his goals, reveal him to be a human being and teacher of exceptional sensitivity.

Nature

As has been noted already, R. Bunim is of the opinion that Torah is aligned with nature.[30]

---

[27] *Ramatayim Zofim* (AZ), chap. 3 §114; *Torat Simhah*, §227.

[28] Thus his hesitancy in saying too much: see, e.g., *Kol Simhah*, par. Vayetze, 32; par. Va'era, 58; par. Mishpatim, 73.

[29] In this Rabinowitz, *R. Bunim*, 56, is correct.

[30] R. Bunim's source for this idea seems to be the Maharal; cf. *Netivot Olam*, 1; ibid., *Netiv ha-Torah*, Chap. 14: "A man can feel all the worlds in his soul, if he merits."

He said that the world was created with Torah, which is the world of nature.[31]

Thus, by looking into his own nature,[32] man can discover Torah – the truth. Moreover, through such an alignment a person can come to the level of intuitively understanding what the Torah wants; in fact he himself becomes Torah.

> They ask: How did Abraham our father know that [welcoming guests is more important than receiving the presence of the Divine]?... Abraham knew in his own mind... and since it occurred to him, so it has to be.[33]

"Since it occurred to him, so it has to be" only makes sense if one assumes that a human being can so refine himself that he intuitively knows what the Torah wants of him, without being commanded explicitly by God to do so.[34] He retraces the footsteps imprinted by God in nature,[35] and does so by looking into his own soul.

See our section on Romanticism in Addendum F. Cf. A. Brill, "Grandeur and Humility in the Writings of R. Simhah Bunim of Przysucha," *Hazon Nahum* (NY: 1997), 421, n. 3:
"God's will is to be discovered both in nature, which was directly created by God, and in man's actions, which are governed by God's providence. God's presence in nature demonstrates His providential dominion over the world. The world is not an illusion, or filled with divine sparks ... His stress is on the soul's sensing of God's presence in creation."
"This idea is also to be found in the circle of Rabbi Moses Cordovero, *Or Ne'erav*, Part 2, Chap. 1; Elijah de Vidas (sixteenth century), *Reshit Hokhmah, Gate of Awe* (Sha'ar Yirat ha-Romemut), Chapter 1; and in Habad."
See Roman Foxbrunner, *Habad* (Tuscaloosa: University of Alabama Press, 1992) Chap. 1. On Judaism and natural law, see Kopul Rosen, "The Concept of Mitzvah," Ph.D. diss., University College of London, 1960, 1–12.
[31] *Siah Sarfei Kodesh*, 2:83, §272; see the continuation.
[32] See below.
[33] *Siah Sarfei Kodesh*, 1:48, §218.
[34] *Kol Simhah*, par. Vayikra, 83. "Abraham made a sacrifice before being commanded." Cf. *Hiddushei ha-Rim*, par. Bo, 89: "R. Bunim said that the plague of locusts was the invention of Moses."
[35] *Siah Sarfei Kodesh*, 3:37, §55.

Abraham's limbs were so refined[36] that when he came to do a command, his limbs themselves led him to do the command.[37]

The Kotzker said: "Abraham's hand would extend by itself to [do] the will of God."[38]

ல் ல்

The connection between human nature and Torah was a central element in Przysucha. The Yehudi first expressed this idea by saying:

> God has committed Himself to the Jewish people, as it says, "And you shall seek from there [the Lord your God] and you shall find."... For what is sought after is in truth in the heart of man, for this is His main creation. Therefore it is not that far from him.[39]

R. Bunim developed this idea further when he said:

> The righteous men of old, even before the Torah was given, kept it by themselves, through their simplicity... for they walked in their simplicity, and it taught them what they should do... and without their knowledge, it came about that they walked in the Torah of God. So that when God gave the Torah to His people He commanded them... concerning the same acts they had already practiced in their simplicity.... And from this it seems that God has given us that same simplicity which the righteous men of old had, who were taught through their simplicity to do those same actions which came from the simplicity of God, may He be blessed.[40]

R. Bunim is asserting that prior to Sinai, even before the Torah was given, it was a recognizable approach to existence. It was kept intuitively by those on the level of religious purity and Sinai was essentially God's

---

[36] I am assuming the text is corrupt and the word is *"meẓuhah [im]"* and not as printed.

[37] *Siah Sarfei Kodesh*, 1:129–130, §656.

[38] *Shem mi-Shmuel*, Bamidbar, 105. Cf. *Siah Sarfei Kodesh he-Hadash*, 1:34, Vayera, and 28. The idea has its source in the Midrash: see *Lev. Rab.* 35.1: "My feet led me to the house of learning."

[39] *Nifla'ot ha-Yehudi*, 55–56.

[40] *Kol Simhah*, Vayikra, 83.

174

imprimatur on (or refinement of) a known way of life. R. Bunim's idea, consistently held, is that a human being can attune his very essence to the Divine will.

For R. Bunim, a person can discover the truth of his being by turning inwards, the heart being the source of this wisdom. Once a person touches a certain point of reality within himself – once he discovers the truth of his core being – he is then able to see truth reflected in God's design in nature.[41]

But there is another, more radical conclusion. Since Torah is also truth, then by making contact with the truth of one's being, one can make contact with the as-yet-unstated, uncommanded Torah – whether to develop it by being more lenient or by being stricter. This idea is based on the assumption that Torah is not something artificially imposed on human nature but is, in fact, its real nature.[42] With such a lens, wisdom is all around and can be learned from everything and from everyone.[43]

For R. Bunim, the human being aspires to integrate the spiritual and the physical. He speaks about joining or connecting "both worlds." "Abraham connected the higher and lower worlds."[44] Humanity's role is not to try to escape this world, as some spiritual ascetics would have us think,[45] but to connect with the Divine so as to bring it into this world.[46]

In describing the biblical character Joseph, R. Bunim says the following:

> [Pharaoh] saw that Joseph was good-looking with curled hair, and said: "… Has there been found someone who walks about with nice clothes and curled hair and who has in him the spirit of God"?

In another version of how R. Bunim described Joseph, he said,

---

[41] *Siah Sarfei Kodesh*, 1.48 §222.

[42] On all this see *Kol Simhah*, par. Matot, 100; par. Masei, 103; par. Vaethanan, 107; Tehillim, 114.

[43] See Chap. 4.

[44] *Kol Simhah*, par. Vayera, 21; par. Noah, 13; cf. *Ramatayim Zofim*, Chap. 2 §78.

[45] See R. Elior, "Between Fear and Love" (op. cit., n. 12).

[46] *Siah Sarfei Kodesh*, 3:140 §533, "Ethics," in the name of the Yehudi: "The wisdom… is to be involved in the world."

The righteous Joseph, who was in charge of Potiphar's estate, controlled everything... knew and was fluent in different languages, and nevertheless had the spirit of God.[47] [48]

Would it be excessive to read into R. Bunim's description of Joseph some of his own philosophy and personal history?[49]

The phrase "curled hair" is found in the Midrash, and the phrase "controlling all he has" refers to the Biblical text. These two characteristics of Joseph are easily located. But where did these other two characteristics – "knowledge of languages" and "nice clothes" – come from? These phrases lend themselves to a description of R. Bunim himself. (R. Bunim was well-known for his knowledge of languages and for dressing in Western clothes.[50]) The point is, however, that R. Bunim is describing a religious model, a man of God who is attuned to this world, from which he learns and with which he is engaged. The following is another tradition in the name of R. Bunim:

> They [the Egyptians] knew well about men in whom the spirit of God moved, such as Enoch, Abraham, Isaac, Jacob and similar people. But these were pure people who separated themselves [from the world, to engage in] the service of God and they had no dealings with people in business or in work. Whereas the righteous Joseph, who was in charge of Potiphar's household and ruled over everything he had, whether at home or in the field, and knew various languages – yet in spite of all this had the spirit of God with him – such a thing they had never heard of or seen before.[51]

The contrast is between "pure people who separated themselves [from the world to engage in] the service of God and had no dealings with people in business or in work" on the one hand and, on the other, someone who was completely *au fait* with the world "and knew various languages, and yet in spite of all this had the spirit of God with him." This is precisely the

---

[47] *Siah Sarfei Kodesh*, 1:9 §3.
[48] *Siah Sarfei Kodesh*, 2:85 §285.
[49] See M. Piekarz, *The Beginnings of Hasidism: Ideological Trends Midrash and Mussar Literature* (Hebrew) (Jerusalem: 1978), 286.
[50] See Chap. 3.
[51] *Siah Sarfei Kodesh*, 2:85, §285.

argument used by R. Bunim to defend himself against the vitriolic and personal attacks leveled upon him by R. Meir of Apta.[52] For R. Bunim, Joseph the patriarch is a forerunner of this very type of balance in the world.

Because R. Bunim held the philosophical underpinning that man's nature is aligned with Torah, he is able to develop an approach which can be described as one of "groundedness": the capacity to steer a path clear of religious hubris while maintaining an appreciative broadmindedness with respect to human nature.

∿∿

There is a tradition within Jewish mysticism which denies validity to this world or one's sense of it, arguing that there are many "realities" but only one true "existence." The "holy sparks" that have emanated from God animate the physical world. R. Shneur Zalman of Liady argued: "Even if we perceive the world as 'being,' it is an absolute lie."[53] Kabbalah facilitates such a view.

However, in Przysucha all concepts of "nullifying the self," "divesting oneself of corporeality," "seeing the world as a lie," not relying on one's sensory perception – all this is beyond the pale for R. Bunim. Where kabbalah is muted, so too is the mystical significance of the zaddik. And where both are muted, the focus is more likely to be on the human being living in the world.

---

[52] See Chap. 11.

[53] Regarding the influence of kabbalah on hasidic thought, see Rahel Elior, "*Yesh* and *Ayin* as Fundamental Paradigms in Hasidic Thought" (Hebrew), *Massuot: Prof. Ephraim Gottlieb Memorial Volume,* edited by A. Goldreich and M. Oron, (Jerusalem: 1994), 168–179 says: "One should not observe worldly matters or consider them at all, in order to separate oneself from profane worldliness. 'One should consider oneself as not being, meaning that one should think oneself not of this world.' Materiality and empirical reality are viewed as devoid of all validity, lacking substance and meaning, since the unattainable *ayin* has become the only meaningful dimension of being. This reversal of the laws governing human perception is the core of the matter...

"This transformation of human awareness is known as *bitul ha-yesh, hafshatat ha-gashmiyut, berur, hitbonenut, ha'atakah,* or *hazazah,* and it requires a conscious rejection of material reality. Thus, the Hasidic ethos is based on indifference to mundane existence and earthly concerns, a state which conditions the conversion of sensory perception into the illuminated consciousness of the *ayin.*"

R. Bunim anticipates a number of expressions of twentieth-century thought, as Isaiah Berlin used to say, "Everything is what it is...", by maintaining that "the world is not an illusion or filled with divine sparks but is a manifestation of the Divine... [awareness of] God's presence reflects a conscious experience, and not an egoless *devekut* [a cleaving to the infinite in which one loses one's personality]."[54] For R. Bunim the world is not an illusion, nature is not a threat; rather, the world provides an opportunity for human beings to be engaged with God.

R. Bunim is quoted as saying that:

> Someone who says that he is toiling in Torah – his service is not true. "For the matter is very close to you" (Deuteronomy 30:4)…. All wisdom and all Torah are something natural (*davar kal*), and anyone who fears Me and does words of Torah – all the wisdom and all the Torah are in his heart.[55]

Torah, if accompanied with awe, is the real desire of the heart. And if one has to force himself to learn Torah, then something is seriously wrong. For Torah is a person's real nature.

Sin and Evil

Ramatayim Zofim is one of our earliest sources for the ideas of R. Bunim. It was written by his pupil R. Shmuel of Sieniawa. The opening line of this work quotes R. Bunim as saying,

---

54 Brill, see note 1. This view is at total odds with that of R. Mahler who, in his book *Hasidism and the Jewish Enlightenment* (267, 283) consistently portrays Przysucha as negating "this world," "all material concerns," and as "ascetic." But see the critique of Mahler by J. Katz, "Jewish History through the Eyes of a Marxist-Zionist" (Hebrew), *Leumiyut yehudit: masot u-mehkarim* (Jerusalem: 1979), 243–251. I am not sure whether the Kotzker would agree with the quote. See *Emet ve-Emunah*, §486.
55 *Pri Zaddik*, par. Beshalah, 72 (13).

Adam was called Adam even after he sinned, as Woman was called Woman after being expelled.[56]

This idea is then repeated a second time on the very first page. To say that man and woman are called by the same name even after their sin, is a clever observation which expresses the view that sin is not cataclysmic – that no irreparable change has taken place – man and woman are of essentially the same nature as before their sin.

In R. Bunim's philosophy sin and evil are not demonic. There isn't the slightest allusion in his thought to a kabbalistic explanation of evil as a result of the rupture between the *Shekhinah* and the Godhead.[57] Sin is part of human nature and is not a subject upon which one should dwell too much. Improvement, yes; wallowing in thoughts of sin, no.

> This is the meaning of (the phrase) "depart from evil"; that is, don't pay any attention to evil.[58]

In another formulation we read:

> Get away from evil. Do not think any longer about the bad things that you did until now. Rather, do good, and by doing good the evil will automatically be annulled.[59] [60]

"By doing good, the evil will automatically be annulled" is not the easy alternative to rigorous analysis. It is rather a psychological insight of major significance. The context for change must be a positive frame of reference. In such a framework evil will either become irrelevant ("automatically be annulled"), or possibly one will have the positive emotional strength to deal with the problem. The entire context of how one looks at the past will have changed.

---

[56] *Ramatayim Zofim* 1.1.

[57] As, for example, in the Zohar and Ari.

[58] *Kol Simhah*, par. Hukkat, 95, and see the continuation; the context for change must be positive. R. Bunim continues, "Even though you pursue and don't achieve, nevertheless seek peace... for it is a blessing." This approach is so very different from that of R. Bunim's adversary, R. Meir of Apta; see *Or le-Shamayim*, par. Vayera, 29.

[59] *Ma'amarei Simhah*, n. 17; *Siah Sarfei Kodesh he-Hadash*, 3:126 §60; *Siah Sarfei Kodesh*, 1:52 §243.

[60] The Kotzker (*Emet ve-Emunah*, §227), typically, has a more strident interpretation.

The Yehudi seems to have expressed a similar idea. On the famous difference of opinion between the House of Shammai and that of Hillel as to whether the lights of Hanukkah should proceed from eight to one (decreasing) or from one to eight (increasing), the Yehudi said the following:

> Beit Shammai says one decreases – that is to say, that first one has to correct one's actions [the principle of "depart from evil"]. But Beit Hillel says one increases – that is to say, one learns more Torah and does more good deeds, and thus one automatically departs from evil... for if a man were to wait until he had corrected the bad, he would spend his whole life doing so [literally, "the days will wear out"], but they [the sins] will not."[61]

Przysucha has a deep understanding of the human psyche. Its concern is not theological. It is a far cry from R. Bunim's pupil, the Ishbitzer, who seems obsessed by questions of good and evil, as to whether a person can ever really know the truth, and what God intended. Here the concern is with helping a human being. There is no hubris in Przysucha, other than the belief that human beings, with all their frailty, have the ability to navigate a personal path toward God.

It was another pupil of R. Bunim – Hiddushei ha-Rim – who gave the most forceful expression to his master's philosophy. In the context of sin, confession, and repentance on the Day of Atonement, he says:

> If a person has committed a serious sin and initially focuses on "depart from evil" (what he has done wrong), he is in fact thinking all the time of this act. And where a man's thoughts are, there he is, thinking of his sinful act. He definitely won't be able to do teshuvah because his mind has become dulled and his heart atrophied and he is likely to fall into depression. And even if he didn't perform a grievous transgression and his mind didn't become dulled, nor his heart atrophied; but if a person focuses on "depart from evil" and on the muck, **he who thinks about muck will remain in the muck.** And whether a man has sinned or not, what does God gain

---

[61] *Ilana de-Hai*, par. Mishpatim, §25 (*Torat ha-Yehudi*, 112 §3).

from that? While thinking of sin, he could be stringing pearls, adding something to the Kingdom of Heaven.[62]

What ought to be the approach in trying to improve human character? Is it a direct attack, so to speak, on the negative quality, with all the concomitant self-flagellation, in which all one's energy and resources are commandeered to dwell on the sin? Even Przysucha, which places such a high value on self-analysis, does not want to lead people down a path of self-obsession. Man is not the center of the stage: God is. The way to change a bad quality is to change the context of life. As Hiddushei ha-Rim puts it, "to string pearls": not because one is trying to evade the challenge of self-analysis, but because the framework of one's being is now changing. It is in the context of the Divine that a person realizes that the triviality of his day to day life cannot continue. A hundred years earlier, the Maggid (d. 1772) had articulated the same idea – namely that dwelling on the past was misguided and deflected a person from his primary task, that of achieving closeness to God. Perhaps it is those who are most self-analytical who are most acutely aware of the dangers of over self-analysis. It is this very awareness that causes them to stress the belief that intimacy with God is the primary context for significant change.[63]

Personality

At the heart of Przysucha's understanding of a person's thought processes is a new definition of personality. Medieval thought, understood "personality as a collection of separate attributes," each one independent of the others. A person might have a certain amount of black bile (i.e., he was depressed), but they did not talk about a depressed personality. The modern understanding of personality, which was shared by Przysucha, is that a human being is a

---

[62] See *Hiddushei ha-Rim,* Day of Atonement, 261.

[63] *Zava'at ha-Rivash,* 11–12, quoted in Rivka Schatz-Uffenheimer, *Hasidism as Mysticism,* 105, cf. 93–94, 101–105 (in Hebrew: 49–50; cf. 41, 47–50): "Focusing on the past inhibits the focus on serving God."

complete entity, comprised of various elements. Each characteristic influences and is influenced by all the others to create the self.[64] [65] [66]

ॐ ॐ

The following observation is found at the beginning of *Kol Simhah,* the first published book of R. Bunim's thought:

> All existence other than [that of] man, can only comprehend itself. But God created man, who contains within himself the higher and lower worlds, **so that he can imagine everything in his soul.** This is the essence of man – that he can understand and imagine something other than himself.[67] And that is the meaning of "Let us make man in our image, in our likeness...."[68]

Neither the faculty of speech, nor the power of the intellect is the hallmark of the Divine in the human being; rather, according to R. Bunim, it is the ability to use his imagination, and self-reflection, which reveal his *imitatio dei.* A human being has a personality that is uniquely designed to comprehend and reflect. The imagination is God's gift to human beings.

---

[64] It has been said that medieval man "treated personality as a collection of attributes with more or less independent states... that the valid references were vertical, intersecting the field of human experience at every turn and separating it into discrete instances that had no interesting relations to each other." – Gabriele Spiegel, quoted in Elizabeth Dees Ermarth, *Realism and Consensus in the English Novel,* Chap. 1, "The Premise of Realism" (New York: Princeton University Press, 1983), 8.

[65] Along with the awareness of personality comes an emphasis on certain values. The self becomes the source of understanding. Brill, *Thinking of God: The Mysticism of Rabbi Zadok of Lublin* (NY: 2002), "Modernity," 637. Brill says, "It is important to note that the simultaneous discovery of the unconscious in nineteenth-century Polish hasidic thought and in western Europe was not coincidental, or based only on western influence." Ibid, 365.

[66] The awareness of self stimulates a concern regarding purity of motive. In R. Bunim's thought, a human being is a creature that has personality and is reflective. If he has sullied his personality he cannot gain intimacy with God. *Kol Simhah,* par. Bereshit, 9. Depression is not a new concept, but one notes a recurrent concern with it in the thought of R. Bunim.

[67] *Kol Simhah,* par. *Bereshit,* 8. The play on words is on *adama, adam, dimyon.*

[68] The play on words is *kidmutenu, dome, dimyon.*

The source of a person's understanding lies within himself. But in contradistinction to the solipsism of the romantics (who maintain that all truth lies within a human being alone), human beings must render an account to the Divine that stands outside and above them. R. Bunim understands that the apprehension of the self is not the be-all and end-all of religious behavior. The manner in which one relates to other people stands as the litmus test.

> "A man didn't see his brother nor did one get up for another" (Exodus 10:23). Said R. Bunim: "Because they didn't see each other, therefore they didn't get up for one another."[69]

If you do not see someone either emotionally or physically, you do not relate to him. R. Bunim once saw a farmer building a house with two planks that were not the same.

> He[70] stood to see what the farmer would do. The farmer made a hole in one of the planks so that the other one would fit. And R. Bunim said to his hasidim, "Look how one can make peace between two sides – not to force them to be the same, but rather for one to fit the other.[71] [72]

R. Bunim said the following insightful gem:

> When a young man wraps himself in a prayer shawl he thinks and imagines that he [is complete]. But isn't his wife also standing with him beneath the prayer shawl?[73]

---

[69] *Siah Sarfei Kodesh*, 1:13 §36.

[70] *Siah Safrei Kodesh*, 5:114. My free translation according to the sense of the piece.

[71] The Yehudi said the same thing. *Torat ha-Yehudi*, 149 §2, mentions the source as *Or ha-Ganuz* manuscript; see also in the name of the Seer (*Siah Sarfei Kodesh*, 2:95–96 §341).

[72] On the perception of the evil inclination in Hasidism, see Ze'ev Gries, *Conduct Literature: Its History and Place in the Life of Beshtian Hasidism* (Hebrew). (Jerusalem: 1989), 182–230.

[73] *Siah Sarfei Kodesh*, 4:38 §2; see also *Ramatayim Zofim*, chap. 11 §21; *Torat Simhah*, §197. Boem and others explain the meaning of this quotation as referring to man's problem with his own sexuality.

Only when one engages the "Other" (in this case, his wife) does one begin to develop one's own humanity. The young man's self-containment reveals the immaturity of one who has not developed a sense of relationship with others. The resultant danger is a false sense of completeness born of ego.

Balance

R. Bunim had a sense of balance which flowed from his understanding of human nature. This is exquisitely expressed in the following well-known aphorism:

> A person should have two pieces of paper, one in each pocket, to be used as necessary. On one of them [is written] "The world was created for me," and on the other, "I am dust and ashes."[74]

This pithy expression encapsulates a religious paradox. On the one hand, a person must develop a sense of individuation, of his own uniqueness, as if he is being personally looked at. On the other hand, he needs to be aware of his utter insignificance in the face of God. The wisdom of life is to know when to use one insight and when to use the other.

R. Bunim's goal is to teach us that each person must function in the context of his own reality. Thus, be it the afore-mentioned[75] story of R. Isaac of Cracow (i.e., that the treasure lies within a person's own heart),[76] or his famous remark that he sees no value in duplicating Abraham (because what would God gain by there being two Abrahams?),[77] or the assertion that a person can only hope to connect with the patriarchs[78] while treading his own path, all these insights are part of the balance. He once said:

> "A wise man is a heretic, a man with a good heart is a hedonist... a frum person who prays a lot is bad for society." And they asked him,

---

[74] *Maggid Devarav le-Ya'akov*, par. *Noah*; *Siah Sarfei Kodesh*, 1:50 §233; *Torat Simhah*, §193.

[75] See Chapter 6.

[76] *Ma'amarei Simhah*, §30.

[77] *Ma'amarei Simhah*, §41.

[78] *Siah Sarfei Kodesh*, 1:9, §6.

"If so, what is good for a man?" The answer was "All three together...."[79]

With this insight, the teacher expresses his aversion to any extreme. R. Bunim projects his desire for a wholesome balance, in joining all these three qualities in one personality. "Thus he can serve God properly." [80] [81]

⇢ ⇣

When R. Bunim was dying, he heard his wife crying in the next room and he said:

Why is she crying? All my life I've been preparing myself for this![82]

It is the manner in which a person lives their life which creates the framework for how one eventually meets death. The very expression of one's true essence is revealed at precisely this moment – one reaches the crescendo of life. Such an utterance must belong to the ultimate wisdom of *Torat Adam* – the psychology of the human soul: to know how to meet one's Maker.[83] Within the same genre is the Kotzker adage:

Death is like moving from one room to another.[84]

⇢ ⇣

There is an amazing piece in the name of R. Bunim – amazing for its earthiness and self-mockery.

R. Bunim once[85] said that it would be very nice to have a big salon with beds and sofas and tables, with wine and roast turkey, and to

---

[79] *Siah Sarfei Kodesh*, 3:6 §14; *Siah Sarfei Kodesh*, 1:49 §229.

[80] *Ma'amarei Simhah*, §10.

[81] R. Bunim remarked somewhat whimsically that "he loved very much the *mufkar*, only a person should be *mafkir* himself and not the other" (*Ma'amarei Simhah*, §54).

[82] *Ramatayim Zofim*, Chap. 31 §104; *Ma'amarei Simhah*, §46; *Torat Simhah*, §294.

[83] This was totally misunderstood by R. Mahler (*Hasidism and the Jewish Enlightenment*, 283), who understood R. Bunim's statement as implying a denial of corporeal needs. It is not. Rather, it is an insight into how to live in this world, the litmus test being how one meets one's Maker.

[84] *Siah Sarfei Kodesh*, 2:94, §326.

[85] *Hashavah le-Tovah*, *Shabbat*, 99.

say a little Torah. And whoever wanted to sleep could sleep a little and eat roast meat and drink wine and say a few more words of Torah. That would be very nice. For when everything is taken to its right place it is very good. And it is not necessary to be a recluse; all things can extend.... And God said to Moses: "Take off your shoes"; no more to be a recluse, rather extend in everything and elevate it to what is fitting...."[86]

This sense that holiness extends is connected with R. Bunim's view of the world and of nature. He criticizes those whose spirituality is lived only by withdrawal, by those who would like to escape this world. And in a self-mocking, but very healthy way, he describes how everything should be in a state of balance – without extremes – a little bit of everything: "a little sleep, a little meat and wine, and a few more words of Torah." Only someone who has a deep sense of self-confidence, both in himself and in his philosophy, could make such nice fun of himself.[87]

With the Yehudi one has the sense that he was always alert to the dangers of corporeality, and with the Kotzker there is also the feeling that he is in a constant state of dissonance with the world. With R. Bunim one is aware of his sense of his at-one-ness with the world (while at the same time being well aware of its pitfalls).[88] This view is clearly reflected in the following:

> There are those zaddikim whose way of behaving is to afflict their bodies; and there is a[89] zaddik who eats and drinks and doesn't afflict himself at all. He is also a holy great zaddik, exalted; as is known from the Taz Even ha-Ezer, n. 25.[90]

---

[86] The root *na'al* is understood as "restriction" or "closure," and not as "shoe" This interpretation is more akin to the Besht than to the Maggid – the latter is more ascetic.

[87] See also *Or ha-Niflaot* p. 2. R. Bunim was not ascetic (unlike the Yehudi) and seems to have enjoyed life; see Chapter 11.

[88] See Chapter 11.

[89] Is it by chance that R. Bunim changes to speaking here in the singular?

[90] *Torat Simhah*, 289. See chapter 11; *Turei Zahav (Taz)*, at E.H. 25.1. The subject there is modesty during sexual intercourse. The *Taz* quotes the *Bet Yosef*, who cites two opposing opinions as legitimate and leaves the matter to the individuals' discretion so long as their intention is "for the sake of Heaven."

In *Kol Simhah*, we read (concerning the Jewish people),

> Wealth should not disturb them from the service of God... on the contrary, it should increase holiness....[91] [92]

Antagonism to the corporeal, which has so bedeviled Jewish philosophy and mysticism alike, throughout the ages, is absent in the world of R. Bunim.

R. Bunim insists that the human being, rather than some cosmology or system of metaphysical knowledge, is the point of departure. R. Bunim initially looks inside rather than outside. Such an approach not only produces insights into human weakness, but also creates an earthiness that teaches people how to navigate life.

---

[91] *Kol Simhah*, par. *Noah*, 12.
[92] For further examples of R. Bunim's groundedness, see *Hashavah le-Tovah, Ethics*, 95.

TORAT ADAM: THE PSYCHOLOGY OF THE SOUL

"Depression is the cause of all sins."

The Yehudi'

Self-Analysis

ONE OF THE MAJOR contributions made by Przysucha to the world of Hasidism was the prominent position given to the psychology of the soul. Przysucha placed supreme emphasis on introspection, self-analysis, and the exposition of ulterior motives.[1] This was by no means a self-indulgent process: but rather a recognition of the necessary requirement for a person to understand his self, to take the lid off and disclose just what was going on inside. If one wasn't prepared to do this, then one's religiosity might very well be motivated by an unidentified self-centeredness. And, if one was indeed serving oneself – the most obvious form of idol worship – one was in effect carrying out the very opposite of serving God.

The entire atmosphere in Przysucha was to mock, rib, and prod away at anything that smacked of pretentious piety, anything that reeked of self-interest – not in a destructive way but in order to cleanse the personality of its excess. It was in no way instigated by cruelty, although it could be hurtful. It was done with an awareness of a person's human frailty; a sardonic prick of the pompous pose, with an earthiness that asked, "What is really going on?"

---

[1] *Siah Sarfei Kodesh*, 3: 5 §1; *Siah Sarfei Kodesh he-Hadash*, par. Behar 95: "A hasid is one who doesn't fool himself" (my free translation).

Any person who undertakes the service of God with a certain degree of introspection will at some stage or other ask himself: what motivates me? What are my weaknesses and fears? What was special about Przysucha (and was perhaps taken to an extreme in Kotzk) was the sharp focus – the laser-like analysis, the predominant emphasis on purity of motive which had the ability to transform a quantitative difference into a qualitative one.

> R. Bunim said, "All the efforts… that a human being makes may be coming from the externality [the delusions] of the heart, for the heart has limitless ante-chambers."[2]

The initial obligatory first step was to be aware of self-delusion, to know that "the heart has many ante-chambers" and that whatever one was experiencing might very well be superficial. One of the requirements was an awareness of possible ulterior motives.[3] The would-be member of Przysucha had to be prepared to receive criticism. "A person should listen to his disgrace, and be silent and endure everything."[4] Moreover, as has already been noted, to engage in this as an on-going process, one needs friends. It is not a one-time act of spiritual masochism. It is rather an educational approach designed to develop the soul.[5] R. Bunim said that "Every person should have a reliable and beloved friend[6] to whom he can tell [the secrets of] his innermost heart, even his shameful actions."[7] It was the dart-like aphorism, the sharp, piercing observation of personality that, within the context of love, could help build a foundation of service not based on illusion. On the contrary, R. Bunim argued:

---

[2] *Ramatayim Zofim*, chap. 6 §28; *Torat Simhah*, §136. The continuation is "but if it comes from Heaven, it literally revives them."

[3] *Siah Sarfei Kodesh he-Hadash*, 1, par Matot, 119. The pun is on the word *tehaltzu*. The continuation reads: "If you release yourself from your ulterior motives… that is to say, from your corporeality."

[4] *Siah Sarfei Kodesh he-Hadash*, par. Hayyei Sarah, 1:36.

[5] See as a parallel *b. Arakhin* 16b, R. Yohanan ben Nuri's statement about the criticisms he made of R. Akiva.

[6] The continuation in the Gemara (ibid.) is exactly this idea: namely that in the right context, criticism leads to greater love.

[7] *Ma'amarei Simhah*, §14.

> When hasidim get together, each one sees the qualities of the other and feels sorry for his own bad behavior. But if he does not go [with others], he does not feel regret for his bad behavior.[8]

In the context of truth and love, the other's excellence is itself a stimulus to personal improvement.

R. Bunim said that his job was "to arouse everyone to make known to him [i.e., the hasid] the things that are hidden from him, his failings that he is unaware of – and that is what I do continuously."[9]

It is reported that R. Hanoch Heinich, who was among those who spent more years of his life in Przysucha than any other person, said, "In my youth I was often unable to slumber. For how could a person conclude his day without making an analysis of his soul? And I haven't succeeded in making my analysis, to know really who I am, where I am in the world and what is the goal of my action...."[10] [11]

The primary question is "Who am I?" and from that question comes "What are my characteristics, strengths, and weaknesses, and what are my motives?" Without these sorts of questions, Przysucha argues that a person is functioning in a fog, worse, under the danger of illusion.

> The Yehudi said to me [concerning the verse, "Justice, justice you shall pursue in order that you shall live" (Deuteronomy 16:20)] that this is the essence.... A person is given life in order to correct what needs to be corrected until his last breath... and that is why it says "justice" [a second time]. This means that even if one has corrected oneself, one must try [further], with even more effort, with greater holiness and purity.[12]

For the Yehudi, a person comes into this world for a purpose, with a role, possibly to correct some aspect of his personality. This process continues until one's dying breath. And even though one might imagine that one has completed this process, the Yehudi demands an additional supreme

---

[8] *Siah Sarfei Kodesh*, 4:43 §24. See also *Siah Sarfei Kodesh*, 1:10, §10: "When Jewish people eat together, they learn from each other the fear of the Creator."

[9] *Or Simhah*, §110.

[10] *Sefer Alexander*, 18; *Hashavah le-Tovah, Hasidut*, 122.

[11] See also *Ma'amarei Simhah*, §40; §38.

[12] *Nifla'ot ha-Yehudi*, 56.

effort. Because without sincerity and self-correction, one is not being true to what one could be, that is, one is not truly authentic.

> My grandfather the Yehudi once said that there are three levels of service. The highest level is that of one who does good acts the whole day and yet feels he hasn't achieved anything. The second level is someone who, though he hasn't done anything, knows that he hasn't corrected anything in this world. This is good, and there is hope for him that he might correct his ways. However, someone who is righteous in his own eyes deceives himself all his life; his good deeds will be lost.[13]

What the Yehudi found intolerable was the smug self-righteousness of religiosity. Such smugness does not allow for the introspection that the Yehudi believed to be critical. The sham, the hubris of self-righteousness is the worst quality, the path that leads to hell (*avadon*).

This quality comes from the absence of self-analysis, which in turn stems from a lack of humility. Without humility and self-analysis a person ends up being static, given to a process of atrophy. There must be continual renewal.[14] This demand for renewal flows from introspection, and real introspection can only take place in a context of humility.

Depression

The problem was that such penetrating analysis could easily lead to despair. Here we come to a central idea in Przysucha's psychology of the soul: Revealing one's muck to one's self is only the beginning of a process, one that can easily slip into depression. Though depression is not a sin for Przysucha, there is no greater "satanic" force, no greater danger than depression. Therefore, if the equation is that one moves from analysis to despair to depression, then one of the antidotes (though not the only one) must be joy. For if depression leads towards inactivity, then joy and passion lead to movement. Said R. Bunim,

---

[13] *Or ha-Ner, Seder Avodat HaYom*, 4; *Tiferet ha-Yehudi*, 179 §101.
[14] The Yehudi continually stresses the need to start afresh each day. *Siftei* Zaddik, par. Vayera, p. 59 (*Torat ha-Yehudi*, 233, §18). See chapter 2.

One needs both modesty and humility, but also not to fall into despair through the intrigue of the evil inclination.[15]

Hasidism draws a distinction between two qualities, which might at first glance appear to be similar. There is controlled self-analysis that brings with it a certain "bitterness" – a reflective sorrow when one realizes that one was unable to respond; a sense of missed opportunity. This is positive. However, there is an alternative type of brokenness that leads to despair.[16] The distinction is between, on the one hand, controlled bitterness of the one who recognizes that he is flawed and, on the other, a sense of despair that leads to resignation, apathy, and hopelessness.... "They fool him by saying that he is already entrapped in the coils of sin"[17] so that the person becomes unable to act.

> R. Bunim said,[18] "He who heals the broken-hearted" (Psalms 147:3); a broken heart is a good thing. And the healing is that he is cleaned from depression, so that the heart remains without any depression... in a state of joy.... One needs a broken heart, but one also needs it complete. One needs both together, brokenness and completeness.[19]

The Yehudi had said a similar thing:

> "He who heals the broken-hearted and binds up their wounds" (Psalms 147:3). One needs to understand: Isn't the quality of being broken-hearted a good thing? Why then does it need to be healed? One can say this: In truth, it is known that a broken heart is a good thing, but only in joy. "For of what benefit is sorrow?" (Proverbs 14:23). And this is what Scripture is saying. "He who heals the broken-hearted" – that is, the one whose broken-heartedness does not come, Heaven forbid, from depression. That is the healing: namely that he remains with broken-heartedness, but in joy.[20]

---

[15] *Ma'amarei Simhah*, §66.

[16] *Sefer Tanya*, chap. 31 for an articulated exposition of the same idea.

[17] *Hiddushei ha-Rim*, 272.

[18] *Torat Simhah*, §128; *Ramatayim Zofim* 10.19; *Kol Simhah, Psalms*, 115.

[19] *Ramatayim Zofim*, chap. 5, §11.

[20] *Shoshanim le-David* on Psalm 147, 334 (*Torat ha-Yehudi*, 308 §4).

The Kotzker likewise quoted this idea in the name of the Yehudi.[21] In fact, all three generations promoted this idea. Which of the three originally said it cannot be proven, but it was clearly part of the manifesto of Przysucha.[22]

The force and frequency in the Yehudi's thought is striking. The danger involved in *torat ha-adam* – in human self-reflection – is specifically this sense of despair.

> And it shall be, if you surely forget (*im shakhoah tishkah*) the Lord your God" (Deuteronomy 8:19). One needs to understand this duplication of the word "forget." And one can explain it according to the [known exegetical] idea that vehayah ["and it shall be"] is an expression of joy. That is, if one forgets joy, then one will come to forget God, because it is impossible to serve God via depression.[23]

Or again:

> Depression is the cause of all sins.[24]

> Since the day that the Temple was destroyed the gates of prayer have been closed, but the gates of tears were not closed" (b. Berakhot 32b). For if, Heaven forbid, the gates of tears were to be closed, then tears couldn't enter. And that is why they are never closed. For tears are of the quality of depression, and they can only enter with difficulty. But the other gates, even though they are closed – one can break their locks with joy.[25]

The tone of this piece might suggest that the Yehudi is talking about himself. And indeed, we have such a quote.

> The Yehudi said about himself that he was born with a tendency to depression, which impeded his service of God. And all his days, his

---

[21] *Siah Sarfei Kodesh*, 3: 20; *Emet ve-Emunah*, §148. See *Shem mi-Shmuel*, Vayikra, 155b.

[22] See the continuation in *Ramatayim Zofim*, chap. 5, §11.

[23] *Likkutei Maharam Shick* 23.1. (*Torat ha-Yehudi*, 308 §2); See also *Emet ve-Emunah*, §564 where the Kotzker argues that, as an antidote to depression, one must believe that one's actions are important to God.

[24] *Maggid Meisharim, Kitvei ha-Kodesh*, 62.

[25] *Tiferet ha-Yehudi*, 180 §107.

service was to come to a state of joy. And were it not for this depression, he could have achieved higher levels.[26]

One can dispute which trait presents the greatest danger. But what concerns us is what, whether exaggerated or not, the Yehudi and R. Bunim felt. They saw depression as the enemy and they realized that depression can easily derive from the very practice that they lauded – namely self-analysis.

The other danger of over-introspection is that one can wallow in the self. (There may be nothing more egocentric than the person who spends his time trying to nullify his ego). Introspection, the framework for change, must be in the context of something greater than oneself, a sense of the grace of God. Ultimately a person has to believe that the Divine can pull him out of the muck and dirt.[27] The satanic force, namely, the evil inclination, will try to persuade him that the Divine has rejected him – that he is too far gone. But a person needs to believe in God's essential compassion, and in himself.[28]

A recurrent theme with R. Bunim is that there should be no depression. He states that:

> Even though one has a life of distress, nevertheless there should be no depression; rather, one should be in a state of happiness and vitality.[29]

R. Bunim had a *joie de vivre* which couldn't tolerate depression and which allowed him to engage the world. As we have mentioned before, in *Keter Kehunnah* we read:

> He was critical of [the performance of] commandments without inner feeling and thought, and he censured those who afflicted their souls and did not wish to delight in the pleasures of this world and

---

[26] *Tiferet ha-Yehudi*, 170 §69.

[27] *Hashavah le-Tovah*, par. Yitro, 23. See R. Schatz-Uffenheimer, *Hasidism as Mysticism*, 93, 101–106; Hebrew: 41, 47–50: "Focusing on the past inhibits the focus on serving God."

[28] *Siah Sarfei Kodesh he-Hadash*, 1:24.

[29] *Nifla'ot Hadashot, Seder ha-Yom ha-Katsar*, 8. The Mishnah in Avot states, regarding the life of Torah study, that "you should eat bread with salt." This is understood by R. Bunim, not as a goal per se, but rather something one must be prepared to do if one doesn't have a better alternative. See chapter 11.

withheld themselves from the delights of the senses as long as it did not contradict our religion and the laws of ethics and modesty. Therefore, we saw the Hasidim of Przysucha going out day by day to listen to the tunes being played by the soldiers... they did not know depression... they didn't walk in the street in tatters or with thick hats full of feathers, nor with torn shoes... their clothes had no stains... their hair was combed... and their whole appearance was one of dignity.[30] [31] [32]

---

[30] *Keter Kehunnah*, 128.

[31] R. Bunim noted that sometimes the name of the Patriarch Abraham is mentioned first, and sometimes that of Jacob; but Isaac's name is never mentioned first. The reason for this, says R. Bunim, is that Isaac embodies the quality of judgment (*Likkutei Kol Simhah*, 13).

[32] It is argued that the nineteenth century was marked by what has been called "an internalization of religion." This is reflected in the use and frequency of certain kinds of language. If one keeps on talking about a subject, then clearly it is an issue. Thus, it is noticeable that all three generations of Przysucha continually talk about the danger of depression. Its frequency clearly reveals that depression was the enemy.

But in addition, certain terms used in the Talmud are reinterpreted. They become clothed with a different garb. Thus, for example, the root *ng'* is mentioned four times in the Talmud, as in the phrase *nogea' be-eidutan,* which is used in a juridic sense – namely, that a person is disqualified from giving testimony because of "self-interest." Among the Rishonim (the medieval halakhic authorities) it is used infrequently. But in Przysucha and later on throughout nineteenth-century pietistic literature, such as that of the Musar movement, it is used to convey something akin to the subconscious – that is to say, a stratum in the human being of which the person is not initially aware. It is almost impossible to imagine Przysucha without a term meant to convey "ulterior motive." Its agenda is thus revealed both in the frequency of the terms used and in their nuanced reinterpretation. I suspect that one could show this phenomenon, namely of giving old words a new meaning and/or noticing the change of frequency of their usage, if one analyzed for example, *shelihut* – not in the standard sense of "messenger," but in the sense of being sent into this world to fulfill some personal role; or *penimiyut*=internal, *or amok*=depth, to describe not a physical space but a multi-layered inwardness of the person.

Joy

The antidote to dejection, depression, and despair is the love of God. And a crucial first step in this process is "*simhah*," joy. Hasidic tradition attributes the following seminal piece to R. Hanoch Heinich of Alexander, a pupil of R. Bunim.

> Depression is not a sin, but [even] the greatest sin cannot dull the heart in the way depression can. When we speak of happiness, we do not mean the happiness of [fulfilling] a commandment, for that is a [certain] level [of religiosity]. We mean by happiness not to be depressed. Quite simply, a Jew who does not walk happily because he is a Jew is an ingrate to Heaven. It is a sign that he has never understood the meaning of the blessing "He who has not made me a gentile." Why does one have to ask oneself, "Am I a hasid or not?" That's pride. What is a hasid? It is that I am a Jew.
>
> Depression is the lowest part of hell. And what really is depression? "I deserve it." "I am lacking," whether physically or spiritually. It's all "me." Bitterness implies a broken heart because one cannot be a faithful servant without total commitment (literally, self-sacrifice). "I haven't done anything and yet I still live in the world; I breathe the air." Behold, that is happiness; the opposite is depression. But there is only a hair's-breadth between depression and bitterness. The entire Torah stands on a hair's-breadth. If the greater part [i.e., just over half of the arteries in the neck are severed], then [the animal] is ritually kosher; but if only [exactly] half, then the animal is unfit to be eaten.… For a person can fool himself with his own intelligence. And that's the difference between depression and bitterness. From depression comes heaviness of the body. A person lies down to sleep and he can't endure himself, he can't endure another Jew. He is irritable with himself. But bitterness doesn't allow one to sleep. "Behold, I haven't even begun to achieve anything." One snatches a prayer, some learning, a commandment. One feels the presence of another Jew; one has pleasure from seeing him.

And despite all of this, even the most delicate bitterness has some connection to depression. But happiness, even if not refined, has its source in holiness.[33]

Human beings have no claim on God. They must therefore be grateful for the air that they breathe. They should be aware of the blessing of being. And Jews should thank God for giving them the gift of the Torah – the path of intimacy with the Divine; for giving them a sense of consciousness, not simply of existence. Depression is rooted in ego; in the imagined sense of having a claim on God; in not having a sense of blessing. The very definition of happiness is, at its most basic level, not to feel depressed. However, there is a fine line dividing depression from the bitterness over missed opportunities brought about by self-analysis (which sometimes is also rooted in ego). But for the grace of God, a person can easily cross that line. It is far better to be in the state of simple joy – that is, to have a sense that God is breathing music through the flute of one's being. It is reported of R. Bunim:

> One can achieve more through prayer with joy than one can achieve with crying. It once happened when [R. Bunim] was in Danzig that he saw someone drowning, and he said to him in Yiddish "Give my regards to the Leviathan." And afterwards, God helped him – he got hold of a plank and [the man] was saved.... And he [R. Bunim] said that he couldn't help him because the man was in a state of great distress until he told him a joke; from which he had a little joy; then he was able to save the drowning person."[34]

In modern parlance, we would say that joy gives one the adrenaline, the energy, to achieve something, whereas distress, whether mental or physical, contracts a person. In R. Bunim's opinion, "All evil stems from the fact that one does not serve God with joy."[35]

Why is someone exempt from sitting in a booth on the feast of Tabernacles if he is in distress? Because, says R. Bunim, "If a person has

---

[33] *Hashavah le-Tovah*, 201–202, *Siah Sarfei Kodesh* vol 1. 115. See Aescoly, ed. D. Assaf, 108, n. 32. *Knesset Yisrael*, quoted in the name of R. Aharon of Karlin, 73 (145). See *Hashavah le-Tovah*, Shabbat, 88–89 for the idea that all a person can do is to be a receptacle to receive blessing, see also *Shem mi-Shmuel* Haggadah, 39.

[34] *Ma'amarei Simhah*, §49.

[35] *Hiddushei ha-Rim*, *Shavuot*, 191.

distress from being in the Sukkah [the festive booth], God doesn't want it…
a mitzvah must be done with joy."[36]

The state of joy was an essential element in R. Bunim's educational
approach.[37] Joy is the armament in the struggle against the dangers and side-
effects of self-analysis which can so easily lead to dejection.

R. Bunim said:

> "The light-hearted are fortunate in this world, because they are
> constantly in a state of happiness. But the fearful, because they are in
> a state of concern and depression the majority of the time, draw
> upon themselves judgments…."[38] [39]

R. Bunim's solution is one of balance between a person's sense of
significance or insignificance.[40]

Both non-Jewish sources and those of the *maskilim* describe the hasidim
of Przysucha as being rather boisterous and full of merriment, to say the
least. The following is a report of a complaint registered by the Parczew
Police chief in 1823, regarding some twenty Hasidim of Przysucha:

> They do not attend synagogue, but rather choose to celebrate
> services in rented houses, where sometimes throughout the whole
> night they make great noise, and celebrate services with various
> songs, jumps, dances. It has frequently been seen that, in this same
> place chosen for prayer service, they played games in which different
> drinks are drunk and songs are sung, and they fly out into the street
> singing, jumping and producing various shouts, which the mayor of

---

[36] *Siah Sarfei Kodesh*, 2: 97 §346; *Kol Mevaser*, 3: 51; *Kol Simhah*, par. *Toldot*, 31; *Siah Sarfei Kodesh he-Hadash*, par. Nitzavim, 1: 138; but see *Ohel Torah*, 95 and *Emet ve-Emunah* §10 for a much harsher interpretation by the Kotzker.

[37] *Torat Simhah*, §56. This is reflected in the following story:
"When I was with him to mention my son, may he live, before him, who was then very dangerously ill, he said that he had no advice for me, just that I should be in a state of joy. And I listened to his advice and I gave some money to the hasidim to eat and drink together in happiness with the love of friends, and immediately he got well."

[38] *Derekh* Zaddik*im*, §23 (*Kol Mevaser*, 2:206).

[39] See *Kol Mevaser*, 2:206 for further sources on joy in the philosophy of R. Bunim.

[40] *Torat Simhah*, §193.

the city cannot tolerate, and they are punished by the police for disturbing the peace at night.[41]

In *Keter Kehunnah* we read, inter alia, the following:

> They laughed and played cards. There was a rumor, that didn't stop, that in a box at the bottom of the Holy Ark, with the Shofar and other religious objects, were a bottle of spirits and some playing cards. And when asked about this, they replied in a rather poetic way, "These are the angels that emanated from the Shofar."[42]

Though one need not take these sources too literally, nevertheless one is left with a general impression that *joie de vivre* was very much part of the Przysucha ethos.[43]

In the world of Przysucha, joy is not some sort of palliative or "feel-good factor." Real happiness comes from being connected to the Divine, believing that there is an umbilical cord between humanity and God that cannot be severed.

R. Bunim said:

> The slightest [sense of] depression is clothed in pride.[44]

Yet on a deeper level, *simhah* (joy) is born of an awareness of *kedushah* (holiness). It is the loved one responding to the lover. Said the Kotzker, "Simhah is an extension of holiness."[45] [46]

Humility

One of the values most prized in the world of Przysucha was genuine humility. Humility, for R. Bunim, derives from the experience of being in the

---

[41] G. Dynner, "Men of Silk: The Hasidic Conquest of Polish Jewry, 1754–1830." Ph.D. diss. (Brandeis University: 2002), 79.

[42] *Keter Kehunnah*, 129–130.

[43] But one wonders whether the Kotzker could have identified with such playfulness.

[44] *Yekhahen Pe'er, Kedoshim*, 117 (=*Kol Mevaser*, 2:206).

[45] *Shem mi-Shmuel, Vayikra*, 55a.

[46] See Azriel Shohat's study: "On Joy in Hasidism" (Hebrew). *Zion* 16 (1951): 30–43.

presence of God. Humility is the result of feeling the grandeur of the Divine.[47] The idea of humility as a basic component of a religious personality is not new. It was the Seer, however, who emphasized the connection between humility and truth, which is our main concern. The idea is that if a person doesn't recognize his own insignificance, he is living a lie. This connection was paramount in the thought of the Yehudi and was what so attracted him to the Seer.[48]

The Yehudi was known for making humility a cardinal element of his faith. He would note that the numerical value of "Amalek" equals the numerical value of the word "pride."[49] The significance of humility as a seminal quality in Przysucha is the following: Humility is the gateway to self-analysis, and self-analysis is the gateway to truth. If one is not prepared to look into the mirror of one's personality with humility, then the whole mission of Przysucha cannot begin. The assumption that one needs to correct one's character traits is a prerequisite for the quest for truth. The function of the intellect is to bring a human being to a place of awe – an awareness of God's presence. It is in the context of "divine light" that humility can begin.[50]

---

[47] This aspect of Przysucha has been dealt with by Alan Brill in an article entitled, "Grandeur and Humility in the Writings of R. Simhah Bunim of Przysucha." In *Hazon Nahum: Festschrift for Nahum Lamm.*

[48] See Chapter 2.

[49] *Zikhron Shmuel,* par. *Lekh Lekha,* 9.2; *Torat ha-Yehudi,* par. Bo, 27.

[50] One of the famous ideas in the world of the Yehudi is his understanding of the word "mah" ("what," by extension "nothingness"). But there is a basic difference in the way in which Habad and Przysucha relate to the word "mah." In Habad, "mah," as in hokhmah – wisdom = "koah mah" – alludes to a primordial, intuitive sense of wisdom, almost before consciousness and definitely before articulation. It is essentially something prior to a concept. But in Przysucha "mah" is the human experience of worthlessness (i.e., humility) as one stands before the Divine. The distinction is critical. The former is dealing with something prior to a thought process; the latter is dealing with a very earthy reality.

One is reminded of the story (*Emet ve-Emunah,* §80) of the encounter between a follower of Habad and Menahem Mendel of Kotzk. The Habad hasid gave a lengthy analysis of "contraction," "emanation," etc., at which point the Kotzker is supposed to have interjected, "But where is the *pipik* [the belly-button]?"

When a man serves God with great clarity, he nevertheless feels that
he hasn't achieved anything... and that was Jacob's blessing to his
children.[51]

This is almost word for word what the Seer had said about Jacob.[52] The
Yehudi had said the same thing about Abraham:

The way of zaddikim is that they always see the excellence of their
friends and their own unworthiness.... Abraham [thought] that he
hadn't achieved anything.[53]

It is precisely the one who has achieved a degree of clarity who begins to
appreciate what it means for the finite to stand before the Infinite, who feels
the concerns of the ego to be irrelevant and consequently they simply melt
away.

A person who peers into the greatness of God needs to look with all
the parts of his soul. And the test of this is that, at the time of his
understanding, he doesn't know if he sees or not; for all the parts of
his soul are clothed with the seeing. That is to say, he has divested
himself of everything. The reward for this is that he sees.[54]

Moses reaches a point where he dissolves in the light of God – "He
[Moses] does not know whether he sees or not." The one who achieves such
a state of unity is the one who really sees and therefore knows that his ego is
irrelevant. It is impossible, says R. Bunim, to sing to God if one hasn't
gotten rid of the quality of pride.[55]

God owes a person nothing. ... [B]ut someone who knows that
nothing is due to him, but [what he receives is] only as a gift, given
to him out of pure love and kindness, then he is assured of all...."[56]

---

[51] *Kol Simhah*, par. Vayehi, 50.

[52] *Or le-Shamayim*, 25.

[53] The first part of *Mishmeret Itamar*, par. *Vayera*, §8 (*Torat ha-Yehudi*, par. *Vayera*, 7
§1).

[54] *Kol Simhah*, par. Shemot, 54.

[55] *Kol Simhah*, par. Beshalah, 66.

[56] *Hiddushei ha-Rim, Likkutim*, 374. Levinger (*Torato shel ha-Rebbe mi-Kotzk*, 419–420)
thought that this was typical only of Kotzk; cf. *Ramatayim Zofim*, Ch. 2, §104.

The point seems to be that a person has no claim in dealing with the Infinite. It is this very non-claim that allows one into His presence:

"If I go down to the depths, behold, You are there." (Psalms 139:8). That is to say, someone who reckons himself to be in the depths because he knows what he deserves from the King of Kings because of his sin, then God goes there, as it says, "I dwell with the crushed" (Isaiah 57:15).[57]

ॐ ॐ

The intolerance of pride is a theme throughout the three generations of Przysucha. Said R. Bunim: "Pride blinds the eyes of human beings."[58] Whenever the Yehudi sensed pride he would react.

The holy R. Yeshaya from Farshedborz was once involved in a dispute with a son-in-law of the Rabbi of Lublin, which led to adjudication. And the holy R. Yeshaya displayed his sharp acumen and originality and won the case. The Yehudi said to him, "Don't you realize that we too know the Torah? But the purpose of knowledge is to know that we don't know."[59]

The Yehudi was not impressed by R. Yeshaya's aptitude. When he smelt ego he was quite direct in pointing it out. He once said to a disciple of the Seer:

I saw that you had pride and therefore the Holy Spirit cannot dwell [in you].[60]

And whenever pride entered into learning the Torah, the Yehudi was critical.[61]

For the Yehudi, the gateway to God was through inner humility:

---

[57] *Torat Simhah*, §116.
[58] *Hiddushei ha-Rim*, par. *Korah*, 213; *Siah Sarfei Kodesh he-Hadash*, 1:110.
[59] *Nifla'ot ha-Yehudi, mi-Kitvei Teuda*, 16.
[60] *Nifla'ot ha-Yehudi, mi-Kitvei Teuda*, 15 (*Torat ha-Yehudi*, 254).
[61] "When a Jew creates new ideas in Torah with a fear of God, new worlds are created, as it says in the Zohar. However, someone who creates new ideas mixed with pride and other impure bad qualities...." *Tiferet ha-Yehudi*, 153 §19.

If one writes two dots together, not one on top of the other, then one creates the name of God. But two dots, one underneath the other, are not the name of God. From this I learnt that when two Jews come together, with neither trying to lord it over the other, they create a Godly quality.[62] [63]

On the other hand, pride and ego meant that a human being was an outsider to the Divine.[64] [65] True humility is the result of one's awareness of being in the presence of God (who created the world from nothing). The closer a man is to the Divine, the more he has a sense of God's presence, and consequently, the greater his glimpse into reality. Only he who truly has a sense of Infinity realizes that he himself is infinitesimal.[66]

---

[62] For further sources on the value of humility, see *Sefer Alexander,* Y.L. Levin, Jerusalem: 1969, 20; *Torat Simhah,* §§8, 141, 189; *Hashavah le-Tovah,* 121; *Kol Mevaser,* 3:70 §10.

[63] *Nifla'ot ha-Yehudi,* 85.

[64] Said the Yehudi: "And how much more a person should never glorify himself, blessing himself in his heart saying that he has already achieved and ascended the ladder of knowledge and perfection." *Siah Sarfei Kodesh,* 2:85 §284. See *Hashavah le-Tovah,* Shabbat, 98 for the idea that all that a person can do is to be a receptacle for blessing from God.

[65] R. Bunim said, The world was created from nothing, and therefore God's praise rests on (someone who is) nothing. *Kol Simhah,* par. Hayyei Sarah, 26.

[66] There is a paradox within humility. This paradox was expressed in a most penetrating way by Franz Rosenzweig.
Humility too is, after all, a kind of pride. Only haughtiness and humility are contradictory. That humility which is conscious of being what it is by the grace of a Superior, however, is pride, so much so that it was possible to consider this consciousness of the grace of God as itself veritably a haughty consciousness. Humility rests secure in the feeling of being sheltered. It knows that nothing can befall it. And it knows that no power can rob it of this consciousness which carries it wherever it may go and by which it is perpetually surrounded. Humility is the only kind of pride which is secure against all surgings, which needs no expression, and which means an altogether essential attribute for him who has it, an attribute in which he moves because he simply does not know differently any more.
(*The Star of Redemption*: Franz Rosenzweig, 168, translated from 2nd edition (1930), by William W. Mallo; Britain 1971.)
Humility comes to one who has peeked beyond the veil. It is a consciousness of one who has had a glimpse of Divine reality, the experience of grace of one who feels blessed that he has been allowed in and who then feels utterly unworthy. Thus humility is a dance between human significance and insignificance.

Equanimity and Simplicity

There are two qualities that, for Przysucha, come in the wake of humility, qualities that are sometimes misunderstood, namely equanimity and simplicity. For Przysucha, equanimity meant that a human being could be so attuned, focused, and centered on God's presence that whatever happens to him does not fundamentally disturb that focus. Equanimity may be seen as a destination. Once you have reached that destination, there is really no other place to go, and that is why things don't move or change one's core.

In hasidic thought there are different understandings of the concept of equanimity (*hishtavut*). For some,[67] it meant indifference to society and indifference to the world (kabbalah can have the effect that one sees the world as a non-reality),[68] but for Przysucha it did not imply that. It is rather the stage a person reaches in which the reality of God puts everything else into perspective. Equanimity is thus the hallmark of someone who is "there," who has reached the point of authenticity and this has consequent implications for the way he relates to society. The Ba'al Shem Tov had already said very much the same thing.[69]

> On the verse "and Aaron did so" (Num 8:3, in the context of lighting the candelabrum).... R. Bunim said: "Aaron did not get excited at all, and though he had come to an elevated position, there was no conceit whatsoever on his part. He remained the same modest person as before."[70] [71] [72]

---

[67] For the Maggid's understanding, see Schatz-Uffenheimer, *Hasidism as Mysticism*, 77–78; Hebrew: 30. M. Idel, *Studies in Ecstatic Kabbalah*, 128–133: "For cleaving and connecting one's thought with God causes one not to feel any honour or disgrace done to him by man" (132). See also ibid., 152–158, for indifference to both the praise or disgrace of men.

[68] Schatz-Uffenheimer, Ibid, 89–90, Heb.: 39, "The World Is Not Real."

[69] *Tzava'at ha-Rivash*, Introduction and p. 216; *Sefer Ba'al Shem Tov*, par *Metzora*, 415 §12; par. Bereshit, 62 §123. *Encyclopedia Hebraica* (Hebrew) 17:808.

[70] *Siah Sarfei Kodesh*, 1: 10 §7; *Torat Simhah*, §257. See also *Ohel Yitzhak*, 45 §104 in the name of R. Yitzhak of Vorki.

[71] R. Bunim echoes this idea in explaining the verse, "And the blessings will reach you" (Deuteronomy 28:2): They will reach you as you are; you will not change with conceit. *Hiddushei ha-Rim*, Hanukkah, 63; par. Ki Tavo, 250; *Siah Sarfei Kodesh he-*

Humility is a prerequisite for equanimity, for only someone with true humility is immune to the influences of success and failure.

On the sentence "and to make you higher than all the nations" (Deuteronomy 26:19), R. Bunim said *"as one lifts up a box from a low place to a high place."*[73] Just as a box is an inanimate object, and has no pride if it is lifted up, so the Jewish people should not feel an ounce of pride when God elevates them, for in God's eyes the lowly of spirit are as precious as any other.

> Joseph was continuously on one level, "and God was with Joseph," for even when he had reached the most exalted heights he was lowly and humble, and even when he was in a low state he was happy, for the celestial Presence doesn't dwell with someone unless they are in a state of joy.[74]

Equanimity is the result of humility and humility is the result of the awareness of the Divine presence, which brings a state of joy.[75]

But with equanimity, one can easily come to a lack of concern for what other people think of you. Or, to put it another way, someone who has touched his inner core can develop a sense of self-confidence outside the theater of public ego massage, in which other people's approval is of no major consequence. This is not because he is antisocial (though he may be). It is because, for the religious mystic, the sense of Divine presence simply puts everything else into proportion. In addition, for the world of Przysucha, the awareness that other people are looking at one's religiosity is an inhibiting factor. All this encourages an inner center of gravity where the focus, as with everything else in Przysucha, has been inverted from outside to inside the human being.

Hadash, 1, par. Bereshit, 17; *Torat Simhah,* §196; *Siah Sarfei Kodesh he-Hadash,* 1, par. Ki Tavo, 134; *Siah Sarfei Kodesh,* 3:5 §5.

[72] "He who brings low the proud and elevates the lowly" (prayer book) – someone who is proud remains so even when brought low; and the lowly, though he is elevated, remains humble. *Hiddushei ha-Rim,* par. Tzav, 151; see also *Ramatayim Zofim,* chap. 3 §3.

[73] *Hiddushei ha-Rim,* par. Ki Tavo, 249; see also par. *Korah* 213; *Ramatayim Zofim,* chap. 2 §59; *Siah Sarfei Kodesh He-Hadash,* 1: 58; *Torat Simhah,* §6.

[74] *Torat Simhah,* §59, see also 67.

[75] See R. Bunim's comments on Laban. *Kol Simhah,* par. Vayetze, 35; *Hiddushei ha-Rim,* par. *Vayetze,* 44.

Equanimity, which flows from the quest for authenticity, can be expressed both positively and negatively. Positively, it means "I know who I am irrespective of how I am perceived by others," or possibly "I don't care how I am perceived by others." Negatively, it means, "I am antagonistic to the whole apparatus which doesn't judge a person for what he really is."

The Yehudi's view was: "If a person knows who he is, he isn't frightened by anybody."[76]

Regarding the phrase "and everything high will bow down before You," R. Bunim said, "If a person is in a state of nullification (i.e., humility), then even if he stands erect – he is still bowing before the God of glory."[77] Equanimity is thus born from the awareness of God's reality. For R. Bunim, one who is humble is not affected by praise or honor. In this context he is reported to have said:

> It is as if one lifts a box from the ground and puts it on the table – it remains as it was.[78]

ॐ ☙

In order to understand Przysucha's view of simplicity one has to differentiate between two concepts, which might be called simpleness as opposed to simplicity. Simpleness is the quality of naive faith which doesn't challenge or try to understand and that is wary of the intellect (and can be anti-rationalist). Simplicity, on the other hand, is the ultimate awareness that a human being does not know truth, that after all his intellectual efforts he stands, as it were, at the abyss of ignorance. It is the minimalist epiphany of the intellectual; revealed as "I don't know." Even though both positions in a certain sense arrive at the same conclusion, the distinction between the two is not just a process. Simpleness is essentially not interested in the rational; whereas simplicity senses that there is something beyond the rational. In many religious traditions, part of the teacher's educational role lies in getting the disciple to be aware of simplicity. In the kabbalistic tradition, for example, there is a view that all mystical preparation is prior to action, but that once one is engaged one should be in a state of "a child one day old."

---

[76] *Tiferet ha-Yehudi*, 171 §76.

[77] *Tiferet Shmuel, Passover Haggadah (Kol Mevaser*, 3:70).

[78] *Bishishim Hokhmah*, 94 (*Noam Siah*, 145).

By some, this awareness has been given the term, a "second innocence," and it is clearly articulated both by the Yehudi and by R. Bunim:

> On one occasion our holy teacher (the Yehudi) took away all the high levels and understandings of his pupil, the holy R. Simhah Bunim of Przysucha, so that he became a person of simplicity. And he would pray and look into a prayer book like a simple person. And he placed his trust in God to be his help. And by this he merited to re-attain all his understandings, completely as at first.[79]

Some scholars infer from this story a difference between the Yehudi and R. Bunim,[80] but this is not so. The teacher must guide his pupil and the pupil knows that this must be done. The Seer said the same to the Yehudi, and R. Bunim would have done the same to Menahem Mendel. Nor is the value being expressed here one of anti-rationalism. On the contrary, the story ends by saying: "And by this he merited to re-attain all his understandings, completely as at first." Ultimately, R. Bunim remains the intellectual sophisticate, but now enriched by having touched simplicity.

The value of the mind is that it acts as a safety net through which one then ultimately works to go beyond it. Mind is a gift of God. R. Bunim, like the Yehudi, would argue, however, that the mind alone cannot bring one into intimacy with the Divine. This view is not anti-rational but meta-rational.

This second innocence is evoked in the following quote:

> During one of the days of Pentecost the Yehudi said Torah at his table and he was burning like a boiling pot. After his fear and trembling he concluded his words of Torah with the following. "'Ultimately, after everything has been heard, fear God and keep his commandments, for that is all that is required of man' (Ecclesiastes 12:13). After all the understanding and after all the insights, one has to begin from the basics: to be a simple Jew."[81]

---

[79] *Yismah Yisrael, Simhat Torah*, 90 (*Torat ha-Yehudi*, 345 §43).
[80] Rabinowitz, "The Yehudi," 94. See, however, ibid., 43–44.
[81] *Ohel Shlomoh*, 2: 17; = *Torat ha-Yehudi*, 238.

Simplicity is the essential "you." It is the essence. The simpleton doesn't understand simplicity. But there is simplicity beyond complexity that brings clarity.

> Once a simple person who had learnt with our teacher together in their youth came [to the Kotzker]... He said "Surely his honor remembers that we learned together; but his honor has become a Rebbe and I am a simple person." To which he [the Kotzker] replied, "You, simple? You are twisted. I am simple."[82]

There is a clarity vouchsafed to great people which allows the Kotzker to describe himself as simple.

Simplicity is the consequence of standing before God in all one's nakedness with an understanding of who one is. The implication is that only if you understand who you are, can you understand what God wants from you. Simplicity is the quality that the Yehudi most admired. In fact, he was the epitome of it.[83]

Real insight is the point at which, after the entire process of learning, which one cannot short-circuit, one stands at the abyss of ignorance, in one's simplicity. As we mentioned earlier, when the Yehudi was once asked by R. Baruch Frankel-Teomim why he spent time with the Seer, since he, the Yehudi, could learn Torah better than the Seer, he replied:

> I learned from the Rebbe that when I lay myself down to sleep, I fall asleep immediately.[84]

This sort of response would have elicited the astonishment of a talmud scholar, as it would of a hasid, who would have expected to hear about some miracle performed by the Seer. But the Yehudi's service of God was expressed also in the ability to fall asleep with a tranquil soul.

Yet the Yehudi, and Przysucha in general, did not idealize the quality of simplicity to point of simple-mindedness. Przysucha sees the intellectual study of Torah as an essential ingredient of Judaism. Yet when it comes to prayer, after all the preparation, simplicity takes over. For then one has

---

[82] *Emet ve-Emunah*, §845.
[83] Introduction to *Torat ha-Yehudi*, Publisher Y. Orner; *Siah Sarfei Kodesh*, 4:67 §17 (*Torat ha-Yehudi*, 238).
[84] *Nifla'ot ha-Yehudi*, 65 (*Torat ha-Yehudi*, 286).

reached the simplicity of someone who has been through the analytical process. Said R. Bunim:

> A person should never be conceited, imagining that he has reached some elevated stage on the ladder of perfection.[85]

Yet even here R. Bunim's groundedness brings him back, as it were. He said:

> It is true that hasidim are humble and make themselves as nothing; but one must accept God and His unity. In the place where he annuls himself, the area that is open, there he has to receive God and His Lordship. For of what benefit are humility and annulment if not that God's Mastery should dwell there?[86]

What a remarkable inversion. Humility and self-abasement are not ends in themselves, nor are they dynamic enough to affect a transformation. The critique is not enough. The negative only creates a space, an opportunity.

> Even if a person rejects the desires of the world, that is not yet perfection. For the main thing is for a person to enter into the yoke of Torah and service.[87]

Przysucha, like Hasidism generally, is God-intoxicated. The dynamic for change, for the service and presence of the Divine, must be a positive one,[88] carried out by human beings.[89]

---

[85] *Siah Sarfei Kodesh he-Hadash*, 1, par. Kedoshim, 95.

[86] *Torat Simhah*, §153; *Kol Simhah, Likkutei Inyanim*, 124.

[87] *Torat Simhah*, §91.

[88] *Siah Sarfei Kodesh*, 5: 63, on the idea of having to draw on something positive to create the context for change; also *Hiddushei ha-Rim, Festivals*, 326.

[89] This same psychological insight is found in the collection entitled *Ohel Torah* (27). Why, it is asked there, didn't the Torah inform us of Esau's deathbed requests? Surely we could have learned some insight from him.
Why wasn't it written?... even though it is good to know how to keep distance from evil, that is not the goal... for if a person distances himself from evil alone and imagines that is good; he won't attain the holiness of the service of God.
Ohel Torah is the first collection of sayings attributed primarily to Menahem Mendel of Kotzk, published in 1909 by Eliezer Zvi Zeligman. Levinger, *Tarbiz* 55/3 (1986): 417 is scathing about its lack of authenticity.

TORAT HA-ADAM: THE PSYCHOLOGY OF SERVICE

"It's not how you fast; it's how you break your fast!"

Kopul Rosen

Preparation

KABBALAH MADE THE HUMAN being the pivotal point of the universe. A person's actions came to have cataclysmic consequences, even to the extent of injuring or repairing the *Shekhinah*. So too in the world of Przysucha the emphasis is on the centrality of the human being, as the mystic who seeks God's presence within his own soul. For R. Bunim, "A person can feel 'all worlds' within his soul."[1] The great drama takes place neither in the Godhead nor in the celestial worlds, but rather in the human soul. In a language that is philosophically reminiscent of Maimonides, R. Bunim says, "All angels are (created) by the actions of people,"[2] and "all blessings of goodness are refracted through the physical world."[3] However, R. Bunim maintained that although a human being is pivotal, his holiness is not intrinsic – it depends upon his behavior.

---

[1] *Rabinowitz, R. Bunim*, 63 §14.
[2] *Kol Simhah*, par. Vayishlah, 36.
[3] Ibid., 37.

> Holiness is not found in the human being in essence unless he sanctifies himself and according to his preparation for holiness, so will the fullness come upon him from on high.[4]

> A person does not acquire holiness while inside his mother; he is not holy from the womb, but one has to labor from the very day one comes into the air of the world.[5]

For Przysucha, unlike other streams of Hasidism, there is no *a priori* holiness. The human being must achieve it himself. The main principle in the psychology of service is that authentic service requires preparation. Unless a person first prepares himself, his service is a sham; in effect, either a routine or an illusion. The revolution in the psychology of service began during the lifetime of the Yehudi and motivated personal attacks on him. He was uncompromising in his belief that everything depends upon the degree of preparation. Only as a result of preparation can one feel that what has been created in one's religious service might have a semblance of truthfulness.

The Yehudi clearly articulated the idea that preparation for a commandment (*mitzvah*) was tantamount to its actual performance. Preparation is the vehicle by which a person brings his totality to engage a mitzvah. It allows him to attune himself to the act, to enter into an act with *kavvanah*.

> Preparation for a mitzvah is like the mitzvah itself.[6]

This is a mind-shattering concept within the halakhic context. However the Hasidim of Przysucha might try to justify this idea (and try they did), it is ultimately antinomian, anti-halakhic. For it is saying that the principle of personal authenticity, which by definition (or at least by their definition) means that one first has to prepare oneself, overrides the value of time-defined commandments. And even if one is willing to turn a blind eye to this, as in the case of an exceptional human being such as the Yehudi, once this approach is accepted as a norm and applied to everyone, becoming part of a movement, the factor of individuality becomes entirely definitive.

---

[4] *Kol Simhah*, par. Miketz, 47.

[5] *Mesharatav Eish Lohet*, 228, quoted in *Noam Siah*, 263.

[6] *Shem mi-Shmuel*, par. Hayyei Sarah, 238; *Siah Sarfei Kodesh*, 4:119 §216.

Preparation, getting oneself attuned, became of supreme importance in Przysucha – especially when it came to the question of the correct times for prayer:

> Preparation of prayer, so that one's entire being is involved...[7]

According to the Yehudi, we must prepare ourselves on the night before *Shavuot* (the giving of the Torah at Mt. Sinai) before we study it because "*derekh eretz* preceded the giving of the Torah."[8] One has to bring oneself to "the giving of the Torah" so that the experience will be real. Preparation, therefore, is not merely a technique but a state of mind.

Preparation means the assimilation of what is given to a person and that which he creates for himself. One has to continually hew oneself out in order to become a vehicle that can receive the blessing which may come one's way. How one does this is a secret that each person is obligated to uncover for themselves.

By stressing preparation as the supreme value, Przysucha effectively, rejected, although it remained unarticulated, the rabbinic norm of "Do a mitzvah even without a pure motive, for by doing it even insincerely, one will come to do it sincerely." Przysucha would respond to this by saying: "If it's insincere, don't do it." Insincerity is falsehood and is essentially a form of idol worship. This attitude was the root of one of the essential criticisms leveled against hasidism by the *mitnaggedim* – that they placed the service of the Almighty before obedience to Jewish law. The Kotzker said that the *mitnagged* served the *Shulhan Aruch* (the Law), but the hasid served *Ha-Kadosh Baruch Hu* (God).[9]

R. Bunim is totally at one with this principle of preparation as formulated by his teacher. He said:

> A man must prepare himself for prayer with awe and love and a great holiness, with all his capabilities; for he is the vessel that is to be prepared for the meal of the King.[10]

All the Prophets needed to prepare their minds, as is known.[11]

---

[7] *Tiferet ha-Yehudi*, 161 §29.
[8] *Ramatayim Zofim*, chap. 18, §58. On all this see Chap. 6.
[9] *Siah Sarfei Kodesh* 5:44.
[10] *Kol Simhah*, par. Beha'alotkha, 87.

> For if a person wants to attune his mind some time before the performance of a command of Torah or service, then he is able to (properly) fulfill a commandment by God.[12]

The clear implication is that, if one does not attune one's mind before the performance of a commandment, then one is unable to fulfill that commandment properly, if at all. This implication is what aroused the ire of the Yehudi's antagonists. For them, it smacked of hubris and, as a norm, was dangerous. For the Yehudi there really was no other option, without preparation, it was all meaningless.

The critical value of preparation is expressed with the same clarity by Menahem Mendel of Kotzk.

> It is not rational to assume that a person's actions are preferable to those of the angelic world.... [However,] it is only with regard to preparation that one can reach true perfection of an action, through which one can come to cleave to God – thus the actions of human beings are preferable. For a human being is enmeshed in snares of powerful drives which surround him – this pinch of earth. But not so the celestial angels, who are intrinsically holy and pure....[13]

Preparation is thus the hallmark of being a true human being. It is the quality of preparation which elevates a person from the dregs of the mundane and raises him above the world of the angelic. Przysucha is not the Hasidism of momentary enthusiasm, of the experience that comes without context. For Przysucha, the human being creates the context, and preparation gives him the ability to internalize and maintain his intensity. Said Menahem Mendel, "The essence is... according to the preparation."[14] Preparation need not be an artificial or laborious process. It is essentially a "concentration of the mind," an antidote to the superficial. On the sentence "and he took for an offering for Esau what came to his hand," Menahem Mendel said:

---

[11] *Kol Simhah*, Shmuel, 111.

[12] *Torat Simhah*, §19; *Siah Sarfei Kodesh he-Hadash,* 1, par. Vaethanan, 124.

[13] *Ramatayim Zofim* (AZ), chap. 14, §2. *Ohel Torah*, par. Tzav, 52.

[14] *Shem mi-Shmuel*, Shemot, vol 1, 229a.

Whenever one takes what comes to one's hand without intentionality, without attending to whether it is good or bad – this is nothing. Even though he thinks it is a mitzvah, it is not. It is an offering to Esau.[15]

Preparation is a process that takes place before the action. Once within the action itself, there has to be total immersion. It is not the time for self-consciousness, or self-reflection.

Only preparation for a commandment needs restraint; but as for the commandment itself, it is better that it should be done quickly.[16]

This is the exact description of how the Yehudi prayed after a long period of preparation.[17]

Groundedness

For R. Bunim, one who strives to be a spiritual being must learn to function in this earthly world. R. Bunim was described by the Seer as "the wise R. Bunim." He is at home in the world. He has what may be described as a sense of groundedness with an awareness of human frailty. This sense mellows even the principle of *kavannah*. With tongue in cheek, he says:

Why don't we recite a blessing over the command to give charity? Because if one had to make a blessing like any other positive commandment, it would require preparation, cleanliness and dipping in the *mikveh* with the proper *yihud* (mystical meditation on unification) or something similar, and in the meantime the poor person would starve to death....[18]

---

[15] *Siah Sarfei Kodesh he-Hadash*, 1, par. Vayishlah, 43.
[16] *Ohel Torah, Song of Songs*, 98; *Meir Einei ha-Golah*, §284; *Ohel Yitzhak*, 100 §235.
[17] See Chap. 10.
[18] *Siah Sarfei Kodesh*, 1, 130 §657.

The groundedness of R. Bunim engenders a healthy distaste for what he called *"frumkeit"* – religious posturing or ignorant religiosity. R. Bunim is acutely aware of the dangers of religious illusion, of fooling oneself.[19]

> The Rabbis say that the gates of tears are not locked. If so, why are there gates? Only if an idiot comes crying – then the gates are locked.[20]

As mentioned:

> It once happened that a person was leading the service for the Day of Atonement and cried profusely, and as a result he was unable to look into the prayer book and made a lot of mistakes. R. Bunim told him that it would be better that he not cry but be able to look into the prayer book and say the words correctly.[21]

A similar distaste for religious posturing is expressed in *Ohel Torah:*

> A person can cry to God, flow with tears with prayer and supplication and imagine that he has drawn near to God.... But it could be that with all the outpouring of his soul and his bitterness, God is still outside his heart.[22]

The psychology of service requires a person to realize that his problems are not solved by the apparent devotion of a pious religious act, it is equally possible for a person to hide himself within the effort of emotional extravagance, his difficulties lie within.

> There are hasidim who sometimes cannot pray, so they go to another place. But that is no solution.[23]

The problem lies within a person,[24] and moving to another location does not solve the problem. The problem, like the solution, lies within the human being. As R. Bunim said about the Exodus:

---

[19] R. Bunim tends to disparage the righteous idiot; see *Torat Simhah,* §177; *Siah Sarfei Kodesh,* 1: 55, §257.

[20] *Ma'amarei Simhah,* §79.

[21] *Ramatayim Zofim,* chap. 31, §95.

[22] *Ohel Torah, Psalms,* 108.

[23] *Ramatayim Zofim* chap. 7, §2; *Or Simhah,* §69.

[24] *Or Simhah,* §106.

God saved them by getting them to eliminate Egypt from their hearts.[25]

More difficult than getting the Jews out of Egypt was trying to get Egypt out of the Jews. We tend to assume that if a physical situation would change, then our problem would be solved. But it could be that many problems are not physical, but lie within the human psyche.

The three generations of Przysucha expressed an aversion to negating the physical (a practice so dominant in mysticism). This was true even of the Yehudi, who had ascetic tendencies.

> A person once accepted upon himself to be silent and for some years only spoke words of Torah and prayer. All other discourse was regarded by him as useless. The Holy Yehudi said to him, "Any word can be useless, and even words of Torah and prayer can have personal motives and pride. Whereas in contradistinction, words not of Torah and prayer can have the power to contain elevated thoughts and can unite for holiness."[26]

With this idea, the Yehudi (following the Besht) was laying the foundation for the Hasidism of Przysucha. *Kedushah* (holiness) is not created by a negative. Abstinence is not to be confused with purity. Wisdom is to be garnered from all around. God did not create human beings to negate the world.

> Once they told R. Bunim about somebody who recited the entire book of Psalms every day. To which he responded, "If in the middle of the book (of Psalms) it says, 'and they seduced Him with their mouths, and with their tongue they denied Him' (Psalms 78:36); someone who finished all the Psalms – all the more so!"[27]

---

[25] *Kol Simhah*, par. *Beshalah*, 64–65.
[26] *Or ha-Ganuz*, 398 (Hebrew).
[27] *Siah Sarfei Kodesh*, 2:13 §14.

Said R. Bunim:

> The Nazirite, who accepted upon himself to be abstinent, and
> forbade himself permitted things because of frumkeit, had impurity
> suddenly come upon him.[28]

R. Bunim is explaining why the Torah (Numbers 6:9) describes the
Nazirite becoming impure by coming into contact with a dead body. He
suggests that the Nazirite had sinned in his very desire to accept upon
himself the restrictions of a Nazirite. His exaggerated form of religious
abstinence is punished by having "impurity suddenly come to him," whereas
when impurity suddenly comes on a priest, there is no suggestion that the
priest did anything wrong.

In a line of tremendous significance R. Bunim said,

> from the Garden of Eden to Hell is only a hair's breath.[29]

The human drama is made up of uncertainty and great fragility, for a
human being can easily slip between Eden and Hell. R. Bunim, more than
any other Rebbe, is recognizable for his insights into the frailty of human
nature, and this more than any other quality is what marks R. Bunim as a
supreme teacher. The simplicity, by which he understands what a human
being is, enables him to maneuver in the world.

The following incident is told:

> It once happened on Purim night that the Seer of Lublin found that
> he could not move. His strongest pupils tried to carry him, but they
> were unable to do so. The Seer commanded that the wise Bunim lift
> him up, and so he did and carried him in his arms to the Study
> House.... The Yehudi asked R. Bunim what "intentions" he had
> when he carried the Seer... R. Bunim replied, "My intention then
> was that I am commanded to carry a simple piece of wood."[30]

What special intention did R. Bunim have when he carried the Seer? Did
he prepare himself by going to the *mikveh?* Did he say Psalms? When he

---

[28] *Siah Sarfei Kodesh,* 2:14 §17.
[29] *Torat Simhah,* §68.
[30] *Or Simhah,* §83.

carried the Seer was he attuned to some greater force? R. Bunim replied that what was needed was simply to carry the great man from one place to another, and it wasn't a question of attunement, but of simply getting the job done.

❧ ❧

R. Bunim's aversion to *frumkeit* has a flip-side. To use modern language, R. Bunim argues that if a person has an inner-directed religious personality, he doesn't need the reassurance of religious stringency, (as in the case of the nazirite).

> Someone who had not reached perfection in the fear of God needs a lot of fences and to have added many stringencies and boundaries. But someone who is wholesome (lit., *shalem*) in the fear of God doesn't need this.[31]

In addition, if a person develops a sense of autonomy, he doesn't have to rely on pedigree (*yihus*). He can look his antecedents in the face. Said the Yehudi:

> Good lineage can help someone a lot in the service of God, so that when God hides His face from him, that person has to make a great effort, so that what he achieves is by his own effort and not by that of his pedigree. For, someone that eats that which is not his (that he has not earned) is embarrassed to look at it.[32]

Ultimately, one has to make one's service one's own.[33]

---

[31] "In the name of R. Bunim..." *Siah Sarfei Kodesh*, 5:70; *Siah Sarfei Kodesh he-Hadash*, 1:121, par. Va-ethanan.

[32] *Tiferet ha-Yehudi*, 144 §5.

[33] There is a passage in the name of the Yehudi, according to which this autonomy seems to lead to an independence from God. The Yehudi explains the argument between Pharaoh and Moses (Exod. 10:8) along the following lines: Pharoah maintained that the Almighty doesn't need sacrifices, to which Moses responds (according to the Yehudi) by saying: God might not need sacrifices, but we do in order to serve Him with the quality of total commitment. Even before the giving of the Law, the human being seeks a way to serve the Creator. For the Yehudi, humanity is a partner with God (*Tiferet ha-Yehudi*, 154 §22).

The following is a tradition of R. Bunim:

> My rebbe, R. Bunim, would always prod the hasidim [i.e., set them
> goals], and through this prodding they argued and came closer...
> and if they could not respond, they could go and burst.[34]

No spoon-feeding here. R. Bunim wants all those who can to become
autonomous. "And if not, then they can go and burst";[35] but eventually they
will become independent.

As mentioned,[36] there is a tradition that the Yehudi had a premonition of
his own death. After discussing this with the Seer, the latter asked him to
spend Rosh Hashanah with him, with the assurance that if he did, he would
not die. The Yehudi refused, because he sensed that by spending Rosh
Hashanah with the Seer he would lose his autonomy. No tradition could give
stronger expression to the Yehudi's sense of independence. Without the
ability to serve God independently there is, for the Yehudi, no meaning to
life; and R. Bunim would concur.

The religiosity of Przysucha is firmly rooted in the earthiness of this world.

> I heard from (R. Bunim) that if somebody asks (God) for fear (of
> heaven) but doesn't ask for livelihood, this is a sign that even his
> request for the fear of heaven is not really sincere, for one is
> impossible without the other.[37]

Once again one hears the self-confidence of someone who realizes that
all spiritual aspiration takes place in the context of earthly reality.

When R. Bunim first came to Kozienice, it happened that year that the
festival of *Shavuot* (Pentecost) fell on a Sunday and Monday. The Maggid had
asked his hasidim not to indulge in idle talk until after the reading of the Ten
Commandments (on the morning of Shavuot), so as to extend, as it were,
the holiness of the Sabbath until after the receiving of the Law. For some
reason R. Bunim needed to speak, and the hasidim indicated to him that they

---

[34] *Hashavah le-Tovah, Hasidut,* 124.
[35] I have used Boem's translation of the Yiddish (*Kol Mevaser* 2:292).
[36] *Nifla'ot ha-Yehudi,* 86–87.
[37] *Ramatayim Zofim,* chap. 5, §111.

were extremely displeased with his behavior, to which R. Bunim said the following:

> Idiots. If I need a glass of coffee, shouldn't I ask the servant girl to give me one?[38]

R. Bunim is saying: "You take the words of the Maggid literally to mean don't speak at all. However, I understand the Maggid's prohibition as an objection to 'idle talk,' but clearly, if one needs a glass of coffee or the like, asking for it in no way interferes with the Maggid's desire to extend the holiness of the Sabbath by not speaking." Such autonomy fits uneasily in a world of religious conformity, which tends to discourage personal initiative. That was R. Bunim in approximately 1792, when he began to enter the world of Hasidism.[39] For the next thirty years, he practiced and developed his grounded approach of individuality.

Fasting

One way of uniting R. Bunim's human psychology, his psychology of the soul, and his psychology of service is to focus on his attitude towards fasting. Because R. Bunim believed in the essentially positive nature of human beings, he was not too enthusiastic about fasting as a normative religious practice.

In general, fasting is a dubious religious mode that lends itself to self-delusion. One imagines that by the act of fasting one has achieved a level of purity, whereas in fact it may be that all one has done is to suppress a physical desire. It's rather like pressing down a spring which, upon removing one's hand, bounces back with double vigor.

A man once told R. Bunim:

> "Time and again I have mortified my flesh and done all I should, and yet Elijah has not appeared to me." In reply the zaddik told him this story: "The holy Ba'al Shem Tov once went on a long journey. He hired a team, seated himself in the carriage, and uttered one of

---

[38] *Or Simhah* §15.
[39] Boem, 89.

the holy Names. Immediately the road leaped to meet the straining horses and hardly had they begun to trot when they had reached the first inn, not knowing what had happened to them. At this stop they were usually fed, but they had scarcely calmed down when the second inn rushed past them. Finally it occurred to the beasts that they must have become men and so would not receive food until evening, in the town where they were to spend the night. But when evening came and the carriage failed to stop, but raced on from town to town, the horses agreed that the only possible explanation was that they must have been transformed into angels and no longer required either food or drink. At that moment the carriage reached its destination. They were stabled, given their measure of oats, and they thrust their heads into their feed bags as starved horses do."[40] Similarly, one who fasts and thinks that he has become like an angel, to merit the revelation of Elijah: the main thing is that, after he has completed the number of fasts, when they give him to eat he shouldn't grab and stuff himself like a horse, because if he does so, then he remains a horse as he originally was.

As my father used to say, "It's not how you fast, it's how you break your fast!" Like other Hasidic leaders, R. Bunim didn't believe in the value of fasting.[41] Fasting is only a mechanism, and one pregnant with delusion.[42]

The hasidim of Przysucha were accused of not keeping the four annual fasts properly. The following is written in *Keter Kehunnah*:

> Our eyes saw, and not on one occasion alone, how they sat together on the benches, mouths full of laughter, with clouds of smoking incense coming from their throat, while the others sat in mourning for the destruction of the Temple, with tears on their cheeks. They

---

[40] *Ma'amarei Simhah*, §36. I have used Buber's rather free translation until this point. The continuation in his translation is too sanitized and loses the earthiness of the Yiddish.

[41] *Kitvei Hasidim, (Kol Mevaser,* 3:31). J. Fox, *Rabbi Menahem Mendel of Kotzk* (Jerusalem: 1967), 21 cites the following quote in the name of the Apta Rav (*Irin Kadishin le-R. Yisrael mi-Ruzhin,* par. Vayikra (Warsaw: 1885): "Were I able to annul all the fasts, I would do so."

[42] *Emet ve-Emunah*, §770 reads: "What is a 'frume' (a pietist)? – someone who confuses the main thing with the minor thing."

said, "All the fasts have lost their credibility except for the Day of Atonement. As for the Ninth of Av, that is a matter which remains to be decided." Therefore every year, on the Fast of Gedaliah, in the morning they ate a hot bagel while the community was saying prayers of supplication.[43]

Whether or not we accept this testimony, what cannot be denied was R. Bunim's opposition to fasting in general.

He once said, "If I had the power, I would abolish all the fasts with the exception of the Day of Atonement and the Ninth of Av. For on the Day of Atonement who needs to eat, and on the Ninth of Av who can eat?"[44]

Fasting is not a goal in itself; rather, it is a mechanism, a means toward an end, which is connection with God. But if that mechanism becomes dominant, then it interferes with the goal. Therefore R. Bunim expresses the idea that it would be better to abolish fasting altogether, with the exception of the Day of Atonement and the Ninth of Av, when in any event fasting is of secondary concern.[45]

We know that in the school of Kotzk, even on the eve of the Day of Atonement, the hasidim deliberately behaved in a provocative way in order to get themselves to internalize why they were fasting, to clarify their motives, to push everything to the edge of clarity, to ask whether it was really for God's sake. There is a riveting testimony called *Ha-Sarid ha-Kotzkai ha-Aharon* (The Last of the Kotzker Hasidim),[46] which describes how a bright young Talmudic scholar was drawn into the world of Hiddushei ha-Rim. The climax of the story is the following: just before the beginning of the Day of Atonement, after returning from the Rebbe's *tisch* (table) where he had been in a state of merriment with his fellow Hasidim, he came home and fell fast asleep. His parents came back from the synagogue and were unable to enter their house. When they eventually woke him up, he washed his hands and began to pray the *Kol Nidre* evening service by himself. This

---

[43] *Keter Kehunnah*, 129.

[44] *Kol Mevaser,* 3:31.

[45] On maintaining a sense of balance in the service of God, see the Yehudi as quoted in *Maggid Meisharim, Kitvei Kodesh*, 62 (*Torat ha-Yehudi* 5 §6).

[46] S. Bergamintz, "*Ha-Sarid ha-Kotzkai ha-Aharon.*" In *Digleinu* (Warsaw: 1927).

was too much for his parents, who slapped his face and threw him out of the house.

The Day of Atonement is the holiest day in the Jewish calendar. The Bible mandates a full twenty–four-hour fast. The *Kol Nidrei* is the most evocative prayer. And yet this "last of the Kotzker Hasidim" is not overwhelmed by the awesomeness of the fast day, for he knows that the ritual of fasting is essentially a methodology to bring one close to the Divine. And if in order to achieve that, he needs to sleep first and then pray the *Kol Nidrei* service by himself – so be it!

The Yehudi and Menahem Mendel might have agreed with R. Bunim's reservations about fasting, but they probably would not have expressed themselves so sardonically, as in the story of the horses. This reflects a certain degree of asceticism in the Yehudi, and an apparent dissonance with the world in the personality of Menahem Mendel of Kotzk. But with R. Bunim, what dominates is the aspect of wholesomeness.

There is an inner coherence to these ideas of Przysucha – almost a logical sequence. The main question in the world of Przysucha is a theocentric one. The question resounds in the world of Przysucha: "How does God want a human being to stand before Him?" The process is anthropocentric, for what flows from that question is another one: "What does a human being have to do to stand before God?" With no theosophy, the drama takes place in the human soul. But this approach is predicated on a rabbinical understanding of the nature of the human being, namely, that he is capable of responding to the call, and the subsequent demands of the Divine. Because he has the capability; therefore there is the demand. But if a person can respond, what is the mechanism to help him with the response?

The answer seems to lie in an apparently innocuous value, which nevertheless reveals itself to be a kind of religious dynamite, namely, the value of preparation, of finding one's own way. It is the safety net, if there is one, for sincerity and purity of motive, as well as, the antidote for routine and self-delusion. It is the process by which the finite (that is, the human being) can have the effrontery to stand before the Infinite with any sense of integrity. It is this essential process which facilitates a drama that revolves solely around the person.

The Impact of R. Bunim as a Teacher

Within the world of the Hasidim, hagiography or legend-making is the proven norm, and as a rule, the later the source the greater the embellishment. The character and personality of the man himself remain on the other side of a veil. Every source remains at best a refraction, representation or rendering of the teachings and persona in which they were cultivated. What's passed down are, if not the man and his Torah, the closest equivalent we can come to, the impressions of those who experienced the passion and spiritual acumen of the protagonist. And while our second-hand experience remains far from that of sitting at R. Bunim's table, for the third meal on Shabbat, after bringing several observations from different sources, what becomes unmistakably clear is the personal impact R. Bunim had on his *talmidim* (students).

৵ ৶

Yitzhak Miesis, a student of R. Bunim who later became an enthusiastic supporter of the Enlightenment, once said of R. Bunim:

> He spoke with passion and with such an inner confidence that he believed that he had the capability to bring all the deniers back to the fold.[47]

In *Keter Kehunnah* (a work consisting mainly of anti-hasidic polemics), the author describes R. Bunim thus:

> We remember in our youth how the Rebbe-Philosopher charted a new path for those drawn after him. For his army of followers, he took only men of excellence – exceptional Torah scholars who were especially intelligent.[48]

---

[47] Rabinowitz, "R. Bunim," 41; see note 5 there for biographical details on Yitzhak Miesis.

[48] A. Zederbaum, *Keter Kehunnah* (Odessa, 1868), 128; also Weissenfeld Avraham Yaacob, *Exchange of Letters between Avraham Yaacob Weissenfeld and His Friends* (Hebrew) (Cracow, 1900), 80. Aescoly describes the social upheaval created by R. Bunim as follows:
"There developed with R. Bunim a new type, which later became famous in Kotzk – the sharp young man – who left his wife without saying goodbye and went to the

Another source quotes this description:

> He was one of the outstanding men of spirit of his age – throughout
> Europe.[49]

From a source totally within the hasidic world comes the following
narrative:

> Once R. Bunim was sitting with his students discussing matters of
> repentance. R. Bunim became very animated and he stood up and
> said, "Maimonides says, 'And what is repentance? It is that the
> sinner should forsake his sin, remove it from his mind and decide in
> his heart never to do it again, so that He who knows the innermost
> secrets of a man's heart can testify that he will never do that sin
> again.' Someone who cannot do repentance like that has no place
> with me.... The students were terrified by the awesomeness of this
> teacher and they fled. Only R. Mendel of Kotzk remained, and he
> said, "I have no strength to flee."[50]

Though the words themselves are not that original, what is evident is the
impact of R. Bunim on his pupils. What makes his words so real and
powerful is the force of his own religious integrity and enthusiasm. When
once asked what was so special about R. Bunim, his pupil R. Yisrael Yitzhak
of Vorki (Warka) said the following:

> When R. Bunim takes the hand of a pupil, even of a simple Jew, he
> immediately becomes infused with Judaism as if he were on fire so
> that the person feels that nothing is important other than cleaving to
> God.[51]

---

rebbe, spending months there absorbed in Hasidism, dancing, drinking and
conversation of camaraderie, breaking all sorts of norms of society. In all towns and
homes there were fathers-in-law who cursed Przysucha for destroying the family."

[49] See Rabinowitz, "R. Bunim," 41, quoting A. Marcus. See *Or Simhah*, n. 11.
"Someone who has not seen R. Bunim has never seen the light that existed in the
First Temple.... He had all the keys of the firmament."

[50] Rabinowitz, "R. Bunim," 75, n. 14. A similar story is told by Hiddushei ha-Rim
about the Kotzker himself (*Meir Einei ha-Golah*, n. 236).

[51] *Ohel Yitzhak*, 19, n. 43.

The effect of R. Bunim was that he inspired a hasid to become more of himself. The following is an early description of R. Bunim:

> I heard from my father-in-law the following. They slandered the hasidim, saying that they were drunkards, libertines, and of bad character. The person in charge of the Enlightenment in those days... visited R. Bunim of Przysucha, and was amazed to find in the rebbe (who had been slandered as a visionary) things that he hadn't found amongst all the rabbis of the time: a philosopher, and a critical scholar. He was completely amazed to discover a wise man who spoke German, Polish and Latin fluently. He found this man a great scholar who had everything, who illuminated a new path, whose whole approach was to purify the mind and practical commandments.[52]

It is this quality of someone whose presence generates a religious response in the other – the supreme quality of a teacher – that seems to be the greatness of R. Bunim.

> [The Rabbi of Alexander] told the following [about Hiddushei ha-Rim]. After he [Hiddushei ha-Rim] had been in Przysucha a number of times, he [the rebbe of Alexander] wanted to know what was on his mind and how committed he was to the rebbe [R. Bunim]. And on the holy Sabbath, before the Third Meal, he himself stood behind our teacher [Hiddushei ha-Rim]. During the Third Meal, when the Study House was completely dark, he felt the holy brow [of Hiddushei ha-Rim] and his entire face was full of tears. Then he knew that he was completely one of them.[53]

Hiddushei ha-Rim (a prodigy of talmudic learning) was conversant with other rebbes (R. Moishe of Kozienice [Kuznitz] and R. Meir of Apta), but he seems to have been totally captivated by R. Bunim.

---

[52] See above, Weissenfeld, "Exchange of Letters," 81 (which Zederbaum, in *Keter Kehunnah*, 130, had misreported).
[53] *Meir Einei ha-Golah*, n. 114. See also n. 121.

In order to appreciate the charisma of R. Bunim, one should consider the following disturbing and painful story. *Meir Einei ha-Golah* is an authorized family history of Yizhak Meir Rottenberg Alter, known as Hiddushei ha-Rim. He was the founder of the hasidic dynasty known as Ger (Gur). He had thirteen children,[54] twelve of whom died at an early age.[55] The book *Meir Einei ha-Golah* gives the following explanation for this tragedy.

Hiddushei ha-Rim had been a hasid of R. Moshe of Kozienice. When he decided to leave Kozienice to learn with R. Simhah Bunim, R. Moshe never forgave him. As a result, each time he journeyed to Przysucha, one of his children died.

> Our teacher had a son who at the age of four revealed himself as a prodigy. Our teacher foresaw great things for him. When our teacher was preparing himself to journey to Przysucha, his wife, the rebbetzin, implored him not to endanger the child. But our teacher did not pay attention. The child was then seven and he accompanied our teacher on his journey to Przysucha to the outskirts of Warsaw. When our teacher returned from Przysucha he found his child on his sickbed, and in a few days he died.[56]

He is reported to have said:

> Seventeen times I journeyed to Przysucha and there were seventeen reasons for my losing my children, and I well know that this was a punishment – namely that the holy Rabbis of Kozienice and Apta held a grudge against me. But I have no regrets for my actions.[57]

When asked why he continued to go to Przysucha, seeing that it was so dangerous for his family, he replied

> that with regard to the truth in the service of God he was not prepared to consider anything else.[58]

---

[54] *Meir Einei ha-Golah*, part 2, n. 438; Aescoly, p. 101 also mentions the figure 17.
[55] The father of the *Sefat Emet,* however, died when he was thirty-nine.
[56] *Meir Einei ha-Golah*, n. 124.
[57] *Meir Einei ha-Golah*, n. 122; see also notes 101, 106, 125–126; part 2, n. 434, notes.
[58] *Meir Einei ha-Golah*, n. 94.

These traditions preserved by the family of Hiddushei ha-Rim are very powerful, for they depict someone willing to jeopardize so much in order to come in contact with something greater than himself. And even if one rationalizes the matter, explaining the tragic deaths of his children as a result of the high mortality rate of the time, one is nevertheless compelled to acknowledge the fact that Hiddushei ha-Rim himself believed that all these tragic events came upon him solely as a consequence of his traveling to be taught by R. Bunim.

𐅋 ɔʅ

R. Bunim's biography may be summarized by saying that, with R. Bunim, Przysucha challenged its rivals for the dominance of Polish Hasidism and, under his leadership, it became the major force in the main center of Hasidism – Poland. R. Bunim revolutionized Hasidism in Poland, and many of the basic ideas of nineteenth-century Polish Hasidism have their source in his exegesis.

It is this aspect of supreme teacher which stands out above all else. And it is simply impossible to evaluate nineteenth-century Polish Hasidism without understanding R. Bunim's world. The Yehudi was distinguished by the charisma of his spirituality and his Talmudic acumen, which so thrilled his students. The Kotzker had the ability to galvanize his pupils through his fiery extremism, which demanded that his followers respond. But R. Bunim was the teacher par excellence – the one who understood the psychology of the soul. He was the one who could help others travel their path. The Rebbe of Kotzk said of his teacher:

> R. Bunim of Przysucha lifted up and helped all those that came to take shelter in his shade. And I want each person to raise themselves [without help].[59]

R. Bunim could bring out what was inside the hasid, not so much by charisma or by demand, but by getting the hasid to discover what was in himself.

---

[59] *Hashavah le-Tovah,* par. Yitro, 20. *Emet ve-Emunah* 21.

PRAYER

A pupil who wants to progress should not wish to behave in a way which contradicts any law from our holy Torah: for example, to annul the time of (for the) reading (of) the Shema' or the times of prayer fixed by the Rabbis. **Even though some people, clever in their own opinion, might entice you, saying that one should wait until one feels the beautiful abundance of expanded consciousness, you should know, my beloved, that this is the advice of the evil impulse.**

R. Zvi Elimelech of Dinov

The Centrality of Prayer

FOR HASIDISM, THE FOUNDATION of a man's service of God is his ability to come close to the Divine, and the medium is prayer. Prayer is so fundamental in the hasidic world that any ostensible discussion as to whether its format or times were biblical or rabbinic is secondary. R. Shneur Zalman of Liady (1747–1813), founder of the Habad group in Hasidism, makes the point explicitly in a letter addressed to Alexander of Shklov.

> Those who argue that prayer is only binding by Rabbinic law have never seen the light. While it is true that the forms of the prayers are Rabbinic and that prayers must be recited three times a day, the concept of prayer and its essential idea belong to the very foundation of the Torah – namely, to know the Lord, to recognize His greatness and His glory with a serene mind and, through contemplation, to have these fixed firmly in the mind. A man must reflect on this theme until the contemplative soul is awakened to love the Lord's name, to cleave to Him and to His Torah, and

greatly to desire His commandments. Nowadays, all this can only be achieved by reciting the verses of praise and the benedictions before and after the Shema with clear diction and in a loud voice so as to awaken the powers of concentration. All this, and then perhaps! It was otherwise with regard to R. Simeon b. Yohai and his colleagues. For them, the recitation of the Shema alone was sufficient for them to attain all this. It was all achieved in a blink of the eye, so humble were their hearts in their covenantal loyalty. But, nowadays, anyone who has drawn near to God and has once tasted the fragrance of prayer knows and appreciates that without prayer no man can lift hand or foot to serve God in truth, unlike the (service) of men who learn by rote.[1]

Because Przysucha does not operate in the world of theurgy, prayer was not undertaken for the sake of the *Shekhinah* – the kabbalistic understanding that the hasid has an obligation to aid and help fix the Godhead. In the same vein, it would be a form of spiritual beggary to focus prayer solely on personal interests (though R. Bunim was not oblivious to the needs of temporal well-being). Prayer was the path to intimacy with the Divine. Though not indifferent to the world, the occupation of prayer is spiritual – the soul humming in tune with its source.

In his paper, "Hasidic and Mitnaggedic Polemics," Mordechai Wilensky summarizes the clash between Hasidism and its opponents as follows:

> The essence of the conflict over prayer resulted from a difference in approach to the concept of prayer, its value and importance. The *mitnaggedim* opposed hasidic elevation of prayer to the highest level of Jewish values. This, the *mitnaggedim* opposed in principle; hence their strong reaction.[2]

Scholem, writing about hasidic prayer, says:

---

[1] "The Hasidic teachers were not unaware that their elevation of prayer over all other duties was a departure from what, at least, was held to be the tradition and they sought to justify their innovation by seeking to demonstrate, as religious innovators are wont to do, that the tradition, rightly understood, was really in line with their attitude." Louis Jacobs, *Hasidic Prayer* (New York: 1978), 18–31.

[2] Mordechai Wilensky. "Hasidic and Mitnaggedic Polemics in the Jewish Communities of Eastern Europe: The Hostile Phase." In *Essential Papers on Hasidism: Origins to Present*, edited by Gershon D. Hundert, 252. New York: 1991.

For the soaring flight of the soul from the worlds created in the act of tzimtzum there are no limits. "He who serves God in the 'great way' assembles all his inner power and rises upwards in his thoughts and breaks through all skies in one act and rises higher than the angels and the seraphs and the thrones, and that is the perfect worship." "In prayer and in the commandments which one keeps, there is a great and a small way... but the 'great way' is that of right preparation and enthusiasm through which he unites himself with the upper worlds." [3]

If the rabbinic world saw the Torah as God's gift to humanity, then the Hasidic world saw prayer as humanity's gift to God. In Przysucha, prayer was a state of mind, a person's quest to enter into the presence of the Divine. The intellect alone, whether focused on Talmud or on any other body of knowledge, could not truly get a person "inside," even if that knowledge is God's gift. That was the function of prayer. But just as "mind" was not limited to the study of Talmud, so prayer was not limited to a particular ritual act at a certain time. Rather, it was a consciousness of God.

This consciousness was critically important for Przysucha. It became an imperative. It demanded a type of sincerity which could not be controlled by normative halakhic rules. Prayer, in this wider sense, is the oxygen of the soul; it is the spiritual life force, the umbilical cord connecting the soul with its Source, between the finite and the Infinite. And the challenge remains how to maintain spontaneity within a *halakhic* system without compromising one's authenticity or halakhic norms.

Przysucha is unique in its refusal to sacrifice authentic prayer or sensitivity to halakhic requirements. Przysucha's attitude to prayer distinguishes it from that of the hasidic world surrounding it. It wasn't mitnaggedic because of the importance it placed on prayer and on the heart. But neither was it traditionally hasidic, due to the emphasis it placed on learning, on the intellect, and on self-analysis. In order to fly, it had to use both wings within the *halakhah.*

---

[3] Defining what was special about Hasidism, he says: "The new element must therefore not be sought on the theoretical and literary plane, but rather in the experience of an inner revival, in the spontaneity of a feeling generated in sensitive minds by the encounter with the living incarnations of mysticism." G. Scholem, *Major Trends in Jewish Mysticism* (New York: 1967), 335, 338.

R. Hanoch Heinich explains the word *va-et'hanan* ("And I beseeched"; Deuteronomy 3:23), noting that it is phrased in the reflexive form, on the basis of an exquisite interpretation by R. Bunim of the phrase *va-ani tefillah* ("and I am prayer"; Psalms 109:4). R. Bunim says[4] that when a person really prays he becomes the prayer. T.S. Eliot said about listening to music: "Music heard so deeply that it is not heard at all but you are the music while the music lasts." Prayer is therefore not a form of spiritually begging, of asking God for goodies. It is rather a process by which a human being develops himself in order to be worthy of a more intimate relationship with God. Whereas mainstream Hasidism would see prayer as a mystical means *to be used*, Przysucha sees prayer as a mystical means *to be* – and what will follow will follow. Not to use prayer, but to be prayer.

Delaying the Times of Prayer

We have multiple sources all testifying to the fact that the Yehudi (not to mention R. Bunim and the Kotzker) delayed praying at the "fixed" time, in accordance with his state of mind. If this had been limited to the Yehudi alone, it might have been tolerated as an idiosyncrasy of a great spiritual personality. In general, a society that feels confident in itself can tolerate a certain deviance from the norm. But what was at stake here was not the Yehudi's personal behavior. His opponents recognized that he was promoting a challenge with philosophical underpinning. The delaying of prayer expressed a far larger concept, and it was this that threatened the Hasidic establishment.

Some argue that "delaying the time for prayer" began with the Seer rather than with the Yehudi.[5] In fact, as Mordechai Wilensky has shown, delaying the times of prayer was one of the original accusations made by the *mitnaggedim* against the hasidim (i.e., before both the Seer and the Yehudi). As he says:

---

[4] *Hashavah le-Tovah*, 60.
[5] *Zichron Zot*, par Pinhas. See Rachel Elior, "Bein Yirah ve-Ahava, be-Omek ve-Gavan," *Tarbiz* 62–63 (1993): 391 n. 14.

The *mitnaggedim* saw the Hasidic lack of precision with regard to the established times of prayer as a violation of Halakha. We find criticism of this custom even before 1772.[6]

In terms of the norm, the implications of the Seer's delaying the time for prayer and the Yehudi doing so were vastly different. What motivated the Seer was his unique role as a zaddik. The spiritual ecstasy which flowed from a state of "love" would be limited to the exceptional individual. But for Przysucha, the delaying of prayer was motivated by a desire to be attuned, and was therefore applicable to anyone who could follow such a path. It was therefore not the domain of the exceptional, but rather the norm for anyone choosing to join Przysucha.[7] Such an approach was far more threatening to the Hasidic establishment.

Alan Brill writes:

> This delay of prayer is one of the distinguishing social features of the followers of R. Simhah Bunim of Przysucha. In the beginning of Siah Sarfai Kodesh, the editor places an excerpt from a responsum by Radbaz (David ben Solomon ibn Abi Zimra, 1513–1573) on not attending synagogue if the other congregants' talking is found distracting. Based on the rabbinic requirement for intention (*kavvanah*) as codified by Maimonides, "a person should not pray in a place that distracts his mind or at a time that hinders his intentions," the followers of Polish Hasidism extended this delay into a positive procedure of preparation for prayer and ritual performance.[8]

---

[6] See "Zivato shel R. David mi-Makov," in Wilensky, *Hasidim u-mitnaggedim*, II: 246, ad loc n. 43. R. David complained that the Hasidism in "Lublin and Kozienice pray close to midnight, and (pray) the afternoon prayer after the appearance of the stars, as I saw in Zelechow...." Regarding The Seer of Lublin, he says, "Around him gather herds and herds of hasidim... he is late for the afternoon prayer." II:195.

[7] Scholem, in "*Devekut,* or Communion with God," in his *The Messianic Idea in Judaism* (New York: Schocken, 1971), 203–227] argues the same distinction for *devekut*: namely, that for the kabbalists it was a method for the exceptional, but in Hasidism it became a norm. However, A. Rapoport-Albert in "God and the Tzaddik as the Two Focal Points of Hasidic Worship," *History of Religions* 18:4 (1979), 311, thinks that in Hasidism too it was the domain of the elite.

[8] A. Brill, "Grandeur and Humility in the Writings of R. Simhah Bunim of Przysucha." In *Hazon Nahum* (1997), 436.

Nothing could be a guarantee for spiritual experience. What the Yehudi wanted was for prayer to be genuine, and not a lifeless ritual act – passion via preparation, rather than *frumkeit*. The *Mei Shiloach* said about the Yehudi:

> In every generation, the zaddik of the generation sees God's will... and the Yehudi saw that God's will in this generation was to delay the time of prayer... so that it would not be lifeless.[9]

Friend and foe agreed that the Yehudi delayed the times of prayer. His grandson said:

> It is known that my grandfather would make the time of prayer his own, alone, and his prayer was with total commitment.[10]

The Yehudi came to the defense of others who also delayed prayer (even though their prayers extended beyond the correct time) on the basis that "Such prayer can be reckoned as if it was all done during the correct time."[11]

Hasidism saw prayer as personal mysticism.[12] Scholem writes:

Mysticism in the world of Przysucha did not mean trying to unify God, but rather unifying with God. It is the experience of the soul being drawn to its source like filings to a magnet, and it must come from one's essence (one's *kishkeh*).

In *Kol Simhah*, we read:

> Prayer is only acceptable if it comes from the depths of one's heart; if one prays from the essence of one's soul, then prayer is acceptable.[13]

In the world of Przysucha, the zaddik does not pierce the heavens on behalf of his disciples, thereby redeeming all their prayers that were said without intention. Nor is the solution to be found in some body of

---

[9] *Mei Shiloah,* par *Beha'alotkha*, 2:29 (§57).

[10] *Aron Edut, Shavuot,* 24.

[11] Responsa Eretz Zvi, §121, 406.

[12] "The distinctive feature of the new school is to be found in the fact that the secrets of the divine realm are presented in the guise of mystical psychology.... What has really become important is the direction, the mysticism of the personal life. Hasidism is practical mysticism at its highest." (Scholem, *Major Trends,* 340–341)

[13] *Kol Simhah,* par. Vayigash, 49.

knowledge. Prayer is "the service of the heart," a drama that takes place in one's existential being.

What stands out in Przysucha is the idea that prayer should be internal and not external, or at least that the external should be a consequence of an internal process. Hiddushei ha-Rim encapsulated this by saying that the following was the message in Przysucha:

> The main work is inside. One shouldn't work on the outside. One should draw on an inner life force in all action. When human beings do the inner work, their external limbs automatically become subservient to them.[14]

The same idea is found, in the name of R. Bunim, from another pupil.

> When one prays, the soul alone needs to pray and the body is drawn after it like a bale of hay.[15]

While one is in the moment of experience, one is oblivious to everything else. Once, when R. Shmuel of Sieniawa complained that he couldn't pray because his head hurt, R. Bunim replied, "What has the head got to do with prayer? The main thing is the service of the heart."[16]

R. Bunim said:

> Prayer should take place when one's mind and heart are at one. It should flow from the heart and soul and shoot like an arrow from all one's senses without any effort or work. All the work is before prayer....[17]

The analytical and emotional preparation takes place before the moment. In the moment one has to be totally within, "All the work is before prayer." Preparation is essentially self-conscious; whereas to be really "inside" means that only in retrospect does one have an awareness of self. It is those who do not prepare themselves before prayer who require the use of prayer itself as a stage in a process of preparation. But if someone is attuned, intimacy is not

---

[14] Boem, 1:268; see also *Siah Sarfei Kodesh*, 3:46 §104.
[15] *Hashavah le-Tovah*, par. Terumah, 28; *Kol Simhah*, par. Tetzaveh, 77.
[16] *Ramatayim Zofim*, chap. 3, §19.
[17] *Torat Simhah*, §226.

by definition limited to the amount of time given to the preparation, nor is it self-conscious.

R. Bunim's description of prayer as something that "shoots like an arrow... without effort" is very similar to a description of how the Yehudi prayed:

> The Yehudi would take a long time until he was ready to pray, but then he would pray in a short space of time.[18]

Time was not a quantitative factor but a qualitative one. Once one was ready, then, and only then, could prayer begin.

The Style of Prayer

Over the following two generations, during the period of R. Simhah Bunim and Menahem Mendel, the style of prayer of Przysucha became distinctive. It was restrained, with an aversion to external manifestations, such as wild gesticulations and praying in a loud voice. R. Simhah Bunim looked down on what he perceived as something essentially superficial, though even he recognized that sincerity should win the day. As Przysucha developed, so did its antagonism to externals and those who paraded them.

It is true that the Yehudi was known for his ecstatic style of prayer. Sometimes the Yehudi's personal sense of the presence of the Divine became so overwhelming that his prayer would reduce him to the point of fainting from physical exhaustion.

> R. Moshe of Rozodov said of the Yehudi: "He prayed with all his strength, with total commitment; and when he reached the passage

---

[18] *Tiferet ha-Yehudi*, 165 §46; *Hiddushei ha-Rim*, par. *Noah*, 11. See *Torat Simhah*, §204. "When he comes to pray, that is to say he comes before the King, there falls upon him a great sense of awe and shame. For he sees the glory of the King of Kings, the Holy One, blessed be He, and knows that he is a lowly creature of meager knowledge before Him Who is of perfect knowledge. And because of this great shame he hides his vessels; that is to say, he cannot open his mouth to pray; and that is the matter of prayer."

'And David blessed,' one could almost see his soul departing... his strength nearly expired from awe."[19]

But notwithstanding his personal ecstasy, the Yehudi emphasized quietness in prayer. In this he followed in the footsteps of the Ba'al Shem Tov.

> One should train oneself to pray even "songs" in a soft voice and to cry out quietly. And one should say one's prayer, whether in song or in learning, with all one's strength, as it says, "All my being shall say." The cry that comes from intimacy is one of quietness.[20]

The Yehudi asked: how did Pharaoh's daughter recognize that the child in the bulrushes was Jewish? Playing on the change between the word "child" and the word "youth" in the biblical text, the Yehudi said, "The real proof of a Jewish child is that his voice is not heard (in prayer)."[21] Pharaoh's daughter realizes that the child is Jewish because it cries quietly.

The style of the Yehudi's prayer also fitted this quest for genuineness. The Yehudi is reported to have usually prayed alone (personal authenticity doesn't always sit neatly with community). In this respect as well R. Bunim followed the example of his master.[22]

The truth is that for the Yehudi, the ultimate goal was to have a sense of being in the Divine presence. For him, sincerity was like a revelation of the *Shekhinah*[23] – and this was the supreme state.

> He related in the name of the Holy Rabbi of Przysucha (R. Bunim) that he once saw R. Natale Helmer on Rosh Hashanah and he did not pray, neither by night nor by day. Amazed, he asked the Holy

---

[19] *Tiferet ha-Yehudi*, 171 §74; *Meir Einei ha-Golah*, §283.

[20] *Tzava'at ha-Rivash*, 4b.

[21] *Emunat Israel*, par. Beshalah, 20.2. *(Torat ha-Yehudi*, par. Shemot, 22)

[22] *Torat Simhah*, §170.

[23] *Migdal David* (Piotrkov, 1893) par. *Re'eh*, 54.

"As I heard from... my teacher, R. Jacob Isaac of Przysucha: 'with great awe' – this is the revelation of the Shekhinah. He explained that a man cannot come to great awe, which alludes to higher awe, without Divine revelation. Through having the greatness of God revealed to him, man comes to great humility and lowliness in his eyes."

Yehudi of Przysucha, who said that it was because of his (sense) of awe (of the Divine).[24]

R. Bunim sees the person whose sense of the Divine is so real that he cannot open his mouth to pray, even though he is obliged to according to Jewish law, and he turns to his teacher in amazement. But the Yehudi, far from criticizing this person, endorses his behavior, believing that to have a sense of the reality of God's presence is the greatest form of prayer achievable.

It was well-known that R. Bunim disdained loud, wild prayer. However, if the passion was the result of a reflective individual (as in the case of his teacher the Yehudi), then that overrode the norm. And if he felt that what motivated this style of prayer, as in the case of Hanoch Heinech,[25] was sincere, he would defer. But his position was clear.

> With our own ears, we have heard that... R. Bunim... would pray without any movement whatsoever; but would stand like a column of bricks – his eyes flowing with tears without respite.[26]

In a similar vein we have a most reliable description of the prayer of R. Menahem Mendel. The *Shem mi-Shmuel* related how his father, R. Avraham of Sochaczew, the son-in-law of the Kotzker, reported to him the following:

> My father told me that in his youth when he was weak and spitting blood, my grandfather took him to pray with him in his room on Rosh ha-Shanah next to the great bet ha-midrash. And he saw him recite the standing prayer of Rosh ha-Shanah... without movement or (visible) emotion – but his face was on fire.[27]

---

[24] *Siah Sarfei Kodesh*, 1:19 §90; *Ramatayim Zofim*, 31:100. *Tiferet ha-Yehudi*, 166 §55. R. Natale Helmer was an in-law of the Seer. See Y. Alfasi, *Ha-Hozeh mi-Lublin,* 274. In *Shem mi-Shmuel*, Rosh ha-Shanah 1911, p. 13b, this story is told about R. Natale Helmer when he was in Lublin with the Seer.

[25] Y.L. Levin, *Sefer Alexander; ha-Admor R. Hanoch Heinich ha-Kohen* (Jerusalem: 1949), 19; also *Torat Simhah*, §333.

[26] *Shem mi-Shmuel*, par. Vaethanan (1915), 35.

[27] *Shem mi-Shmuel*, par. Korah, 267b. The phrase "face on fire" is used in *Vayikra Rabba* 21:12 to describe the High Priest in the Holy of Holies on the Day of Atonement.

If that isn't God-consciousness in prayer, then what is? In R. Bunim's opinion, prayer came from the heart, not from the head.[28] It was acceptable when it came "from the depths of the heart, from the essence of one's soul – then it was desirable."[29] This attitude of R. Bunim's was, of course, picked up by his hasidim and became part of the behavior that they mocked in others.

> Our teacher (Hiddushei ha-Rim) used to make strange movements in preparation for prayer… once, when he was preparing himself to pray, one of the prominent hasidim grabbed his phylacteries.[30]

Antagonism to external manifestations in prayer was an attitude which everyone in Przysucha, including Hiddushei ha-Rim, learned sooner or later:

> Once, after the Day of Atonement had ended, (R. Bunim) said that he had had a good Day of Atonement – that from when the Day of Atonement came in until it went out he had stood on one level without any movement whatsoever, not even for a second.[31]

The problem with external manifestations of prayer was fundamentally the following: Externals detract from the internal; however, if the external ecstatic movements were the result of something occurring inside the person that was another matter. But without the process starting from within, the external was thought to be a shallow display. As Hiddushei ha-Rim reportedly mentioned to his hasidim what he had learned from Przysucha. "When a person does the work inside, his external limbs automatically become subservient."

R. Bunim said:

> When one prays, only the soul should pray; and the body should be drawn after it like a bale of hay. Then "I will dwell in them" refers to those who create the Tabernacle – the soul and the body together.

---

[28] *Ramatayim Zofim*, chap. 3, §19.

[29] *Kol Simhah*, par. Vayigash, 49.

[30] *Meir Einei ha-Golah*, §113.

[31] *Ramatayim Zofim*, chap. 31, §100.

But if they are not together, then the Tabernacle is merely a piece of wood.[32]

R. Bunim once reprimanded a *sheliah tzibbur* for crying so much that he forgot the words of the Yom Kippur prayers. As was explained, the danger with crying (as with fasting) is that one confuses the medium with the message. One gets mixed up between the goal (*teshuvah*) and what is purely a mechanism (fasting or crying).[33]

There was a similarly negative approach to *kavvanot* (kabbalistic intentions). Once R. Bunim asked someone to blow the *shofar* (the ram's horn) on Rosh Hashanah, but before he did so he began to engage in "intentions" to help him to be in the right mode for the blowing. However, preparation is something that is done beforehand, not when the community is ready to blow the *shofar*. R. Bunim said to him "Look what is written in the order between the blowing: *shin bet*. This alludes to *"Shoteh, bloys"* – 'Idiot, blow!'"[34]

The time of prayer became a *casus belli* for the opponents of Przysucha because they saw quite correctly that, in that crucial area which Hasidism had made its own, namely prayer, the issue was whether personal authenticity alone would function as the determining factor. Delaying the time of prayer because of one's personal readiness, or lack of it, was the one area in which all three generations of Przysucha broke the law. Though they tried to justify their behavior halakhically,[35] the fact remains that it was their one area of antinomianism. Perhaps one of the dangers perceived by the others was that this sort of behavior would extend to other areas. Not being punctilious over the times of prayer extended for the Yehudi to the time of blowing the shofar.[36] Was there a danger entailed in everyone taking the rules into their own hands in order to be authentic? Certainly, the Yehudi's contemporaries were highly disturbed.[37]

---

[32] *Hashavah le-Tovah*, par. Terumah, 28.

[33] On *"frumkeit"* and "groundedness," see chapter 9.

[34] *Siah Sarfei Kodesh he-Hadash*, vol. 1, *Rosh ha-Shanah*, 187.

[35] *Kol Mevaser*, 2:179–180.

[36] The essential idea is to be found in *Sha'arei Aryeh*, 64 §8 *(Torat ha-Yehudi*, 89).

[37] Regarding R. Bunim, see *Siah Sarfei Kodesh*, 1:53 §249.

This behavior of the Yehudi aroused criticism even from R. Yisrael, the Maggid of Kozienice,[38] who was positively disposed towards him. On the issue of delaying prayer he is reported to have been angry at the Yehudi. Those less well disposed towards the Yehudi had fewer qualms and were openly critical:

> A person once came to a certain zaddik for help in a state of distress, asking him to pray for him. The zaddik asked him what Rebbe he usually visited. When the person replied, "The Yehudi," the zaddik said that if he would, from now on, accept upon himself not to delay the times of prayer, then certainly salvation would shortly come.[39]

One of the Yehudi's main opponents, R. Yehuda Leib of Zelechów, pulled no punches:

> There is a simple approach in the service of the Creator to do each mitzvah as it should be done, to pray with the community and in its time... that is the way of the righteous. But there is an alternative approach, namely, not to always pray with the community and sometimes to delay prayer in order to pray with the intention of hubris and the like. And these are called genuine acts of the wicked.[40]

One of the ways of blunting religious radicalism is to argue that it is fitting only for an exceptional person, or for the exceptional few, but not as the norm. Some of the Yehudi's antagonists[41] and those of later generations might certainly have believed that, possibly out of piety. But the Yehudi and R. Bunim[42] would have rejected this. The Yehudi was promoting a definite approach, not something limited to him alone. Later generations (within

---

[38] *Nifla'ot ha-Yehudi*, 64; *Tiferet ha-Yehudi*, 160 §29; *Mikhtevei Teuda*, 17; *Tiferet ha-Yehudi*, 172 §80.

[39] *Nifla'ot ha-Yehudi*, 83.

[40] *Likkutei Maharil*, par. Bereshit; Rabinowitz, *The Yehudi*, 103–104.

[41] *Tiferet ha-Yehudi*, 142 §2.

[42] Typical of this approach is the addition in *Siah Sarfei Kodesh*, vol. 5, p. 45 (end). "The above is true for the great righteous zaddikim who would prepare a lot before prayer; and preparation and the commandment are one in the same. But we orphans of orphans, who only prepare a little before prayer, are not allowed to transgress the time (of prayer), Heaven forbid."

Przysucha) tried to tone down this radicalism and argued that the delaying of the times of prayer only applied to exceptional personalities of earlier generations. But that sort of argument was part of the retrogression that set in after the Kotzker died.

Describing R. Bunim's philosophy of prayer, *Keter Kehunnah* says the following:

> He angered the old guard [by saying] that a person wasn't a machine ready and prepared to function... that it diminished the glory of God to think that He stood as if with a watch to see if a Jew had fulfilled to the moment and to the hour what was placed upon him... and that He expressed displeasure if there was delay in bringing a thanksgiving offering or in seeking His mercies.[43]

The author of *Keter Kehunnah* was an "enlightened Jew" (a *maskil*) who had an agenda of his own. Nevertheless the essential idea rings true. The implications of the place of honor given to preparation and to the world of the heart go beyond the simple question of delaying the time for prayer until one is ready, for to be "ready" assumes a frame of mind, a context of consciousness. This approach might entail doing things that would be simply incomprehensible, if not downright sacrilegious, to someone who either did not understand or did not share this concern for personal preparation. Przysucha Hasidism is thoroughly grounded in reality. It is too earthy to entertain the hubris of using such grandiose terms as "emanations" and "contractions" (which come with kabbalistic jargon). For Przysucha hasidim, one needed to start with basics, that is to say, to enter into a state of consciousness even if that might entail dismissing social or religious niceties.

We thus find the following description of the hasidim of Przysucha in prayer in *Keter Kehunnah*:

> In the main, they sat in the study houses of the *mitnaggedim* and, in spite of their displeasure, during prayer, they smoked a pipe. They paid no attention when the leader reached Kedushah or Barechu...

---

[43] *Keter Kehunnah*, 128–129.

They said the morning prayers after midday and stood with tallit and tefillin, with holy emotion, for only a few moments.[44]

There is something anarchic in the psyche of such a totally individualistic service. To smoke during prayer, in front of others, with no apparent sense of awe of the Almighty, let alone a sense of respect for religious decorum, strikes other people as downright provocative. But it all makes perfect sense if one assumes that the phrase of the rabbis, "God wants the heart" or the phrase "prayer is the service of the heart" is taken literally, in the most intimate way. Under this condition only the heart alone can determine the how, and when. This sort of behavior might be seen as self-indulgent, but it can also be seen as an expression of a world that is confident in its own religious identity without having to justify its credentials (at least to itself). Inevitably, therefore, we find that the hasidim of Przysucha did not pray with a quorum. The continuation in *Keter Kehunnah* reads:

> And if they have a special place (to pray) they don't pray there in a quorum, but rather when they are alone.[45]

This description strikes us as being correct, not just for the internal reason, as described above, but because hasidic tradition says something similar:

> R. Bunim warned the hasidim that on the eighth day (of the Festival of Tabernacles) they should all pray together. By this, they would correct all the prayers that had been prayed individually.[46]

The issue of delaying the time of prayer was one of the arguments used by the opponents of the Yehudi during his lifetime.[47] Those who opposed the Yehudi with regards to delaying the time of prayer continued this opposition with his pupil R. Bunim. But by then, Przysucha's opponents had bigger fish to fry and the kid gloves had been taken off.

---

[44] *Keter Kehunnah*, 129. One cannot rule out the possibility that part of this description projects Zederbaum's own agenda.

[45] Ibid.

[46] *Hiddushei ha-Rim*, 268.

[47] For sources justifying the delaying of prayer see *Kol Mevaser*, 2:179–180; *Siah Sarfei Kodesh*, 1:53 §249; *Torat Simhah*, §322; Rabinowitz, "R. Bunim," 26; see also *Torat ha-Yehudi*, 333, notes.

There is another element that needs to be added to this discussion. The kabbalist has a map with rules and regulations. He must make sure that his thinking and intention correspond in an exact way – via unification, combination or numerical value – to a specific structure which has cosmic significance. He has an intricate and involved manual that he must navigate with trepidation. If done incorrectly, it could create a cataclysmic crisis. For the kabbalist, therefore, preparation before prayer includes "getting it right." But in Przysucha there is no Kabbalah. Remove the mystical roadmap and one is left alone as an individual needing to make one's own solitary path towards the Divine. Instead of preparation focusing on the esoteric, it now focuses on a person's consciousness. The process is thoroughly anthropocentric. There is no "getting it right." There is only man's frail attempt to come a little closer.

As we have said, Przysucha is a fusion of two worlds: the world of Talmud study – i.e., the cognitive, as expressed by the *mitnaggedim*, and the world of prayer – the experiential – as expressed by the hasidim. Hence it should not surprise us if we encounter statements in the world of Przysucha that extol the value of learning *Gemara* above all else. This may be because any other approach in the service of God is potentially subject to delusion. But there might be a more nuanced understanding. The inner world, the quality of being, appears nebulous, whereas studying Talmud is something that seems to be tangible. What is happening inside oneself is far more difficult to gauge. What has one achieved? How can one measure it?[48] Yet it is the most real thing. Ultimately, for R. Bunim, tranquility of the soul, inner peace, does not come from some body of knowledge – not even from learning Torah. It comes from intimacy with the Divine, and intimacy with the Divine is another word for prayer.

Extraneous Thoughts during Prayer

One of the issues that occupied the founders of Hasidism was what to do with extraneous thoughts that enter one's mind during prayer. The literature detailing the hasidic-mitnaggedic polemic also includes accusations against

---

[48] See *Meir Einei ha-Golah* 2:109.

the doctrine of "elevation of strange thoughts" during prayer.[49] Because prayer was perceived by them as the oxygen of the soul, anything that detracted from this intimacy was of major concern for them. It has been noted that, in the compendium *Sefer Ba'al Shem Tov al ha-Torah*, the number of aphorisms on the subject of extraneous thoughts exceeds all others, with the exception of those dealing with prayer itself.[50]

The Ba'al Shem Tov is quoted as teaching a number of techniques for dealing with alien thoughts.

1. Ownership

One approach is what might be described as taking ownership: that is, that a person asks himself why this thought has occurred specifically to him:

> Therefore when a person stands in prayer or is involved in Torah, extraneous thoughts stand to confuse him. For the extraneous thoughts are his sins, and they stand before him to do battle. But their intention is that he should rectify them and take them out from the depths of the husks, and this via his trembling, when he senses that they are his sins, and he is distressed on account of them.[51]

2. The Cosmos

Recognizing that there are holy sparks in alien thoughts which need to be liberated and elevated.

> There is nothing in the created world that does not contain holy sparks that need to be purified.... There is a cosmic need for the work of human beings to rectify and purify them and to raise them from level to level... for a person has the ability to return the holiness of the spark.[52]

---

[49] See Mordechai l. Wilensky, *Hasidic-Mitnaggedic Polemics in the Jewish Communities of Eastern Europe: The Hostile Phase* (Hundert "Essential Papers," n. 7).

[50] M. Kallus, "An Examination of the Term 'Thought' in the Teachings of the Besht, and His Thought Transformation Practices." Paper delivered at the AJS Conference, 2001. I have drawn upon his ideas and copied some of his translations. See also Yehuda Yifrach, "The Elevation of Foreign Thoughts in the Tradition of R. Israel Baal Shem Tov," MA thesis, Bar Ilan University: 2007.

[51] *Sefer Ba'al Shem Tov*, 203 §109.

[52] Ibid., 217–218, §116.

3. Divine Providence

It is believed that extraneous thoughts came to a person in the first place via Divine providence, and that this was not coincidental, but significant, and that a person must be responsible for them:

> When at the time of prayer, an unseemly or distracting thought occurs to a person, (he should realize that) it came to him in order that he rectify it and raise it up.... There is not a single thought which does not have the entire cosmic structure present within it – even an evil thought that comes to a person in order to be repaired and raised up. But if the person casts the destructive thought away, it is as if he has cast away and killed an entire cosmic structure.[53]

This entire approach of the Besht stands in stark contrast to that of the kabbalist. The kabbalist, prior to the Besht, advocated "either the forced dismissal of negative thoughts, or the counteraction by the recitation of scriptural verses, or the contemplation of Divine Names that erase the effect of the thought."[54]

But R. Bunim's approach is different from that of the Besht. We have a tradition in the name of R. Bunim on this very topic, and it rings true to what we know about his general outlook on life.

> I heard from my master from Przysucha that once he heard, through a wall, someone praying with a lot of strength, and he understood with his wisdom that the person was making an effort to remove strange thoughts. He waited for him until after his prayer, and asked him why he made such a commotion during prayer. He remained silent, and didn't answer. And my master, because he understood that this was because of strange thoughts, said to him, "My son, let me give you some advice – listen to me and it will be good for you. When a strange thought comes to you, such as a horse, or a similar thing, do not reject it; but rather, settle your mind and clarify whether there is a horse, or something similar. For in truth, there is nothing there; and through this, the thoughts will be annulled."

---

[53] Ibid.

[54] Kallus, ibid., 3. Though the Besht argues that there are times when "thoughts come to a person that should be cast away."

What is R. Bunim's approach to extraneous thoughts during prayer? Our understanding of this piece shows that, unlike the Besht, he is not concerned with redeeming "holy sparks." Nor it is necessary to always take ownership or to give thought some significance, and definitely not to fight it like the kabbalists. Rather, one should look at it for what it is, and in that way it may simply evaporate. R. Bunim does not attribute any cosmic significance to extraneous thoughts; he does not see them as traumatic. Unlike the Besht, "thought" does not necessarily have any significance for R. Bunim. The way to deal with these thoughts – this interference – is to take them for what they are; to look at them and realize that there is in fact no "horse" – it was a mirage. Then the thought will simply dissolve.

THE REACTION AGAINST
PRZYSUCHA

> I am traveling to Kozienice, and the hasidim of Kozienice say that
> one should make a blessing every day: [Blessed be He] who did
> not make me a Hasid of Przysucha.
>
> Hiddushei ha-Rim

The Reaction against Przysucha

IN THE YEAR 1822,[1] an attempt was made to excommunicate Przysucha
from the world of Hasidism. Within the lifetime of the Yehudi,[2] there were
deep tensions between Przysucha and the wider Hasidic world, and over the
course of time they became increasingly exacerbated. After the death of the
Seer an attempt was made by the leaders of Polish Hasidism to rein in R.
Bunim and when that failed, the entire leadership of Polish Hasidism
erupted into a public melee – a concerted attempt to excommunicate
Przysucha as a movement in general and R. Bunim, its leader, in particular.

Hasidic sources relate the following tradition:

> On Tisha be-Av, after midday, in the year 1820, on the anniversary
> of the Seer's death, many of the hasidic leaders of Poland gathered
> together to create a plan against Przysucha which, according to many
> of them, had deviated from the accepted path. Witnesses, who

---

[1] This date is based on the tradition (*Meir Einei ha-Golah*, §155) that R. Eliezer Baer,
the spokesman for the Przysucha delegation, died shortly after the event because of
his rudeness to the Rebbe of Apta.

[2] See *Meir Einei ha-Golah*, §§81–86; Boem, 521–525.

appeared in the eyes of the assembled as reliable, spoke exaggeratedly about the atrocious behavior of the pupils of Przysucha, which was reaching levels of unrestrained [rejection] of all norms of social behavior, with neither fear of Heaven nor fear of sin. Some gave evidence against the hasidim of Przysucha, stating that they treated the obligation of laying tefillin lightly. Others gave testimony about actions that bordered on the desecration of the Sabbath and requested to "permit their blood," to view them as people who were lawless to whom one must apply the principle of "We push them [into the pit] and do not bring them up." Some suggested that they impose a grievous ban of excommunication. Those assembled were unable to reach an agreement and they decided to await another opportunity.[3]

The occasion was not late in coming. In 1822, at the famous Hasidic wedding in Austila where there was a gathering of hasidic notables, an attempt was made to remove Przysucha from the family of Hasidism once and for all.

The main arguments leveled against R. Bunim and Przysucha are known to us through the citations of three groupings of primary sources. To begin with, R. Yitzhak Meir (Hiddushei ha-Rim), one of the main protagonists at the wedding in 1822 and, one could safely assume, somewhat biased in favor of Przysucha, is quoted in *Meir Einei ha-Golah*.[4] The second source is from R. Zvi Eliezer Harlap[5] of Tiktin, a *mitnagged,* who for the most part can be assumed to have stood somewhat apart from the fray. Finally, there are various works by the Hasidic opponents of R. Bunim such as R. Meir of Apta, who was the heir to the throne of the Seer,[6] and R. Yehudah Leib of Zelechów.[7] Regarding these sources we would do well to assume a certain degree of prejudice against Przysucha.[8]

---

[3] See Y.L. Levin, *Sefer Alexander* (1969), 21; cf. *Meir Einei ha-Golah,* §86.

[4] This seems to be the most reliable version; cf. Aescoly, *Hasidut be-Folin,* ed. David Assaf, 84 §17, Jerusalem: 1999. *Meir Einei ha-Golah* was written by his grandson.

[5] On R. Zvi Eliezer Harlap, see note 12.

[6] R. Meir of Apta. See Rabinowitz, *From Lublin to Przysucha,* 381–382.

[7] *Likkutei Maharil.* See *From Lublin to Przysucha,* 277.

[8] The value of vitriolic language is that, by discounting courtesies, it reveals what the opponent is really thinking.

ॐ ঔ

This first citation is a description, from R. Yitzhak Meir (Hiddushei ha-Rim), of what happened at the wedding as reported in *Meir Einei ha-Golah:*

> When the opponents of R. Bunim saw the honor given to our teacher and his companions, by the Apter, they were very angry and they decided to arraign their case in public… to excommunicate R. Bunim and all those that followed him. [The case was as follows]: They have departed from the way of Hasidism, they speak falsely and ridicule all the zaddikim[9] and their students; they are lenient concerning a number of forbidden things; they delay the time of prayer until after mid-day; they have almost ceased to learn the revealed Torah [the Oral Law]; every day is a festival for them; they eat, drink, sing, and dance; and because of this Hasidism has become a joke and a derision amongst the ordinary people, so that God is disgraced."[10]

The same work goes on to reports that:

> There were some who slandered the hasidim of Przysucha [saying that] they were not careful to keep explicit laws in the Shulhan Arukh; they were lenient publicly in not fasting on the four fast days; they do not wait the fixed time between milk and meat."[11]

The following quote is from the correspondence between R. Zvi Eliezer Harlap[12] and R. Bunim.[13] In a letter written by R. Harlap to R. Bunim, he states, inter alia, that R. Bunim should use his influence on his hasidim:

---

[9] *Meir Einei ha-Golah,* §140.

[10] *Meir Einei ha-Golah,* §150; also §138–163.

[11] *Meir Einei ha-Golah,* §86.

[12] R. Zvi Hirsh Eliezer Harlap was an outstanding Talmudic scholar, quoted with effusive praise in the *Gilyon ha-Shas* on the *Yerushalmi Terumot,* end of Chapter One, and in the *Bi'ur Halakha* of Rabbi Israel Meir of Radin, *Orah Hayyim* 27:9. He was Rabbi of Tiktin-Bialystock and later of Mezerich. He clashed with the Kotzker's hasidim as well; see *Siah Sarfei Kodesh he-Hadash,* 3:171 n. 17.

[13] This letter was copied by his nephew. The copy consists of some thirty-six closely-written pages and is today in the possession of Rabbi Zevulun Sacks of Jerusalem. Rabbi Sacks is the grandson of R. Moshe Yaacov Harlap, who showed the letter to Zvi Meir Rabinowitz (see his *R. Bunim,* 33 §12). Rabinowitz copied

To submit before Torah scholars, so that they may suck from the breasts of Torah the discussions of Abbaye and Rava, via whose words we walk; and not to depart, neither to the left nor to the right, from the traditional laws of the Rabbis and from the Shulhan Arukh. Horror has taken hold of us; they do not honor one another, the young dishonor the old and think it meritorious to give them nicknames. The hasidim of Przysucha openly transgress the laws of the Shulhan Arukh; they shoot barbed arrows to dishonor scholars. All the scholars of the Gemara are in their opinion of no consequence. On the seventeenth of Tammuz they eat while it is yet day, and on the ninth of Av mourning has become joyous.

R. Bunim replies very courteously but, as we will discuss later, does not respond to the criticism in any substantive way:

His [honor's] voice, a powerful voice hewing flames, walking between stones of fire, has been heard and understood by my ears, a clear reproach [and a hidden love]. Dear are the wounds of the lover of God and His holy Torah, let a righteous man strike me with reproach even more. I know that he speaks not from jealousy nor enmity, but rather from flames of fire of God that are in his midst with the love of perfect knowledge – the torch of God.[14] [H]is wisdom and awe and his great knowledge: my ear has heard from the mouth of... R. Yitzhak of Lublin and also from his honor the Gaon, the teacher Ya'acov Yitzhak, the Yehudi... who hardly moved from his love, and his praise was continuously in his mouth. Therefore my

---

some ten lines from these thirty-six pages, from which I have translated these excerpts. Rabbi Sacks told me that R. Moshe Yaacov Harlap expressed a dying wish not to publish the letter because it was so critical of certain named individuals. I have glanced very briefly at the thirty-six pages and can confirm the genuineness of Rabinowitz's quotations.

The letter is dated 1826 and not, as claimed by Boem (628–629), between 1822 and 1824, relating its context to governmental investigations into Hasidism. More important, it implies that the criticisms of Przysucha did not abate after the attempt to excommunicate it in 1822 (assuming that date is reliable). By implication, therefore, it suggests that the radical behavior of Przysucha had in no way mellowed.

[14] R. Bunim is referring to the greatness of R. Harlap, of which he had heard from the Seer and the Yehudi.

spirit has kept his honor's command and perhaps I can achieve more, and so for the sake of His Holy Name and his love as my heart; and love covers all sins; and peace be with his honor and his Torah.[15]

The third category consists of various sources from R. Bunim's hasidic contemporaries. These are the most vitriolic and personal.

- R. Yehuda Leib of Zekilkov's criticism which has been previously mentioned:

  There is an alternative approach (to conventional prayer), which is not always to pray with the community and sometimes to delay prayer in order to pray with the intention of hubris and similar such matters. And this is called genuine acts of the wicked.[16]

- R. Meir of Apta said:

  A man should not seek greater understanding than his station, even if his intentions are pure; [rather] he should clarify and purify the first [steps].[17]

He sent the following message to R. Bunim:

They say of R. Bunim of Przysucha that he is a very wise man. Tell your Rebbe in my name that I ask from God the request mentioned by Moses... that is to say... Give me mind and understanding, but only from your book; that the understanding and elevation should come from learning Torah, but not from business activities and the theatre in Danzig."[18]

---

[15] *Torat Simhah*, 148–149. For an analysis of R. Bunim's reply, see below. Noteworthy is the fact that R. Bunim describes the Yehudi as "Gaon" but doesn't use that term for the Seer.

[16] *Likkutei Maharil*, par. *Bereshit* (Lvov, 1862). The Maharil had been an opponent of the Yehudi as well; see *Or Simhah*, §47.

[17] *Or le-Shamayim*, par. Shemot, 70. Re R. Meir of Apta's opposition to R. Bunim, see, e.g., *Torat Simhah*, §249.

[18] *Meir Einei ha-Golah*, §99.

- The nature of the relationship between Hiddushei ha-Rim (R. Yitzhak Meir) and R. Moishe of Kozienice is discussed in another portion of the book.[19] Hiddushei ha-Rim relates the following anecdote: that, while he was still a young hasid in Kozienice, he said:

> I am traveling to Kozienice, and the hasidim of Kozienice say that one should make a blessing: "Blessed be He who did not make me a hasid of Przysucha."[20]

From this quip one can gauge the level of animosity between Przysucha and its opponents.

- R. Zvi Elimelech of Dinov wrote:

> A pupil who wishes to progress should not behave in a way which contradicts any law from our holy Torah – for example, to transgress the times for reading the Shema or the times for prayer fixed by the Rabbis. Even though some people, clever in their own opinion, might entice you, saying that one should wait until one feels the beautiful abundance of expanded consciousness, you should know, my beloved, that this is the advice of the evil impulse.[21]

As mentioned,[22] an incident that occurred at the wedding in Austila involving a silken belt (a talisman from the Rebbe of Apta) that had been smeared with black paint was referred to. The delegation sent by R. Bunim to defend Przysucha was quick to rebut these accusations. But in spite of their denials, one wonders whether the lady does not protest too much, as the incident is consistent with what we know about the disposition of Przysucha, namely that the followers of R. Bunim, as a matter of principle, trampled the social norms of reverence and respect that were assumed within the hasidic world. Irreverence, or challenging authority, was by no means some anarchical impulse rumbling within Przysucha; rather, it flowed from the first principle of authenticity.[23] [24]

---

[19] See Chapter 12.

[20] *Meir Einei ha-Golah,* §89.

[21] *Derekh Pikudekha,* negative commandment §16.

[22] See chap. 1. *Meir Einei ha-Golah,* §151; also, §§141, 150.

[23] Boem, 524–525.

[24] *Ramatayim Zofim* (AZ), chap. 4, §118.

The second type of argument that runs throughout these sources is that the hasidim of Przysucha are lax about various rabbinic laws codified in the *Shulhan Arukh*. The world of Przysucha was not in fact antinomian, and was, by and large[25] halakhically observant. However, at times their philosophy of "purity of motive" resulted in the concealment of piety as a matter of principle. An outsider was liable to arrive at a diametrically opposite understanding of what the hasidim of Przysucha were in fact doing (and such was precisely their intention). Przysucha was not interested in outside approval; it was in fact antagonistic to it. This might easily have been misinterpreted by a *mitnagged* such as R. Harlap as sacrilegious behavior when in fact it was an educational methodology.

As a point of fact, it was absurd to accuse Przysucha of not learning Talmud or Rabbinics.[26] If there is one movement in Polish Hasidism which asserted the primacy of the value of learning, it was Przysucha. But to learn for some ulterior motive and to be seen to be learning (to be pious because one longed for approval) was something to be avoided. Accusations about not keeping the laws of ritual purity[27] or not being particular about waiting between meat and milk[28] must either be understood in the above context or seen simply as examples of slander used to achieve the goal of de-legitimizing Przysucha within the world of Hasidism.

The argument about not keeping the fasts is more interesting, since we know that R. Bunim played down the significance of fasting. Moreover, we know that in Kotzk,[29] even on the eve of The Day of Atonement, the hasidim behaved in a deliberately provocative way in order to bring themselves to internalize the first principle of why they were fasting in the first place; to push the motive to the edge of clarity. Namely, was it for God's sake? – and to hell with what anybody else thought.

The hasidim of Przysucha were accused of not keeping the four annual fasts properly. As we have mentioned, the following is written in *Keter Kehunnah*:

---

[25] See below note 31.

[26] *Siah Sarfei Kodesh he-Hadash,* 4: 170 §19.

[27] *Meir Einei ha-Golah,* §86.

[28] See S. Bergamintz, "*Ha-sarid ha-aharon le-hasidei Kotzk,*" in *Digleinu* (1927).

[29] *Keter Kehunnah,* 129.

They said, "All the fasts have lost their credibility except for the Day of Atonement. As for the Ninth of Av, it is a matter which still has to be decided." Therefore, every year on the Fast of Gedalya, in the morning they ate a hot bagel while the community was reciting prayers of supplication.[30] [31]

These accusations stemmed, in the main, from a deep-seated clash of philosophies – a fundamental misunderstanding of Przysucha's objectives. Przysucha's opponents had in a fundamental way confused the medium with the message.

ॐ ॐ

As we stated earlier, the one area in which Przysucha broke the rules of halakhah was the delay in the time for prayers. This was acknowledged during the lifetime of the Yehudi: For Przysucha the supreme value of authenticity overruled Jewish law here in regard to the time of prayers.

To all the above, must be added a certain innate suspicion of R. Bunim as an outsider. He did not come from a hasidic background; his business activities had taken him to the West; he had, for whatever reason, participated in its culture, dressed accordingly, and was concerned with assimilated Jews. He was interested in medieval Jewish philosophy. He was fluent in a number of languages and last, but not least, had a secular profession.[32]

What was never stated, but was perhaps the underlying cause for the animosity to R. Bunim, was the fact that the hasidic leadership was involved in a power struggle with him, for it was he who, by dint of his wisdom and

---

[30] See above Aescoly, 80; *Or Simhah* §36; *Keter Kehunnah*, 128.

[31] In "The Fluidity of Categories in Hasidism" (*Hasidism Reappraised*, 319 [9]), Yehoshua Mondshine says: "For Hasidic departures from the strict rule of Halakhah see Kamelhar, *Dor de'ah*, the chapter dedicated to R. Simhah Bunem of Przyshcha, where the author condemns the 'Hasidic digressions' from the rule of halakhah in no uncertain terms. However, his condemnations were omitted from subsequent editions of the work, largely as a result of the remarks by R. Meir Jehiel Halevi of Ostrowiec, to the effect that Przyshcha hasidim had long abandoned the practice of 'digression' and were now toeing the line advocated by R. Isaac Meir of Gur, urging a return to the full rigour of the *Shulhan Arukh*. See on this Y. Mondshine, *Ha-zofeh le-doro* (Jerusalem: 1987), 243–244."

[32] On all this, see chapter 3.

organizational abilities, had made Przysucha into a formidable movement. It was R. Bunim who attracted the intellectual and spiritual cream of Polish hasidic Jewry, and it was R. Bunim who created alternative centers throughout Poland, which bore allegiance, not to the local hasidic rebbe, but rather to R. Bunim himself. The difference between R. Bunim and the Yehudi may perhaps be understood by analogy to that between the Maggid and the Besht. The Yehudi, by force of his charisma, intellect, and piety, started Przysucha, but it was R. Bunim who organized, strengthened, and disseminated its values that now posed a challenge for the dominant role in Polish Hasidism.[33]

There may be a further factor that led to the enmity between Przysucha and other types of Hasidism in Poland. The Seer was regarded by his disciples in messianic terms. There was thus a certain analogy to the line of David, including the expectation that the Seer's son, R. Yosele, would continue his dynasty, even though that didn't happen. As R. Yehuda Leib of Zelechów, one of the Yehudi's antagonists, put it:[34]

> When a righteous person establishes a son who is righteous, his work is not interrupted, for it is as if he did not die and did not depart from this world, for the power of the father is in the son. Thus, when the son performs a service and it is accepted by God, it is as if the father himself is still performing his service without interruption.[35]

Finally, attention should also be drawn to the nature of R. Bunim's defense, specifically, to the letter that he sent in response to R. Harlap. There is no ideological discussion or justification of his position, nor does he try to deflect criticism by attributing excessive behavior to hasidim who might have misunderstood his educational message. There is tremendous significance, not only in what is said, but also in what is not said. R. Bunim doesn't back down on any ideological principle: his compass of integrity remains

---

[33] Boem, 523.

[34] *Likkutei Maharil*, par. *Vayera*, 4b; interestingly enough, it was R. Meir of Apta who wore the mantle of leadership of the Seer and not R. Yossele, the Seer's son.

[35] *Tiferet ha-Yehudi* 177, n. 95, suggests that an additional factor was the role played by R. Bunim in getting the Yehudi to break with the Seer. This too played its part.

steadfast.[36] What we do have is a letter of deference, of respect, acknowledging the passion and concern of the one making the critique – but no more. As for the criticism of R. Meir of Apta[37] that R. Bunim had learned alien wisdom from the West, R. Bunim made no excuses. He replied with a totally authentic response, which reflected his own world:[38]

> He is a holy man from his youth and doesn't know how people sin. When people come to him, how can he know what they lack? I have been in Danzig, in the theatre, and I well know the essence of the sinner. When I come home and see a crooked tree, I cut and prune it on all sides to make it erect like a plank, and then I put into it a holy soul.[39]

The attack against Przysucha was essentially internal, not external. It was led by other hasidic groups and not by the *mitnaggedim* (just as Przysucha's critique was aimed within the hasidic family). But by and large, their criticisms are but a précis of the original polemics against Hasidism made by the *mitnaggedim* during the second half of the eighteenth century. Wilensky says the following:

> In its proclamation of 1781, the community of Sluck claims that the hasidim allowed shaharit, the morning prayer, to continue "until midday." In Zemir Aritzim, R. David of Makow accuses the hasidim of Kozienice and Lublin of reciting minhah, the afternoon prayer, after the stars have already appeared. R. Hayyim of Volozhin in his Nefesh ha-Hayyim criticizes this new custom, whereby "… they have almost forgotten the time for the afternoon prayers which was determined by the rabbis of blessed memory." In his book Sefer

---

[36] With all the respect bestowed by R. Bunim on R. Harlap, a letter of thirty-six closely-written pages elicited a response of only eight lines. But cf. *Siah Sarfei Kodesh*, 1:117, §614 for a slight retraction.

[37] Regarding R. Meir of Apta's opposition to R. Bunim see *Siah Sarfei Kodesh*, vol. 3, 93 §309.

[38] *Or Simhah*, §43.

[39] On R. Bunim's perception of hatred and dissension, see *Siah Sarfei Kodesh*, 4, 39 §5; *Siah Sarfei Kodesh*, 3:134 §505.

Vikuah, R. Israel Loebel maintains that hasidim "tell stories and gossip and obscenities among themselves before prayer and consequently are late in beginning to pray."

Wilensky mentions the criticism of the Hasidim for their irreverent behavior, such as doing somersaults in public, which they justified on the basis that "when a man is afflicted with pride, he must roll himself over." However, he argues that the wrath of the *mitnaggedim* was because "the new sect caused neglect of Torah studying and disrespect for Torah scholars."

> When the leader of the Vilna hasidim, Meir ben Rafael, was summoned by a special committee to account for his membership in the hasidic sect, he was asked, "Why did you ridicule, insult, and belittle scholars and students of Torah?"

In a letter to R. Levi Yitzhak of Berdyczew:

> R. Katzenellenbogen voiced strong opposition to the members of the sect "who despised the Oral Law and think of the Talmud commentators as nothing and are contemptuous of them."[40]

How ironic all this is! What was originally a polemic of the *mitnaggedim* against Hasidism, is now being leveled – almost word for word – by the hasidic establishment itself against Przysucha. The revolution has now become staid and evinces the same insecurity and fear as any other establishment. *Plus ça change, plus c'est la même chose.*

Hasidic tradition too has preserved reports of those who were critical of R. Bunim's leadership.

> When he led the community following the death of his teacher, the Holy Yehudi, people drew near to him with such passion that they abandoned themselves and were not concerned with providing for their families. Because of this, his reputation fell in the eyes of the ordinary people who opposed him more than other zaddikim of his generation. But the more they persecuted him, the more people

---

[40] Mordechai Wilensky. "Hasidic and Mitnaggedic Polemics in the Jewish Communities of Eastern Europe, The Hostile Phase No. 7." In *Essential Papers on Hasidism Origins to Present,* edited by Gershon David Hundert, 244–271. New York: 1991.

drew near to him. And once, an outstanding young man came to be with him; and his father-in-law journeyed after him, and he came before R. Bunim rudely and said, "You are corrupting people of excellence, for through… being with you, they cast off everything else. And you say that you teach them the fear of Heaven! Don't we have the book Reshit Hokhmah and the Rokeah? What's written in these books is more than what you are!"[41]

One is reminded of Solomon Maimon's depiction of the Maggid's hasidim, in which he bemoans the fact that young people forsook parents, wives, and children and went en masse to visit these leaders and hear the new doctrine from their lips.[42]

అం అం

The real criticism of Przysucha was the one which was not stated, and could not be stated. Positing authenticity as the supreme value opened the hasidic establishment itself, the rebbes et al., to the focus of criticism. But such a criticism could not be articulated by the disciples of the Seer and R. Elimelech, for they could not criticize the value of being honest, nor would they want to admit the problem. Therefore what was crucial was what was not stated – namely, that the value of being honest inevitably meant that the hasidic world too was put under the microscope.

Przysucha demanded that a person be honest about himself. For those with an introspective character, this must have been hypnotic. But for many others, and particularly their leaders, it must have been the greatest threat a person could face – or else something totally incomprehensible. The consequence of such a service is of course to weaken and possibly to destroy any hierarchy. The hasidic world could not accept these values without admitting its own shortcomings.

అం అం

R. Bunim was invited to the wedding in Austila (circa 1822). Although he[43] knew what awaited him, nevertheless he quite typically intended to go to the

---

[41] *Or Simhah,* §36.

[42] See S. Maimon, "On a Secret Society." In Hundert, *Essential Papers,* 20.

[43] *Meir Einei ha-Golah,* §150.

wedding and argue his case. Ultimately, his pupil Menachem Mendel of Kotzk insisted that R. Bunim not go[44] and a delegation was sent on his behalf to debate the issues. Hiddushei ha-Rim, then a young man who served as part of this delegation, has preserved the fullest version of what then took place. Interspersed between the "teachings" of the Rebbe of Apta, a public debate erupted between the opponents of Przysucha and its proponents, involving accusations and counter-accusations. It is interesting to note that, throughout the various stages of the debate for and against Przysucha, no substantive issues of ideology were raised or discussed. What was taking place was essentially a discussion of the religious credentials of Przysucha in general and of R. Bunim in particular. There was no verbal shootout, no climax. Rather, as time went on the opponents of Przysucha were discredited.[45] If there was a critical moment, it was when the Rebbe of Apta turned to R. Yerahmiel,[46] the oldest son of the Yehudi, and asked his father's opinion of R. Bunim.[47] Turning to R. Yerahmiel was particularly sensitive since relations between R. Bunim and R. Yerahmiel, both of whom had centers (courts) in the town of Przysucha, were strained. This was therefore a critical moment. R. Yerahmiel is quoted as saying that his father, the Yehudi, stated that R. Bunim was the "apple of his eye" and that he (the Yehudi) had deposited a treasure of the fear of heaven into his beloved R. Bunim. With this statement, endorsing R. Bunim in the name of the Yehudi, the debate ended, with Przysucha victorious.

The Differences between R. Bunim, the Yehudi and the Kotzker

There are at least two areas in which there appear to be major differences between the Yehudi and R. Bunim – asceticism and style of prayer. Interestingly enough, in one such case Menahem Mendel of Kotzk is closer

---

[44] Ibid., §144.

[45] Ibid., §§150, 154.

[46] Ibid., §153. The fact that the Rebbe of Apta turned to R. Yerahmiel to clarify what his father thought of R. Bunim suggests that the Yehudi's integrity was never questioned and that any criticism or misgiving that one might have had of the Yehudi and his approach was overridden by his exceptional reputation.

[47] *Meir Einei ha-Golah*, §86.

to R. Bunim, and in the other he is closer to the Yehudi. Regarding the asceticism of the Yehudi, it is related that:

> Once our Rabbi ate some bread and borsht after prayer and he imagined that he had pleasure from the food, and he accepted upon himself punishment.[48]

Even if we presume some degree of exaggeration, the tone, the perception is nevertheless clear. This is confirmed by another incident related by his son.

> He (R. Nechemiah) told him that once during the winter his father journeyed to the holy R. Menahem Mendel of Rimanov, taking his son R. Yerahmiel with him. During the journey they lost the way and traveled all night. In the morning, at the break of dawn, they continued on the main road, and close to midday they came to a village where the Yehudi knew someone who had an inn. When they came in, our holy teacher prepared himself for prayer and his holy son prayed in another room. After praying, because he was very weak, the holy R. Yerahmiel took a potato and threw it into the oven and quickly took it and ate it. While doing so, our holy teacher opened the door of his room, called him, and said to his son, "All night long we were lost and journeyed until midday and now thank God we have arrived at the settlement. Is this your 'settling of the mind,' to eat quickly and lustfully?" He punished him, not allowing him inside the carriage but making him stand outside on the platform, even though it was very cold, until they came to Rimanov.[49]

In contrast to these passages there is a tradition that:

> R. Bunim once said that it would be very nice to have a big salon with beds and sofas and tables with wine and roast turkey and to say a little Torah. And whoever wanted to sleep could sleep a little and eat roast meat and drink wine and say a few more words of Torah. That would be very nice. For when everything is taken to its right place it is very good. And it is not necessary to be a recluse; all things

---

[48] *Or ha-Ner,* 12 (*Torat ha-Yehudi,* 161 §9).
[49] *Tiferet ha-Yehudi,* 148 §9.

can be done expansively.... And God said to Moses, "Take off your shoes" – No longer be a recluse, but rather be expansive in everything and elevate it to what is fitting.[50]

In this piece, R. Bunim advocates the idea that holiness is expansive – an idea connected with R. Bunim's view of the world and of nature generally. His criticism is directed against those who believe spirituality is only found through withdrawal,[51] or that the ideal is to escape or shun this world.[52] But it also reflects his at-one-ness with the world. At the very least, one can say that these sentiments do not express (whether consciously or not) the sense of dissonance with the physical realm that one at times senses with the Yehudi or with the Kotzker. R. Bunim's sense of at-one-ness with the world is clearly reflected in the following source:

> There are those Zaddikim whose way is to afflict their body; and there is a Zaddik who eats and drinks and does not afflict himself at all. He is also a holy, great and exalted Zaddik; as is known from the Taz on Even ha-Ezer §25.[53]

This is not the only example of R. Bunim's attitude towards what might be called issues of corporeality:

> As was his way, when he was wealthy, he was very spoiled and he ate and drank there a number of weeks until it amounted to the sum of twenty-five rubles.[54]

R. Bunim had a negative attitude towards fasting. This attitude was encapsulated in a worldly-wise remark:

> I heard from... R. Simhah Bunim that he saw in the Gemara that R. Zaddok fasted forty years and was a tanna; but he saw there another tanna who ate fatted calves. He said: Since one can be a tanna even

---

[50] *Ma'amarei Simhah*, §36.

[51] *Kitvei Hasidim* (*Kol Mevaser*, vol. 3:31).

[52] *Hashavah le-Tovah*, par. Sabbath, 99.

[53] *Turei Zahav* (Taz), subsection 1. The subject discussed is one of modesty during sexual intercourse. The *Taz* quotes the *Bet Yosef*, who gives legitimacy to two opposing opinions and leaves the matter to the individuals' discretion so long as their intention is "for the sake of Heaven"; see *Torat Simhah*, §289.

[54] *Or Simhah*, §56.

though one eats fatted calves, it is better that I should eat and be a tanna than fast.[55]

R. Bunim's *joie de vivre* would not tolerate depression and allowed him to be involved in the world. As has already been mentioned, in *Keter Kehunnah*, we read:

> He was critical of [the performance of] commandments without inner feeling and thought, and he censured those who afflicted their souls and did not wish to delight in the pleasures of this world and withheld themselves from the delights of the senses as long as they do not contradict our religion and the laws of ethics and modesty. Therefore, we saw the Hasidim of Przysucha going out day by day to listen to the tunes being played by the soldiers... they did not know depression... they didn't walk in the street in tatters or with thick hats full of feathers, nor with torn shoes... their clothes had no stains... their hair was combed... and their whole appearance was one of dignity.[56]

It is difficult to evaluate the reliability of this description, as its author, Alexander Zederbaum, had his own critical agenda, but it fits the general impression that one draws of R. Bunim. R. Bunim, like the Yehudi (not to

---

[55] *Torat Simhah*, §318. "R. Bunim taught his hasidim the kavannah of eating," *Hiddushei ha-Rim, Likkutim*, 370; see also *Torat Emet* vol. 2: 54b. I am inclined to think that this is not some mystical illusion, but more the ability to function in the physical world. On this difference between the Yehudi and R. Bunim, see Y. Schiper, "The History of Hasidism in Central Poland," in *Hasidism in Poland*, 32.

[56] *Keter Kehunnah*, 128. On page 127, note 4, we read: "R. Bunim loved the life of pleasure, and only when he returned three times a year did he in his wisdom give money to the zaddik in his town so that the hasidim would not ban him and burn his house down." For a playful critique of sadness by R. Bunim, see *Siah Sarfei Kodesh* vol 1, pages 52 and 240.

mention the Kotzker), knew the dangers of corporeality.[57] [58] Still, the music is not the same.[59]

The difference between them is also felt in their attitude to and control of money. It is related that the Yehudi never went to bed with a single coin in his possession, since he had given it all to charity.[60] For the Yehudi, money blinded people more than anything else.[61] R. Bunim, on the other hand, did not share this antipathy to wealth. There were stages in his life when he was quite rich.[62] Though like any sensitive person, he was aware of the hold and power of distraction of money,[63] money per se was not distasteful to him, as it was to the Kotzker.

> On one occasion in Przysucha, our holy Rabbi R. Bunim… gave… a certain sum of money to R. Shraga Feivel of Gariza to distribute to the poor students of Torah. Suddenly the Rebbe of Kotzk entered the house of study with worn and torn clothes… poor and needy…. And when R. Feivel saw him he was very distressed that he had forgotten him. And he said to the Rebbe of Kotzk, "My dear friend, I can't restrain myself from the distress and pain that I feel. For I have distributed all the money I had and forgot you completely." The Rebbe of Kotzk replied, "What are you talking about? Money?! Pfeh, money is disgusting."[64]

---

[57] *Hiddushei ha-Rim*, Prophets and Writings, 273. See also *Ramatayim Zofim*, chap. 3 §5, chap. 5 §5.

[58] *Amud ha-Emet* 97 relates the following incident when the Kotzker first came to meet the Yehudi. The Yehudi greeted him and said, "It is good for a man to bear a yoke in his youth." (The Kotzker said:) "These words penetrated all my limbs. *I detested eating and drinking* and my food was very sparse."

[59] R. Bunim loved beer: thus *Or Nifla'ot* 2 (*Kol Mevaser*, 3:50, §6); The Yehudi loved to smoke: *Meir Einei ha-Golah* §75, *Tiferet ha-Yehudi*, 142 §2, 152 §14; *Keter ha-Yehudi*, 38 §13.

[60] *Tiferet ha-Yehudi*, 176 §94; 190 §132; *Siah Sarfei Kodesh*, vol. 4, 67 §22.

[61] *Tiferet ha-Yehudi* 176 §94.

[62] *Or Simhah*, §56.

[63] *Ramatayim Zofim*, chap. 5 §5; *Or Simhah*, §116.

[64] *Eser Nifla'ot*, sect. Kotzk §34; *Niflaot Haddashot*, *Likkutim* 92. *Shem mi-Shmuel, Vayikra* 301a. Dynner, "Men of Silk," 158, n. 208 says R. Menahem Mendel of Kotsk, dealt in hides, albeit unsuccessfully: *Siah Sarfei Kodesh*, 1:59, 271. But in 1826, according to Schiper, he was "married to a daughter of a certain Warsaw moneylender and traded in textiles (or rather his wife traded in textiles)." R.

Was that reply just sour grapes? Or did it reflect a genuine sense that money, and everything it stood for, was disgusting? There is an asceticism in the Yehudi[65] which is shared by the Kotzker.

Relying heavily on the work *Emet ve-Emunah*, Mahler[66] says the following about Menahem Mendel:

> R. Mendel of Kock went to the greatest lengths in his denial of worldly life. His attitude is summed up in his well-known saying, "The entire world is not worth even one sigh." No doubt the tragic circumstances of his life contributed to this pessimistic attitude.... [His difficult personal life] is clearly marked by the fact that he lived apart from his first wife for twenty-five years.[67]

But here too the "sources" do not speak with one voice. *Emet ve-Emunah* quotes the following in the name of Menahem Mendel.

> By going to do physical things (business activities)... via this, one has added strength to long for the Torah.[68]

That is to say, our so-called antagonist to the corporeal is quoted as giving the following psychological insight: when one has life force, energy even for some mundane activity, it can be channeled to the holy. Business activities need not be shunned, but rather utilized. (One should qualify the above statements by adding that whatever one attempts to say about the

---

Menahem Mendel owned a store on Wolowej street and a home and prayer-house on 1027 Grzybowie Street. Schiper, *Zydzi Krolestwa Polskiego w dobie powstania*, 28.

[65] Though even here there were different nuances. If the Kotzker is supposed to have said, "The entire world is not worth even one sigh," (*Emet ve-Emunah* §337), the Yehudi is reported to have said (*Torat ha-Yehudi*, 176 §7; *Hasidismus*, 229): "The entire lowly world is not worth even one sigh; all the time falsity rules." That's not exactly the same thing. *Siah Sarfei Kodesh* vol. 3:109, §389, *Emet ve-Emunah* 742 relates that once the Kotzker went to visit the grave of the Yehudi and said: "I want to lead like the Yehudi." For the Kotzker's relationship with the Yehudi, see also *Siah Sarfei Kodesh* vol. 5:93, §1.

[66] R. Mahler, *Hasidism and the Jewish Enlightenment*, 283. See also *Emet ve-Emunah* §716.

[67] *Emet ve-Emunah*, §708. See also §827; *Ohel Yitzhak*, 120 §280.

[68] *Emet ve-Emunah*, §445. For further examples of the Kotzker advocating functioning in the physical world, see *Siah Sarfei Kodesh he-Hadash*, vol 1, 229, n. 13, *Sefat Emet* par. Mishpatim, 1872, *Niflaot Hadashot Seder ha-Yom Katzar*, 9.

Kotzker must be stated with reservation knowing that, without primary sources, they remain only suppositions.)

Nor is the view that the Kotzker is intolerant of human frailty true without qualification. Hiddushei ha-Rim thought that the demand by the Russian government to change Jewish attire had to be resisted at all costs. The Kotzker made it very clear that he didn't think that so-called Jewish dress was sacrosanct.[69] He noted the attraction of the army; "he saw young children running after the soldiers singing tunes."[70] He seems to have given "advice" about worldly matters,[71] encouraging business activities.[72] We should also note his criticism of the zealotry of Pinhas.[73] All this should temper us in viewing the Kotzker through a one-dimensional prism of irascibility.

The Yehudi's asceticism stems from an issue that has bedeviled religion since time immemorial; the issue of the body and one's relationship to it.[74] The antagonism towards the corporeal is missing in R. Bunim, and Mahler does an injustice by lumping R. Bunim and Menahem Mendel together on this issue when their attitude to the matter is very different.[75]

The difference between R. Bunim, and both his teacher the Yehudi and his pupil Menahem Mendel, can be highlighted by the following quotation. In *Ethics of the Fathers* 6:4 we read:

> This is the way of the Torah: eat bread with salt, drink water in small measure, sleep on the ground, live a life of deprivation – but toil in the Torah.

Neither the Yehudi nor Menahem Mendel would have any difficulty with taking this statement literally. Not so R. Bunim. For him, physical deprivation is not a goal. Typically, therefore, he explains the above passage

---

[69] *Meir Einei ha-Golah*, §409, *Emet ve-Emunah* §§140, 270.

[70] *Emet ve-Emunah* §736.

[71] *Emet ve-Emunah* §734.

[72] *Emet ve-Emunah* §741, 805.

[73] *Emet ve-Emunah* §861.

[74] The Yehudi could also express tolerance for human frailty. See *Nifla'ot ha-Yehudi*, 80.

[75] Could R. Bunim's more relaxed attitudes be a reflection of what he said to R. Meir of Apta to the effect that the latter had led a sheltered life and therefore was unacquainted with sin? Maybe we fear what we do not know.

to mean that, despite physical hardship, one should relate to the world with joy, without sadness. Abstinence is not to be confused with purity.[76]

Ȕ ș

Levinger[77] tries to draw a distinction between R. Menahem Mendel and both the Yehudi and R. Bunim. One of his arguments is based on Menahem Mendel's attitude towards Torah – namely, that for him learning Torah alone was the main path in the service of God.

We are reluctant to accept this argument because it was precisely the Yehudi and R. Bunim who restored the primacy of learning Torah in Polish Hasidism. Therefore, this process did not start with Menahem Mendel. It was the Yehudi who said, for example, that "learning a page of *gemara* is like going to the *mikveh*."

All three generations of Przysucha are pietistic in the sense that they acknowledge the inadequacy of the intellect alone to improve personality, to purify one's being. The challenge, therefore, is how one translates the cognitive into the affective – that which is apprehended by the mind into the body? Here there is a change. Unlike the Yehudi, R. Bunim promoted the study of medieval Jewish philosophy (which he had inherited from his father). R. Bunim felt that his alter ego, so to speak, was the Maharal of Prague.[78] That is, he attached great significance to pietistic, philosophical works that dealt with the nature of a human being. But what did the Kotzker think about the study of Jewish philosophy? Piekarz brings the following story:

> Once the Kotzker found his sick son-in-law R. Avraham involved in (learning) an ethical work called *Behinat Olam* (the doctors had forbade him to learn gemara, which required too much effort). R. Menahem Mendel said to him: "Learning (analyzing) such a book is of no value, because all its ideas appeal only to the intelligence – but

---

[76] *Nifla'ot Haddashot* 4b; Boem, vol 2, 119.
[77] Levinger. "The Torah of the Rebbe of Kotzk," 422.
[78] On all this see chap. 3. R. Bunim did not accept the kabbalah of the Maharal.

the body does not give in to them. But learning *gemara* forces the body to give in."[79]

If the source is reliable, it implies that the Kotzker saw little value in works other than the *Gemara*. Perhaps it expresses the view that intellectual engagement which fails to be integrated, which can merely be thought about and fails to enter into the body is ultimately lacking in value, no matter how interesting. But other sources paint a different picture. We have first hand testimony by a hasid who was himself in Kotzk who said that during Menahem Mendel's leadership hasidim learnt Maimonides's *Guide to the Perplexed*.[80] Schiper and Mahler maintained that Menahem Mendel followed in the steps of his teacher R. Bunim and studied the works of Yehuda HaLevi, Ibn Gabirol, Maimonides and Ibn Ezra. *Emet ve-Emunah*[81] quotes Menahem Mendel as saying in a positive way (as if it were their normal habit), "We weary ourselves [trying] to understand every word of the Maharal."[82]

Keter Kehunnah (published in 1866) states the following about the Kotzker:

> He set limits to free investigation and analysis of works of inquiry which R. Bunim had set; though he himself and his exceptional

---

[79] Piekarz, *Ideological Trends*, 59, who quotes: "*Eretz Zvi's*... statements... words of piety and Hasidism..." (1, [Tel Aviv, 1960] 157); *Mareh Deshe* 51, n. 15. See *Shem mi-Shmuel*, Vayikra, 300a. On the supremacy of Torah, see also *Shem mi-Shmuel: Bereshit*, 96a and 121a; *Emet ve-Emunah*, §440. For the idea that only learning is real, see the quote by Hiddushei ha-Rim, *Meir Einei ha-Golah*, vol. 2: 109.

[80] *Ginzei ha-hasidut: da'at Torah: der kvitel fun Kotzker hasid*: Yaacov Yitzhak (Zelig) of Valezlavek, 61, Jerusalem: 1967.

[81] Schiper, 34. R. Mahler, 282, quoting *Emet ve-Emunah* says the following: "R. Mendel of Kock even encouraged the study of the *Yad ha-Hazakah*, recommended the writings of the Maharal (of Prague), "which provide intelligence and reason for the understanding of the Gemara and the *Posekim*," and saw the perusal of the *Guide of the Perplexed* as beneficial to those who had already had their fill of studying *Shas* (the Talmud) and *Posekim*. Indeed, following in the footsteps of their masters from Przysucha and Kock, the Hasidim would study Maimonides, the *Kuzari*, the works of the *Maharal* and other writings in religious philosophy." See also *Emet ve-Emunah*, §781.

[82] *Emet ve-Emunah*, §450; see also §762; also Bezalel Safran, "Maharal and Early Hasidism," in *Hasidism: Continuity and Innovation*, ed. B. Safran, (Cambridge, MA: Harvard University Press, 1988).

disciples delved into our ancient philosophical works like the books Me'or Einayim, Ikarim and similar works. He even gave permission to the exceptional few to analyze and become absorbed in the Guide for the Perplexed.[83]

If we were to rely on the above quote by Piekarz, then we might say the following: The emphasis on the body "giving in" is reminiscent of the Yehudi and not of R. Bunim. According to the aforementioned source, Menahem Mendel sees the study of ethical works as a waste of time because they don't work! Their impact on the human personality was questionable. It is not so much a question of the primacy of Torah. Rather, it is whether there are any other methods or sources that can be used in the enterprise of building one's character and purity of motive apart from Torah. On the other hand, in the quote from *Keter Kehunnah* it is clear that the Kotzker, like R. Bunim, was also involved in the study of medieval Jewish philosophy. It is possible that the Kotzker changed his position. That earlier on, while still under the influence of R. Bunim, he was in favor of medieval Jewish philosophy. Later, however, as he withdrew personally, so his perception of wisdom contracted as well. Nevertheless, there is a greater openness in the attitude and atmosphere of R. Bunim.

છે જી

Another significant distinction between R. Bunim and the Yehudi is the difference in the nature of their activity in regards to relations with "assimilated Jews." Although the Yehudi might have approved[84] of R. Bunim's efforts, it is difficult to imagine that he would or could have done the same.

> When he (R. Bunim) was a young man journeying to Danzig, a businessman asked him to look after his son.... Suddenly, he (the son) disappeared and R. Bunim went looking for him. And his heart sensed that the businessman's son had gone into a brothel. So he went in, and in the outer room stood a lyre and a woman singer sat

---

[83] *Keter Kehunnah*, 130.
[84] *Meir Einei ha-Golah*, §153.

there. He paid her to sing a song that he (the young man) knew, so that via the attraction of the song, he would come out.[85]

One can hardly imagine the ascetic Yehudi going into a brothel or having the street wisdom to entice the young man away through music. As for the Kotzker, it was in line with his character to have burnt the house down. This incident was not a one-time event. It was entirely at one with R. Bunim's attitude to those who had fallen by the wayside.

The following incident is told about the Yehudi:

> In Cracow there was once an enlightened scholar who, God forbid, inclined towards heresy.... One of the hasidim suggested that they journey in the world together, and he agreed. During their journey they came to Przysucha and there the hasid entreated him to meet our holy teacher under the pretense that he would have something to make fun of. He agreed. When they came to our holy Rabbi he was very friendly toward the enlightened Jew and took off his [own] hat and covered the head of the enlightened Jew [with his hat] and then took it away again [when he left]. From that time on, the enlightened Jew changed and became a great person.[86]

So the Yehudi was also prepared to deal with heretics. But the similarity only highlights the difference. In the case of the Yehudi, the wayward Jew came to him. But in R. Bunim's case he was pro-active: he would consistently go out himself, as well as sending his Hasidim to engage the secular world. There is a distinctive difference in the accent of their philosophy in regard to "assimilated Jewry," as articulated by R. Bunim, who said:

> Don't think that Abraham our father behaved like other Rebbes. They sat at home and the Hasidim journeyed to them. But he [Abraham] didn't behave like that. Rather, he moved around the

---

[85] *Or Simhah*, §42. Buber, in *Tales of the Hasidim: Later Masters*, 241 has a more expanded and embellished version, though the import is essentially the same.
[86] *Tiferet ha-Yehudi*, 174 §86.

270

streets, shouting in a loud voice that there is one Creator – unique, who oversees everything.[87]

On the verse (Genesis 18:24) "Perhaps there are fifty righteous people within the town," R. Bunim said that the meaning is that there are zaddikim for whom it is not sufficient just to be in the house of learning, but rather they are in the middle of the town, moving around in the streets doing business. If there are zaddikim like that, then He will save the place for their sake, because the real goal is to draw the simple people closer.[88]

The other major difference between the Yehudi and R. Bunim was the difference in their style of prayer. This was not merely a difference of temperament. In the two generations after the Yehudi, during the period of R. Simhah Bunim and Menahem Mendel, the style of prayer of Przysucha became distinctive. It developed into a style characterized by its restraint; an aversion to external manifestations. R. Simhah Bunim looked down on what he perceived as something he discerned as being essentially superficial (though even he recognized that authenticity should win the day).

The following sources, many of which have already been mentioned, convey a clear educational approach as represented by R. Bunim which is different in respect to the Yehudi. In this respect Menahem Mendel followed R. Bunim.

> R. Moshe of Rozodov said of the Yehudi that "he prayed with all his strength, with total commitment; and when he reached the prayer 'And David blessed,' one could almost see his soul departing... his strength almost expired from awe."[89]

---

[87] *Siftei Zaddikim*, par. *Lekh Lekha*, 37 (*Kol Mevaser*, vol. 2: 224–225). See also *Emet ve-Emunah*, §541; and §699 for the Kotzker's "outreach."
[88] *Shem mi-Shmuel*, Pentecost, 116.
[89] *Tiferet ha-Yehudi*, 171 §74.

For the Yehudi, the ultimate was to have a sense of being in the Divine presence. Authenticity came from this sense, from what he called the "revelation of the *Shekhinah*."[90]

> And he related, in the name of the Holy Rabbi of Przysucha (R. Bunim), that he once saw R. Natale Helmer on Rosh Hashanah and he did not pray, neither by night nor by day. And he was amazed. And he asked the Holy Yehudi of Przysucha, who said that this was because of his (sense of) awe (of the Divine).[91]

There are a number of sources relating how the Yehudi, when praying, would come to a point of ecstasy and total physical exhaustion in which he would literally faint. All this is in contrast with R. Bunim[92] and the Kotzker[93] – although it is known that the Yehudi, as well, was against loud prayer.[94]

As mentioned, we have a most reliable description of the prayer of R. Menahem Mendel. His son-in-law, R. Avraham of Sochaczew, told the following:

> My father told me that in his youth when he was weak and spitting blood, my grandfather took him to pray with him in his room on Rosh Hashanah next to the great Beit ha-Midrash and he saw him praying the Standing Prayer of Rosh Hashanah… without any movement or (visible) emotion – but his face was on fire.[95]

Hiddushei ha-Rim said the following:

> The Hasidism of Przysucha taught us that the main work is internal and one should not work on the external limbs. Rather the inner life force should extend to action. When a person does the work inside, his external limbs automatically become subservient.[96]

R. Bunim said:

---

[90] *Migdal David* (Piotrkow, 1893), par. Re'eh. 54.
[91] *Siah Sarfei Kodesh*, vol. 1, 19 §90; *Ramatayim Zofim*, 31.100; *Tiferet ha-Yehudi*, 166 §55 (*Torat ha-Yehudi*, 87).
[92] *Sefer Alexander*, 19; *Torat Simhah* §333.
[93] *Shem mi-Shmuel*, par. Va-et'hanan, 35b.
[94] *Emunat Israel*, par. Beshalah, 20.
[95] *Shem mi-Shmuel*, par. Korah, 267b; see also *Siah Sarfei Kodesh he-Hadash*, vol. 1. 104.
[96] *Siah Sarfei Kodesh*, vol. 3: 46 §104.

When one prays, only the soul should pray and the body should be drawn after it like a bundle of hay. Then "I will dwell in them" refers to those who create the Tabernacle – the soul and the body together. But if they are not together, then the Tabernacle is merely a piece of wood.[97]

ॐ ≪

Finally, there are additional areas (though of less significance) that are more typical of R. Bunim than of the Yehudi or the Kotzker. For example, R. Bunim was known for his use of parables and stories as a normative educational practice. The Yehudi and the Kotzker hardly ever used parables or stories to illuminate an idea (and we are not speaking here about telling the story of an actual incident). To this it should be added that, although the Yehudi believed in the use of the mind, it was R. Bunim who promoted the study of medieval Jewish philosophy[98] and who was concerned with *peshat* – the literal meaning of the text. And it is safe to say that of the two, R. Bunim possessed more of a philosophical inclination.

There is no mistaking that Menahem Mendel stands for an uncompromising, searing quest for truth. By contrast, R. Bunim is a more multi-faceted personality. If we analyze his pupils, we find a range of different personalities in his entourage. Yet all saw themselves as disciples of R. Bunim and considered him their rebbe. Clearly they found a personal resonance with this man. They identified with him but translated his teachings through the prism of their different personalities. When R. Bunim died, his pupils divided into two groups. There were the firebrands, who were attracted to Menahem Mendel; but then there were other pupils of a softer mien, such as R. Yitzhak of Vorki, who followed R. Bunim's son, Avram Moshe. Yet they were all contained within the enterprise of R. Bunim.

The truth is that while there were significant differences between the three distinctive personalities that developed Przysucha, when compared with what they share in common – uncompromising religious intensity

---

[97] *Hashavah le-Tovah*, par. Terumah, 28.

[98] See *Emet ve-Emunah* §710 for the Kotzker's approval of Maimonides, and §762 regarding the Maharal, and §819 regarding *The Guide for the Perplexed*, for those ready for it.

grounded in authentic behavior – these differences dissolve into insignificance. There is a complete resonance in terms of shared values and religious philosophy. If they were all seated around a table, each would feel inspired by the other; each would hear their essence in the other – the same philosophy the same essential values.

THE END OF THE HOLY
REBELLION

Hiddushei ha-Rim

IMMEDIATELY FOLLOWING the death of the Kotzker (1859) there was a
change, if not a retrogression, from the values established in Przysucha, even
among its closest associates. The sharp insight of R. Bunim had become
softened and in many cases was tempered to a complete reversal in meaning.
A mass movement was created where the individual was sacrificed to the
enterprise of producing one truly great Torah scholar. This was a complete
retrenchment from the individuality and sense of personal autonomy that R.
Bunim espoused as obligatory upon any human being who desired to come
close to God. **It is as if the whole enterprise of Przysucha came to an
end with Hiddushei ha-Rim.**

As mentioned earlier, R. Yitzhak Meir Rottenberg Alter, known as
Hiddushei ha-Rim, had thirteen children,[1] twelve of whom died at an early
age.[2] In his perception, this tragedy was caused by his leaving R. Moshe of
Koznitz. Yet when challenged, he replied that:

> With regard to the truth in the service of God I wasn't prepared to
> consider anything else.[3]

---

[1] *Meir Einei ha-Golah*, part 2, §438. Aescoly, 101, also mentions the number 17.
[2] *Meir Einei ha-Golah*, nos. §124, §122, 101, 106, 125–126; part 2, §434, notes.
The father of the *Sefat Emet,* however, lived till the age of thirty-nine.
[3] *Meir Einei ha-Golah*, §94.

Whatever one might think of this behavior, it depicts a person willing to jeopardize even that which was most precious in order to come into contact with something greater than himself.

&ℴ ◌֍

It was Hiddushei ha-Rim who, after the death of R. Bunim, deferred to the leadership of Menahem Mendel of Kotzk,[4] and then, when Menahem Mendel went into semi-seclusion for some twenty years,[5] maintained the world of Kotzk.[6] It was also he who stood by Menahem Mendel when the Ishbitzer broke with Kotzk in 1839 and, according to some, was responsible for persuading the majority of the hasidim who left with the Ishbitzer to return to Kotzk. All this suggests a radical personality unwilling to compromise, someone for whom "life is no life" unless it is engaged in the ultimate quest for the Divine.

&ℴ ◌֍

There are nevertheless a number of sources in which Hiddushei ha-Rim cites his teacher, R. Bunim, only to disagree with him. What is even more disconcerting is that these disagreements reflect an intellectual retreat from the radicalism of his mentor.

For example,

> He related that he heard a number of times from our master Hiddushei ha-Rim who said, in the name of R. Bunim, that nowadays the world runs after rebbes... and that is a punishment.... But in the last winter he related this again in the name of R. Bunim and concluded with the following. "It appears to me that it is not a punishment, for because the world thinks that a zaddik is an upright man of truth, they run after him and cleave to him."[7]

This is a very sweet value that in any other hasidic school would be entirely acceptable, but with regard to Przysucha, it is not too severe to assert that it is as if truth had fallen to the ground. The very quality which R.

---

[4] *Meir Einei ha-Golah*, §§187–191.

[5] *Meir Einei ha-Golah*, §§235, 251.

[6] *Meir-Einei ha-Golah* 241–247; *Emet ve-Emunah* 651, 361; see n. 19 below.

[7] *Siah Sarfei Kodesh*, 5: 22, §9; see also *Hiddushei ha-Rim*, Hasidut, 352, 356.

Bunim was criticizing, namely the inability to recognize and demand a true zaddik, became, under the conciliation of Hiddushei ha-Rim, a point of praise that at least people "believe" that they are attracted to an upright man.

This retrogression of Hiddushei ha-Rim from the penetrating analysis of R. Bunim is not an isolated example. The following parable related by R. Bunim, illustrates this point.

> A king had an only son whom he loved exceedingly. It happened that the son sinned against the father and was exiled to a distant land where he wandered around. On one occasion the king decided to inquire about his only son and sent a minister to find him. The minister found him in an inn, in a village amongst farmers, drinking and dancing barefoot without clothes. The minister asked him how he was doing. And he (the son of the king) replied, "If only I had shoes and warm clothes, nothing could be better." He had become so coarsened that he did not feel the lack of anything else. Understand this, for it is a parable about the Exile. And the holy Hiddushei ha-Rim said about this, that presumably it was good, for it aroused greater compassion.[8]

R. Bunim is reflecting on how the Jewish people had become bruised by their exile. Through this parable, he is illustrating that a person is no greater than his dreams (than the place which he believes himself to be hewn, cut out from, the throne of God or a pinch of earth). Our dreams often reflect exactly who we are and consequently reveal just how small a world we maintain; spiritual midgets, our desires are all too banal.[9] For Hiddushei ha-Rim to say, as it were, "Yes, but there is value in the cry," no doubt defends the honor of the Jewish people but completely misses the point. One might ask who, in essence, believes in the Jewish people more: a person who accepts mediocrity or one who seeks to arouse the hearts of the Jewish people to awaken them from the deep slumber of exile.

In a similar vein R. Bunim comments on the word *sevel* ("suffering"; Ex. 6.6). Regarding the servitude of the Jewish people in Egypt he says,

---

[8] *Siah Sarfei Kodesh* 1:52, §244.

[9] The parable predates by two generations that of the Jewish author I.L. Peretz in his story "When the Angels Wept."

They endured it and did not feel the harshness of their servitude.[10]

R. Bunim is making an important insight into the nature of man. A person can sink so low that he becomes habituated to a particular mental state. But regarding this very remark it is reported in the name of Hiddushei ha-Rim that he said,

> The word "sevel" means that at least they could not tolerate the impurity of Egypt.[11]

Once again, the sharp insight of R. Bunim has become softened and Hiddushei ha-Rim's remark is the exact opposite of what R. Bunim wanted to communicate.

Seminal to R. Bunim's thought is the idea that man has to dig for himself the wells of his own inspiration:

> Every Jewish person who draws near to God needs to dig by himself a well whereby he can cleave to the Creator.[12]

But on the same theme of "wells," Hiddushei ha-Rim says:

> Our role is not to toil in [personal] service; only from the wells of our fathers.... The desired goal is the glory of heaven **and not to think by oneself**.[13]

☞ ☜

As mentioned, one of the most exquisite ideas of R. Bunim is that God cherishes the emotion that cannot be expressed because of its intensity – the song that therefore has no voice.[14]

With this in mind, he makes the following comment on the Biblical verse (Ex 36:5): "The people bring more than enough for the service of the work."

---

[10] *Siah Sarfei Kodesh he-Hadash*, par. Va-era, 64.

[11] *Sefat Emet*, par *Vaera*, 1871 and 1876, Shabbtai Weiss, *Me-Otzar Ha-Mahshavah shel Ha-Hasidut* (Tel Aviv: 1949), 130.

[12] *Kol Simhah, Toldot*, 29–30.

[13] *Siah Sarfei Kodesh* 3: 48, §116. Alternatively, the phrase "lahshov be-azmo" might mean "to think about oneself." However, it is clear from the full quotation that Hiddushei ha-Rim would agree with both interpretations.

[14] Chap. 6.

The Jewish people had such a desire to build the Tabernacle – they were so generous – that they brought too much, and some of their offering was left over. How is one to view this generosity? According to R. Bunim, it is precisely this "left-over" which is so precious in God's eyes.[15] Hiddushei ha-Rim, however, offers the following reservation:

> Generosity and desire need containment so that the desire and passion do not extend to other (undesirable) things.[16]

Expressed here is the need for restraint – for structure. The enthusiasm of passion is sacrificed for the more staid and controlled emotion. It's not a bad comment, and his grandson the *Sefat Emet* follows in his footsteps.[17] But the radicalism of R. Bunim is lost. The value of the ecstatic has been quieted.

In addition, whereas both R. Bunim and Menahem Mendel had a deep ambivalence about having too many hasidim, Hiddushei-ha-Rim had no such reservation.[18] According to him, the mass movement was necessary to produce the one exceptional person. R. Bunim however, wanted a Torah that related to each individual. The individual was not a means to another end.

⇛ ⇚

One of the indications of change after the death of the Kotzker is the reintroduction of kabbalah, as seen in the use of the Zohar, the Ari and other mystical works. During the three generations of Przysucha, kabbalah hardly existed for them. However, in the work *Hiddushei ha-Rim* on the Torah, or in the work *Neot Deshe* (a collection of teachings attributed to the Kotzker's son-in-law, R. Avraham of Sochaczew), kabbalah abounds. The Ishbitzer (a pupil of R. Bunim) the author of the *Mei Shiloah* was a theologian who, buttressed by the kabbalah, deals with determinism and free will. But all this is muted in the world of R. Bunim. Even the basic terminology of kabbalah is absent.

Another aspect of retrogression from the principles of Przysucha after the death of the Kotsker was the reinstatement of dynasties amongst the

---

[15] *Hiddushei ha-Rim*, par Vayakhel, 144.
[16] *Sefat Emet*, par. Va-Yakhel 1875, 339.
[17] Ibid.
[18] *Siah Sarfei Kodesh* 1:96, §526.

pupils of R. Bunim, such as the rebbes of Warka (Vorki), Gur, Ishbitz (Izbica) and Alexander.

ও৽ ৵৩

In the year 1844, after things had subsided somewhat in Kotzk,[19] Hiddushei ha-Rim journeyed throughout Eastern Europe,[20] meeting with both hasidic and non-hasidic leaders. (In fact, what characterized Hiddushei ha-Rim throughout his life was his ability to bridge these divides). One of the leaders he visited was R. Yisrael of Ruzhin.[21] It is not clear whether these two men even understood each other.[22] Nevertheless, Hiddushei ha-Rim was very impressed and stayed two weeks in Ruzhin, where he was shown great deference. Now, there are few streams of Hasidism more removed from the world of Przysucha than that of Ruzhin, which is essentially Hasidism for the masses. It would be difficult to imagine the Yehudi[23] or R. Bunim having the same reaction as Hiddushei ha-Rim. When he described to the Kotzker how the Ruzhiner played with gold coins, the Kotzker was not impressed. And when he reported to the Kotzker the fact that Ruzhin was critical of Kotzk, the Kotzker replied, somewhat laconically:

But what will they do if the Messiah is a hasid of Kotzk?[24]

How is one to reconcile these apparent contradictions in the personality of Hiddushei ha-Rim? The obvious explanation is to suggest that, though as a young man he was prepared to risk much, however, later in life, when he saw the tragic consequence of the "passion of truth" as played out in the

---

[19] According to *Meir Einei ha-Golah,* nos. 361–362, Hiddushei ha-Rim held the fort after the Kotzker's withdrawal from public life.

[20] *Emet ve-Emunah,* §863. D. Assaf (*The Regal Way: The Life and Times of Rabbi Israel of Ruzhin* (Hebrew). Jerusalem: 1997, 234–235), relying on the work *Siah Sarfei Kodesh,* says that the journey was at the instigation of the Kotzker. This does not ring true. Meir *Einei ha-Golah* §362 implies that the initiative came from Hiddushei ha-Rim himself. One should be wary of relying on one source alone, especially *Siah Sarfei Kodesh.*

[21] *Meir Einei ha-Golah,* §§371–379.

[22] *Meir Einei ha-Golah,* §375.

[23] Even though the Ruzhiner thought highly of the Yehudi (*Tiferet ha-Yehudi,* 152, §14, *Ma'ase Nehemyah* p. 64); cf. Assaf, *Hasidut be-Hitpatshuto,* 289, §74.

[24] *Siah Sarfei Kodesh,* 3:18; *Emet ve-Emunah* 863. This might also be an allusion to the fact that Ruzhin had a tradition that one of their descendents would be the Messiah.

persona of the Kotzker, he resigned himself to a more staid sort of Hasidism; one that undercut the radicalism of Kotzk. It may be possible to explain his position as a delayed reaction to his own terrible losses. Even so, it would appear that the truth lies elsewhere. In a personal letter, written in the year 1844, to his family, Hiddushei ha-Rim exposed his inner world. He said:

> Learn Torah continuously… for everything else is worthless. What a man can achieve with calm composure when he learns Torah is greater than what he can achieve via prayer. For passionate prayer is full of illusion and doesn't endure; whereas composure clarifies for him the difference between good and evil.[25]

With this statement, the revolution started by the Yehudi came to an end. Wisdom was to be found in the text alone, not in the encounter of a being immersed in life who then brings himself to the text. Anything other than the text was "worthless," "full of illusion" and therefore one sought safety in learning. This seems like a rejection of Hasidism itself in favor of mitnaggedism.

After the death of the Kotzker, Hiddushei ha-Rim became Rebbe. He complained that the role of being a rebbe was injurious to his learning *Gemara*. In his opinion, the Yehudi was able to combine both, but not he.[26] The Kotzker, when faced with the tension between being a Rebbe and personal authenticity, eventually found the strain too great, and chose the latter. Hiddushei ha-Rim, when faced with the tension between "learning" and being a rebbe, reluctantly chose the role of the rebbe (he had always been reluctant to play that role, and his demands on his hasidim were benign). One can understand his *cri de coeur* because he is essentially a *lamdan* (a Torah scholar), as at home in the world of *mitnaggedim* as in the world of hasidim.[27] His journeys and visits to various Jewish leaders are indicative of this aspect of his personality. He was not interested in leading a radical Jewish renaissance. On the contrary, it was he who brought Przysucha back into the main stream of Hasidism and of the Jewish world. It was now a safe package which didn't make waves.

---

[25] *Meir Einei ha-Golah*, 2:109.

[26] *Meir Einei ha-Golah*. §71

[27] *Meir Einei ha-Golah*, §460–461.

There is conservatism in the personality of Hiddushei ha-Rim. When the secular authorities demanded that the Jewish community modernize its dress, Hiddushei ha-Rim thought that to do so was *yehareg ve-al yaavor* (i.e., a cardinal principle for which one ought to sacrifice one's life rather than acquiesce), though he knew that Menahem Mendel did not think it was so terrible.[28] This suggests that Hiddushei ha-Rim's halakhic decision had a lot to do with his conservatism.[29]

అ ఆ

It was said in the name of the Kotzker that the difference between a mitnagged and a hasid was this:

The *mitnagged* serves the *Shulhan Arukh* (the Law) and the hasid serves God.[30]

But it was reliably reported in the name of R. Meir Jehiel Ha-Levi of Ostrowiec that Przysucha hasidim had long abandoned the practice of "digression" (from halakhah), and were now toeing the line advocated by Hiddushei ha-Rim, urging a return to the full rigor of the Shulhan Arukh.[31]

---

[28] *Meir Einei ha-Golah* §409; *Emet ve-Emunah,* §§140, 270. Another factor contributing to this may have been the growth of the haskalah, in addition to his own innate conservatism.

[29] In the year 1859, Hiddushei ha-Rim wrote an approbation to the work *Kol Simhah.* This work, written by R. Zusha of Plozk, was supposedly a collection of ideas uttered by R. Bunim. It was severely criticized as in no way reflecting R. Bunim's greatness (see Addendum A). The work *Meir Einei ha-Golah* (vol. 2, p. 386, ed. 2005) quotes this approbation. After a few complimentary words about R. Bunim, Hiddushei ha-Rim goes on to support the publication of the work and says:
"Presumably even now, his [R. Bunim's] words will arouse the hearts of the Jewish people" ("Umistoma gam ata devarav ye'oreru libot bnei Israel").
This is a remarkably lukewarm endorsement. The word "presumably" seems to me to suggest that presumably Hiddushei ha-Rim no longer identified with Przysucha.
How interesting that this approbation stands in stark contrast to his more effusive one given to R. Israel of Kozienice's work *Avodat Israel,* published in 1842 (*Meir Einei ha-Golah,* p. 382). To give a more admiring approbation to a work from Kozienice than to one from Pryzsucha surely indicates that Hiddushei ha-Rim has come full circle.

[30] *Siah Sarfei Kodesh* 5:44.

[31] Yehoshua Mondshine. "The Fluidity of Categories in Hasidism." In *Hasidism Reappraised,* p. 319. Cf. Chapter 11, n. 31.

෨ ෨

When Hiddushei ha-Rim moved from Warsaw to Gur, he noticed that in a certain *bet midrash* the *shofar* was not blown after the morning service during the month of Elul. After some inquiry, it transpired that the people in this *bet midrash* were Kotzker hasidim and weren't particularly concerned with this custom. Hiddushei ha-Rim told his *gabbai* to order these Kotzker hasidim to blow the *shofar* and he added the following:

> If heaven still approved of such behavior, why did it take away its leader (i.e., the Kotzker)?[32]

From this vignette it is clear that Hiddushei ha-Rim repudiated the approach of the Koztker, the very person he had stood by when Kotzk had been in danger, as soon as he became Rebbe. The radicalism of Kotzk was now over.

Summary

The pre-modern mind believed that there was some body of knowledge – be it philosophy or kabbalah – that could tell us something about God. The modern mind has no such illusion. Maimonides, for example, described proper thinking about God by using the metaphor of a castle. There are those who see the architecture of the castle, but have never been inside; there are others who have entered the castle, but have never seen the king. For Maimonides, divine science (metaphysics not Talmud) brought one into intimate contact with God. But we are more akin to Kafka and even if we have the language to describe the architecture of the castle, we still have no idea which door will bring us into the presence of the King. Modern man has no body of knowledge with which to establish a relationship with that which is beyond, or to explain God. Nor is there any corpus of law which could possibly contain all the permutations and combinations of life. And even if there were such a book of divine knowledge, Przysucha maintained that learning such a book alone would remain inadequate, unless one made it

---

[32] *Meir Einei ha-Golah*, 543; A. Rubinstein (*Encyclopedia Hebraica*, 17:763) says, "Hiddushei ha-Rim basically liquidated the approach of Kotzk."

one's own through experience. Therefore, it wasn't "right thinking," but rather "right being" or "right living" that moved one inside. And no text, no matter how important, could be a substitute for life.

But there are also moments of grace. One such moment is the experience of coming into contact with greatness or spiritual grandeur. It is as if one was living on the second floor of an apartment block and all of a sudden one became aware that someone else was living on the fourth floor of the same building. "Wow," one might say, "I never knew that there was a fourth floor or that somebody could live there!" In the world of Przysucha, the hasid's experience of the rebbe was not one of being pampered, as it was for the rest of Polish Hasidism – a guaranteed check that would allow the hasid to enter the kingdom of heaven on the coattails of the zaddik. In Przysucha, it was both disconcerting and thrilling to meet one's zaddik, for the encounter with spiritual grandeur demanded a response.

There is a belief in Judaism that the human being cannot be relied upon; the only thing this "pinch of earth" is capable of is to obey the law which has been imposed upon him from without. They depict a Creator which fashioned a being locked in a traumatic struggle – between body and spirit – "unto death." The mystic longs to extricate himself from the physical prison of his body. The implication being that, since in this corporeal world the body is dominant, it is "unnatural" for a person to be spiritual.

For the religious person, such a view produces a deep sense of guilt about enjoying life. The equation then becomes, "if it hurts, it must be good; and if it is enjoyable, it must be sinful." This causes the secular person to ask, "Why be religious unless, of course, you have a problem – unless there is something wrong with you?"

The above recipe for neurosis is totally absent in the philosophy of R. Bunim. There is no dualism in his thought. The world is not divided between body and soul: God's intention is that human beings learn to function in a world of imperfection, in which the physical is a partner (albeit one to be refined) in the service of God. Prayer is the medium for this music. R. Bunim might very well have made the following argument: How does one develop personality, if not by learning how to function through trial and error? How does one develop a moral sensitivity if not by relying on one's own inner nature? For those who see nature only as animalistic, it becomes an object to dominate, not a partner with which to develop. It is either something to control or escape from. But R. Bunim follows the Rabbinic tradition that "holiness dwells within one."

છે જ

There is a Torah of God and there is a Torah of the human being. By the Torah of God we mean the issues that theology tries to answer, such as the problem of evil or divine providence. As the psalmist says (73:11), "Is there knowledge on high?" But there is also the Torah of human beings. By this we refer to such questions as "What credibility can I give to my experience?" or "Is my prayer illusory?" These are questions asked by any sensitive and intelligent person. The human Torah grapples with these issues, and though these have no ultimate answer, they at least function within and inform the very framework of human experience.

Przysucha asks, "If Torah is that which changes one's essence, then is that happening to me?" In fact, "What is my essence – who am I?" All this assumes sensitivity to one's inner world. But though one's inner world appears to be nebulous and unquantifiable, it is, in fact, the most real. Przysucha believes that when a person dies, his individual soul, his essence, lives on. But his essence is also the cumulative effect of his engagement with the Divine (or the lack thereof) in this material world and no tradition can supply such an encounter unless people are willing to seek it out for themselves. What lives on after a person's death – unless he has experienced something of the Divine from the seat of this world, as Job says, "In my flesh I will see God" – is not how much Torah he has learned or how many commandments he has kept but what he has become. One might well argue that "what a person is" is the effect of how much Torah he has absorbed, how many commandments he has kept. Still, the most important question remains, "Who am I? What have I become?"

Przysucha is Judaism without crutches. As the Yehudi said, "There are no rules in the service of God, and this itself is no rule." Przysucha poses the question, can a Jew be part of the tradition and yet challenge it? That they challenged the establishment is obvious. But the real issue is the existential one. To what extent can a tradition become mine; to what degree can it so resonate within me that in a sense it is no longer a tradition, but is *me*?

Przysucha is the world of *"Torat ha-Adam."* When a person comes to serve God, what are his motives? How can they be purified? The quest of

Przysucha is the quest by a human being to discover the truth about himself, though God is the intention of service. But the quest is not focused on the nature of God but on the human being himself. Przysucha produced psychological insights into the nature of man that presaged Western culture at the turn of the twentieth century. It contains a genre of "vortlech" (sharp observations) that in a few words encapsulated the quintessence of the nature of human beings. This genre became immediately recognizable as the Torah of Przysucha-Kotzk. And if, hagiography and tradition have ascribed to Menachem Mendel statements he might never have made, in another sense, they are the best indication of what was understood as being the Torah of Kotzk, and successfully convey the style of thought for which he stood (see Addendum A).

Przysucha's agenda was a quest for personal authenticity. That meant self-analysis, and not self-indulgence. Reality is not contained in the human being alone, but just as a person works to develop an independent intellect, so too, he works toward the development of his own soul. The spirituality of Przysucha is a spirituality of intimacy with God, not of trying to affect God or unify Him, but by making God a reality within oneself. The drama of service takes place within the reality of human frailty – in the heart of the human being, and not in the Godhead. Therefore, kabbalah is virtually non-existent in the thinking of Przysucha. Even kabbalistic terms that we would have expected to be used in religious language are simply not found.

The insistence on purity of motive became radicalized during the lifetime of R' Bunim. It expressed itself as an antagonism to anything external, anything conformist, anything "*frum*" (religiously conventional). This demand for a person to be honest and to purify himself, had of course, always been part of Jewish piety; but in Przysucha it was raised to a value of supreme importance. It wasn't one of a series of values, it was **the value**. Without it, one's service was literally an abomination, an amalgamation of self-interest, i.e., idol worship. Przysucha-Kotzk is the passion for truth, the intolerance of the superficial and ecstatic demand to unite heaven and earth without illusory trappings and without concern for what anyone else might think. The concern of Przysucha was, "How do I want to stand before the Divine?" or "How does God want me to stand before Him?"

It was this value that led the Yehudi to promote the principle that "Preparation for a commandment is the equivalent of doing the commandment itself." Rabbinic Judaism is patently clear about how and when a commandment should be performed. The Yehudi's formulation is iconoclastic; it was recognized as such by friend and foe alike. If prayer is the medium by which one is drawn to the Divine, then a person needs to prepare himself, to attune himself. Only then is there hope that his experience might indeed be real and might endure afterwards. Time and preparation allow a person to enter into a deeper state of mind and purify his consciousness.

$$\approx \, \ll$$

In the second half of the nineteenth century, Hasidism turned inwards. A movement that a century or so earlier had engaged the Jewish world now found itself unable to cope with the onslaught of the secular enlightenment, unable to grapple with the issues of the time. What remained of Hasidism after this forced retrenchment was a richness of insights into the soul, but with little understanding of how to apply them in the modern period. The major hasidic figures might well have been concerned with poverty, but they did not develop any philosophical or pragmatic approach as to how to eradicate it. There was thus no response, for example, to the challenges of Socialism or Zionism.[33] The leaders of Przysucha were not uninvolved with the larger world. Both R. Bunim and his pupil R. Yitzhak of Vorki represented the Jewish community in dealings with the secular authorities. Moreover, both Menachem Mendel and Hiddushei ha-Rim were overt supporters of the Polish rebellion of 1831. When that uprising failed they had to change their names to evade the Russian authorities. Menachem Mendel changed his name from Halperin to Morgenstern and Yitzhak Meir changed his name from Rottenberg to Alter.[34] Even hasidic Torah became totally spiritualized, unable to guide the hasid in the earthly world.

Hiddushei ha-Rim brought the world of Przysucha and Kotzk to a close. With him there was a reassertion of kabbalah. One need only compare the

---

[33] See *Mareh Deshe,* 94–101, 235–238 for the interesting connection between the descendents of Kotzk and Zionism.

[34] *Ha-Rebbe mi-Kotzk ve-Shishim Gibborim,* Y. Rottenberg, M. Shenfeld, vol 2, p. 549. Tel Aviv: 1959. Rabinowitz, *From Przysucha to Lublin,* p. 530.

popular *Sefat Emet*, his grandson, with R. Bunim to realize that his radicalism had been entirely blunted. The short epigram, the sharp observation of human nature, now became a more traditional Torah with a dose of kabbalah which any self-respecting *mitnagged* could have taught.

But what would R. Bunim have done had he lived fifty years later? After all, here was a man who, though he had experienced the cultural breadth of Western Europe, chose the spiritual depth of Eastern Europe. Would R. Bunim have been able to lead an Eastern European community to navigate modernity? He once said that "only a hairbreadth separates heaven from hell." A human being has no alternative but to tread that narrow bridge, for not to respond to the challenge is to create one's own hell. And the only support is the belief that his efforts are not worthless in the eyes of the Creator, and that He beckons each person to come a little closer to Him – as a human being.

In the post-Auschwitz era, there are various responses taken by the religious world towards modernity. One is simply to deny it (unless it can be used technically). In such an atmosphere of threat it is natural to rely only on *halakhah* and on the belief in the zaddik (nowadays called *"emunat hakhamim"*). Another response is to adopt the consumerism of the Western world and apply it to religion. Religion becomes a palliative. Every question can be answered, and Judaism is sold successfully like a bar of soap as long as the packaging is right. Both approaches are frightened of making a creative mistake – afraid of their own shadow. But R. Bunim's approach is closer to the following:

> Grow up with faith and the ability to face life. Face it with its challenge, its triumphs and defeats and sorrows. With true faith in God you will not be inflated by success nor shattered and reduced to impotence in hours of defeat and unhappiness…. "Know Him in all thy ways."[35]

---

[35] Kopul Rosen, *"Dear David,"* published in *Memories of Kopul Rosen* (London: 1970), 27.

To summarize, we will formulate thirteen principles of faith in the world of Przysucha. These are:

1. Learning Torah in particular and the use of the intellect in general are crucial values.

2. These values must be accompanied by a personal purifying process; otherwise mind alone is inadequate to achieve intimacy with God. This purifying process requires an analysis of who one is and what one's motives are.

3. Performing a commandment for the sake of personal interest or because of what other people think is not acceptable.

4. Only those who have an understanding of themselves can come to the supreme value of personal authenticity; otherwise, one is living a lie.

5. All actions have to be done with sincerity in a state of personal truthfulness. Przysucha rejected the Rabbinic value that one should perform a command even for an ulterior motive because eventually one will come to do it sincerely. Przysucha utterly rejects what is insincere, sham, pretence, external, and superficial, whether it is reflected in the leader or in his adherents.

6. The seat of truth and truthfulness is inside one's heart, which is allied to nature and Torah. It is not to be found in some book of knowledge outside oneself. Because Przysucha focuses on human beings, anything theological or esoteric is not its concern. Therefore, the Zohar, the Ari and kabbalah are muted. Theology is simply not the issue – the issue is the human being.

7. To be true to oneself requires not only an awareness of one's true essence but primarily a sense of Divine presence, aware that this sense might be a delusion without some degree of self-analysis. The vehicle for this awareness is prayer. Prayer is therefore so critical that even normative halachic restrictions of time are ignored.

8. Preparation is critical for a person to be able to fulfill a commandment authentically. Preparation means that one can only perform a commandment such as prayer when one is ready. Without preparation, the likelihood is that the experience will be a sham, and any emotion will evaporate and nothing of value will remain after the act.

9. The ultimate purpose of Torah and the commandments is to draw a person close to God. This approach to the Divine can only be achieved within the context of humility and with a sense of awe,

which is the experience of being in His presence. Where there is no humility there can be no true self-analysis. Haughtiness, pride, self-righteousness and self-satisfaction are all to be rejected. The greatest enemy in the psychology of service is depression, the antidote to which is joy and passion.

10. No rebbe or zaddik can usurp the role of the individual. All they can do is to help a disciple to become what he could be. Imitation, especially of a zaddik, is therefore the kiss of death. Because purity of motive leads to a challenge to or a weakening of external authority, Przysucha shows no respect to zaddikim if they exhibit any of the qualities of insincerity, ignorance or pride.

11. Each individual must assume personal responsibility for standing before the Divine presence. Belief in zaddikim cannot absolve a person from personal responsibility and finding his own path.

12. One must never be static or in a state of routine. Rather one is to be in a continual state of renewal striving for sincerity and genuineness. The role of the group and the rebbe is to ensure this renewal.

13. The quest for truth as the supreme value means that norms and customs no longer have credibility per se, for social behavior encourages parading one's religiosity, whereas the search for pure motive would tend to lead the devotee to hide his quest for spirituality.

Postscript

In this book, I have tried to show that there is an inner coherence to the thought of Przysucha – not simply a cluster of ideas. Once one understands where they were coming from, one can see how everything fits together, and how it was all quite coherent. Even though none of their ideas was original, nonetheless, while in other forms of Hasidism this collection of ideas served as an element within a larger picture, for Przysucha it was the picture itself. Therefore, one can speak of a Przysucha profile – an educated projection of the kind of idea they would have espoused.

The main protagonist of this book is R. Simhah Bunim, but I have tried to show that the essential ideas of his thought can be paralleled with his teacher the Yehudi of Przyshcha. However, there is a shadow which hovers over this story – it is the shadow of what ultimately happened to R. Bunim's pupil – the Kotzker.

When R. Bunim died in 1827, Kotzk became the main magnet of Polish Hasidism and Menahem Mendel was its pillar of fire. But then in spite of, or possibly because of his success, Menahem Mendel removed himself from active leadership for some twenty years until his death in 1859. This seems to have happened at the same time that R. Mordechai Joseph Leiner (the Ishbitzer) broke with him in 1839 – though the process seems to have started earlier.[36] Some have claimed that the rift between Menahem Mendel and the Ishbitzer was occasioned by the so-called "Friday night incident." But the Ishbitzer's grandson, R. Yeruham, states explicitly, "There was no such incident. It was an utter lie, motivated by the *Maskilim* and others."[37] Fairstein, too, has shown that later interpretations of this withdrawal were malicious inventions motivated by political considerations.[38]

It is difficult, from the various sources, to gauge Menahem Mendel's behavior during the last twenty years of his life. On the one hand, *Meir Einei ha-Golah*[39] conveys an image of someone who has virtually withdrawn from society. On the other hand, there are sources[40] that convey the impression of someone who is on fire and dissonant rather than someone who has totally removed himself from his Hasidim – of someone still functioning – but in an active state of withdrawal. *Meir Einei ha-Golah*[41] itself describes how, after R. Yitzhak of Vorki died in 1848, many of his important hasidim, including his eldest son Mordechai Menahem, came to learn from the Kotzker. It was the Kotzker who eventually told him to return home and to wear his father's mantle of leadership.[42]

---

[36] Y.L. Levin, *Ha-Admor me-Ishbitz*, 30.

[37] Quoted in S.Z. Shragai. *In the Paths of Hasidism*. Izbica-Radzin, 185 (Jerusalem: 1972), quoting *Tiferet Yeruham*, 149.

[38] Faierstein, *All Is in the Hands of Heaven,* appendix entitled "The Friday Night Incident in Kotzk: History of a Legend" (93).

[39] §429, 430, 432, 487.

[40] *Meir Einei ha-Golah*, §§235, 236, 323, 360; *Emet ve-Emunah*, n. 264; Levinger in "The Torah of the Rebbe from Kotzk: Authentic Statements by the Rebbe of Kotzk" (Hebrew). *Tarbiz* 55 (1986): 130 (n. 7).

[41] §394–395.

[42] §324.

There is a dark side to the personality of the Kotzker. When as a young man he came to Lublin, the Seer told him, "Your path is the path of darkness."[43] It may be that the Kotzker was continually at war with the dark side of his soul. The Kotzker's withdrawal might be due to his depression.[44] But the question is whether this withdrawal was an inevitable consequence of his extreme passion for truth. Is it inevitable that someone who brooks no compromise in matters of truth simply cannot function in society? Was it inevitable that Przysucha could last no longer than these three generations? These questions are haunting for those who see Przysucha as an educational paradigm for our time.

I would like to make an apology to R. Bunim. I have tried, to the best of my ability, to give a coherent structure to his thinking. But I know that ultimately, it is impossible for me to render his greatness as a teacher – the magic of his engagement with his pupils – and the thrill of being in the presence of a great man. As Walt Whitman said, "I and mine do not convince by arguments, similes, rhymes; we convince by our presence."

---

[43] *Nifla'ot ha-Yehudi*, 71.

[44] For a first-hand account of the Kotzker's withdrawal and what it was like in Kotzk, see B. Mintz, *The Last of the Kotzkers*, in *Ketuvim* 26, p. 177. Faierstein, ibid., says: "Finally Gliksman indicates that the story of Menahem Mendel's seclusion has been greatly exaggerated. He cites a wide variety of evidence to show that he did not cut himself off from the world during his last twenty years. He did not hold public gatherings or grant audiences, as was customary for a *rebbe*, but he kept in close touch with events in both the Jewish community and the world at large. Gliksman quotes a number of letters written by Menahem Mendel during this period in which he comments on world events, and in one case offers advice on who should be appointed to a particular rabbinic position. He continued to see his close disciples regularly and spent every Sabbath afternoon examining his grandsons on their studies of the previous week. Gliksman paints a picture of Menachem Mendel in semi-seclusion, yet keeping a close watch on events around him."
Faierstein summarizes Heschel's position (Kotzk, 2:568–570). "According to an oral tradition, he suffered a nervous breakdown on the Sabbath of Parshat Toldot 5599 (1838). Menachem Mendel was ill during the whole winter and following spring" (See *Meir Einei Ha-Golah*, n. 361).

ADDENDA

METHODOLOGY

Towards a Methodology of Dealing with the Sources of Przysucha Hasidism

AN ACADEMIC APPROACH towards the study of Przysucha Hasidism confronts serious problems of methodology. In general, the hasidic sources tend towards hagiography: lines of dissension are smoothed over and radicalism is softened by later generations, who attribute those tensions that existed to pupils who did not understand the master. But in the case of Przysucha we have an additional problem. One of the characteristics of all three generations of Przysucha was that they never published any written work of their own. This was not true of their predecessors (the Seer of Lublin and his teacher, R. Elimelech of Lyzhansk), nor was it true of the generations immediately after Menahem Mendel. There are thus no primary sources for the three major teachers. That is, we have nothing written by the Yehudi, by R. Simhah Bunim, or by R. Menahem Mendel.

Said R. Bunim:

> I thought of writing a book about the generations of man that would contain his role and his essence; but on further reflection I decided not to.[1]

In the case of R. Bunim there are two extant works by people who knew him personally. The first, *Kol Simhah*, was written by R. Zusha of Plozk (Breslau, 1859), a disciple of R. Bunim. But this work was severely criticized by his contemporaries as being totally inadequate. Weissenfeld relates the following reaction by his father-in-law, who knew R. Bunim personally, to this work:

---

[1] See Chap. 7, n. 2.

Recently a book has been published in the name of the Rabbi [R. Bunim], called *Kol Simhah*.... I brought it to my father-in-law in the year 1864, and after having glanced at it, he said that the above work does not have an ounce of the wisdom of the great man, that insipid things have been written in his name, and that one can't learn anything whatsoever [about R. Bunim] from the book.[2]

The other major source is a work entitled *Ramatayim Zofim*, compiled by R. Shmuel of Sieniawa (Warsaw, 1882), which is a collection of teachings that he heard from a variety of teachers. But as R. Shmuel states of himself, "When I first met him [R. Bunim]... I was eighteen or nineteen years old," so that the subtlety of R. Bunim's teachings might not have been sufficiently appreciated by a teenager.[3] In general, based on these two works, one would not at all understand what was so radical about the teachings of R. Bunim nor why there was a concerted effort made by the majority of Polish hasidic masters and virtually all those of Galicia to excommunicate Przysucha.

Moreover, even such noted disciples of R. Bunim as R. Yitzhak Meir Alter (Rottenberg) of Ger and R. Hanoch Heinich of Alexander did not write the works published in their names (*Meir Einei ha-Golah; Hiddushei ha-Rim* or *Hashavah le-Tovah*).[4] Later compilations such as *Simhat Israel*, with its

---

[2] Weissenfeld, Avraham Yaacob. *Exchange of Letters between Weissenfeld Avraham Yaacob and His Friends* (Hebrew). Cracow: 1900, 81. Also Rabinowitz, "R. Bunim" (40) who quotes Yitzhak Mieses, a pupil of R. Bunim, as saying "There is no comparison between the wisdom of R. Bunim and his Torah as published in *Kol Simhah*." See also *Siah Sarfei Kodesh he-Hadash*, 4:175 §46.

[3] *Ramatayim Zofim*, chap. 3 §2. Compare our understanding of the very first quotation of R. Bunim with R. Shmuel's somewhat bizarre interpretation (see Chapter 7 section on "Sin and Evil"). Boem (28) mentions that both R. Zusha of Plozk and R. Shmuel of Sieniawa were among those hasidim who, when R. Bunim died, followed his son Avraham Moshe rather than Menahem Mendel of Kotzk. They were the less radical followers of R. Bunim.

[4] See M. Piekarz, *Ideological Trends of Hasidism in Poland During the Interwar Period and the Holocaust* (Hebrew) (Jerusalem: 1990), 60, n. 19; cf. Avraham Yissakhar Binyamin Eliyahu Alter, *Meir Einei ha-Golah*, 2 pts. (Tel Aviv, 1954; first published: Piotrkow, 1928–1932). This work is based upon documents owned by the family and used with their permission, a kind of official biography of Hiddushei ha-Rim. Cf. Yitzhak Meir of Gur, *Hiddushei ha-Rim al ha-Torah; Moadim ve-Likkutim*, ed., Yehudah Leib Levin, revised and expanded version (Jerusalem: 1987). *Hashavah le-Tovah*, pt. I, consists of novellae of R. Hanokh Heinich ha-Kohen of Alexsander (Piotrkow:

three sections, *Or Simhah*, *Ma'amarei Simhah* and *Torat Simhah*, were published in Piotrkow 1910, and the compendium *Siah Sarfei Kodesh* (Lodz-Piotrkow) was published in 1923–1924. As for the first generation – the Yehudi, the founder of Przysucha and teacher of R. Bunim – works attributing teachings to him were published a hundred years or so after his death.[5]

The fact that we have nothing written by the Yehudi or R. Bunim means that we must rely (at best) on secondary material. But that does not necessarily imply that this material is to be dismissed as hagiographic. What it does mean is that *we must not give too much credence to any one source. Rather, we need to build our thesis on the basis of multiple quotations from different sources in order to begin to paint the contours,* an approximation of this movement. We can never know for certain whether the person actually said the words ascribed to him. But if there are a number of sources all indicating the same general idea, then we can have more confidence in its overall reliability.

At times, an idea is ascribed to the Yehudi or R. Bunim or the Kotzker. This might indeed be true. It may be that the Yehudi was the original source but that the idea was developed and became typical of R. Bunim as well. Even if neither of them actually expressed it, the fact that we have sources attributing such sayings to them suggests that later generations considered these sayings typical of their teachings. Therefore, even if a given idea was not actually expressed by the master, the idea might encapsulate what the master stood for – and that ultimately is what interests us. Even if we have no proof that a given quotation was in fact expressed by one of these three masters of Przysucha, the material is still useful. There is a genre of interpretation that is identifiable as belonging to that world. Przysucha has certain seminal values, which are recognizable, so that we can create a context, a discriminatory sense, which allows us to evaluate whether an idea, rather than a specific quotation, was part of the *oeuvre* of Przysucha or not.

Nor is oral tradition to be dismissed. In his work *From Lublin to Przysucha*, Zvi Meir Rabinowitz says:

> When I started my investigation of Przysucha, I set myself the goal of using those books whose sources are reliably those of pupils of Przysucha, but especially I drew on a living tradition of this Hasidic

---

1929); *Sefer Alexsander*, by R. Hanoch Heinich ha-Kohen, ed. Y.L. Levin (Jerusalem: 1969), second edition.
[5] See our bibliography for works on the Yehudi.

school. I knew a number of elderly Hasidim whose parents had known personally all the great Hasidic leaders, including R. Simhah Bunim.[6]

A living culture is reluctant to commit itself to the written word. Its vibrancy, its reality, is not easily confined to the pages of a book. Thus, though an oral tradition might be frustrating for the academic who wants to know "what they actually said," a living oral tradition conveys "what they actually meant." We might not be able to know precisely whether it was the Yehudi or R. Simhah Bunim or R. Menahem Mendel who made a particular comment. However, one can say that such a comment emanated from the world of Przysucha.

Yaakov Levinger[7] is dismissive of Abraham Joshua Heschel's book on Kotzk. But Heschel's argument, though frustrating for the academic, has a powerful ring. He says:

> Whoever attempts to describe Hasidism on the basis of literary sources alone without drawing upon the oral tradition, ignores the authentic living source and is dependent upon material artificial in character. In the absence of the oral tradition and a proximity to Hasidic personages, one can scarcely describe Hasidism. Its essence was rarely expressed in writing, and that which was written down was translated into Hebrew in a style which seldom captured the living tongue of the masters. Hasidic literature is a literature of translation, and not always successful translation. In order to understand Hasidism one must learn how to listen and how to stand close to those who lived it.[8]

One should be forewarned not to rely upon any single source, even if it is an authentic one. For example, to construct a thesis that there is a difference in philosophy between R. Bunim and R. Menahem Mendel because we have an example of different interpretations by these two masters of the same verse – even if both interpretations are authentic – is inadequate and possibly misleading. It is possible that a master gave a particular interpretation one year, but may

---

[6] Z.M. Rabinowitz, *From Lublin to Przysucha*, 293.

[7] Y. Levinger, *"Imrot autentiot shel ha-rebbe mi-Kotsk"* (Hebrew). *Tarbiz* 56 (1): 111.

[8] A.J. Heschel, *The Circle of the Baal Shem Tov: Studies in Hasidism,* edited by S. Dresner. Chicago: 1985, Introduction, 23.

have equally well have given an alternative one. The real question is whether the difference between these two interpretations is substantive. Do we know from other sources that this difference of interpretation is consistent with their philosophy? One example proves nothing.[9] In our opinion, the essential ideas of Przysucha, from the Yehudi through R. Bunim to R. Menahem Mendel, are consistent throughout.[10] There are one or two variants, but these seem due more to differences in personality than to ideology.

Even if we assume that many of the aphorisms were invented by later generations, they still have value, for they reflect at least what later generations considered to be the values of a particular master (and that too cannot be dismissed). They may therefore be used as corroborative support, as additional material to add to an already established profile. One cannot simply dismiss the vast collection of homilies found in *Siah Sarfei Kodesh* simply because they do not have the introductory phrase "I heard from [the Master]."[11] One needs to be a little bit more flexible and use this material, albeit with caution. The living oral tradition can also play a complementary role in providing shadow in order to bring out the light of a personality. Even hagiography can capture what a person epitomizes without him necessarily articulating it.[12]

This sense of insecurity, of never being quite sure who said what, of the absence of reliable primary sources, was highlighted by Yaakov Levinger in his article "Authentic Statements by the Rebbe of Kotzk." He writes:

> No less than ten works have been devoted to R. Menahem Mendel of Kotzk and to his teachings; no less than five special collections of his statements have been published; however, it is extremely difficult to evaluate the academic value of this vast literature.

---

[9] Y. Levinger. *"Torato shel ha-Rebbe mi-Kotsk le-or ha-imrot ha-meyuhasot lo al yedei nekhdo R. Shmuel mi-Sochaczew." Tarbiz* 55/3 (1986): 418–421. He consistently falls into this trap.

[10] Compare Aescoly, *Hasidut be-Folin*, edited by David Assaf. Jerusalem: 1999, 32.

[11] Levinger dismisses all statements attributed to the Kotzker unless they have the introductory phrase "I heard from (the Master)."

[12] On some level there is an analogy here with the attitude of modern scholars as to whether one can derive anything historical from the Talmud.

Referring to two works on the Rebbe of Kotzk written by academics, he writes:

> They cannot be regarded as scientific. They describe his life and his teachings without differentiating between reliable sources and those that are not; what statements attributed to him were indeed expressed by him and which attributed to him by later generations. The Rebbe of Kotzk did not write anything; at least we have nothing written by him.... Statements attributed to R. Menahem Mendel of Kotzk have sprouted and multiplied like mushrooms, for each collection has only increased the number of statements. In 1881–1882 – that is, twenty-two years after the death of the Rebbe – there was published in Warsaw for the first time the work *Ramatayim Zofim* by R. Shmuel of Sieniawa, one of the disciples of R. Simhah Bunim and one of the adherents of the Rebbe of Kotzk... in which are included thirty statements by him. In 1909 the first collection of statements exclusively his was published in Lublin. The collection *Ohel Torah* by R. Eliezer Zvi Zeligman now included more than three hundred statements by the Rebbe. In 1940 there was published in Jerusalem the collection *Emet ve-Emunah,* which now included 906 statements. In 1956 there appeared in Tel Aviv a collection, *Amud ha-Emet,* which now included one thousand statements. In 1961 there was published in Bnei Berak a collection, *Emet mi-Kotzk Tizmah,* which now included 1,113 statements and in 1980 a collection... now in excess of twelve hundred statements... with the name of *Lehavot Kodesh.*[13]

Thus, R. Menahem Mendel of Kotzk is clearly a growth industry. This ironic piece by Levinger only highlights the methodological problems we are dealing with when we have no primary sources. Whatever one might think of Levinger's own rigid and somewhat arid methodology,[14] his point is well taken and applies with equal validity to Menahem Mendel's teachers, R. Bunim and the Yehudi.

---

[13] See note 7.

[14] See Pinchas Sadeh, *Ish be-heder sagur.* Jerusalem: 1993, 15–16.

A good example of the morass in which we find ourselves is the following. Rabinowitz builds an entire thesis on the alleged difference between the Yehudi and R. Bunim, remaking them in the images of R. Judah ha-Levi and Maimonides. But this very difference is quoted in the exact opposite fashion in an earlier work. Rabinowitz writes:

> The holy Yehudi taught, like R. Yehudah ha-Levi, that the foundation of Judaism was the Exodus.... By contrast, his disciple R. Bunim taught that the foundation was contemplating the verse, "Lift up your eyes on high and see Who created all these" (Isaiah 40:26).[15]

The version quoted by Rabinowitz is found in *Siah Sarfei Kodesh*, in the work *Hiddushei ha-Rim*, and also in *Ramatayim Zofim*.

> The Yehudi once asked R. Bunim whence he derives his inspiration for the service of God. R. Bunim replied: from the verse, "Lift up your eyes on high and see Who created all these." The Yehudi replied that the Jewish people do not need this sentence because they have the Exodus.[16]

Now, we know that the use of the verse, "Lift up your eyes on high and see Who created all these" (Isaiah 40:26) was typical of R. Bunim.[17] But what are we to do with the fact that we have an earlier source, which has a contradictory version? In *Shem mi-Shmuel* (written by the grandson of the Rebbe of Kotzk) we read the following:

> One can explain this on the basis of what R. Bunim of Przysucha once asked my grandfather of Kotzk: from where does he derive his inspiration for the service of God? And he replied: from the verse, "Lift up your eyes on high and see Who created all these," and R.

---

[15] See above Z.M. Rabinowitz, 332–333. Even his understanding of the way R. Bunim uses the sentence is inadequate. R. Bunim's philosophy is that one first looks inside the person and is thus enabled to then see outside the design of the Divine in nature.

[16] *Siah Sarfei Kodesh*, 3:37 §55 (but see below note 20); *Hiddushei ha-Rim*, par. Bereshit, 5. See also *Ramatayim* Zofim, chap. 14. §35.

[17] The phrase was almost his motto: he quotes it in the very first comment in *Kol Simhah*. See above Rabinowitz, 332, n. 6.

Bunim replied that after the Exodus, one's inspiration should come from the Exodus.[18]

Either these traditions are contradictory or they are not. Either R. Bunim accepted the Yehudi's correction and changed his mind, and it just happened that Menahem Mendel thought in the same way as R. Bunim originally thought before the Yehudi corrected him (in which case, if R. Bunim changed his mind, what value is there in Rabinowitz referring to R. Bunim's earlier opinion?); or, alternatively, these traditions are contradictory. Yaakov Levinger,[19] in his article on the teachings of the Rebbe of Kotzk, asserts that *Shem mi-Shmuel* is the most reliable source we have for knowing what Menahem Mendel said or thought. Thus, if we had to choose between these two sources, we would choose the one by the grandson and assume R. Bunim had changed his mind. Or, alternatively, perhaps we simply cannot build too much on any single source, especially where there is a lack of clarity or a certain dubiousness.[20]

We are inclined to adopt Levinger's caution, but reject his conclusions. Levinger relies heavily on *Shem mi-Shmuel* as the cornerstone of authenticity, or on those quotations that have an introductory phrase, such as "I myself heard." While this is a safe approach, it is hardly adequate to bring out the personality or thought of the world of Przysucha. Therefore, Levinger himself admits that he isn't quite sure as to what the special contribution of Menahem Mendel was.[21]

---

[18] *Shem mi-Shmuel*, par. Vaethanan, 44. Cf. *Emet ve-Emunah,* 34; *Amud ha-Emet,* 99.

[19] See above J. Levinger.

[20] Confusion is reflected in *Siah Sarfei Kodesh* itself. See *Likkutei Yonatan, Siah Sarfei Kodesh,* 4, 41-42, §17; cf. *Siah Sarfei Kodesh,* 3.5 §7.

[21] Levinger, "*Torato shel ha-rebbe mi-Kotsk le-or ha-imrot ha-meyuhasot lo al yedei nekhdo R. Shmuel mi-Sochaczew,*" 422, asks the following question: "What therefore differentiates R. Mendel of Kotzk from his teachers the holy Yehudi and R. Simhah Bunim?" This somewhat begs the question. Who says there is a significant difference between them? Levinger goes on to say, "The answer is not that simple, but maybe we can note two things." Levinger argues that unlike the Yehudi and R. Bunim, who both thought that learning Torah alone was inadequate in the service of God, Menahem Mendel thought that learning Torah alone was the main path in the service of God. This is somewhat surprising coming from someone who on page 414 (at the beginning of the article) says that he "cannot say for certain that R. Mendel of Kotzk was a great talmid hakham in talmudic literature." In addition, we

note that the revolution of bringing the learning of Torah back into the Polish orbit of Hasidism, was accomplished precisely by the Yehudi and R. Bunim.

But more important, what is the basis for thinking that R. Mendel thought that "learning alone is the main path"? There is a quote in his name (*Shem mi-Shmuel*, par. Lech Lecha, vol. 1, 121a) which says the following: "There are many paths to draw near to God, but they all have a danger. Only the path of Torah is the one in which you can feel sure." We would suggest that the Kotzker means the following: any other path taken alone is prone to delusion (for one can never know if one's experience is fake or not), but learning Torah is the one path that is objective. Therefore, spirituality without Torah is dangerous. One's spirituality must first pass through the intellect. And that is exactly what the Yehudi and R. Bunim would say as well. Menaham Mendel's statement is not so different from what R. Yitzhak Vorki is supposed to have said on his deathbed: "The gemara is the greatest purification" (*Ohel Yitzhak*, 107.259).

Levinger argues that, unlike the Yehudi, whose prayer was ecstatic, R. Mendel's prayer was not. We might add that in this respect R. Mendel followed his teacher, R. Bunim, who looked askance at exaggerated styles of prayer. However as we have mentioned before the Kotzker's son in law, R. Avraham of Sochachzew tells the following story (*Shem mi-Shmuel*, par. *Korah* 267, [1914]; par. Vaethanan 35 [1915]): "My father told me that in his youth when he was weak and spitting blood, my grandfather took him to pray with him in his room on Rosh ha-Shanah next to the great bet ha-midrash and he saw him pray the standing prayer of Rosh ha-Shanah… with no movement or emotion – *but his face was on fire.*" If that isn't a form of ecstatic God-consciousness via prayer, then what is?

Levinger's second argument is that, whereas for the Yehudi and R. Bunim the ultimate in faith is the sense of "*ayin*," we don't find such a belief in the thought of the Kotzker. However, for the Yehudi or R. Bunim the concept of "*ayin*" is not a theological one, as it is in the case of the Maggid (see R. Schatz-Uffenheimer, *Hasidism as Mysticism* [Jerusalem-Princeton, 1993], 67-79). It is more akin to a phrase used by Abraham Marx who said, "Scholarship is like standing on the abyss of ignorance." "*Ayin*," or the quality of "*mah*" for Przysucha in general, is an intuitive sense of merging with the Divine, which contains elements such as human worthlessness, of no claim on God – and in this R. Mendel would totally agree.

The truth is that there is an inconsistency in Levinger's two works. In the earlier one, "*Authentic Statements by the Rebbe of Kotzk*," *Tarbiz* 55 (1986): 121, he says:

If we consider, analyze and compare them (the statements attributed to Menaham Mendel) with those of his teachers, the holy Yehudi and R. Simhah Bunim of Przysucha, we won't easily find anything which differentiates R. Mendel of Kotzk from his teachers…. *There is nothing original in the Kotzker from his aforementioned teachers.*

For sources on Menahem Mendel's knowledge of Torah, see the introduction to the work *Eglei Tal* and *Avnei Nezer, Orah Hayyim,* §453, by his son-in-law, R. Abraham of Sochaczew.

Oral tradition has its own vitality and rationale. For example, there are many anecdotes about R. Bunim that might easily be misconstrued, or seen in a negative light, or at least considered highly unusual for someone who became a rebbe. What motive would there be for hasidic tradition to have preserved these stories? On the contrary, one would have expected that these stories would have been censored, or at least explained away. If they had been invented by, say, a *maskil* who was trying to besmirch Hasidism, why would they have been published at the end of the nineteenth century by people whose fathers might well have known R. Bunim personally? Why would Hasidim, of all people, have preserved and not denied such traditions?

In our attempt to describe R. Bunim's essential ideas, we have used the Yehudi as the major point of comparison. But of course the figure of R. Menahem Mendel of Kotzk also looms large. Here Levinger's words resonate loudly. There are various "collections" of sayings attributed to the Kotzker, such as *Ohel Yitzhak* (which is the only collection to attribute its sources) *Emet ve-Emunah* and *Amud ha-Emet*. By and large, we have only used these in a secondary way, to reinforce and support an idea or value already quoted by a more reliable source.

But there is another question. What inhibited these three masters from writing? Did they feel that the written word became fossilized too easily and would mitigate against personal authenticity – for example, that once the rebbe advocated a particular approach it would simply be accepted slavishly by his followers? Or did they believe that *torat adam* – the individual human psyche – precludes, by definition, any given path, book or canon? More likely, it was a conscious decision based on a philosophy of education. If the role of the zaddik is essentially to arouse in the disciple, by his personal example, what the disciple needs to become, and not, God forbid, to imitate the zaddik, then there cannot be any handbook, because each person must travel his or her own path. Thus, this lack of writing is part of a totally coherent approach, consistent with Przysucha.[22]

Finally, it is belaboring the obvious to say that there is a danger that one will project one's own agenda onto a master. In trying to describe a master, one uses loaded words. For example, to speak of Menahem Mendel as being

---

[22] For further details, see chap. 7.

"individualistic" is true – but the word "individualistic" might in itself convey the impression that he was antinomian. Now, while there are seeds of antinomianism in mysticism, in Przysucha's case it was limited by and large to the area of times of prayer. One need not make a philosophy of one's own weakness by projecting it onto someone else.[23] Or, for example, one might speak about Przysucha and the Romantic movement, but we must never forget that their entire world, their self-perception, was one that was totally and unselfconsciously halakhic. Przysucha is highly individualistic and totally within *Klal Yisrael.* If it stresses personal redemption, it knows that this takes place within the context of the wider redemption of the Jewish people – before God.

The Prejudice and Agenda of Scholars of Hasidism

Methodology relates not only to the reliability of sources, but also to the bias or historical context of the historian. A case in point might be the question: What was the attitude of the Yehudi to the hastening of the coming of the Messiah? Rabinowitz[24] correctly states that there are only a few sources to indicate his view. There is a famous quotation in the name of the Yehudi that we have already mentioned, but is worth repeating:

> With the greatest of respect to those zaddikim who reveal the time of the Messiah: in truth it is a great secret and anyone who knows it cannot, under any circumstances, reveal it. And if one does reveal it – that is proof that he does not truly know it.[25]

This source suggests that the Yehudi is critical of those people who try to hasten the time of the coming of the Messiah. But how reliable is this source? What credence can we give it, and how much can we build on it? It is our thesis that the three generations of Przysucha are not to be understood as a series of separate ideas. It is not enough to observe that

---

[23] See M. Fairstein's critique of Shaul Magid's *Hasidism on the Margin: Reconciliation, Antinomianism, and Messianism in Izbica and Radzin Hasidism* (Madison: University of Wisconsin Press, 2003). "This may be Shaul Magid's theological enterprise, but it is not that of Mordecai Joseph of Izbica or Gershon Heinokh of Radzin."

[24] Rabinowitz, *The Yehudi*, 121.

[25] *Atarah le-Rosh* Zaddik, 136 (*Torat ha-Yehudi*, 183 §13).

Przysucha throughout these three generations emphasizes truthfulness, personal integrity, introspection, and a disparagement of the miraculous, interesting as these characteristics might be. What needs to be stressed, and cannot be stressed enough, is that these values all derive from one seminal value: that of personal authenticity (within the context of Rabbinic Judaism).

If our understanding is correct, then we have an approach that can help us methodologically. In spite of the differences (and there are such) among the Yehudi, R. Bunim, and Menahem Mendel, we maintain that there is a basic profile of the Przysucha personality. On the basis of such a paradigm, we can say with some degree of confidence, even without any sources whatsoever, that the Yehudi's view would probably be to the question of attempting to bring the Messiah.[26]

Buber wrote a romantic novel *For the Sake of Heaven* in which he portrayed the Yehudi as opposing those who would try to hasten the coming of the messiah. This portrayal is correct[27] – that is to say that the Yehudi was not part of any enterprise to hasten the coming of the messiah. Trying to force God's hand is a venture that can take place within a Kabbalistic frame of reference, and that was simply not the Yehudi's agenda.

&ppar; (

No historian is entirely objective, but on the issue of Hasidism one feels that there are excesses of subjectivity that need to be corrected. One may perhaps forgive the nineteenth-century exponents of the Science of Judaism who thought that anything spiritual was some sort of deficient gene that would be rendered obsolete by "Enlightenment." But the problem is one of methodology. Without attempting to enter the mindset of a spiritual movement with some degree of empathy, one is reduced to being a type of voyeur. Worst, without according a spiritual movement its own inherent

---

[26] Regarding Przysucha and Messianism, see chap. 4.

[27] Regarding Buber's *Gog and Magog* (*For the Sake of Heaven*), cf. David Assaf's notes to A.Z. Aescoly's *Hasidut be-Folin* (Jerusalem: 1999), 15, n. 16.

On Buber's book (that first appeared in 1944), the views implied therein and its impact, see Shmuel Werses, "Hasidism in a Belletristic Light: Studies in Martin Buber's *For the Sake of Heaven*" (Hebrew). In Zaddik*im ve-anshei ma'aseh*, ibid., 317–356; A. Shapira, "Two Paths of Redemption in Hasidism in Light of Martin Buber" (Hebrew), *Masu'ot: mehkarim be-sifrut ha-kabbalah u-ve-mahshevet Yisrael* (Jerusalem: 1994), 429–446.

integrity, one seeks to explain its phenomena by purely external reasons. The modern scholar of religious phenomena must *combine being apart from with being a part of.* Otherwise he is either too much inside or too much outside to be of value.

Some academics are fond of quoting, in connection with Hasidism, the phrase "Nonsense is nonsense, but the history of nonsense is history." As cute as this is, it simply won't do. One is reminded of what Wittgenstein said about Frazer's *Golden Bough* to the effect that it reflected the limitations of an Anglican cleric living in England at the beginning of the twentieth century.

Recently, Glenn Dynner[28] has challenged the assumption that Hasidism was born of crisis. In a section of his work, *Men of Silk,* entitled "What Crisis?," he surveys the various interpretations given to explain the rise of Hasidism. These include Dubnow's view, connecting it to the Chmielnicki massacres of 1648[29]; Mahler's theory, relating Hasidism to economic poverty[30]; Ben Zion Dinur's suggestion that early hasidic leaders were members of a disenchanted secondary intelligentsia[31]; that of Chone Shmeruk, who suggests that Hasidism may have filled a vacuum created by the abolition of the Council of Lands in 1764[32]; and Katz's view that the Enlightenment in Eastern Europe sent ideologically besieged traditional Jews floundering towards Hasidism.[33] Dynner rebuts all these theories:

---

[28] G. Dynner, "Men of Silk: The Hasidic Conquest of Polish Jewry, 1754–1830." Ph.D. diss., Brandeis University, 2002, 38–45. The essential critique of the bias and prejudice of previous historians of Hasidism was already detailed by Shmuel Ettinger, "Hasidism and the Kahal in Eastern Europe" (64–65) and Imanuel Etkes, "The Study of Hasidism and New Directions" (447–464) in *Hasidism Reappraised.*

[29] Dubnow, *Toldot ha-Hasidut,* 8–9, 36. See also Rabinowitz, *Lithuanian Hasidism* 1.

[30] R. Mahler, *Hasidism and the Jewish Enlightenment* 1–16.

[31] Benzion Dinur, "The Origins of Hasidism and its Social and Messianic Foundations." In *Essential Papers on Hasidism,* edited by G. Hundert, 86–208. New York: 1991. Cf. R. Mahler, *Essential Papers, ibid.,* 401–498.

[32] Chone Shmeruk, "Hasidism and the Kehillah." In Antony Polonsky et al., *The Jews in Old Poland, 1000–1795.* London: Taurus, 1993, 186–198.

[33] Jacob Katz, *Tradition and Crisis.* Edited by Bernard Dov Cooperman. New York: Schocken, 1993.

Several of the possible causal factors introduced by Dubnow may be quickly dismissed. The massacres in 1648 occurred over a century before the rise of Hasidism, and Jewish populations in town were replenished fairly quickly.... Had standards of living even decreased at the end of the eighteenth and beginning of the nineteenth centuries for the bulk of Polish Jewry? This contention has been rejected by Hundert, who finds that "the middle decades of the eighteenth century saw the beginnings of a general economic recovery from the nadir reached at the turn of the century."[34]

According to the English traveller Robert Johnston, in 1815 "the whole retail trade of Lithuania and Poland is carried on by the Jews."[35] J.T. James, another English traveller from 1813 to 1814, reports that the Jews of Cracow, "notwithstanding the oppressive hand of government, seem everywhere to thrive; some, indeed, have amassed large fortunes in spite of all the difficulties."[36]

Dynner demonstrates, on the basis of fresh archival material, that there was a direct correlation between Hasidism and the wealth and development of an area. He summarizes thus:[37]

> The impact of Hasidism on local populations may be demonstrated using several towns for which the data is available before and after the arrival or departure of Hasidic courts: From 1765 to 1790, the period of the arrival of Zaddikim in these towns, the Jewish population of Kozienice and Lublin rose. This growth contrasts favourably with other towns in the district. By the same token, Ryczywol's and Zelechow's Jewish population fell in the years comprising Levi Isaac's departure from the cities. Wieniawa's Jewish population fell by more than seventy percent when R. Jacob Isaac left for Lublin. These figures only reflect permanent settlement.

---

[34] G. Hundert, "The Contexts of Hasidism." In *Essential Papers,* op. cit., 176.

[35] Robert Johnston, *Travels through Part of the Russian Empire and the Country of Poland.* New York: 1816, 382.

[36] J.T. James, *Journal of a Tour: 1813–1814.* London: 1827, 420–421.

[37] See Dynner (above), 114–115, 123; cf. Moshe Rosman, "Medzhibozh and R. Israel Ba'al Shem Tov (Besht)" (Hebrew). *Zion* 52:2 (1987); also, *Essential Papers on Hasidism,* 209–226; idem., *Founder of Hasidism: A Quest for the Historical Baal Shem Tov* (Berkeley: 1996).

They do not represent the masses of pilgrims, who undoubtedly impacted local economies as well....

Polish Jews unquestionably figured prominently in the modest industrialization which fuelled the wars and uprisings of the period. This increase in Jewish economic self-sufficiency and involvement in large-scale international trade coincided with the collapse of Poland's nobility-dominated grain trade, inspiring an enormous amount of envy and resentment.[38]

Contemporary observers found that most of Warsaw's merchants were Jewish. A British traveller named Robert Johnston writes in 1815, "The present population of Warsaw is estimated at fifty thousand individuals, of whom twenty thousand are Jews, and who seem to manage all the trade of the city."[39] Harring was struck by Franciscan Street, which reminded him of the busy Jewish districts in Frankfurt, Prague, Rome, Amsterdam and Leghorn.[40] According to the 1792 census, about one quarter of Warsaw's Jewish population was involved in commerce....[41]

This is not to deny that much of Polish Jewry endured a great degree of economic pain.... But the mistaken assumption in so much of the literature on the rise of Hasidism is that they only appealed to that segment of the population. To the contrary, the Hasidic sources portray a full socio-economic range of supplicants....[42] Scholars have begun to downplay the effectiveness

---

[38] On the collapse of the grain market in the 1820s and the ruin of the Polish nobility see R.F. Leslie, *Polish Politics and the Revolution of November 1830*. London: University of London, 1956, 85.

[39] Johnston, *Travels, ibid.,* 381-382. An allegation about Jewish "arrogance" and the "conquest of all trade, crafts and distilleries" in Warsaw is included in Wladyslaw Smolenski, *Mieszczanstwo warszawskie w konscu wieku XVIII.* Warsaw: 1976, 295–296.

[40] Haro Harring, *Poland under the Dominion of Russia.* Boston: 1834, 125. Like the Jews of those other locales, those in Franciscan Street are "characterized by the same peculiarities, viz. uncleanliness and the love of finery, avarice, and dishonesty; while the persecutions and insults to which they are exposed render them real objects of pity."

[41] A. Eisenbach, "Jews in Warsaw: The End of the Eighteenth Century." In *The Jews in Warsaw: A History.* Oxford: 1991, 95–126.

[42] For one example of the full socio-economic range of hasidic supplicants, see Moshe Menahem Walden, *Nifla'ot ha-Rebbe* (Warsaw: 1911). See also Gershon Bacon, "Prolonged Erosion, Organization and Reinforcement: Reflections on

of the Council of Lands near the time it was abolished, while others have argued that Jewish communal life remained basically intact after its demise.[43]

There remains the question of the crisis of the Enlightenment put forth by Katz.... Emancipation did not apply in the case of Eastern and East Central Europe. Enlightenment ideology without the realistic promise of emancipation was bound to be a hard sell.... One should heed Mihail Berdychevski's lone dissent from back in 1899: "Hasidism was not created due to the crisis of Haskalah, nor was it even aware of it."[44]

So how does one explain the phenomenon of Hasidism? Dynner says (inter alia):

> Hundert posits "the appearance of a similar geist at a similar zeit among both Jews and Christians." These movements were not a reaction to the Enlightenment, but rather shared with the Enlightenment "the emboldening of the individual to independence of thought and feeling in matters of spirit."[45] Religious individualism characterizes an inexplicable eighteenth century zeitgeist that applied equally to Hasidism and other contemporaneous movements.[46]

The same prejudice – namely, that the desire for spirituality has to be motivated by a problem (otherwise why would a normal person be religious?) – underlies Idel's critique of Scholem and his school. Scholem

---

Orthodox Jewry in Congress Poland." In *Major Changes within the Jewish People in the Wake of the Holocaust*, edited by Yisrael Gutman, 75. Jerusalem: Yad Vashem, 1996.

[43] For a summary of these views, see Eli Lederhendler, "The Decline of the Polish Lithuanian *Kahal,*" in *Polin* 2 (1987): 153.

[44] He continues, "It was created due to an independent and natural reason." Mihail Berdychevski, "Le-Korot ha-Hasidut," in *Ozar ha-Sifrut* III (1899), 55. Yet we must temper Berdychevski's enthusiasm by noting that R. Nahman of Bratslav is clearly aware of the "dangers" of Haskalah. See M. Piekarz, *Hasidut Breslav*, Addendum 1, "Reshimu shel *Sefer Ha-Brit* be-divrei R. Nahman." Divrei R. Nahman

[45] See Hundert, "The Contexts" (op. cit.), 172–173.

[46] Torsten Ysander, *Studien zum Bestschen Hasidismus in Seiner Religious geschichtlichen Sonderart* (Uppsala, 1933), 372-392; Yaffe Eliach, "Jewish Hasidism, Russian Sectarians; Non-conformists in the Ukraine, 1700-1760," unpublished PhD Dissertation (1973).

relates the quest for messianism to the context of crisis. But it does not have to be. Idel says:

> There is another historical model of explanation that may more successfully illuminate the essence of the awakening of a messianic awareness. Instead of positing catastrophe and the despair that follows as the main causes of eschatological ideas and events, it is possible to stress, at least in certain cases, the kindling of hope as a prelude to a messianic awareness. Thus the appearance of Jewish apocalyptic behavior in the seventh and eighth centuries might be explained as the result of great waves of hope that spread in the wake of the Arab victories over the Christians.[47]

The end result of the linear historical approach is that it understands religious phenomena exclusively via external factors. This leads Aaron Zeev Aescoly to explain the Seer's (supposed) messianism as being motivated by crisis.

> The longing for redemption in Lublin was an expression of the great crisis in Hasidism. The Seer had to bring the Messiah, or all his world would come tumbling down.[48]

What is the source for such an interpretation other than Aescoly's predetermined view that Messianism is motivated by crisis? One could just as easily have argued exactly the opposite, namely, that the Seer's desire to hasten the coming of the Messiah was influenced by his own overwhelming success and that he felt that redemption was the next stage in this process.

We do not mean to argue that religious movements are not influenced by outside factors. A spiritual movement does not arise in a historical vacuum. But to argue, as does Brill,[49] for example, that it was the urbanization of Poland that created the revolution of Przysucha, seems to us to fall into the very trap for which Idel criticized Scholem. As Idel says:

---

[47] M. Idel, *Messianic Mystics.* New Haven: Yale University Press, 1998, Introduction, 8–9.

[48] A. Aescoly, *Hasidut be-Folin.* Edited by David Assaf, 57. Jerusalem: 1999.

[49] A. Brill, "Grandeur and Humility in the Writings of R. Simhah Bunim of Przysucha." In *Hazon Nahum* (1997), 444–448.

Most modern scholarship of Jewish messianism has preferred to concern itself more with the public, communal, or historical – in short, outward – manifestations of the Jewish messianic phenomenon than with its inner sources. This approach assumed that the overt facets of Jewish messianism indeed revealed its true character. In contrast to the emphasis upon inner experiences typical of the study of Christian mysticism, whose scholars were apt to ascribe special meaning to those private sensations that are considered to be the precursors of redemption, some of the contemporary scholars of Jewish messianism have depicted their subject essentially as a public affair.[50]

Maybe it is this lack of empathy that causes the Jewish historian to remain an outsider to a movement he is trying to explain. Or perhaps, in understanding religion in general, or spiritual movements in particular, the assumption is that there must be a problem to have caused the spiritual movement. The standard nineteenth-century German interpretation of Hasidism was that it was a response to the Chmielnicki massacres of the previous century that decimated Polish Jewry and that in an atmosphere of crisis, Hasidism appealed to the poor and gave them hope. This *"okh'n vey,"* this lachrymose approach to history is inadequate. Rosman has shown, through an analysis of the increase in rents being paid in Miedzyboz (where the Ba'al Shem Tov resided) at the beginning of the eighteenth century, that at the time the city was growing economically and was doing rather well.[51]

The assumption that religion only thrives when there is a problem is not only inadequate in explaining the rise of Hasidism, but is also totally inadequate to explain why, at the beginning of the twenty-first century, Hasidism should be thriving in Brooklyn, USA – a world as far removed from eighteenth-century Poland as can be imagined.

The historiography of Hasidism is full of the prejudices and agendas of the historian. For example, Scholem points out the rich theoretical literature of

---

[50] Idel, *Messianic Mystics*, 3–4.
[51] See M. Rosman, *Founder of Hasidism – a Quest for the Historical Baal Shem Tov.*

early Hasidism and that Buber consciously/purposefully ignored these primary sources:

> These legends and sayings [chosen by Buber] are certainly most impressive and they just as certainly posses a general human interest. However, if we want to know what they really meant in their original context we would still have to revert to those primary sources which Buber pushes aside as merely secondary. We shall presently see how important this original context is when we come to a discussion of the central point in Buber's interpretation of Hasidism. Although his selection entails certain ambiguities, we willingly grant Buber, as a writer and even as the advocate of a message, the right to choose what appeals to him. But I very much doubt that such a selection can form the basis for a real and scholarly understanding of what most attracted Buber to Hasidism.[52]

Buber's Hasidism is essentially divorced from any historical or social context. Worse, it is divorced from the religious and halakhic praxis of its adherents. In other words, Buber has distilled a sanitized spirituality, which is of significance for assimilated Jews and the non-Jewish world. As Buber told Scholem personally,[53] he wasn't really interested in historical Hasidism. Buber's Hasidism is Hasidism made relevant to the modern syncretistic culture that seeks a universal spirituality without any particular religious form

---

[52] G. Scholem, *The Messianic Idea in Judaism.* New York: 1972, 236. Cf. ibid., "Martin Buber's Interpretation of Hasidism," 248–250; J. Dan, *Gershon Scholem and the Mystical Dimension of Jewish History.* But for a devastating critique of Scholem's own methodology, see H. Lieberman, *"Keitzad hokrim hasidut be-Yisrael"* (Hebrew), *Ohel Rahel,* New York: 1980, 38–49. For a summary of this interchange, see Wilensky, *Hasidim u-mitnaggedim,* 2:377.

[53] G. Scholem, *On the Kabbalah and its Symbolism* (New York, 1969), 32. Regarding the famous difference of approach between Buber and Scholem, see Rivka Schatz-Uffenheimer, "Man's Relation to God and World in Buber's Rendering of the Hasidic Teaching." In *The Philosophy of Martin Buber,* edited by P.A. Schilpp and M. Friedman, 403–434. The Library of Living Philosophers. XII; La Salle, Ill., 1967; Martin Buber, "*Replies to My Critics,*" ibid., 689–744; Moshe Idel, "Martin Buber and Gershom Scholem on Hasidism: A Critical Appraisal." In *Hasidism Reappraised,* edited by A Rapoport-Albert, 389–403. London and Portland: 1996; Jerome Gellman, "Buber's Blunder: Buber's Replies to Scholem and Schatz-Uffenheimer." *Modern Judaism* 20 (2000): 20–40.

(to which Buber was opposed). One is left with Buber's intuitions which, to a spiritual person, are often of significance. Sometimes one feels about Buber what was said about "art": "Art is a lie which reveals the truth."

However, Scholem's historical approach has its own agenda. Scholem believed that messianism was produced by crisis. As he categorically states, "Mysticism as a historical phenomenon is a product of crisis." But this view was influenced, by his own admission, by his commitment to Zionism.[54]

As Idel says:

> The reduction of messianism to historical or external action, which unifies Scholem and Tishby, reduces the equal importance of the inner life as a significant criterion for determining the acuteness of a given phenomenon.... In other words, the modernistic emphasis on external action and thus on verification might distort the understanding of impulses that flourished more on the hidden scene of the inner life.[55]

It is not that historical analysis has no part to play in understanding religious movements. He further says:

> I see no problem in attempting to relate the social, economic, or political background to intellectual developments when such an approach is explicitly mentioned by the authors of the cultural creation, or when the content of the new writings cannot be explained on the ground of earlier traditions. Neither do I demand forensic proof for such a nexus between cultural and paracultural processes. However, in order to advance the plausibility of such a link, some affinity should be explicated beyond the mere statement that two phenomena are close in time. This form of what I have called proximism is a historistic approach that I can hardly accept without additional facts to substantiate it.[56] [57]

---

[54] Idel, *Messianic Mystics,* 413, n. 23.

[55] Ibid., 244.

[56] Ibid., 220.

[57] "I contend that the recourse to Greek psychological concepts and their appropriation has nothing to do with a sense of crisis in public Jewish life or even less with a reaction against an active apocalyptic messianism. It was, in my opinion, part of the enrichment of Jewish messianism by paradigms supplied by medieval theologies and psychologies new to medieval Jews." Ibid., 240.

Instead of positing catastrophe and the despair that follows as the main causes of eschatological ideas and events, it is possible to stress, at least in certain cases, the kindling of hope as a prelude to a messianic awareness.[58]

Idel stresses that the explanation for religious movements should not be reduced to external causal factors, for they have their own inner integrity:[59] "[Hasidism is] more than merely a reaction to historical crises; the vitality of hasidic mysticism draws from the creative appropriations of a full gamut of messianic ideas and models."[60] [61]

Aescoly asks[62] the following question. Why would R. Bunim, an educated, enlightened person who knew Western culture, want to join the Hasidic movement? It seems to me that this question reveals far more about Aescoly himself than it does about R. Bunim. What he is really asking is how can one choose to be an *Ostjude* (an eastern European Jew) after having tasted (like Aescoly) the world of modernity? In that question, all his own prejudices and possibly his own journey are revealed, more than anything else.

The historian is a child of his age – warts and all. It therefore seems imperative, when it comes to the history of Hasidism, to first have a history of the historian.

---

[58] Ibid. 8.

[59] Ibid., 238.

[60] M. Idel, *Hasidism: Between Ecstasy and Magic*, 214 says, rather appropriately, the following:
"The theory of alternating fluctuations of the relative roles of the magical, mystical and theosophical-theurgical is, one could argue, a better description of the 'history' of Jewish mysticism than any linear or Hegelian vision of the development of this mystical lore, in the spirit of Frazer's 'great transition.'"

[61] Idel, *Messianic Mystics*, 242.

[62] See Aescoly, 76; cf. Idel, *Messianic Mystics*, 9: "I would say that many examples of inner messianism... are not a reaction to the despair."

The Messianic Efforts of the Seer as an Example of the Methodological Problems

The methodological problems involved in dealing with the sources of Hasidism are very serious. No example better highlights this than that of the Seer's supposed attempts to hasten the coming of the Messiah and the objections of the Yehudi. Very few incidents in hasidic folklore have gripped the imagination as much as the attempts by the hasidic leaders of Poland to intervene either on behalf of or against Napoleon.[63] The Napoleonic wars were seen by some rebbes as presaging the coming of the Messiah and redemption. Buber's romantic novel *For The Sake Of Heaven* (in Hebrew, *Gog u-Magog*), which portrays this clash of Hasidic titans, inspired many to develop a love of Hasidism. Aescoly went even further and argued that it was this very issue of messianism that was the occasion for the great rebellion of the Yehudi against the Seer. Aescoly writes:

> In a very dramatic way, the Yehudi's rebellion expressed itself with regards to the bringing of the Messiah. During the Napoleonic wars in the 1790's, the Seer had still gathered his pupils and friends and managed to organize a special "unification" with a single intention for all. But behold, this intention had been thwarted. The Seer was in a state of great distress and mental contraction and investigated the matter, concluding that it was all because of the Yehudi who arrived in Lublin in the middle of this unification with the intention of interfering.[64]

We now quote, at some length, from an article by Yitzhak Alfasi:[65]

> There are few Zaddikim in Hasidism to whom there have been attributed such longings for the Messiah as have been attributed to

---

[63] Rabinowitz, "R. Bunim," 7, n. 18, highlights the change in the view of the Maggid of Kuznitz, who was initially a supporter of Napoleon. Menahem Mendel of Rimanov was a fervent supporter of Napoleon; see *Eser Orot*, 74 §32.

[64] Aescoly, *Hasidut be-Polin*, 54 says: "In a dramatic way, the rebellion of the Yehudi was given expression with regards to the bringing of the Messiah," and continues to trace the supposed involvement or non-involvement of the Yehudi in the Messianic aspirations of the Seer.

[65] Alfasi, Yizhaq. "Galut u-geulah be-mishnat ha-Hozeh mi-Lublin." In *Sefer Aviad*. Jerusalem: Mossad ha-Rav Kook: 1986, 85–88.

R. Yaacov Ha-Levi Horowitz, the Seer of Lublin, the foremost Zaddik of Poland. Hasidic folklore has adorned the many efforts of the Seer to advance the time of the coming of redemption; and even his wondrous demise on the ninth of Av, 1815; even his mysterious fall from the window of his room on Simhat Torah earlier that year is described as a result of the battle to hasten the time of redemption... In time, the story of the Seer's attempt to bring redemption became famous in various versions. Buber's book, *Gog and Magog,* is based upon this story, which is one of the most widely known in the folklore literature of Hasidism. **However, in spite of all the beauty of this story, it has no historical truth.**[66] Not only is there no allusion to this in the works of the Seer but he clearly and explicitly states the exact opposite. One should know that the Seer's works were written by himself and not by his pupils, unlike other Hasidic works, so that his works may be taken as authentic....[67] In tracing the source for this wonderful folklore, we are led to R. Aaron Marcus, who was the first to publish this story in his work "Hasidismus." R. Yekutiel Aryeh Kamalher, a fervent admirer of R. Aaron Marcus, used to quote his works extensively. R. Aaron Marcus was an outstanding and exceptional personality. However, his passion seems to have got the better of him. Many have already noted any number of examples of things that are incorrect and mistaken from a historical point of view.... R. Aaron Marcus's love for the land of Israel and for Zionism is the basis of the folk legend mentioned above regarding the wondrous death of the Seer. We should mention, in support of this assumption, that R. Aaron Marcus is [also] the source for telling us that Theodore Herzl's project for establishing a Jewish State was in fact the project of the Zaddik R. Yitzhak Friedmann of Buhusi, who preempted Herzl's

---

[66] For just such a romantic description of the Seer's attempt to bring the redemption, see Alfasi himself, *Ha-Hozeh mi-Lublin* (Jerusalem: Mossad ha-Rav Kook, 1969), chap. 8.

[67] See *Zot Zikaron* 69: "We are sworn not to pre-empt the coming of the Messiah before his time, which is known to God alone." See Ze'ev Gries, "The Hasidic Managing Editor," in *Hasidism Reappraised*, 145, n. 13: "Generally, the written or printed versions of all teachings of the leaders were not regarded as authoritative 'sacred writings' in themselves."

vision of a Jewish State. However, R. Yitzhak of Buhusi was a critic of the idea of settling the land and rejected outright all attempts by Hovevei Zion which sought his support.

This is not to argue that the Napoleonic wars had no impact on Polish Jewry. Clearly, this is not so. The leaders of Eastern European Jewry were divided on the cost-benefit ratio of civil rights on the one hand and of the dangers of openness on the other that lay in the wake of Napoleon's reforms. But not every historical event should be seen through the prism of the Jewish world.[68]

Piekarz[69] argues that the description of the Seer as someone who saw his role as bringing the Messiah (as Aescoly does in fact claim) is wrong. "Not only does it not fit in with his authentic writings, but these writings contradict the eschatological messianic pretensions which historians have attributed to him." Piekarz maintains that there were two seminal ideas propounded by R. Elimelech and his disciple the Seer (which were pursued consistently by his pupils throughout the nineteenth century) – concern for the physical welfare of the Jewish people in the Diaspora, and opposition to any concentrated religious effort in bringing the Messiah. But on the other hand, we know that the Seer believed that only by improving the physical situation of the Jewish people could the Godhead be repaired. It is possible therefore, to be involved in the hastening of the Messiah because one wants to repair the rupture on High.

David Assaf,[70] in his article "The Fall of the Seer..." states that, "A number of sources connect his [the Seer's] physical fall with his personal fall, after his efforts to bring the Messiah and redemption collapsed upon the shattering of his messianic expectations connected with the wars of Napoleon in Russia." But he goes on to show that the problem with this interpretation is that all Hasidic sources indicating such a view were written a

---

[68] See Addendum D.

[69] M. Piekarz, "Ha-Hasidut be-aspaklariat Tiferet Shlomoh, R. Shlomoh mi-Radomsk." *Gal Ed* 14 (1995): 37–58.

[70] David Assaf, "The Mitnaggedim Mocked That He Got Drunk and Fell: The Fall of the Seer of Lublin via the Mirror of Hasidic Memory and Maskilic Satire" (Hebrew). In *Within Hasidic Circles: Studies in Memory of Mordechai Wilensky*. Bialik Institute: Jerusalem, 1997, 161–208. Regarding Napoleon, Assaf maintains that hasidic sources depict the Seer as an opponent of Napoleon (see Berger, *Eser Tzahtzahot* [Piotrokow: 1910], 87, n. 17).

hundred years or so after the fact. The sources of the *Maskilim* (contemporary with the Seer, and other references throughout the nineteenth century), dealing with his fall, prejudiced as they might be, make no reference to any messianic eschatological aspiration on his part,[71] and they would have been only too delighted to have used the incident as a barb if they had in fact known about it.

Shmuel Werses,[72] in his analysis of Buber's *Gog and Magog,* seems less dismissive of these Hasidic traditions regarding the Seer and the Yehudi's involvement in Messianism. Nevertheless, after reading Alfasi's article one feels that, regarding much of the literature of Hasidism, one is so-to-speak building on quicksand (not to mention the prejudices of the historians). Therefore our approach has been not to give any one source too much weight: to be critical, to err on the side of suspicion, but to build up an impression (maybe one can do more than that) based upon multiple and independent sources.

In conclusion, it is also germane to mention David Assaf's observation that,[73] even today, we are still lacking thorough and consistent research into Polish Hasidism, which was the main center of the Hasidic world of the nineteenth century. Assaf notes that academic scholarship of Hasidism has centered on its earliest stages, with a somewhat supercilious attitude to Hasidism of the nineteenth century. Interestingly enough, this attitude is a precise reverse image of the Orthodox world, which is more interested in living Hasidism.

---

[71] The Seer may have changed his mind from the view he expressed in his personal diaries, which were written before he assumed the role of leadership. But it is also possible that he did not do so. *Ateret Menahem* 39 §125 reads "… and the Rebbe of Lublin said that that was not his way" (in the context of trying to bring the Messiah).

[72] Shmuel Werses dismisses Rabinowitz's view as apologetic, albeit he does not substantiate this critique. For a thorough analysis of Buber's *For the Sake of Heaven,* see Shmuel Werses, "Hasidism via the Prism of Belles-Lettres: An Analysis of Martin Buber's *For the Sake of Heaven"* (Hebrew) in Zaddik*im ve-anshei maaseh,* Jerusalem: 1994. See also E. Simon, "Buber and the Jewish Faith" (Hebrew), *Iyunim* 9 (1958): 13–50, in which he concludes that Buber adds material which has no reference in the sources.

[73] David Assaf, "Polish Hasidism in the Nineteenth Century: The State of Scholarship and Bibliographic Analysis." In *Hasidism in Poland.* Bialik Institute, Jerusalem, 1994.

HISTORICAL BACKGROUND

Przysucha in the Context of Hasidism

In a candid observation, Gershom Scholem asks the following question: what was unique about Hasidism that was not present in earlier Jewish mystical traditions? He says:

> If you were to ask me: what is the new doctrine of these mystics, whose experience was obviously first hand, more so perhaps than in the case of many of their predecessors? What were their new principles and ideas? I say, if you were to ask me this, I should hardly know what to answer.
>
> It is precisely this fact which makes Hasidism a special problem for our interpretation. The truth is that it is not always possible to distinguish between the revolutionary and the conservative elements of Hasidism: or rather, Hasidism as a whole is as much a reformation of earlier mysticism as it is more or less the same thing. You can say if you like that it depends on how you look at it. The hasidim were themselves aware of this fact. Even such a novel thing as the rise of the zaddikim and the doctrine of Zaddikism appeared to them as being, despite its novelty, well in the Kabbalistic tradition....[1]

More recently, Mendel Piekarz[2] has delineated some of the essential characteristics of Hasidism:

---

[1] G. Scholem, *Major Trends in Jewish Mysticism*. New York: 1967, 338.
[2] M. Piekarz, *Ideological Trends of Hasidism in Poland during the Interwar Period and the Holocaust* (Hebrew). Jerusalem: 1972, 45–46.

1. The idea of Zaddikism, which runs through all hasidic groups from its beginnings in eighteenth century Ukraine down to our very own period.
2. The idea that a zaddik has metaphysical significance; i.e., that all the Jewish souls are interwoven and dependent upon him in some mystical fashion.
3. that the role of the zaddik is to redeem the masses.
4. that, by extension, the zaddik redeems the physical world by redeeming the sparks of holiness from the husks of corporeality.

Piekarz emphasized that these ideas did not originate with Hasidism, but were its hallmark.

If one were to ask where all of the above exists in the world of Przysucha, one would be hard-pressed to find sources to substantiate any of the above characteristics. As we have seen, in Przysucha the zaddik is essentially a **living paradigm** (albeit a charismatic personality), but at no time did he want the individual disciple to relinquish his autonomy, his judgment, or his discrimination. Quite the opposite is true. The disciple had to learn to develop his own autonomy, and if he became dependent on the teacher, then he was not fit to be a member of Przysucha. If these "hasidic essentials," mentioned by Piekarz, are to be found at all in Przysucha, they are so muted as to be of little significance. Perhaps, if one would have asked the Yehudi, he might have agreed theoretically with the ideological underpinning of some of these kabbalistic concepts, but in practice they played no meaningful role in Przysucha. The ideas of redeeming the masses, metaphysically redeeming the world, and the distinction between the rebbe and his disciples as spiritually different types of human beings are simply not part of the ethos of Przysucha. On the basis of all of the material that is extant, one may confidently say that kabbalah, with all its derivative implications, was not a fundamental part of their consciousness.

In addition, if one were to say that Hasidism can be characterized by spontaneity, by unprepared ecstasy, and a simple, unintellectual attitude towards faith without too much emphasis on the value of learning, that again, while it might be true of Hasidism in general, would be totally contradicted by Przysucha, which opposed all of the above.

A scholar of Hasidism asks:

Is this program of sustained contemplation, attachment, and utter devotion to God really possible for all men? The hasidic answer is generally in the negative. This is why the doctrine of Zaddikism is so important for Hasidism. The holy man, his thoughts constantly on God, raises the prayers of his followers and all their other thoughts and actions.[3]

Once again, this may or may not be true of Hasidism in general. But because in Przysucha the zaddik did not play this vicarious role, this description is decidedly untrue regarding Przysucha. The answer to the above question with regard to Hasidism might indeed be "no." But for the disciples of Przysucha the answer would be a most definite "yes" – at least for their own members.

It was this sort of problem that led Scholem and Buber[4] to wonder whether one could describe Przysucha as a part of Hasidism altogether. But the self-perception of Przysucha, and that of others (whether hasidic or not), was that Przysucha was indeed part of the hasidic movement. Thus, the question becomes irrelevant. Perhaps we should be a bit more flexible so as to not force Hasidism into one definition. Rather, we should acknowledge its lack of homogeneity, which allowed very disparate attitudes to co-exist as part of the hasidic movement. Idel consistently points out that Hasidism is not one-dimensional. He takes Scholem to task by pointing out that the Hasidic masters had a variety of mystical texts open to them and they were not limited to Lurianic Kabbalah alone.[5] There are a variety of hasidic modes. The movement is multi-dimensional. Maybe an alternative definition would focus on the hasidic characteristics of God-intoxication, the centrality of prayer, passion, and involvement with the community and the fact that Hasidism presupposes that learning Torah alone is inadequate. [6]

---

[3] Rivka Schatz-Uffenheimer, s.v. "Hasidism," *Encyclopaedia Judaica* 7:1405.

[4] See also A. Brill, "Grandeur and Humility in the Writings of R. Simhah Bunim of Przysucha." *Hazon Nahum* (1997): 444.

[5] M. Idel, *"Martin Buber and Gershon Scholem: A Critical Appraisal,"* in *Hasidism Reappraised,* edited by A. Rapoport-Albert, 393. London–Portland: 1996. See also *Encyclopaedia Hebraica* (Hebrew) 17:771: "From a conceptual point of view, Hasidism includes different and contradictory points of view."

[6] For the state of Hasidism at the time of the death of the Baal Shem Tov, see *Encyclopaedia Judaica* 7:1392.

&ngrave; &ngrave;

One further point needs to be added. Scholars have described Hasidism as a movement that initially had at its core a group of radical pietists determined to plummet the depths of the human soul. This quest was the domain of an elite (*b'nei aliyah*). Could such a quest be open to everyone? The answer eventually given by Hasidism – at least from the mid-nineteenth century onwards – was a definite no. But perhaps in this sense one can say that Przysucha, during its three generations, was a reversion to the original path of Hasidism, except that what was originally an "inner circle" was now a broader movement.

Hasidism in Poland

Hasidism came to Poland in the second half of the eighteenth century, entering Warsaw during the late 1770s. Y. Schiper[7] asks the following question: Why is it that, while turbulence and an exacerbated atmosphere of accusation and counter-accusation reigned between the *mitnaggedim* and hasidim in Lithuania and Galicia, there was relative calm in Poland? Why was the opposition relatively tolerant to what was initially a hasidic minority? And why was it that, by and large, neither the *mitnaggedim* nor the hasidim of Poland turned to the secular authorities to intervene on their side, unlike the case in other parts of Eastern Europe?

First of all, Schiper maintains that, contrary to the romantic idea that Hasidism challenged the structure of society, in Poland the attraction of Hasidism crossed socio-economic divisions. Hasidism drew support both from what Schiper calls the "plutocracy" as well as from the masses. When R. Yisrael Loebel and R. David Makov published anti-Hasidic tracts in

---

[7] See Y. Schiper, "The History of Hasidism in Central Poland" (Hebrew), in *Hasidism in Poland.* Jerusalem: 1994, 23–59. C. Shmeruk, "Yitshak Schiper's Study of Hasidism in Poland." in *Hasidism Reappraised*, edited by Ada Rapoport-Albert, 17. London: 1997, demures from some of Schiper's conclusions. On the history of Polish Hasidism see: S. Dubnow, *History of Hasidism* (Hebrew) (Tel Aviv, 1967), 175–204, 215–217, 326–327; A.Z. Aescoly, "Ha-Hasidut be Polin." In *Beit Yisrael be-Folin*, vol. 2, edited by I. Halpern, 86–141. Jerusalem: 1953; R. Mahler, *Hasidism and the Jewish Enlightenment.* Philadelphia: 1985, Chap. 9, "The Schools of Hasidism in Poland," 245–314.

Warsaw (1798–1800), the Maggid of Kozienice turned to the wealthy elite in Warsaw to buy out the entire stock.[8] Secondly, Hasidism in Poland expressed a feeling of deep love for the Jewish people, which in turn made it appealing as a force for unity.[9] Thirdly, in Warsaw (and also in Podolia and Galicia) there was a danger from the Frankists, uniting the Jewish community against any would-be internecine warfare. Furthermore, argues Schiper, in central Poland such characteristics of hasidic life as the *shtiebel* and the zaddik's court did not harm the communal structure or the people's allegiance to it.

Schiper questions whether Hasidism ever really challenged the Jewish establishment. The image of Hasidism as "utopian socialism," with all its beauty, was in his opinion not a reality. Bartal agrees.[10] He too does not see Hasidism as some proletariat credo, akin to the radical socialism of the twentieth century. Hasidism in Poland, according to Bartal, didn't challenge the authority of the Jewish establishment. Rather, it worked alongside it, complemented it, and fit into the known functions of Jewish autonomy in Poland.

This whole approach has recently been further developed by Glenn Dynner[11] [12] [13] on the basis of recently available archival evidence. He, too,

---

[8] Schiper, ibid., 25, states that this attempt was successful. Not so, says Dynner "Men of Silk," 128. On R. David Makov, see M. Wilensky, *PAAJR* 25 (1956): 137–156. On R. Israel Loebel, see idem., *PAAJR* 30 (1962), 141–151.

[9] On the role of Levi Isaac of Berdyczow, see Dynner, ibid., 58–60, 126–127; on that of R. Shmuel Shmelka, ibid., 306–308.

[10] Israel Bartal, *The Jews of Eastern Europe* 1772–1881, (Israel, 2002). Cf. Alfasi, *Gur*, 10, based on A. Marcus, *Hasidismus*, 98. J.L. Maimon, *Sarei ha-Meah*, 1:99, suggests another reason why Poland was relatively tranquil in his opinion. It was due to the deep scholarship of the two brothers, R. Shmuel Shmelka of Nikolsberg and R. Pinchas (author of *Sefer ha-Hafla'ah*), Rabbi of Frankfurt. There is a tradition that, due to their reputation as Torah scholars, the Gaon of Vilna omitted them from his fierce opposition.

[11] David Kandel, "Zydzi w dobie utworzenia Krolestwa Kongresowego," in *Kwartalnik poswiecony badania przeslosci Zydow w Polsce* r.l., z.l. (1912).

[12] For the first recent foray into archives pertaining to the Besht, see Moshe Rosman's archival-based *Founder of Hasidism: A Quest for the Historical Baal Shem Tov* (Berkeley: 1996).

[13] The latest work of this type is that by Marcin Wodzin, *Oswiecenie zydowsl w Krolestwie Polsk wobec chasydyzi* (2003), who maintains that all previous historians used only limited or no archival materials.

mentions that the zaddikim preferred to stack communal offices with their devotees rather than supplant the *Kahal*.[14] Furthermore, he is highly critical of those scholars who portrayed the movement's leaders as folk heroes of the allegedly impoverished, uneducated, and backward masses.[15] He says,

> Actually, the Polish zaddikim were not only warmly received by certain prominent members of the Polish Jewish upper classes, but were even financed, promoted, and protected by them.
>
> The foundational role of prominent representatives of the Jewish mercantile elite in fostering the development of Polish Hasidism into a mass movement has by and large escaped notice in Polish Jewish economic historiography.
>
> Their endorsement helps us begin to comprehend Hasidism's repeated triumphs over a myriad of powerful enemies.... Schiper's[16] hitherto lost work, it turns out, constitutes a first step away from the Dubnowian notion of the exclusively folk nature of Hasidism....

[14] Shmuel Ettinger, "Hasidism and the Kahal in Eastern Europe," in Ada Rapoport-Albert, *Hasidism Reappraised*. London: 1997. 63–75.

[15] Dynner, 117, says that we might label adherents to this conception the "Dubnow School." See Simon Dubnow, *Toledot ha-Hasidut* (Tel Aviv: 1975). An embryonic form of the view is contained in Heinrich Graetz, *History of the Jews* (Philadelphia: 1895), V: 383, 392. Joseph Weiss regards the Hasidic leader as a wandering preacher, "a miserable type, who sells his teachings for alms" from whom "a smell of money-grubbing rises." See his "The Dawn of Hasidism," *Zion* 16: 3–4, 46–105. See also idem, "Some Notes on the Social Background of Early Hasidism," in his *Studies in Eastern Jewish Mysticism* (London: 1985). A second tendency is the romanticization of the first stage of the movement. Martin Buber imagines a "religious elite itself arising out of the mass of the people," forming a movement with a "democratic strain" that set aside the "existing 'aristocracy' of spiritual possession." See his *The Origin and Meaning of Hasidism*, translated and edited by M. Friedman, 58, 61. New York: 1960. Ben Zion Dinur characterized the early Hasidic leaders as members of a disenchanted secondary intelligentsia in revolt. See Dinur, "The Origins of Hasidism and Its Social and Messianic Foundations" in *Essential Papers on Hasidism*, edited by G. Hundert.

[16] This thesis of Schiper, Bartal and Dynner may be one of the factors in explaining why Hasidism never seems to have responded in any conceptual way to the issues of socialism and social justice during the second half of the nineteenth century – issues which shook Jewish society to its very core. It isn't just that with the onslaught of secularism, Hasidism turned inwards; it is also possibly due to the fact that, although Hasidism was desperately concerned with poverty on an individual basis, it never evolved a societal strategy for dealing with it.

What distinguished Hasidism and practically guaranteed its triumph was its combination of a popular spiritual message with social and political power, accumulated and preserved paradoxically through both elitism and populism.... The Polish zaddikim eventually proved invincible due to their patronage by prominent representatives of the Jewish mercantile elite, their own membership in the Jewish elite, and their popular support amongst the Jewish masses.... Hasidism appealed to all classes, from the most humble representatives of Polish Jewry to the most sophisticated urban Jews....

Polish Hasidism[17] decidedly inclined towards the Jewish elite, despite its considerable popular attractions. The Polish zaddikim, like their predecessors, made a special effort to attract scions of the East European Jewish aristocracy and members of the mercantile elite, who enjoyed a privileged status as either potential zaddikim or patrons. Although populism was a key component of Hasidism, it did not translate into egalitarianism or increased access to power....

"Polish" Hasidism is a territorial domain that encompassed the densest areas of urban settlement and most advanced industrialized regions in Eastern and East Central Europe, on the one hand, and extensive rural regions consisting of scattered, less-developed small town and villages, on the other... from the wealthiest, most educated and cosmopolitan Jews, to the most rural, impoverished "shtetl" Jews. This versatility entails, in and of itself, a corrective to the misleading portrayal of the Hasidic leader – the zaddik – as an obscurantist who appealed to the more impoverished, superstitious segments of the Jewish populace....

The above analysis further undermines the conception that Hasidism promised the Jewish masses liberation from the prevailing oligarchic leadership. Zaddikim were rarely humble preachers, as Joseph Weiss portrays them, nor the "lowly folk" of Isaac Levitat's description. They do not appear to have had democratic convictions,

---

[17] In his article on R. Shlomo of Radomsk, M. Piekarz says the following (58): "The truth is that Hasidism is a socio-religious movement and not some stage or other in the history of the mystical streams of Israel." But, he also wonders, "didn't R. Shlomo of Radomsk, who was so involved in the life of the community and of the Hasidim around him, react to the social, cultural, and political occurrences of his time?... or have they been censored out by his family?" (39)

as Martin Buber and Harry Rabinowitch argue, but continued to preserve leadership within their own families. They were not strangers to the aristocratic families, as Raphael Mahler implies, but rather members of those very families. Finally the zaddikim were not members of a "secondary intelligentsia," as Dinur would have it, but the offspring of established rabbis and merchants.

What emerges from an analysis of earlier scholarly theories that seek to explain the appeal of Hasidism is the overt or covert agenda of their authors. It is assumed that Hasidism could not have been attractive to anybody enlightened; ergo, its attraction must have been to the ignorant and the uneducated. Hasidism could not have been attractive to anyone well off; ergo, its leaders couldn't have come from the main stream of Jewish society, but must have come from a disenfranchised group; ergo they were upstarts, if not charlatans. Why on earth should anyone enlightened, educated, or capable of living in a more open society want to attach themselves to the backward, obscurantist world of Eastern Europe? Dynner's critique and conclusions seem to have greater credence, based as they are on archival evidence. The other theories, cited above seem to reflect the agenda of the scholars propounding them more than they do a description of historical reality.

CONTRADICTIONS

The central thesis of this book is that there is an inner coherence of ideas running from the Yehudi to R. Bunim to Menahem Mendel. The differences among them have been noted, but our essential claim is that there is such a thing as a Przysucha profile. If that is so, then it would be quite natural to find the basic ideas of Przysucha repeated by all three teachers in one form or another. And that is exactly what we find. There are innumerable cases of an idea or interpretation being attributed to 1) the Yehudi and R. Bunim; 2) R. Bunim and Menahem Mendel; 3) the Yehudi and Menahem Mendel; 4) R. Yitzhak of Vorki and Menahem Mendel (lack of space prevents us from detailing all the examples).

ॐ ॐ

However, there are certain sources that seem to confute this. By this we mean that a specific idea is attributed to one master, and the same idea is contradicted by a statement of the same master in an alternative source.

Such an example has already been mentioned in Addendum A. Rabinowitz argues that the Yehudi and R. Bunim had a fundamental disagreement as to whether one's religious inspiration should come from the Exodus or from Nature. In support of his thesis he quotes *Siah Sarfei Kodesh* vol. 3, 37, 55; *Ramatayim Zofim* 14:35; *Siah Sarfei Kodesh, Likkutei Yonatan* vol. 4, 41–42, 17 and *Hiddushei ha-Rim,* par. Bereshit 5.

But all this is contradicted by the following sources: *Shem mi-Shmuel,* par. Va-ethanan, 44; *Siah Sarfei Kodesh* vol. 3, 5, 7; *Amud ha-Emet* 99; *Emet ve-Emunah* 34, which attributes the same disagreement to R. Bunim and the Kotzker.

ॐ ॐ

Another example is the following. In *Torat Simhah* §7; *Siah Sarfei Kodesh* vol. 1, 32 §155; *Ramatayim Zofim* (AZ) 16.27, we read:

> On the gemara in Berachot …"If he examined himself (as to why he was suffering) and didn't find a sufficient reason, he should attribute it to his not learning enough." And the question is asked, how can one say "he didn't find" if indeed he hadn't learnt enough? To which R. Bunim replied that "not learning enough" is not the reason why he is suffering, but the reason why he can't explain why he is suffering.

But in *Siah Sarfei Kodesh* vol. 5, 63 this same exegesis is given in the name of the Yehudi and, in contradistinction, R. Bunim gives a much more penetrating interpretation on how to deal with suffering. Moreover, in *Shem mi-Shmuel* (Levinger, "Authentic," 127, n. 32), the former of the above explanations is not given in the name of the Yehudi nor in the name of R. Bunim, but in the name of his grandfather, Menahem Mendel of Kotzk.

PRZYSUCHA AND
THE ENLIGHTENMENT

Though a religious community has its own internal integrity, it would be mistaken to assume that Eastern European Jewry was oblivious to the French Revolution, the Napoleonic wars, and the Enlightenment.[1] [2] All of Europe shook with these cataclysmic events. The folk legend of how the Seer tried to bring the Messiah (because the Napoleonic wars were seen as the battle of Gog and Magog) may be of dubious historicity[3] but it may well indirectly reflect the impact these events had on the Jewish psyche. Tradition may be seen as a narrative record of a people's consciousness.[4]

The leaders of Eastern European Jewry were divided in their reaction to Napoleon and viewed Emancipation with mixed feelings. On the one hand, the granting of civil rights and rectification of legal discrimination could only be welcomed. On the other hand, someone like R. Shneur Zalman of Liady

---

[1] Regarding the Enlightenment see Chapter 9 of R. Mahler, *Hasidism and the Jewish Enlightenment*, "The Schools of Hasidism in Poland," 245–314; Iytzhak Schiper, *Zydzi Krolestwa Polskiege, w dobie Powstania Listonapowego* (Warszawa: 1932), str. 7–9, 11; D. Kandel, *"Komitet Strazokonnych' 'Kwartalnik pswiecony badania przeszlosci Zydow w Polsce',"* 1912–1913, *Zeszyt*, 111 quarterly.

[2] Nathan Frank, *Yehudei Polin bi-yemei milhamot Napoleon* (Warsaw: 1913); Mordechai Teitelbaum, *Ha-Rebbe mi-Liady u-mifleget Habad*, 150.

[3] See Addendum A.

[4] The Maggid of Kozienice was initially pro-Napoleon before apparently changing his mind. Cf. Rabinowitz, "R. Bunim," 7, n. 18. R. Menahem Mendel of Rimanov was pro-Napoleon (see *Ateret Menahem*, 38 §§124–125; *Eser Orot*, 74, §32). Assaf (*The Fall*, 163) maintains that Hasidic sources depict the Seer as a staunch opponent of Napoleon (see Berger, *Eser Tsahtsahot* [Piotrkow; 1910], 87, §17).

foresaw that social openness would bring it in its wake social assimilation. He said:

> If Napoleon wins, the Jewish people will be more wealthy… but their hearts will become distant and separated from their Father in Heaven; and if [Czar] Alexander our master wins, though the Jewish people will be poorer… their hearts will be closer and joined to their Father in Heaven.[5]

Though for a brief while Polish Jewry might have naively expected things to change for the better, in reality Emancipation did not apply to Eastern and Central Europe. "Enlightenment ideology, without the realistic promise of emancipation, was bound to be a hard sell."[6] The failure of Emancipation produced the absurd phenomenon of spectacularly wealthy merchants with almost no civil rights.[7]

The Jewish leaders of Poland soon became aware of the motives of the Russian and Polish governments.[8] Czartoryski, the Pole in charge of the cultural system in the annexed territories after the Napoleonic upheaval, wrote the following to the Emperor in a letter dated July 1817:

---

[5] See note 2 above, Teitelbaum, 156.

[6] Dynner, "Men of Silk," 170–171.

[7] Regarding the Enlightenment, Arnold Eisen, *Rethinking Modern Judaism, Ritual, Commandment, Community* (Chicago: University of Chicago, 1999) 3, says:
In a word, the role of Enlightenment, per se – intellectual and ideological upheaval – has not been as predominant among Jews (and, I suspect, others too) in their negotiation of modernity as we might think. But Emancipation – by which I mean the assumption of new sorts of selfhood by Jews in a radically altered social and economic order – has, in contrast, been decisive.

[8] Distinctions must be made between the period when Napoleon was in control of Poland, even though that period was uneven (cf. Rabinowitz "R. Bunim," 35) and what happened from 1813 onwards, especially after 1823, with the government investigation into Hasidism. Cf. R. Mahler, *Hasidism and the Jewish Enlightenment*, 370–371.
"In the archives of Warsaw, Vol. No 1871, there are hundreds of documents relating to the extensive investigations made by the police and government commissions with regards to the Hasidim." On the various stages of the government enquiries between September 29, 1823 and August 15, 1824 and the role played by R. Simhah Bunim, see E. Roset's unpublished draft dissertation on R. Simhah Bunim, 2005.

The Jews are a chief cause of the wretchedness of this country. Your Majesty, out of piety and wisdom, has wished to convert them to Christianity. But that notion must be the Government's secret, as is said in a paper I submitted on this subject.... Otherwise this fine, holy idea cannot succeed. It must be hidden from the Jews; a beginning must be made, by administrative directives, on preparing them for conversion; they must first be made Christian culturally. One can not busy oneself with this matter enough nor too soon, whether considered as a matter of humanity, of politics, or of religion.[9]

As has been noted:

One cannot fail to be struck by this "civilizing" concept, which necessarily involved emptying Jewish culture of its content – and this by means of devious methods – the ultimate goal being conversion![10]

Efforts to modernize and to bring enlightenment to a supposedly backward world were aided and abetted by the Jewish reformers – the *Maskilim*.[11]

Dynner mentions that:

Jacob Samuel Bik estranged himself from his fellow Maskilim by defending the Hasidim. Bik was repulsed by much of the fanatical anti-Hasidism which characterized the Haskalah. He observed that certain Zaddikim, including R. Moses Leib of Sasow and R. Levi

---

[9] A.J. Cazrtoryski to Alexander I, *Bibl. Czart*, Cracow, EW. 1283, quoted in *The Jews in Poland*, Abramsky, Jachimczyk, Polonsky p. 82.

[10] Daniel Beauvois, "Polish-Jewish Relations in the Territories annexed by the Russan Empire in the First Half of the Nineteenth Century," in *The Jews in Poland*, edited by Abramsky, Jachimczyk and Polonsky, 78–90. London: Basil Blackwell, 1986.

[11] Regarding the Maskilim, see H. Nusbbaum, "*Skice historycine z Zycia Zydow, w Warsaw*" (Warsaw: 1881); Shipper, "*Zydzi kroi. Polskiego w dobie pwstania Ilstopadawego*," 488–451. On all this see Rabinowitz, "R. Bunim," 44–47; idem., *From Lublin to Przysucha*, 315–320; and cf. Dynner, 271–285.

Isaac of Berdyczow, evinced a great "love of Israel," and made sacrifices for their poor fellow Jews.[12]

During the period when R. Bunim was a rebbe, there were various governmental inquiries into the nature of Hasidism. For example: in December 1823 the commission on Denominations turned to the Synagogue Supervisory Board for a detailed report on the sect and eventually concluded that Hasidic leaders kept their followers subservient and in a state of darkness and superstition. On March 15, 1824 a decree was issued against "Rabbis residing in Przysucha," which strictly forbade them to "collect fees and give advice or opinions," and generally prohibited "hidden Hasidic prayer gatherings in private homes." On July 8th, a special subcommittee was established under the direction of Stanislaw Staszic to determine whether or not "the Jewish sect Hasidim have harmful principles which are contrary to good customs."[13] It is clear from these archives that Przysucha was seen as the main center of Hasidism in Poland.

R. Bunim made it perfectly clear that:

> The function of government is to benefit the lives of the Jews (i.e., its citizens), to improve their economic position, but not to get involved in their internal affairs (on issues) like liturgy and the essence of Hasidism."[14]

---

[12] Dynner, 285.

[13] Dynner, 164–165; Roset (see note 8). Mahler (271) puts it this way: R. Simhah Bunem of Przysucha was appointed by the government commission of the *wojewodztwo* of Sandomierz as one of the two fellow correspondents of that district to the Advisory Chamber of the Committee for the Affairs of Old Testament Believers. When Abbe Chiarini's project made it clear that the goal of the committee was to undermine the Jewish faith, the Hasidim, headed by the disciple of R. Simhah Bunem, R. Isaac of Zarki (later Warka), were the most active organizers of a vigorous campaign about the imminent danger from the committee. Earlier, in 1826, it was the Hasidim who mobilized the community against the committee's plan to establish a rabbinical school.

[14] See Rabinowitz, *From Lublin to Przyshcha*, 320; also Aescoly, *Hasidut be-Folin*, 76.

But R. Bunim, though an intellectual, was antagonistic to the secular rationalism of Emancipation when it was used as an anti-religious force. Though time and time again we find R. Bunim demanding from his Hasidim the use of the mind, we find expressions of deep reservation about those whose intention (at least as perceived by R. Bunim) was to use rationalism as an enemy of Judaism. R. Bunim said: "If man purifies himself, he will recognize God from within the Torah and he won't need investigations or miracles."[15] For R. Bunim, true insight is not a purely intellectual exercise. Having an understanding of God requires purity.

He recounted the following incident:

> When he was in Berlin to be healed from the pain of his eyes he met someone (who said)… that there was a doctor who can heal within a short space of time and that he is called a wonder doctor. To which R. Bunim replied that the Jewish way should be that one goes to the righteous person of the generation, that he may seek mercy for one. But the world functions according to nature. It would be better for me to go to the Maggid of Koznitz.… The reason why the nations did not believe the signs and wonders that Moses performed in Egypt was because they said that they were performed by natural causes and not because he was a man of God. Therefore God gave them the wicked Balaam, who did everything not according to nature.[16]

R. Bunim navigated between two seemingly contradictory positions. On the one hand, like the Yehudi before him and Menahem Mendel after him, he believed in the use of the mind. On the other hand, R. Bunim felt that it was sacrilegious to use the mind to deny God's existence, to rationalize everything on the basis of natural causes.

It is with this understanding that we note a number of very critical comments made by R. Bunim about doctors. One might have assumed that a practicing apothecary would have some sympathy for doctors – but that

---

[15] *Ramatayim Zofim*, Chap. 17, §47; *Torat Simhah*, §202. The juxtaposition of these two extremes – "investigations" and "miracles" – is interesting. On "investigations," see *Siah Sarfei Kodesh he-Hadash*, par. Emor, 97.

[16] *Siah Sarfei Kodesh he-Hadash*, 1.114; *Siah Sarfei Kodesh*, 1, par. Balak, 10 §9. For similar such sentiments, see *Torat Simhah*, §20, also §133 towards the end and §240.

depends on whether science is being used to deny God's immanence or not.[17]

Said R. Bunim:

> Pharaoh wanted to cause doubt amongst the Jewish people and to implant this bad quality in them, so they wouldn't know how to do repentance.[18]

Is the mind to be used to increase doubt, or is it part of the Divine service? On this issue, secular rationalism has no place in R. Bunim's world view. It is in this context that we should understand such statements as the following:

> All wisdom and investigations to understand God and His unity are called "from there" i.e., from somewhere else. But true wisdom is literally in his heart, if he purifies himself and is fitting.[19]

This sounds anti-rationalist,[20] but it is not. It is rather to be understood within a context of deep reservations about the motives of the Enlightenment.

In the collection *Ohel Torah* (attributed to Menahem Mendel of Kotzk), we read the following:

> Truth is not applicable to something that is known. For if a person said the opposite he would be a liar.... Only if something happens that appears to man to be the opposite of God's word, and he makes an effort and makes all sorts of actions and stratagems to find the word of God in truth – such a person is called "those that call on His name" – a man of truth.[21]

This piece, though a little unclear in all its details, is a sort of manifesto for Przysucha. Truth is not being used in the simple empirical sense of

---

[17] R. Bunim's position is not the same as that of R. Nachman of Breslav (see *Sefer ha-Berit*). R. Bunim is essentially a rationalist who believes that the intellect is to be used as the handmaiden of religion. On R. Bunim's criticisms of doctors, see *Ramatayim Zofim* (AZ), 9.14.

[18] *Siah Sarfei Kodesh*, vol 3, par. Shemot, 129 §479.

[19] *Ramatayim Zofim*, chap. 5 §96; *Torat Simhah*, §133.

[20] Cf. M. Piekarz, *Hasidut Breslav* in addendum 1, p. 193 on *Sefer ha-Berit*.

[21] *Ohel Torah*, par. Shelah, 70.

confirming reality. Truth is being used to clarify the word of God when, to all appearances, it seems to indicate the opposite of reality.

As always happens when battle-lines are drawn, we find R. Bunim taking a position, for polemical reasons, that he would not normally have taken. R. Bunim, who is very concerned with *peshat* – the literal meaning of the text – said:

> I don't want to read the Torah in a grammatically correct way even though according to the law one should do so; because they (the Maskilim) have adopted this so strongly.[22]

One may conclude that R. Bunim's philosophy is motivated by reaction to the Enlightenment. That he was aware of its challenge is clear. That he believed that learning Torah alone was inadequate for his day, he stated articulately. But we must not deny a religious movement its own inherent integrity. Przysucha was not hermetically sealed off from historical circumstances. It would have been bizarre if it hadn't been influenced by the French Revolution. But essentially Przysucha stands in its own right – an internal religious movement.

All three masters of Przysucha believed in the value of the mind per se. But by this they meant an essentially pre-modern attitude, in which the intellect was the handmaiden of religion. But with the growing influence of secular rationalism, they were, to some extent, caught between the hammer and the anvil. We see a growing stridency of language from the Yehudi to R. Bunim to Menahem Mendel, attacking the use of the mind to undermine faith in God. The Yehudi said:

> Someone who creates new ideas (in Torah) which are mixed up with pride and other impure qualities makes a false heaven. However, the spiritual intelligence (of these ideas) wanders around to England and from this intelligence wonderful machines are made.[23]

As we have seen, R. Bunim's language was stronger than that of the Yehudi,[24] but with Menahem Mendel the tone and degree of ferocity change even further.

---

[22] *Siah Sarfei Kodesh*, 5.105 §8.
[23] *Tiferet ha-Yehudi*, 153 §19.
[24] *Torat Simhah*, §133; *Ramatayim Zofim*, chap. 5 §96.

Before the giving of the Torah at Sinai, the Patriarchs comprehended God via the investigation of their intelligence. But ever since God gave the Torah, He forbade us to inquire. For only via the Torah should one comprehend God.... Someone who inquires with the depth of his intelligence... to comprehend God via inquiring forfeits his life.[25]

The phrase "forbade us to inquire" reflects the growing dissonance with secular rationalism. This was not an isolated outburst.

In the year of his death... I will tell you what I heard from our teacher of Kotzk; although I heard earlier many words of Torah, but with this he infused my heart. On the night of the holy Sabbath, after Kiddush, he sat on his chair and his form almost changed with a stripping away of corporeality. And with all his strength he said this: "There are in the world some people who investigate, philosophers; and all of them inquire thinking of the knowledge of God. But they cannot comprehend more than their intellectual capacity. But the Jewish people are holy and they... have the methodology to achieve more than their level – and more than the angelic level."[26]

The onslaught of secular rationalism was one of the major causes of a process by which Hasidism and even Przysucha began to withdraw from the world of assimilated Jewry and the West. Przysucha, especially R. Bunim, had taken an attitude of engagement – in the fullest sense of the word – both philosophically and in practice. But by the middle of the nineteenth century it found the process of navigation between the value of the intellect, on the one hand, and secular rationalism, on the other, too difficult. Thus a generation later, when Hasidism was confronted with major social issues of the day – Socialism, Communism and Zionism – it was essentially unable to respond.[27] To navigate between Scylla and Charybdis became too difficult. But I would like to think that even here, R. Bunim would have known how to navigate.

---

[25] *Ohel Torah, Ethics,* 128; *Nifla'ot Hadashot, Likkutim,* 90.
[26] Levinger, *Imrot Otentiot,* 130–131 n. 7.
[27] See Chap. 12, Summary.

PRZYSUCHA AND ROMANTICISM

"Know then thyself, presume not God to scan;
The proper study of mankind is Man."

Alexander Pope

IN HIS BOOK, *The Roots of Romanticism,* Isaiah Berlin spends the first twenty pages or so "in search of a definition" of Romanticism – specifically, with the question as to what were the characteristics of this "movement." But even this question is not so simple, if only because one needs to differentiate, for example, between German Romanticism and English Romanticism. Moreover, even within English Romanticism, for example, there are varied positions on the issue of belief in God. Scholars differ as to whether or not Blake was a theist, while Coleridge certainly was. But despite all these reservations, there are some basic identifiable characteristics of the Romantic period and, above all, a certain change in consciousness, in the way of thinking. It is this which finds resonance in the thought of R. Bunim. Berlin says the following:

> The values to which they attached the highest importance were such values as integrity, sincerity, readiness to sacrifice one's life to some inner light, dedication to some ideal.... They were not interested, above all, in adjustment to life, in finding your place in society.... What people admired was wholeheartedness, sincerity, purity of soul, the ability and readiness to dedicate yourself to your ideal, no

matter what it was… but the worst of all possible things is compromise.[1]

How is one to explain the fact that such sentiments echo so loudly in Przysucha? This is not to deny the existence of major differences between Romanticism and Przysucha. Przysucha believed in a Divinely revealed truth; its adherents worked within the traditional legal framework of Judaism. And yet, the description of the artist by the German philosopher Herder (at least the first half) could have been uttered equally well by the Yehudi, by R. Bunim, or by Menahem Mendel of Kotzk as by its author:

> His business as a human being is to speak the truth as it appears to him; the truth as it appears to him is as valid as the truth as it appears to others.[2]

And what is one to make of the similarities between the Yehudi and his English contemporary, Blake? Both would argue that the intellect is inadequate to get one "inside" from a religious point of view, and hence the vital need for simplicity.

When we say that there are certain similarities in thought between the Yehudi and Blake, we do not mean to say that the two are the same. It has been observed of Blake that "(he) can hardly be identified as a theist…." In contradistinction, the Yehudi was God-intoxicated. Though the Yehudi might agree with Blake that "man must be raised to a perception of the infinite,"[3] Blake rejects a transcendent deity, whereas for the Yehudi such consciousness is the very purpose of man's life. Nevertheless, despite all their fundamental differences, there remains a certain confluence of values among them, at the same period of history.

Spiritual movements, though not impervious to social or economic factors, are trivialized by being reduced to them alone. Such an approach does not attribute sufficient integrity to a culture, which has its own voice. It presupposes that there is always a linear line of causality from the outside in – in this case, to argue that Przysucha resulted from the industrialization of Poland. Yet, at the same time, we know that R. Nahman of Breslav had read

---

[1] Isaiah Berlin, *Roots of Romanticism* (London: Pimlico, 2000), 8.
[2] Ibid., 66.
[3] Martin Price, quoted in H. Bloom, *The Ringers in the Tower*, 99.

Sefer Habrit[4] – a work in which the latest Western ideas of the end of the eighteenth century were clothed in Kabbalistic garb. Though we know of no source to specifically indicate that the Yehudi had read such a hybrid work, it is not inconceivable that the values of romanticism had filtered into Eastern Europe and buttressed a movement that would have taken place anyhow.[5]

Przysucha exhibits many of the characteristics which we identify as belonging to the cluster of ideas of Romanticism. If we were to ask: "Who said 'There are no rules in the service of God'?", though the answer is the Yehudi, it could as easily have been one of the German romanticists a generation earlier. Isaiah Berlin says:

> The greatest virtue of all is what existentialists called authenticity and what the Romantics called sincerity.[6]

But this is the essential quality of Przysucha, and is precisely what the Yehudi stood for. Or again, Berlin says about Romanticism: "What people admired was wholeheartedness, sincerity, purity of soul." One could imagine any one of the three generations of Przysucha saying exactly the same thing.

---

[4] Cf. M. Piekarz, *Hasidut Breslev,* in Addendum 1, p. 193, on *Sefer ha-Berit.*
[5] The Yehudi was aware of his time. This is clear from the following facts:
a) He would ask R. Bunim about what he heard in Danzig (*Shem mi-Shmuel,* Yitro, 268). *Meir Einei ha-Golah,* §153, relates how, at the wedding at Austila, R. Yerachmiel (the son of the Yehudi) gave the following testimony:
"I remember that once when R. Bunim came from Danzig and entered into my father's room, he spoke with him for many hours, and told him about different matters concerning simple things which he saw and learnt there in Danzig."
b) His critique of secular rationalism (*Torat ha-Yehudi,* 169 §§1, 2).
c) His contacts with "enlightened" Jews (*Tiferet ha-Yehudi,* 174 §86); and how miracles would be explained away in rational terms (*Torat ha-Yehudi,* 171 §9).
d) Phrases and terms (e.g. *Tiferet ha-Yehudi,* 153 §19).
Schiper, 23–59, relates that when R. Yisrael Loebel and R. David Makov published their anti-Hasidic tracts in Warsaw (1798–1800), the Maggid of Kozienice turned to the wealthy elite of Warsaw to buy out the entire stock. Likewise, I. Etkes, in his *Rabbi Israel Salanter,)* 135–146 [English: 123–134], mentions that Menahem Mendel Lefin published a booklet entitled *Sefer Heshbon ha-Nefesh* (Warsaw: 1792) containing suggestions for improving the situation of Jews in Poland. See also Etkes's article, "On the Harbingers of the Enlightenment in Eastern Europe" (Hebrew), 109. It is possible that the Yehudi might have known about the above, but it is clear that the Yehudi was not as *au fait* with the culture of the age as was R. Bunim.
[6] Ibid, p. 139.

What is one to do with the following fact? One of the characteristics of Przysucha which was so difficult for the outsider (whether Hasidic or not) to understand was the break with social norm. This led to near-anarchic behavior, in which everything was challenged and pushed to its limit, with total disregard for what society thought. The motive was to discover the core of truth – at least within oneself. Now on some level (not the religious one) this is again parallel to what was happening with contemporary romanticism, propelled as it was to discover its own authenticity.

The points of similarity between Przysucha and Romanticism therefore seem to be the following:

- Disregard for anything even slightly suggestive of imitation;
- Questioning of and breaking with established authority and traditional behavior; scorn for accepted social norms.
- Assuming aspects of bohemianism and utter lack of concern for what other people think, for outer appearances, for the hauteur of scholars of the religious bourgeois, contempt for anyone who puts on airs.
- A great emphasis on relying on one's personal judgment.
- Learning from everyday life, from the mundane. "The mundane is the mundane" (even though sometimes it can be used as a metaphor).
- Simplicity as a value, connected to a sense of the real "you" – the essence of a person.
- The value of equanimity, since it also reflects a lack of concern with what the outside world thinks.
- The use of the aphorism – the *vort* – which became a hallmark of Polish Hasidism. This was typical of Novalis.[7]
- The importance of passion.
- The importance of original ideas.[8]

---

[7] Heschel, *The Circle of the Baal Shem Tov* (Chicago: 1985), xxii, says the following: "One of the qualities of the Kotzker Rebbe was a marvelous gift in formulating his thoughts in a tense, sharp and brilliant manner. Reading those of his aphorisms which have been preserved in the distinctive manner in which they were uttered, that is, in Yiddish, reveals an extraordinary style and power."

[8] Cf. *Ohel Yitzhak*, 64 §164.

However, it is not so much a question of points of similarity as it is that the essential direction of change – the paradigm shift – is the same. If Romanticism said that the drama of art now occurs within the human soul, then, in a deep way, Przysucha evinces the same value – albeit in a religious garb – arguing that the human soul is the arena for the drama of religious intimacy. The point of departure is that the human being's unique personality is the realm of revelation.

About Romanticism, Abrams says the following:

> From the dawn of speculation of art through the greater part of the eighteenth century... the poet was regarded primarily as an agent who holds a mirror up to nature. Or as the maker of a work of art according to universal standards of excellence.[9]

What became crucial for Romanticism was literature as a revelation of personality; art was now an expression of the artist's state of mind. The change of mind-set effected by Romanticism was that art was the product of a unique individual. The artist asked something like "What does this mean to me?" He was concerned with his own inner resonance. The focus of reality lies within the artist. Thus, Schleiermacher wrote in 1800:

> If the introspection of the spirit into itself is the divine source of all plastic art and poetry, and if the spirit finds within its own being all that it can represent in its immortal works, shall not the spirit, in all its products and compositions, which can represent nothing else, also look back upon itself?[10]

Now let us compare Schleiermacher's statement that "the introspection of the spirit into itself which is the divine," with what R. Bunim says:

> All existence, other than man, can only comprehend itself. But God created man, who contains within himself the higher and lower worlds, so that he can imagine everything in his soul. That is the

---

[9] A. Abrams, *The Mirror and the Lamp: Romantic Theory and the Critical Tradition.* New York: 1958, 226.
[10] *Monologen*, ed. F.M. Schiele, 22.

essence of man – that he can understand and imagine something other than himself.[11]

It is thus neither the power of speech nor that of the intellect which is the hallmark of the Divine in the human being. Rather, according to R. Bunim, man's *imitatio dei* is revealed in his ability to use his imagination, his reflectiveness. Man has a unique personality, capable of comprehending and reflecting, and this is God's gift of imagination.

If one were to substitute the words "service of God" for Schleiermacher's "art," "poetry," and "literature" in the above quote, one would have something very much akin to R. Bunim's philosophy. In *Kol Simhah* we read:

> "And you shall seek from there and find" (Deuteronomy 4:29) – that is to say, all wisdom and analysis to comprehend God and His unity is called "there'" – that is, from somewhere else. But the real truth is literally "in its place" – that is to say, in his heart. For when a person properly purifies his character traits, he will find the Divine in his heart. And that is the "finding," for you should know that you do not need to inquire about God, to seek and search from anywhere, except in your heart and in your soul.[12]

The Divine is revealed within the human soul. Of course, for R. Bunim the Divine is transcendent as well as immanent. God is not found only within the human soul, but the individual souls of human beings are the only means they have to make contact with the Divine, and that means that ultimately each soul must find its own path, its own style – in short, its own authenticity to commune with God. The above quotation by R. Bunim involves the same shift of focus as the following statement by Herder: "The deepest ground of our being is individual in feelings as well as in thoughts... all the species of animals are perhaps not so distinct from one another as a man is from [other] men."[13] And R. Bunim would have concurred.

In a religious context, what would then flow from this shift would be the demand that the individual find his religious authenticity within his own soul. If there is one crucial idea in the thought of R. Bunim, it is the demand for

---

[11] *Kol Simhah*, par. Bereshit, 8.
[12] *Kol Simhah*, par. Vaethanan, 107.
[13] *Vom Erkennen und Empfinden der menschlichen Seele* (1778).

human beings not to imitate, not to try to be anyone else other than their own selves, thereby enabling their unique divine spark to shine through. And all this would take place essentially within themselves.

When Herder says "One ought to be able to regard each book as the impression (*abdruck*) of a living human soul,"[14] one is reminded of R. Bunim who said "Everyone should make a book of himself, what a person does. Indeed, he should be a book himself."[15] Or, as R. Yitzchak of Vorki said, "Every Jew is a book."[16]

For Przysucha the drama of religious service had turned away from trying to repair the Godhead or influence the Divine will. The drama of service – the real creativity – now lay within the human heart, within the human being's inner world.[17]

When Novalis speaks about "poetry," "art," or "spirit," he is within the same frame of reference. He says that "Poetry is the representation of the spirit of the inner world in its totality."[18] He wrote in his Fragmente, "In all genuine art an idea a spirit is realized produced from within outward.[19]... Poetry is the representation of the inner world in its totality. The musician takes the essence of his art out of himself."[20] To see the parallel with R. Bunim, all one has to do is substitute the concept of intimacy with God for the words "poetry," "art," or "spirit."

---

[14] Abrams (above), 236; 374 n. 31.

"Herder's Samtliche Werke, WXXX, 207–208; cf. Xii, 5–6. Schleiermacher's Monologen later exhibited a similar reasoning. He had long believed, he says, in the essential uniformity of human nature, until there dawned upon him his 'highest intuition' that 'each man is meant to represent humanity in his own way, combining in elements uniquely.' On this basis Schleirmacher concludes that 'language too should objectify the most interior thoughts... Each of us needs only make his language thoroughly his own and artistically all of a piece, so that (it)... exactly represent the structure of his spirit....'" (Soliloquies, trans. H.L. Fries. Chicago: 1926, 30–31, 66).

[15] Cf. Chap. 7.

[16] *Ohel Yitzhak*, 8 §8.

[17] I am inclined to think that the perception that redemption cannot come from a body of knowledge alone (whether Talmud or Kabbalah), but is rather a transformation from within, is also part of the same paradigm shift.

[18] Abrams (above), 50.

[19] Ibid., 90.

[20] Ibid., 93.

Thus to the Romantic mind all genuine art represents a spirit that is realized from within outward. Compare this with the subject of prayer which, Przysucha would argue, is the most creative form of art – the impossible rendezvous between finity and Infinity. This is what Przysucha has to say about the creative process:

> The main work is inside. One shouldn't work on the outside. One should draw on an inner life force in all action. When a man does the inner work his external limbs automatically become subservient to him.
>
> When one prays, the soul alone needs to pray and the body is drawn after it like a sheaf of hay.

The theological underpinning of this idea would appear to be the following: According to R. Bunim, a person can discover the truth of his being by going inwards – the heart being the source of this wisdom. Once a human being touches a certain point of authenticity within himself, once he discovers the truthfulness of his core-being, then he is able to see truth reflected in God's design in nature. If only a person would purify himself, he could discover the footprints of the Divine in himself and in nature. This has a similar ring to what Schelling said:

> So long as I myself am identical with nature I understand what a living nature is as well as I understand my own life.... As soon, however, as I separate myself... from nature, nothing more is left for me but a dead object.[21]

Keble[22] tells us that the "Author of Scripture" is the "Author of Nature." "The book of nature declares to us its author" or, in R. Bunim's words, "God's name *Shaddai* conveys the idea that it is sufficient (*she-dai*) for man to recognize the Divine from the world He created." Or, as Schelling said, "The world of thought has become the world of nature."[23] And Coleridge put it this way: "Man sallies forth into nature only to learn at last that what

---

[21] Abrams, *Natural Supernaturalism: Tradition and Revolution in Romantic Literature* (New York: W.W. Norton, 1973), 181.

[22] See Abrams, *The Mirror and the Lamp*, 240.

[23] Schelling, *Samtliche Werke*, Part I, vol. 7, p. 32.

he seeks he has left behind."[24] R. Bunim certainly would have agreed, for that is essentially what he said to any would-be devotee. Everyone who came to Przysucha was told the story of R. Isaac the son of R. Yekilish (who went to seek treasure under the bridge in Prague only to be told that it lay in his own home, i.e., within his own heart).[25] In describing Romanticism, Abrams talks about "the transformation of theological history into the process of human education."[26] This encapsulates Przysucha's move away from esotericism, towards psychological insights into the nature of the human being.

Needless to say, R. Bunim would take issue with certain romantics and argue that only by moral perfection (i.e., *teshuvah*) could human beings sense the Divine within themselves and that the Divine is outside themselves as well. But all would agree that this sensitivity is immanent within man. The change from thinking outward to thinking inward is essentially the same.

But it isn't the amalgam of examples which is the point. It is rather that the *Weltanschauung* of Przysucha, though thoroughly theocentric, reveals itself in a very fundamental way as being a product of its age. This, coming from within traditional Eastern European Jewry, is remarkable.[27]

---

[24] *The Friend*, ed. Rooke, 1:508–509.

[25] See Chapter 1 above.

[26] Abrams, *Natural Supernaturalism*, 189. See *Romanticism and the Internernalization of Scripture*, Joshua Wielner in *Midrash and Literature*, edited by Geoffrey H. Hartman and Sanford Budick, 237–252. Yale University Press: 1986.

[27] Regarding somersaulting and rolling over in prayer, Wilensky, *Hasidim and mitnaggedim*, 258, says:

Though Rashaz opposed this practice, he too was criticized by R. Israel Loebel for his behaving, while dancing, like one of the common folk. A Habad source tells us, approvingly of course, that when Rashaz had reached a peak of enthusiasm in prayer, "he would roll on the ground almost without consciousness."

Louis Jacobs, in his work *Hasidic Prayer* (New York: 1973), 56, observes that somersaults were customary among the Shaker sect, which began in England in the second half of the eighteenth century and moved over to America. We may safely assume that the hasidic leaders neither knew of nor were influenced by this English group. Jacobs rightly ascribes these phenomena to the Zeitgeist.

Hundert posits "'the appearance of a similar *geist* at a similar *zeit* among both Jews and Christians.' These movements were not a reaction to the Enlightenment, but rather shared with the Enlightenment 'the emboldening of the individual to

The reader might now conclude that we can explain R. Bunim simply as someone who, while in the "West," was exposed to the world of romanticism, whose values he then assimilated into Judaism. But, as we have stressed, Przysucha started with the Yehudi; the revolution began before R. Bunim, and we have no indication that the Yehudi was influenced by the spirit of the age. It is true that R. Bunim was a conduit to the Yehudi for what was happening in the "West," but this was once the Yehudi was already the Yehudi. The ideas of R. Bunim might well have been sharpened by his experiences, but the essential values are themselves intrinsic to Judaism and would have happened anyhow.

One needs to navigate between two extremes. The first one is an ethnocentric approach which denies any direct influence from the non-Jewish world, so that all one can say about the simultaneous advent of similar ideas is "Zeitgeist." On the other hand, there is an opposing tendency to reduce everything to Hegelian proximity; thereby denying a spiritual movement its own integrity. It is not inconceivable that R. Bunim heard some of these ideas when he was in the "West" and that they jelled with what he had heard from the Yehudi and the movement that the Yehudi had started.

---

independence of thought and feeling in matters of spirit.' Religious individualism, characterizes an inexplicable eighteenth century zeitgeist that applied equally to Hasidism and other contemporaneous movements." See: Torsten Ysander, *Studien zum Bestschen Hasidismus in Seiner Religious geschichtlichen Sonderart* (Uppsala: 1933), 372–392, and Yaffe Eliach, unpublished Ph.D. diss., "Jewish Hasidism, Russian Sectarians; Non-conformists in the Ukraine, 1700–1760" (1973). There are parallels between Przysucha and Western philosophy which are striking. For example, Pope's phrase,

Know then thyself, presume God not to scan;
The proper study of mankind is man

or Kant's argument in his "Religion within the Limits of Reason Alone" that goodness is genuine only if done for goodness's sake, otherwise it is a form of idolatry; or his statement,

Two things fill the mind with awe and wonder
the more often and more steadily we reflect upon them:
the starry heavens above me and the moral law within me

all the above quotations fit perfectly in the study house of Przysucha. In this context a seminal work is that of Charles Taylor, "Sources of the Self: The Making of Modern Identity." His central thesis is that "a modern notion of the self is related to... a certain sense of... inwardness" (111). This is what typifies Przysucha.

Ultimately, however, the religious issues of Przysucha are eternal and would have happened in one form or another in whatever century, with or without any particular social or cultural circumstance; whether R. Bunim had gone to the West or gone to the East. The language, the terms, might reflect the age in which they lived, but the ideas themselves are ageless. [28] [29]

---

[28] R. Mahler, *Hasidism and the Jewish Enlightenment,* 302, says the following: "The original thoughts propounded by the school of Przysucha-Kock as a result of its outspoken trend of religious individualism not only paralled many leading ideas of romantic literature of its generation but also partly presaged the new extreme, individualistic philosophy, particularly that of Nietzsche. In their effort to achieve profundity of religious thought and religious feeling, the spokesmen of regenerated Hasidism also reached a penetrating psychological power of observation."

[29] See M. Idel, "Hasidism," 23: "One must remain sceptical of proposals regarding the religious mentality of Hasidism that attempt to learn too easily from 'history.'"

PRZYSUCHA AND ELITISM

It has been argued that originally Hasidism had been led by an elite group, and not by the zaddik, an outstanding individual.[1] If so, then Przysucha may be seen as a reversion to the original Hasidic approach. However, this elite was not limited to a small fellowship (though at times some might have wished that it was). Przysucha was a movement open to all those who could respond to its call.

Przysucha's becoming a movement (an elitist movement, if you wish) was facilitated by the fact that it virtually removed from its agenda all kabbalistic aspects (unification, combinations of letters, *kavvanot*, and the mysteries of the Divine). It therefore saw the zaddik not as a unique individual (or group of individuals) or as someone who intervened with or knew how to manipulate the Divine, but rather as a living paradigm – a model to be emulated (though not imitated).

Przysucha was a meritocracy, and as such was not limited to any one social group. It was not limited to the founder's family: at each stage of transition, the mantle of leadership was taken up by the pupil rather than by the son. It was a meritocracy because the authority of the zaddik could be challenged and, if the challenger was proven correct, the zaddik would even agree with the challenger. Przysucha was open to all, but its strongest attraction was to those who were prepared to join its quest for truthfulness; for those who were prepared to endure piercing analysis of their own motives, and for

---

[1] Ada Rapoport-Albert, *God and the* Zaddik *as the Two Focal Points of Hasidic Worship.* 312–314.

those who believed in the intellectual endeavor of Talmudic study and the use of the mind in general.

In discussing whether Przysucha was elitist or not, one must be aware that words are loaded. Each generation has its own political correctness and the word "elitist" is a bad word nowadays. But more importantly, there is a semantic problem. As Professor Joad used to say, "It all depends what you mean by...."[2] Is this elite group aloof from the needs of the community, or does it serve them?

The Yehudi saw a superficiality within Hasidism as it existed in his day. He demanded the analytical scrutiny of the mind and the purification of the soul. This invitation was open to anyone who could participate. Przysucha was a reaction to the shallowness of a mass movement. It was not just that it had an aversion to the paraphernalia of the court of the zaddik. It was also the fact that any movement with too large a number of people would inevitably function at a lower common denominator in the service of God.

> Once (R. Bunim) said to our teacher from Kotzk: why do I need so many Hasidim like these? I would be satisfied with a few.[3]

The mass is good for the ego, but it is not good for depth. Couldn't more be achieved by focusing on a smaller group of people? This question exercised the minds of both R. Bunim and R. Menahem Mendel, as is indicated by the famous parable told by R. Bunim as to how the evil urge thwarted the success of the Baal Shem Tov.

> When the Baal Shem Tov made the first hasidim, the Evil Urge was in great straits for, as he said to his followers, "Now the hasidim of the Baal Shem Tov will set the world ablaze with their holiness." But then he thought of a way out. He disguised himself as someone else and went to two hasidim who lived together in a certain town. "Your service is praiseworthy," he said to them, "but there ought to be at least ten of you, so that you can pray in a quorum." He fetched eight of his people and joined them to those two hasidim. And since

---

[2] Professor Joad was an English philosopher who, after World War II, became famous for his participation in a radio program on the BBC called "The Brain's Trust." He was known for always giving an answer which started with the phrase "It all depends what you mean by...."

[3] *Siah Sarfei Kodesh*, 1:25 §122; cf. ibid. 1:49 §226.

they had no money to purchase a (Torah) scroll and other things they needed, he brought them a rich man – also one of his devotees– who provided them with whatever was necessary. He did the same everywhere. When he had finished he said to his followers: "Now we no longer need be afraid of anything, for we have the majority, and that is what counts."[4]

What is someone who tells such a story thinking of? Surely this reflects R. Bunim's unease with the state of Hasidism in his day; his feeling that with numbers, the movement had lost its raison d'être.

Scholem, taking a swipe at Buber's sanitized Hasidism divorced from any social historical or religious practice, says the following:

> … nor did Hasidism declare such a "simple man" its highest ideal.… But hasidic teachings know nothing of his representing the highest ideal which the disciple is to realize. Quite to the contrary, it tirelessly repeats the teaching of the necessary reciprocal relationship between the truly spiritual man – who always appears as a gnostic initiate – and the simple people. These two types of men can bring about the true Hasidic community.…[5]

Hasidism, possibly unlike earlier forms of mysticism, emphasized the combination of the horizontal (direct service to the community) with the vertical (personal depth). The balance of these two axes is not fixed and changes according to circumstances. But, essentially, the commitment of Przysucha to the entire Jewish community (klal Israel) was always there.[6]

---

[4] *Siah Sarfei Kodesh*, 1:44, §34.

[5] G. Scholem, "Martin Buber's Interpretation of Hasidism," in his work, *The Messianic Idea in Judaism*, 237.

[6] Schiper, in "The History of Hasidism in Central Poland" (26), argues that the original founders of Polish Hasidism stressed "the love of Israel and the love of Zion." Faierstein on personal redemption says on this the following:
"Hasidism has been a bifurcated movement from its inception. It was both a popular movement centered around the charismatic figure of the zaddik who reached down to all strata of the community to elevate them spiritually, and at the same time a continuation of the kabbalistic tradition for a spiritual elite."

One of R. Bunim's outstanding characteristics was his active concern and involvement with assimilated Jews,[7] even if his children or hasidim did not always approve of this.[8] He said, "It is important to see that not one Jewish soul is lost."[9]

But what encapsulates this idea of combining the vertical with the horizontal is the following statement:

> R. Bunim said that the real goal is to draw the simple people after God. Men of elevated consciousness are the vessels for drawing the simple people. Therefore they shouldn't lord it over them.[10]

Any act having to do with holiness, said R. Bunim, starts with a formula that relates to the Jewish community in general and in their name: "Even Torah and prayer, when praying alone, is together with all Israel."[11] The stress was on personal redemption, while never forgetting for a moment that the goal was communal redemption. Even Menaham Mendel, for whom there was no compromise, said much the same thing:

> All matters related to holiness should be done with the totality of Israel and in the name of Israel. Therefore the language (of prayer) is plural.[12]

And:

> With regard to the entity of the Jewish people you will never find a blemish.[13]

The following story is told:

---

[7] *Or Simhah,* §§22, 42, 43, 63; *Torat Simhah,* §64 101.

[8] *Or Simhah,* §29.

[9] *Siah Sarfei Kodesh,* 3:60 §186.

[10] *Shem mi-Shmuel, Bamidbar, Shavuot,* 115 (1919).

[11] *Ramatayim Zofim* (AZ), chap. 14, §3. On three occasions, *Ramatayim Zofim* (chap. 8 §70, chap. 9 §15, chap. 31 §104) mentions in the name of R. Bunim that although there are Jews who do not have a place in the World to Come as individuals, collectively, as part of the Jewish people, they do.

[12] Levinger, *"The Torah of the Rebbe from Kotzk,"* 123, n. 8. The continuation, however, shows the difference between R. Bunim and Menaham Mendel, for the latter continues, "But in things physical, even if they eat together, the food goes into each person's body and he doesn't know about the body of his friend."

[13] *Ohel Torah,* par. Balak, 74. (*Sefer Likkutim Hadashim,* 18a).

I heard in the name of the Admor... from Kotzk... that he said about a certain contemporary zaddik that he is a zaddik in an overcoat (*im pelts*), meaning that there is one who makes for himself warm clothing for the winter and there is one who warms up the house. What is the difference between them? Although the one who makes himself warm clothing is warm, it is of no benefit to the others, while the one who warms up the house – that is good for others as well.[14] [15]

In *Emet ve-Emunah*, the Kotzker is quoted as saying, "I only look for the good qualities in every Jew. That way I come to love him."[16]

One could argue that we cannot be sure of the reliability of these quotations, but our claim is that we have a number of sources, all of which express a deep commitment on the part of Przysucha to the wider community, i.e. *klal Israel.*

Even an intellectual and spiritual aristocrat such as the Yehudi never removed himself from the people. If there was one quality that epitomized the Yehudi, it was that of giving charity to the poor. For him, giving charity was not some spiritual act that did not engage one with the "other." The Yehudi would wear the clothing not of a scholar but of a simple Jew. He went to the marketplace and mixed with the masses. He did not engage in his personal quest at the expense of concern with the uneducated.

> The Yehudi would dress in simple peasant's clothing – cap and gown... and would journey to the markets to seek Elijah, who would reveal himself in the markets.[17]

As we have mentioned, it was the Yehudi who noted that:

> When two Jews come together, with neither trying to lord it over the other, they create a Godly quality.[18]

---

[14] *Nifla'ot Hadashot, Seder ha-Yom ha-Katzar,* 9.

[15] See also *Shem mi-Shmuel, Shemot* par. Tezaveh, 2:125a, *Emet ve-Emunah,* §124.

[16] *Emet ve-Emunah,* §620. See also §663 on the Kotzker's tolerance for mistakes.

[17] Buber, *Or ha-Ganuz,* 397; cf. *Tiferet Shlomoh, Avot,* 153b. "The Yehudi said that he had accepted the words of R. Dovid of Lelov not to admonish people with strictures to make them repent, but to be with them with words of kindness and draw them near with love to arouse in them the fear of heaven."

For the Yehudi there was a clear yardstick by which one could evaluate whether one was in the right dynamic in the service of God, and that was: Did the act – the *mitzvah* – lead to a greater love of the other?

> In everything there is a way of evaluating whether it is being done correctly.... Similarly, with regards to the service of God and love of Him, a Jew can determine whether he is walking in the correct path and whether he is one of those who love God and love Israel. If a person sees that his love of Israel increases daily, that is proof that he is rising in his service of God – and that is the yardstick in his service of God.[19]

In very simple language, but in a way that in the world of Przysucha reverberated with significance, R. Bunim said:

> A Rebbe is called a "good Jew" because a Rebbe must have the quality of the love of Israel for all Jews. He must have a soul of love to find merit in every person.[20]

Possibly taking aim at the world of the *mitnaggedim* and definitely expressing the concern of Hasidism for the "other," R. Yitzhak of Vorki (Warka) pointed out: "The obligation of *limmud Torah* is specifically to teach others."[21]

∾ ∿

In conclusion, let us reiterate that Przysucha was open to anyone – rich, poor, young, old, from a religious or non-religious background – as long as they were prepared to submit and participate fully and sincerely. And if they showed ability, they could ascend as far as their ability allowed, irrespective of parentage, wealth, and so on.

Some have argued that

---

[18] *Nifla'ot ha-Yehudi*, 85.
[19] *Tiferet ha-Yehudi*, 174 §87.
[20] *Siah Sarfei Kodesh*, 4: 44 §28; but note the contrast of this interpretation with that of Menahem Mendel of Kotzk; Levinger (*"Torato"*), 134, n. 10.
[21] *Ohel Yitzhak*, 85 §201.

Right from the start, Hasidism confined the possibility of direct access to God to a specific class of supreme spiritual men.[22]

Such a description is simply not true of Przysucha. There was no vicarious redemption in Przysucha. Przysucha demanded the analytical scrutiny of the mind and the purification of the soul. This demand was open to anyone who could participate in the quest with Przysucha.

In his concluding remarks as to what is new in Hasidism, Idel says:

> While the ecstatic Kabbalist would consider his own achievement as religiously paramount and meaningful in itself, though it may also have social implications, Hasidic masters would in most cases consider the mystical experience as a stage on the way toward another goal, namely the return of the enriched mystic who becomes even more powerful and active in and for the group for which he is responsible.[23]

Przysucha would concur with this description of Hasidism, but it would argue that the Zaddik, as a result of his mysticism, is "more powerful and active… for the group" by being a living paradigm.

Yet with all its concern for the people, it must be said that the average Jew would not have found his place in Przysucha. The Kotzker might have been more strident, but the value system of Przysucha by definition excluded the Jew who did not want to think deeply, who did not want to extend himself, who wanted neither the agony nor the ecstasy, but who just wanted to

---

[22] Rapoport-Albert (n. 1 above) says:
"If, right from the start, Hasidism confined the possibility of direct access to God to a specific class of supreme spiritual men, and denied it to the ordinary person, what did it offer the ordinary person that seemed so attractive to vast sections of Eastern European Jewry of the time as to account for its rapidly increasing popularity?" She concludes:
"As was suggested earlier on, while it denied him direct access, it guaranteed access to God to the ordinary person by means of his adherence to those who enjoyed it directly" (22).

[23] M. Idel, *Hasidism: Between Ecstasy and Magic,* 209 ("Concluding Remarks").

identify and feel *heimish* (at home).[24] There was no place in Przysucha for the Jew who simply wanted to pay his dues to the religious party, as it were, without being forced to ask himself the question, "But why?" The Seer understood that people need to belong, that they need a group. The Seer was prepared to make the personal sacrifice that such a role demanded. The three generations of Przysucha were not – indeed, could not make such a sacrifice.[25]

By its very nature, membership or identification with a group entails some personal compromise. Przysucha was strongly opposed to such compromise. Thus its very nature entailed a dilemma, and perhaps the seeds of its end. However, for many of those who have a reflective personality, the quest for authenticity must have been almost irresistible.[26]

---

[24] It was precisely this that the Kotzker opposed. See *Siah Sarfei Kodesh he-Hadash*, par. Vayikra, p. 90.

[25] It is not inconceivable that a movement whose credentials were truth and purity of motive might have spun off from the Jewish community or at least been indifferent to it. There are indeed one or two statements by the Kotzker that express indifference, but by and large this world is too rooted in the Jewish people to have allowed itself to become indifferent to it.

[26] A quest for personal authenticity is beset with many difficulties, the least of which is the relationship between teacher and student. If it is too loose, the student will receive too little; if it is too close, the student may never achieve personal responsibility.

רשימת ציטוטים ראשיים פרקים א–יב (לפי מספר הערה בספר)

הציטוטים מובאים בצורתם המקורית ללא תיקון

פרק א'

הקדמה

(1) אז התאזרו חיל מתנגדי הרר״ב זצ״ל ויאמרו כי אין כוונתם לדון עפ״י השמועה אך יוכיחו דבריהם בראיות נאמנות ויספרו מעשים שונים מבזיונות שנעשו לצדיקים ע״י חסידי פרשיסחא ואיש א' הי' שם מחסידי הרה״ק מאפטא והעיד כי בן קרה דבר שהי' לו רח״ל סיבות שונות ונתן לו רבו סגולה של משי לבנה כשלג שיהי' לבוש בה תדיר, וסמוך לביתו הי' דר שכן א' מחסידי פרשיסחא, והיה רגיל לבוא לביתו ולהתלוצץ מהסגולה, ופ״א כאשר לא היה האיש בביתו בא השכן הנ״ל ולקח את האבנט ומשח אותה כולה בצבע שחור ואח״כ מילא פיו שחוק ממנו מדוע יתן אומן בסגולות כאלה וכו'. והרבו המתנגדים להביא עוד דוגמאות כאלה איך כבוד צדיקי הדור מושפלים בעיני חסידי פרשיסחא, אשר בוודאי כן הורה להם רבם כי רק דרכו דרך אמיתי... (מאיר עיני הגולה,קנא)

(15) ...אדמו״ר ר' וואלף מסטריקוב ישב פעם בגסיסתו של אחד מזקני חסידי קוצק. הרכין עצמו ר' וואלף ושאלו : ״ ישראל, האם היצר הרע עדיין שולט בך״? -״ כן״ - נענה הזקן בראשו - הוא משדל אותי שאגיד ״שמע ישראל״ כדי שיאמרו אחרי, ״נשמתו של הצדיק יצאה בטהרה, באחד״ (עיטורי תורה 1, עמ 81)

(16) ...ויאהב יצחק את עשו כי ציד בפיו (כ״ה, כ״ח) ופירש רש״י, לצוד ולרמות את אביו בפיו, ושואלו אבא היאך מעשרין את המלח ואת התבן, כסבור אביו שהוא מדקדק במצוות. ובמדרש (דברים רבה א, טו) אמר רבי שמעון בן גמליאל, לא כיבד בריה את אבותיו כמו אני את אבותי, ומצאתי שכיבד עשו לאביו יותר ממני. כיצד, אמר רבן שמעון בן גמליאל, הייתי משמש את אבי בבלכים צואים, וכשהייתי הולך לשוק הייתי משליך אותן הכלים ולובש כלים נאים ויוצא בהן. אבל עשו לא היה עושה כן, אלא אותן כלים שהיה לובש ומשמש בהן את אבא הן הן מעולים, עיין שם. ובאמת, וכי לא היה רבן שמעון בן גמליאל יכול ללבוש מלבושים נאים לשמש את אביו. אך הענין הוא, כי בלבושים נכלל כל הלבוש וההגוון שאדם מציב לו בצורת נפשו ותכונתו, וזהו שמצינו שעשו שימש את אביו בכלים מעולים, היינו שהציב לו לבוש נאה נגד אביו, וכמו שנאמר עליו ״כי ציד בפיו״, שרימה אותו בשאלו היאך מעשרין את התבן ואת המלח. ואף שרימה את אביו, ובשורש לא היה יצחק אבינו ע״ה מסכים שירמה אותו, ואדרבה היה רוצה לראות חסרונו, כדי שילמדנו אורח מישור, אך לפי שעה בשעתו היתה דעת יצחק אבינו ע״ה נוחה, שנדמה לו לפי שעה שבנו הולך ישר. וזהו שאמר רבי שמעון בן גמליאל, שהוא אינו יכול לעשות בזה כמעשה עשו, שהוא אינו מסתיר חסרונותיו מפני אביו, ואדרבה היה לובש בגדים צואים, היינו שגילה לפני כל הדברים שהיה לבו דוה עליהם, וכל דבר שלא היה נראה יפה בעיניו היה מגלה לפני אביו. והגם שבשורש היתה דעת אביו נוחה מזה, שעל ידי זה למדו דרך ה' ויעצו האיך יישר מידותיו, אבל לפי שעה היה בה גם אביו מצטער מה קצת, ולכן לא היה יכול לכבד את אביו באופן שכיבד עשו את אביו... (אורחות חיים ע׳. מ)

18) ...הי' מרגלא בפומי' דהרה"ק ר' חנוך העניך מאלכסנדר ז"ל לומר בשם רבו הרה"ק הרבי ר' בונם ז"ל שאמר אשר כל אברך אשר בנוסעו פעם הראשון אל הצדיק, ולהסתופף בצל החסידים, צריך לידע המעשה מרבי אייזיק ר' יעקעליס מקרקא, שכנה הביהכנ"ס בקרקא הנקרא ר' אייזיק ר' יעקעליש שוהל וזהו כי הר' אייזיק ר' יעקעליש חלם לו כמה פעמים שיסע לפראג, ושם סמוך לחצר המלך תחת הגשר יחפור בארץ וימצא אוצר גדול ויתעשר, הוא נסע לפראג ובבאו שמה הלך אל הגשר אשר אצל חצר המלך, אבל שם עמדו אנשי חיל ההולכים על המשמר לילה כיום, והי' ירא לחפור בארץ ולחפש במטמונים. אבל מרוב צערו כי עמל כ"כ בדרך רחוקה, ועתה ישוב לביתו בחוסר כל, הי' הולך כל היום סמוך להגשר אנה ואנה, תפוש במחשבותיו וכשחשכה הלך אל האכסניא לנוח, וביום השני וכן ביום השלישי שוב בא בבוקר אל המקום הזה, וטייל שם כל היום, ולפנות ערב הלך לאכסניא, השר העומד שם בראש האנשי חיל שומרי ראש המלך, בראותו כי יום יום הולך איש יהודי שחוח ותוארו כעני המעוטף בצער ובינגון, סובב סובב אצל הגשר כל הימים, קראו אליו ושאלו בדברים רכים מה אתה מחפש ועל מי אתה ממתין זה כמה ימים במקום הזה, סיפר לו כל העניין כי כמה לילות רצופים חלם לו כי כאן טמון אוצר גדול, ולמטרה זאת בא לפראג ברוב עמל וטורח. אז פתח השר את פיו שחוק ואמר לו האם הי' כדאי שתסע דרך רחוקה כ"כ ע"י חלום, מי זה אשר יאמין לחלומות, הלא גם אני בחלומי אמרו לי שאסע לעיר קראקא ושם נמצא א' הנקרא בשמו אייזיק ר' יעקעליש ואם אחפור שם בבית היהודי ר' יעקעליש תחת התנור וכיריים אז אמצא אוצר גדול, אבל הכי אתן אומן לחלומות אשר שוא ידברו. ולנסוע בשביל זה לקראקא, ואתה עשית שטות כזה לבא לכאן, הי' כששמוע ר' אייזיק ר' יעקעליש דברי השר הבין כי עיקר ביאתו לכאן הי' למען ישמע דברים אלו ושידע כי האוצר נמצא לא כאן רק בביתו וכי עליו לחפור ולבקש במטמונים בביתו ושם ימצא האוצר. חזר ונסע לביתו וחפש ומצא בביתו תחת התנור וכיריים את האוצר ונתעשר, ובנה בהונו את הבית הכנסת הנודעת בשם ר' אייזיק ר' יעקעליש שוהל, כן הדבר צריך לידע כי ע"י בואו אל הצדיק והרבי, נתודע לו שהאוצר אין לו לחפש אצל הרבי רק בביתו, ויהי בנוסעו לביתו שם יחפש ויחפור עד מקום שידו מגעת, ויגעת ומצאת תאמין כי קרוב אליך הדבר בפיך ובלבבך לעשותו, אצלו ממש. (מאמרי שמחה ל)

פרק ב'

<u>המרד הקדוש</u>

הצדיק הזה רוצה להמשיך דרך חדש מלמעלה למטה לליבות בני ישראל, איך שיעבדו את ה' בתורה ותפלה יחדיו, ודבר זה עדיין לא היה בעולם. (אמרי קודש השלם אות סח)

7) ...והנה בימים ההם היתה עיר לובלין מלאה סופרים וחכמים גדולים בתורה ויראה. אולם כולם היו מתנגדים ולא דרכו בדרכי החסידות וכמו זר נחשב אצלם ההולך בדרך הזה. ולא הבינו כי החסיד ג"כ עובד ד' בכל לבב רק דימו וחשבו כי החסידים עוברים על דת משה ויהודית ואינם מתנהגים ע"פ הש"ע. הגם שנמצאו בימים חסידי הרבי ר' אלימלך. אולם היו אחד בעיר ושנים במשפחה. וכאשר שמעו בלובלין כי סמוך לעירם נעשה פרצה כזאת, כי נתיישב שם איש המתנהג בדרך החסידות ומושך ומקרב אליו אנשים ויושבים עמו על שלחנו ולומד עמהם שיתנהגו גם הם בדרכיו, אז חרה אפם עליו מאוד... (עשר אורות עמ' 19)

8) בזמן נשיאותו של המגיד הגדול ממעזריטש לא הי' עוד בווארשא כמעט שום חסיד הגם שמספר היהודים שגרו בעיר זו כבר הי' די ניכר, חסידים מספרים שפעם שההה הרה"ק ר' משה ליב מסאסוב זצ"ל בווארשא בענין פדיון שבויים שהיו אסורים שם, וכשהצליח לשחררם, אותו היום היום ערב שבת הי' ועשה משתה לכבוד זה ועוד באותו יום לפני חשיכה נסע מחוץ לעיר ולא רצה לשבות בתוך העיר כששאלוהו מפני מה אתה נוסע כ"כ, השיב מתירא אני להיות בווארשא ועד עכשיו הגינה עליו המצווה של פדיון שבויים.והמגיד מקאזניץ בבואו בפעם הראשונה להמגיד ממעזריטש, שאלו מאיזה עיר הוא בא? השיבו מקאזניץ שהיא עשר פרסאות מווארשא, אז שמח המגיד שבעשר פרסאות מווארשא כבר אומרים כתר (כנוסח ספרד) וביקש שיזכה עוד לשמוע שבווארשא עצמה יאמרו כבר כתר...(מאיר עיני הגולה,מלואים והוספות,א)

17) פ"א סיפר אדמו"ר מפרשיסחא ז"ל בשם הרבי מלובלין. איך שהגאון האמתי מו' עזריאל ז"ל הורוויץ האבד"ק לובלין שם היה דרכו בכל עת להציק הרבי מלובלין בשאלות. והעיקר אחרי שידע בעצמו שאינו רבי, למה הוא מדריך אחרים באורחותיו בהמשכתו עדה והשיב לו הרבי מה הוא אוכל לעשות בזה. ויגיד לו הרב הנ"ל בשבת הבעל"ט תפרסמו א"ע לעיני כל הקהל ואז ישובו לדרכיהם.וכן קיים והתנצל א"ע מאוד בשברון רוח כי הוא הפחות. ודבריו אלה הלהיבו להכניס הענווה גם בהם עד שנתדבקו ביותר. אח"ז התראו יחד וסיפר לו הרבי שקיים דבריו ולא הועיל. השיב לו הרב הגאון הנ"ל דרכי חסידים לאהוב בעניני ולהתרחק מהגאות בכן תגידו להם מעלתכם כי אתם מהצדיקים האמיתים ואז ישובו לדרכיהם. והשיב לו הרבי אף שאינני רבי אבל אינני גם שקרן ואיך אוכל לומר עלי שאני צדיק היפך האמת. (רמתיים צופים א"יז 22.24)

18) ובספר משמרת איתמר פ' תשא כתב וז"ל. וכן שמעתי מפה קדוש אדמו"ר הרבי מלובלין נ"ע. ברוב ענוותנותו היתרה ובשברון לב בזה הלשין על עצמו.אוי לדור שאני הוא המנהיג עכ"ל. (נפלאות הרבי, 55 כח)

19) ..."וכן אמר אין גרוע בעולם כמותי אפילו יאמר לי מלאך ה' שאני צדיק איני מאמין לו. אפילו יאמר לי הקדוש ברוך בעצמו שאני צדיק,אאמין לו על אותו הרגע ולא יותר, כי בניקל נוכל לדחות לשאול תחתית חיי" (היכל הברכה כי תשא רעו)

20) שאלו תלמידו הרה"ק רבי שמחה בונם מפרשיסחא, הנה תכלית המכוון הוא שעל האדם לידע שהוא כ'אין', ומה תכלית הוא זה, אם ידע שהוא 'אין' והוא (באמת) 'אין'. והשיבו רבנו הק' הנה חותמו של הקב"ה אמת, ואם נתוודע לו שהוא 'אין' דבוק הוא באמת, ודבוק הוא בהקב"ה שחותמו אמת, וזה הוא תכלית המבוקש להיות דבוק באמת. (נפלאות היהודי 60)

24) אם אדם העובד את ה' יתי' רואה בעצמו שכאתמול כן היום, והיום הוא אך באותה בחינה בעבודתו כיום אתמול, ידע נאמנה שעוד נפל ממדריגתו, והיום נגרע מערכו מבחינת עבודתו מיום העבר, כי אדם הוא בבחינת 'הולך' ולא 'עומדי'. (בית יעקב, שבת חוהמ"ע סוכות צא,ב)

25) הרבי מלובלין שאמר שהוא אוהב יותר הרשע אשר יודע שהוא רשע מהצדיק שיודע שהוא צדיק. ושאל אותו הרב הקדוש מפרשיסחא הטעם. והשיב לו כי הרשע שיודע שהוא רשע הנה הוא דבוק בהאמת והקב"ה הוא אמת ונקרא אמת. אבל הצדיק שיודע שהוא צדיק ובודאי אינו כן כי אין צדיק בארץ וכו' ומכש"כ זה שהוא מרגיש שהוא צדיק בודאי אינו צדיק. (נפלאות הרבי 54 קכד)

30) בעת המחלוקת הידועה שהי' בין הרבי הקדוש מלובלין זצוקללה"ה זי"ע עם ההי"ק "היהודי" זצוקללה"ה מפרשיסחא, פ"א נסע היהודי הק' זצללה"ה ללובלין ולקח עמו את תלמידו האהוב לו ביתר שאת הלא הוא ההי"ק הרבי בונם זצללה"ה מפרישסחא ואמר לו בוא ונכנס

להיכל הקודש נאוה קודש של הרבי לקבל פניו, וכאשר באו לבית המקודש של הרבי הק׳ זצללה״ה שמך אתם שמחה גדולה וישבו יחדיו כשבת אחים באהבה ואחוה ורעיות, ואח״כ התחילו לדבר בינהם מהמחלוקת שהי׳ ע״י מלשינות כידוע (שהי׳ אנשים כאלו שהי׳ מלשינים על היהודי הקדוש זצללה״ה לפני הרבי הק׳ זצללה״ה ודברו על צדיק עתק ר״ל) אז אמר הרבי הקדוש ליהודי הק׳ תאמינו לי שאני אוהבכם מאוד. וגם הנני חפץ בחבורתכם, וגם הנכם נאמנים עלי כמאה עדים יותר מהמלשינים עליכם. אכן יען שיש מלשינים השונאים אתכם, וכפעם בפעם יש מלשינות עליכם, לכן הי׳ עצתי נכונה שלא תסעו עוד מהיום לכאן ותתנהגו כטוב לפניכן בעירכם, כי גם אני בעת היותי אצל רבי הק׳ הר״ר אלימלך זצללה״ה הי׳ ג״כ בינינו כדברים האלו ונתייעצתי שלא ליסע עוד לליזענסק ע״כ גם אתם שמעוני, וכמוני וכמוכם ולא תסעו לכאן, ואח״כ פטרם הרבי לשלום. וכשיצאו אמר הרבי בונם זצללה״ה מפרשיסחא להיהודי הקדוש זי״ע שיעשה כעצת הרבי הק׳ מלובלין זצללה״ה אז פתח היהודי הקדוש את פיו הק׳ והטהור, ואמר ואל מי תדמיוני ואשוה, הרבי הקדוש הי׳ יכול לעשות כן אצל רבו הר״ר אלימלך זצוקללה״ה, יען שלא הי׳ רב חכמתו ממנו, כי מקודם קיבל לקח מרבינו הקוה״ט הרבי ר׳ בער זצלל״ה לא כן אני שרוב חכמתי מהרבי הק׳ זצוקללה״ה. (תפארת היהודי עמי קעו. צה)

(34 …וכאשר שמעתי פי׳ הפסוק מפה קדוש כאדמו״ר הק׳ מו״ה יעקב יצחק זצללה״ה מלובלין כי לא אוכל לקום מפניך כי כתיב כי צר צרתם בכל חלילה נחסר כאשר כביכול מאומ׳ לבני״י נוגע החסרון הזה למעלה ובשביל זה עומדות השכינה בשבילנו ומבקשת רחמים וז״ף כי לו בשביל בכל צרתם לו צר ח״ו אוכל לקום ולבקש מפניך וזהי׳ לא באל״ף ויסיר הצער מב״יי (אור לשמיים 6)

(38 …ואמר ששמע מהיהודי הקדוש זי״ע שאמר שהאמת שאנו הולכים במדרגה יותר גדולה מהרבי מלובלין זי״ע, אבל בכל מקום שאנו מגיעים הוא רבי. (ביכורי אביב,הקדמה)

(47 יהודי אחד זקן אבדה לו בדרך לבית המדרש קופסת הטבק. …והנה פגש את התיש הקדוש. התיש הקדוש היה נודד על פני האדמה וראשי קרניו השחורות נשקו את הכוכבים. כשמע את יללתו של היהודי הזקן, הרכין עצמו אליו ואמר: חתוך מקרני כמה שנחוץ לך לקופסה׳. חתך הזקן כדברו, ועשה לו קופסה ומילא אותה טבק. אחר כך הלך אל בית המדרש והציע לכל האנשים סביבו קמצוץ טבק. האנשים הריחו והריחו, וכל מי שהריח קרא : מה נהדר הטבק ! זה בא לו מן הקופסה. מה נהדרה הקופסה! מניין היא? ׳. סיפר להם הזקן אל דבר התיש הקדוש נדיב הלב. מיד יצאו איש אחרי אחיו אל הרחוב וביקשו את התיש הקדוש. התיש הקדוש נדד על פני האדמה וראשי קרניו השחורות נשקו את הכוכבים. ניגש אליו איש אחרי אחיו וביקש רשות לחתוך משהו. פעם אחר פעם הרכין עצמו התיש לפני המבקש. קופסה אחר קופסה נעשתה ונתמלאה טבק. תהילת הקופסאות נתפשטה למרחקים. על כל פסיעה ניגש מבקש אל התיש הקדוש. נטול קרניים נודד התיש הקדוש על פני האדמה״ (אור הגנוז 444)

(49 סיפר ששמע מהרבי מלובלין זצ״ל שאמר שהאמת שדרך היהודי זצללה״ה זי״ע הוא יותר גבוה מהדרך שלנו, אבל מה נעשה שעל דרך זה העמיד לנו הרבי ר׳ אלימלך זצללה״ה זי״ע (הק׳ לספר ביכורי אביב)

פרק ג'

קוים לביוגרפיה של ר' בונים

(1) ...וז"ל "(בונם לעבין) תחזיק את עצמך בי ותהיה לך רוה"ק מעולם האצילות וירוצו כל העולם אליד". (רמתים צופים יח.סג)

(4) ...כי לא הבאתי בחיבור הזה שום דרוש בחריפות רק כדרכי מעולם לשום העקוב למישור ביסודות בנויות על הקדמות מתישבות על הלב בדרך פשוטו, באופן אשר השכל האנושי יסכים עמהן ויעיד עליהן. (עשרה למאה עמ' ג-ד)

(25) ...גם אמר החידושי הרי"מ זצ"ל מורי הרבי ר' בונם ז"ל הי' מכניס א"ע במקומות כאלו בניסיונות אשר גם תנאים ואמוראים לא היו מכניסים א"ע במקומות כאלו. (אור שמחה, יב)

(37) ...אדם גדול, בקי בתלמוד ובספרות האלהית והמחקר העברית, רוקח (אפאטהעקער) מנוסה ומומחה ומבין מעט בחכמת הרפואה ויתר חכמות הטבע הנצרכות למכין רפאות תעלה, וגם שפת גרמניא פוליניא ולטינא, גבר חרוץ במפעליו, ר' בונם ז"ל: אשר ראה רבות בנעוריו ויתערב בין מפלגות שונות, לרגל עסקיו בקבלנות עם הממשלה ומפקדי צבאות החיל במלחמת הפולנים. (כתר כהונה עמ' 127)

(42) ...אחר ש"ק שמעתי פני ללובלין והייתי שם אצלו על ש"ק ואמר תורה בליל ש"ק. ואמר שהוא לא הבין כלום מה שאמר הרבי ז"ל. אך זאת הבנתי שהעולם עליון עוה"ב הוא כאן בעולם הזה אצל הרבי הזה. (רמתים צופים, יח. סג)

(57) ...עוד שמעתי ממנו ז"ל מעשה אחת שהיה בדרך סמוך לווארשא. וכה סיפר שהיה צריך לספר איזו מעשה. אך מעשה זו היה דברי חול וידעתי כי צחוק גדול יהיה כשאספר זאת והעולם היה גדול מאוד. ואמר לי היצה"ר שלא אספר כי אפסיד את העולם ולא יחזיקו אותי עוד לרבי... (רמתים צופים ל. פח)

(58) ...עוד כתב לי הרב שי' מפלונסק הנ"ל שפי"א הי' הרבי ר' בונם בוכה מאוד. ואז הי' בקודש פנימה הרה"ק רח"א מאלכסנדר הנ"ל תלמידו, וקרא אותו אצלו בשמו והוא הי' אז עוד רך בשנים. ואמר לו ידעת מפני מה אני בוכה. בא ואספר לך מעשה. בעת שהייתי אצל הרה"ק ר' אפרים מסדילקוב זצ"ל בעל דגל מחנה אפרים. אמר לי שאין חכמים בעולם רק אני. ועוד איש אחד הדר בכפר פלוני והנה בזו הרגע יצא האיש מכפר פלוני מן הדת רח"ל. ומשום זה אני בוכה. וחקרו הסיבה איך בא לידי כפירה ר"ל. ונתודעו המעשה שהי' כך הי'... (אור שמחה כח)

(60) ...ואז אמר התורה על ויקראו שמו עשו כי הכל קורין לו כן. כי לשון קריאה הוא ענין המשכה. שלשקר הכל נמשכין אבל לאמת אין הכל מבינים ע"כ. (אור שמחה נס)

(62) כתב בספר נפלאות חדשות (דף מח) שמעתי בשם הרב הקדוש רבי ר' בונם על המדרש שהראה הקב"ה לאדם הראשון דור דור ודורשיו דור דור ומנהגיו, והקשה למה הראה הקב"ה הדור קודם למנהיגיו, ואמר שאם הראה השם יתברך לאדם הראשון קודם את המנהיג, יאמר אדה"ר שמחה בונם הוא יכול להיות מנהיג. ע"כ הראה לו תחילה את הדור, ובדור כזה יכול ג"כ אני להיות מנהיג. (מאמרי שמחה פא)

(63) ...מי שיש לו שונאים ומקללים אותו הקב"ה מברך אותו ולא יוכלו לפעול בו ח"ו. ונמצא יש לו יתרון, היינו הברכות יותר מאם לא היה לו שונאים שאז לא היה לו הברכות. והחסיד דוד

המלך ע״ה אמר לגודל ענוותנותו שאף שאינו ראוי לברכות מצד צדקתו כי אם מצד השונאים צריך לחזק אותו כמשל הנ״ל... (קול שמחה קיד)

65) הרבי רבי בונם זי״ע, דיבר פעם אחת בקדשו ואמר: אם לא הייתי מפחד מה״עולם״, הייתי תוקע שופר בראש השנה שחל להיות בשבת, מכיון שבבית דינו של הרי״ף ז״ל, היו תוקעין בר״ה שחל להיות בשבת, והחברייא שלי הם ג״כ חשובים וגדולים כמוהם. (קול מבשר 3. 37)

פרק ד

<u>תורה</u>

5) ...לימוד גמרא ותוספות המטהר את המוח. (תפארת היהודי כט)

6) ...וכיון שנשייר לנו את התורה, יש לנו הכל, כיון דמן התורה נוכל לבוא לכל המדריגות שהיה מקודם ולגילוי שכינה. (נפלאות חדשות, סדר היום ע׳ סו)

7) במקום שאי אפשר להיות במקוה ילמד ׳גמרא׳... (מכתבי תורה, מכתב ס׳)

12) בגמרא אם רואה אדם שיסורין באין עליו יפשפש במעשיו כו׳ אם לא מצא יתלם בביטול תורה. והקושיא ידוע האם זאת נקרא עדיין לא מצא. ואמר שהפי׳ יתלה בביטול תורה. יתלה זאת מה שלא מצא הוא בביטול תורה. כי ההסרה מן התורה מונע אותו ומסמא את עיניו מלהביט בבחינת הרע הצפון בקרבו. ובאם היה עוסק בתורה כראוי בוודאי התורה היתה מאירה לו. ולא היה נעלם ממנו באיזה סוג מצבתו וחסרונו. (רמתים צופים, א״ז טז. כז)

18) ...ופי׳ הרב מפרשיסחא ז״ל בטובו זו התורה שעל ידי התורה יש התחדשות בעולם, בפרט בעת נתינת התורה נתחדש ונתקן כל הבריאה בכח התורה. (תורת שמחה קסו)

22) ...שפ״א הלך היהודי הקדוש זי״ע עם תלמידו הגה״ק מ׳ פרץ ז״ל ע״פ השדה וראה עופות פורחים והבהמות רועות ובכל פעם יגהקו ויצפצפו ואמר לרבו היהודי חשקה נפשי להבין צפצופם ודבורם. ואמר לו כשתשים על לב להבין מה אתה מדבר אז תבין צפצופם ודבורם ג״כ. (תפארת היהודי קנב. טו)

24) ...אכן נראה דכל אחד צריך שיהיה לו רב שילמוד ממנו בין תורה ובין עבודה באיזה דרך ישכון אור וכל חייו בזה העולם צריך האדם לזה. אכן האדם שהוא בזה הבחינה שלומד מכל האדם היינו במה שבני האדם פחותים מדברים בעניני העולם הזה הוא מוציא בזה רמיזא דחכמתא היאך לעבוד השי״ת. האדם הזה אין צריך לרב כלל והבן. (קול שמחה, ויצא לה)

25) ההי״ק הר״ר בונם זצ״ל אמר באם שאדם רוצה הדבר באמת, יכול ללמוד ענין זה אף מהגוי, למשל שאנחנו רואין שגם גוי שחושק ורוצה שיתנהג המדינה כפי הבנתו לטובת המדינה אינו משגיח כלום על עצמו ומסכן נפשו ועושה מלחמות עד שכובש כולם לעשות רצונו... (שיח שרפי קודש 5 .22 . 43)

29) ...כל מי אשר ערב ליבו לגשת אל הקדוש צריך לפלס דרכיו בהשכל ודעת גם במעשים טובים אשר כוונתם שלימה לה׳ שיכוין לרצון השי״ת...אמנם האיש הישראלי הדבוק בהשי״ת ותורתו יוכל להעמיק בדעתו ושכלו הכל במקומו הראוי לו... (קול שמחה עח)

(31) ...נראה הביאור, שעניין חוליים בזה היינו שלא הכירו מחסרונם שהם בעלי מומין באמת על
ידי שהיו בשיעבוד במצרים מקום הטומאה, ועל כן המתין השי"ת ג' חודשים עד שישיב
נפשם ותתישב דעתם עד שיכירו וידעו מחסורם. (אהל תורה לו)

(32) בבואי פעם ראשונה לקוצק קרא לי רבינו ואמר, בא ואגיד לך מהו חסיד, חסיד שואל עצמו-
מדוע. (עמוד האמת עמ' קא)

(42) הרה"ק הרר"ב מפשיסחא ז"צל אמר על הפסוק ולא נתן ה' לכם לב לדעת כו' עד היום הזה,
כי כל הניסים ונפלאות שעשה עמהם השי"י, מ"מ הואיל והיו ע"פ הטבע היה רק לשעה.
אבל אחר שנגמר להם כל התורה ונעשה מכל ההתנהגות תורה נעשה מזה בנין קבוע לדורות.
(חידושי הרי"ם רן)

(43) ...אכן נראה פירושו, דהנה כל הניסים שעשה השי"י היה כדי שיכירו וידעו כי כי הוא
היוצר הכל ומשגיח על כל הנמצאים העליונים והתחתונים לעשות בהם כרצונו ויקבע בלבם
האמונה ההוא וזה היו תכלית הניסים. אכן הכרה זו לא היה רק לפי שעה, אבל לאחר זמן
שעבר הנס לא היה להם הידיעה ההיא בפועל כל כך רק כמאמר הכתוב (תהילים
קי"א, ד) זכר עשה לנפלאותיו. אבל התורה שנתן לנו השי"ת על ידה אנו משיגים אלהותו
ואחדותו ואיך הוא משגיח על כל הנמצאים... (קול שמחה במדבר פד)

(47) פעם אחת נסע הרר"ב מפרשיסחא עם גדולי תלמידיו, וא' שכאו"א יאמר איזו דבר חידוש
בהלכה, וכל שלא יאמר יעשו לו קנס, וכאו"א אמר, ומרן מהר"יי מוארקי א' שלא למד
מעולם ע"מ לחדש, ורצו לקיים בו הפסק, והתחנן להם, וא' הרר"ב שעתה יחוס עליו, ויקבל
ע"ע לחדש עכ"פ דבר א'... (אהל יצחק 64. קסד)

ההגבלות של תורה

(54) הרה"ק רבי חנוך העניך מאלכסנדר נלקח לחתן בהיותו בן י"ג שנה אצל ר' יאקיל פאבטער
שדר בפרשיסחא, ובעת התקשרות ה'תנאים' ביקש מחותנו מרבנו הק' שיבחן אותו. שאלו
רבנו הק' איזו קושיא, ולא ידע רבי העניך להשיב על אתר עד אחר שעה, שנתיישב בדעתו
והעמיק במחשבתו עד שהשיב תרוצו. צבטו רבנו הק' בלחייו ואמר לו : בעת שהייתי בן י"ג
שנים אמרתי חומרא גדולה מזו, ובעת שהגעתי לגיל י"ח שנה הייתי גדול בתורה, אך ראיתי
שמן הלימוד לבד לא יוכל אדם לבוא לתכלית השלימות. ואמרתי לנפשי, שאצל אברהם
אבינו ע"ה נאמר שהיה חוקר מקודם בחמה ולבנה וכוכבים ומזלות עד שנתוודע לו שבכולם
אין ממש אך יש אלהים בשמים ובארץ המושל אליהם ומנהיג העולם כולו, ומזה בא
לתכלית השלימות... (נפלאות היהודי עה)

(58) הרבי ר' בונם זצ"ל סיפר : פעם אחת היה נוסע למרחץ ובשובו לביתו היה בפוזנא אצל הגאון
רבי עקיבא אייגר זצ"ל והלך עמו אל חדר מיוחד, ואמר הרבי ר' בונם זצ"ל לרבי עקיבא
אייגר זצ"ל, אמור לי תורה, והשיב לו אמור אתה, ואמר לו אני סגי נהור בביתי ואיני רואה,
אבל יש לי אדם אחד שהוא אומר לי מה שכתוב בספר, ואני אומר על זה תורה מגידות שאני
מגיד, אבל יש לי קושיא אחת, הלא העיר פוזנא הוא מקום לומדים ותורה מצלת בין בעידנא
דעסיק בה ובין בעידנא דלא עסיק בה, ומפני מה העיר פוזנא אינה ניצלת, ולא היה משיב לו
כלום, ואמר רבינו זצ"ל : אני מתרץ שבאמת קודם עיקבתא דמשיחא די היה התורה בנגלה,
אבל היום בעיקבתא דמשיחא אין די תורה בנגלה אלא צריך שיהיה בנסתר בפנימיות הלב...
(חשבה לטובה קכא)

(59) מה שנא' דפרשה ראשונה, ושננתם לבניך ובפרשה שני ולמדתם אותם, היינו שבפ' והי' אם
שמוע שהוא קבלת מצוות הלימוד שייך אבל פרשה ראשונה שמע קבלת עול מלכות

שמים לא שייך על זה לשון לימוד רק לשון שינון בחרב פיות להביא בתוכו עול מלכות שמים. (שיח שרפי קודש 3. 58)

(66) שמעתי שהה"ק הררמ"מ מקאצק זי"ע שאל למופלג אחד בעת שבא לפניו בפעם הראשון להיות חסיד. ולהסתופף בצל קדשו. מהות למודו. והשיב המופלג הנ"ל בזה"ל איך האב אויס גילערינט שיס. ואמר לו הה"ק זי"ע. בזה"ל ואהס האט שי"ס דיך אויס גילערינט. (שיח שרפי קודש 1 . 72 . 364)

(68) ...פ"א בא א' ממדינת ליטא גדול בתורה. אשר ישב סגור ומסוגר ולמד תורה ביגיעה שלשים שנה, וכעת שיצא שמעו הגדול בעולם של בוצי"ק מווארקי זצ"ל, עלה בלבו שיסע אליו, ובבואו לפניו שאל אותו הבצ"יק, הלא אתה איש למדן ועוסק בתורה זמן רב, הכי ידעת מה אומר ד'. אבל הוא לא הבין מה כונת הה"יק בזה. והשיב לו ד' אומר להניח תפילין ולהתפלל ולעסוק בתורה, והוא זצ"ל שחק ע"יז ואי' לו שאינו יודע מה הוא שואל אותו. והלך ממנו בעצבות גדול. וכן הי' בכל יום כשבא לפניו לא דיבר עמו מאומה רק שאל אותו העוד לא ידעת מה ד' אומר, ולא הי' יודע מה להשיב. ולא רצה לדבר עמו שום דבר אחר זולתו, והתעכב עצמו שם איזה שבועות, ולא עלה בידו לשמוע ממנו שום דבר. ורצה ליסע לביתו והלך ליטול רשות, ושאל אותו עוה"פ במה אתה נוסע לביתך כיון שלא תדע מה אומר ד', והתחיל לבכות במר נפשו, ואי' רבי הלא באתי לאדמור"ר שאוכל לידע שום דבר, השיב לו הה"יק כך אי' ה' הלא אם יסתר איש במסתרים ר"ל שיושב סגור ומסוגר בחדרי חדרים ל' שנה ויושב ולומד תורה, אעפ"כ ואני לא אראנו ר"ל שאינו יכול לסבול אותו, נאום ד', ר"ל שמסיים הכי שכך אומר ה'. וכששמע כך נבהל מאוד ונדהם ונאלם מלהשיב, ולא נשאר רוח חיים בקרבו, כי לא שמע כזאת וגם הוא רחק ממנו יותר ממאה פרסאות ואעפ"כ יודע הרבי מכל זה, אבל תיכף השיב רוחו ואי' רבי שאלה אי' יש לי לשאול, ואי' לו שאל, ואי' היאך הדין כשנונל על הארץ שמות קרועים מספה"ק מה לעשות, והשיב הה"יק הדין צריך להגבי' אותם כדי שלא יבואו לבזיון, ותיכף כששמע זאת הפיל א"ע מלא קומתו על הארץ והתחיל לבכות ולצעוק במר נפשו, רבי רבי, הלא נפל עתה לארץ צנא מלא ספרי תורה ג"כ ש"ס ספרא ספרי תוספתא, כולם נפלו לארץ ועתה אדמו"ר העלי אותם והגבי' אותם כדי שלא יבוזו ולהעלותם למקום שרשם הטהור, ותיכף נטל אותו הרבי תחת הידים והגבי' אותו ועשה לו טובות עד למאד. (אהל יצחק 126. רצה)

קבלה

(77) הרבי ר' מאיר מאפטא, הי' מתנגד הרב"יב וישלח הר"יר בונם לשאלהו, הן קריאת שמע בכל לשון ואיך יכוון סודותיו בפסוק שמע ישראל בשפת פולנית, ויתרגם לו הפסוק כצורתו עכ"ל. (שיח שרפי קודש 3 .7 .16)

(78) פ"א אמר לי בייחוד תדע שאני לא אחיה לעולם. אני אגיד לך איזה רבי שתקח אחרי. כל מי שיגיד לך פשט בזוה"יק חצי עמוד ויתקבל לך הפשט את זה תקח לרבי. (רמתים צופים כט. פ)

(79) פ"א אמר על בעל מקובל אחד מפורסם בזה"יל.(עהר קאן נישט קיין קבלה). והיו תלמידיו אצלו. והבין בחכמתו שאין מבינים דבריו כי ידעו שהיה מקובל מפורסם. ואמר שאינו מכיר הקבלה כמו שאומרים שאינו מכיר העיר כי לא היה שם מעולם. וזה שאמרתי כי אינו יכול לימוד הקבלה כי לימוד הקבלה צריך להשיג האורות. (רמתים צופים ל, פה)

(89) רבינו זצ"ל אמר כי יכול להחיות מתים אבל הוא רוצה יותר להחיות חיים. (אמת ואמונה קלה)

97) ...שמעתי בשם רה"ק מקאצק ז"ל שאמר עוד בתחלת קאצק כי כל איש הלומד זוהר ואין לו
התפשטות גשמיות אינו יודע תיבה א' וכל מי שאומר שהוא יודע מוטעה הוא עכ"ל"ה,
והקאצקער חסידים אשר היו בימי רה"ק מקאצק ז"ל לא למדו זהר רק יחידי סגולה... (גנזי החסדות סא)

ניסים

98) ...דהנה כל הניסים שעשה הש"י היה כדי שיכירו וידעו הכל כי הוא היוצר הכל ומשגיח על
כל הנמצאים העליונים והתחתונים לעשות בהם כרצונו ויקבע בלבם האמונה ההוא וזה היה
תכלית הניסים. אכן ההכרה זו לא היה רק לפי שעה, אבל לאחר זמן שעבר הנס לא היה
להם הידיעה ההיא בפועל כל כך רק בבחי' זכר. (קול שמחה, פרשת במדבר, פד)

100) ...היינו שלא באו להשכלת אמונה על ידי נפלאות ומופתים רק מהרו שכחו מעשיו (שם יג),
כי התפעלות אמונה שעל ידי מופתים הוא רק לפני שעה כנ"ל שהרי לשעה קלה נשכח, מה
שאין כן ויאמינו בדבריו. (אהל תורה, פרשת יתרו לה)

101) ...וירא העם וינועו ויעמדו מרחוק. נראה לפרש שלזה התנועעו ופחדו מחמת שראו שעדיין
הם עומדין מרחוק מצד עצמם אלא שבא עליהם הארת השכינה מה שאינו לפי מדרגתם
עדיין. על כן יוכל להיות ח"ו שלאחר שיפסק זה יפלו בפעם אחת מכל המדרגות... (קול
שמחה, פרשת יתרו 71)

105) אף בעל מדריגה קטנה יוכל להפוך שמים וארץ, אך להיות יהודי הוא קשה. (שיח שרפי
קודש 4. 34 .17)

106) אמר שאם היה יודע שבידו להועיל לאנשי אשכנז באותות ובמופתים, היה נוסע אליהם,
והיה מראה להם מופתים שהראה רבנו ע"ה במצרים. אלא שאי אפשר לשבות לבו של
איש ישראלי באותות ובמופתים. (שיח שרפי קודש, מלואים אות נד)

111) ...וכמו ששמעתי מאדמו"ר מפרשיסחא זי"ע שאמר שהוא יודע מכל אחד מה שעשה מיום
היולדו אך מה שאין אני מגלה זאת. למה זאת כי לא יועיל כלום. רק להודיע כי איש מופת
ובעל רוה"ק אני. וכל אחד בעצמו יודע נגעי לבבו ועושה תשובה. אך זאת אני מחוייב לכל
אחד ולהודיע הדברים שנסתר ממנו ואינו חושב כלל בחסרונו וזאת אני עושה תמיד, עכ"ל.
(רמתים צופים ג.ד)

113) והיה ה' לי לאלקים וכו' היינו בלי נסים ונפלאות ושנוי הטבע יהיה לי השגה כי יהודי אי"צ
לזה, ומה שהיה במצרים הוא עבור המצריים כמ"ש וידעו מצרים. (תורת שמחה, רלד)

115) ...ונראה פירושו, דהנה ידוע דבאורייתא ברא הקב"ה עלמא והקב"ה היה מביט בתורה
וסידר כל הנמצאים כו'. נמצא כי התורה ברא כל הנמצאים כו'. וסדר התורה הוא שיתנהג
עלמא בטבע. נמצא שהניסים והנפלאות שהם למעלה מן הטבע וזו יציאה מסדר התורה.
והרי זה כביכול כמו שהאדם עובר עבירה... (קול שמחה, פרשת מסעי עמי קג)

116) ...הרה"ק הרר"ב מפשיסחא זצ"ל אמר על הפסוק ולא נתן ה' לכם לב לדעת כו' עד היום
הזה, כי כל הניסים ונפלאות שעשה עמהם הש"י, מ"מ שלא ע"פ הטבע היה רק
לשעה. אבל אחרי שגמר להם כל התורה ונעשה מכל ההתנהגות תורה נעשה מזה בנין קבוע
לדורות. (חידושי הרי"ם 250)

119) ...הנס של יעקב בצאן לבן היה מלובש בטבע וכמבואר שפיצל המקלות וכו'. ואף שלא היה
צריך לזה לעשות על ידי טבע (כמבואר בפסוק) אכן זו מדריגה יותר עליונה כי מי שאינו

בשלימות הגמור אף שהוא צדיק צריך לנס כדי שיתחזק בצדקו יותר. אבל מי שהוא בשלימות הגמור אינו צריך שיעשו לו נס מהשמים כי הוא בעצמו עושה מה שצריך והבן זה. (קול שמחה פרשת וישב, לח)

120) ...גופא דעובדא הכי הוי!פ״א בנסיעתי על הדרך והייתי על ש״ק במלון אחד וברכתי שמה ברכת הנהנין אכלתי ושתיתי כמו הרגלי כאשר ידעת אהו׳ אחי כי איש חלוש אנכי ומוכרח לי לאכול ולשתות ולהבריא את גופי לקיים מאמר התוה״ק ושמרתם את נפשותכם! אחר ש״ק רציתי לשלם להבעל אכסניא ולא רצה ליקח מאתי תשלומין. ואמרו כי דרכי עבודתי ותפילתי ישרה בעיניו ומכיר אותי לבעל מדריגה ולא ירצה ליקח מאתי שכר שבת. וד׳ יודע ועד כי לא על זה התפללתי להתנאות חי״י או לקבל פרס להרויח תשלומי אוכל. רק התפללתי ביני לבין עצמי כפי אשר הרגלתי וכמו אשר למדנו אצל רבותינו הקדושים. עכ״ז מה יכולתי לעשות? שאלתי את בעה״ב. עכ״ז במה אוכל להשיב גמולך הטוב? אמר לי. אורח טוב מה הוא אומר? מברך את בעה״ב. וברכתי אותו ואת ביתו ואת כל יו״ח. והלכתי על העגלה שלי ליסע משם. בפתאום נשמע קול מדבר אומר. איי דער רבי האט זיך פארגעסין צי גיזעגענען מיט אונזר טאכטער. און חרה אפי למאוד. כי ידעת כי אני איש חלוש למאוד ומרוב צער תוך כי צעדתי על המרכבה שלי. ועתה אהי׳ מוכרח לצעוד פעם שנית וילך תוך הבית ליקח רשות מבתו של בעל הבית ולברך אותה ביוחד? ואמרתי להם כרב רוגז. ניה איז דען אייהר טאכטער שוואך ארויס צי קומען צי דער בויד צי גיזעגענין? זאל זיא הערויז קימען צי מיר ותומ״י באתה לפני ליטול רשות וכי אברך אותה. אבל זאת לא ידעתי כי בתם היתה נחלית וזה י״א שנים אשר שכבה על ערש דוי ר״ל ולא היתה יכולה לזוז בין ימינה לשמאלה ועתה בפתע פתאום נתרפאה. ותומ״י נעשה רעש גדול והחזיקו אותי לאיש מופת ורבי... (נפלאות היהודי סט)

121) ...עד שא׳ לו המלמד הנך עושה זאת בכדי לרמות אותי מעשיך בליצנות ולא תרמה אותי כי הרבי מלובלין צוה עלי להביאך אליו ומיד נסע ללובלינה. ובבואו קנה לו סכין א׳. ובבואו לפני הרבי א׳ לו באת אלי לפה לקנות סכן? השיב לו. לא באתי לפה לראות רוח הקודש. ולא בזה תקחו אותי... (נפלאות היהודי ע)

122) הרבי ר׳ בונם הסיר מעליו מסוה הנסים והנפלאות למעלה מן הטבע, ורק כמורה דרך ומנהל התיצב בין גדוד מאמיניו ללמדם חוקי חיים. ברכתו לא אצל על חולים ועקרות, וגם לא קיבל מהם כסף הפדיום במספר מכוון לעשות כוונים לסודות הקבלה מעשית. רק עצתו היתה אמונה לבאים לשאול פיו בכל עסק ומסחר, כי היה בקי בהם. גם נתן מועצותיו לידועי חולי וחשוכי בנים ויעש להם תעלות מסמים ועשבים עפ״י חכמת הרפואה, וכל החפץ נתן לו מתנה כאות נפשו. (כתר כהונה 128)

משיח

124) במחילה מכבודם של אותם צדיקים המגלים קץ המשיח. שבאמת הוא סוד- שכל מי שיודע לא יוכל לגלות בשום אופן, וכל מי שמגלה זהו סימן שאינו יודע לאמיתו. (עטרה לראש צדיק ע׳ קלו)

127) סיפר פ״א היה הרב הרב יהודי ז״ל והרב ר׳ דוד מלעלוב ז״ל בלובלין. והיו מדברים בענין הגאולה ובמאמרם בסנהדרין (דף צ״א) אין הדבר תלוי אלא בתשובה. ויהי כאשר שמע אדמו״ר הדברים האלה וילך אל השולחן ולפני היושבים והיה מונח ספר חומש. ונשבע בנק״ח שלא יעשו ישראל תשובה. והגואל בודאי יבא. (רמתים צופים כב. סו)

366

130) ...בשם רבו הרר"ב זצ"ל שאמר פ"א בזה"ל הנני מרגיש בעצמי כעת יכולת להחיש הקץ שיבוא מלך המשיח, אבל ציירתי לעצמי סדר ביאתו איך יהי', כשיבוא המשיח ילך אל ראש גדולי הדור שם יתוועדו כל הגדולים והצדיקים לקבל פניו, והנה הזקן והגדול שבזמננו הלא הוא הרה"ק מאפטא ושם בביתו יתוועדו כל רבני ומנהיגי בנ"י וישבו כולם אצל שלחן ארוך מאוד, גם אני יהי' לי איזה מקום בקצה השלחן ובשני צדי השלחן ישבו כל הגדולים והצדיקים ובראש המסובים ישב מלך המשיח ואצלו ראש הדור הרב מאפטא, ובוודאי תיכף ישאל הרב מאפטא למלך המשיח נא לגלות לנו מי הוא אשר פעל להחיש הקץ ולהביא אתכם, וישיב לו האמת זה פעל בונים פרשיסחער היושב שם בקצה השלחן, ויהי' מזה חלישת דעת גדול להרב מאפטא, ולכן הנני מונע מעצמי מלעסוק בזה שלא לגרום לו חולשת דעת עכל"ק (מאיר עיני הגולה קלט)

133) מה תצעק אלי דבר אל בני ישראל ויסעו. פ"א בא הגה"ק מ' יעקב דוד זצ"ל האבד"ק קאזיגיץ, לקאצק עוד בהיתו בק"ק מעזריטש, והוא הי' מתלמידי ההי"ר הרש"ל מלענטשנא זצללה"ה, שאל אותו ההי"ק מקאצק זי"ע מה שלום רבך אני אוהבו מאוד אבל מה צועק להקב"ה לשלוח את המשיח למה אינו צועק לישראל שישובו, וזהו מה תצעק אלי, דבר אל בני ישראל. (שיח שרפי קודש החדש סח)

פרק ה

תפקיד הצדיק בפרשיסחא

4) כי שמעתי מכאדמו"ר מוהרי"י מלובלין זצלה"ה פי' הגמרא הנותן סלע לצדקה בשביל שיחי' בני ה"ז צ"ג ותוכן הדברים הק' הוא כך כי יש שני בחי' צדיקים האחד שכל רצונו לעבוד את הבורא ב"ה אפילו מתוך דוחק ועוני ושאר יסורים מחמת שהוא מואס בעוה"ז ושני הוא מבקש תמיד לעשות רצון קונו ומבקש ג"כ שיהי' טוב לו ג"כ בעוה"ז בבני חיי ומזוני והבחי' השניה היא יותר טוב כי בכל צרת' לא צר הוא ואם הוא בוחר ביסורין חלילה אזי גורם צער לעילא אבל הבחי' שהוא בוחר שיהי' ג"כ טוב לו בעוה"ז וכוונתו כדי שיהי' למעלה טוב זה הדרך יותר טוב מהראשון וזפה"ג הנותן סלע לצדקה ועושה רצון בוראו ב"ה ואגב זה המצוה רואה שיחי' בניו ג"כ כדי שלא יהי' ח"ו צער למעלה וכנ"ל ה"ז צ"ג ודפחי"ח (אור לשמים 226)

11) ששמעתי מכ"ק אדמו"ר זי"ע ששאל להרה"ק היהודי זלה"ה שהיה המחובר לטהור כו' ושאל לו וכי הקב"ה וותרן כו' ומה סברא הוא זו שבדבר קל יהיה לו מדריגת הצדיק אשר לא נהנה מהעוה"ז. והשיב לו שזה עבודה גדולה מאוד להיות דבק לצדיק האמיתי ויותר קשה מלהיות צדיק בעצמו ואין כאן וויתור כלל. (רמתים צופים ג.לד)

15) ויעש להם משתה וגו' וילכו מאתו בשלום. בשם הרה"ק ר' שמחה בונים זצ"ל מפרשיסחא שדרך בר ישראל כשבא אל הצדיק נשבר לבו בקרבו שרואה החילוק שבינו לבין הצדיק. אבל אבימלך ושאר אנשים שהלכו עמו לא נשבר לבם הפירוש של בשלום שלא היה לב נשבר. (נפלאות חדשות 22)

16) כל המתפלל אחורי ביהכ"נ נקרא רשע וכו'. הרה"ק היהודי מפרשיסחא זצוק"ל אמר ע"ז. אחורי ביהכ"נ הוא החושב בלבו שא"צ להיות כפוף להצדיק לכתת רגליו אליו שהוא יסוד העולם וחושב על עצמו לצדיק. הוא מתפלל אחורי ביהכ"נ ונקרא רשע (נפלאות היהודי עמי ו)

(17)   ...סיפר בשם רבו היהודי הקדוש זי״ע כשיבוא משיח צדקינו אז ילכו לקראתו כל הצדיקים
ומנהיגי ישראל. עם אנשים החסידים אשר שאבו מימיהם ויהי׳ בניהם מנהיגים כאלה אשר
משיח צדקינו יאמר להם גש הלאה עם החסידים שלך. (הוא אמר משיח צדקינו וועט זייא
זאגין פארט דיר מיט דיינע חסידים). ואז יקרבו החסידים ויבכו מאוד ויאמרו משיח צדקינו
מה חטאנו ואשמנו הלא הי׳ לנו אמונה כי הוא צדיק אמת ומה תלונתך עלינו ומשיח צדקינו
ישיב להם כל ימיו של איש מהצורך לבקש מהבוית״ש כי יזכה להתקשר בצדיק אמת.
והבוית״ש לא ימנע טוב מההולכים בתמים. ואם הי׳ רצונכם באמת להתקשר בצדיק אמת
הי׳ מאיר לכם את האמת. ובודאי לא הי׳ רצונכם האמת להאמת. (תפארת היהודי קמה)

(23)   ופ״א נסע היהודי הק׳ זי״ל עם הר״ר בונם ז״ל עלי דרך, ובאמצע הדרך ראה היהודי הקדוש
איש אחד מרחוק, וקפץ מהעגלה והלך אצלו וחזר על העגלה, ושאלו הר״ר בונם ז״ל מי
האיש הזה ואמר שנפטר הוא ורוצה ממני טובה, ושוב שאלו שאלו עשיתם לו טובה? והשיבו
היהודי הקדוש, לאו, ויהי׳ כשמוע הר״ר בונם ז״ל דבר זה אמר א״כ אין אתם רבי שלי, ואני
איני תלמידכם, שהנחתם איש הנפטר הזה בלי עשיית לו טובה, כשמוע היהודי ז״ל דברי
הר״ר בונם ז״ל תלמידו תיכף קפץ פ״ש מהעגלה להנפטר הנ״ל ועשה לו טובה ונתן לו תיקון.
(שיח שרפי קודש 2, 10, 6)

(25)   ...סיפר לו ביחידות הרה״ק מרן מאלכסנדר זצוקללה״ה, שפ״א בהיותו אצל מו״ר הגה״ק
מפרשיסחא זוצקללה״ה התפלל תפילת שחרית בהבית סמוך לבית רבו הגה״ק זצ״ל
הנ״ל, והתפלל בקולות ותניעות מאוד, (כדרך כל המתפללים אז,אולם למו״ר זצ״ל הנ״ל לא
נראה זה הדרך בתפילה), ובתוך כך באמצע התפילה בא מו״ר הק׳ זצ״ל,והפסיק תומ״י
מהקולות ותנועותיו, אולם ברגע התיישב בדעתו לאמר מה לי עתה עסק עם רבי הלא אני
עומד עתה לפני השי״ת ואי״כ מ״יל עסק עם רבי וחזר תומ״י והתפלל בקולות ותניעות
כמתחילה, ואחר התפילה קראו מו״ר זצ״ל לביתו ואמר לו בזה״ל, העניך היום נהנתי
מתפילתך. (שיח שרפי קודש 5,21, 1)

(27)   כי תראה חמור שונאך רובץ תחת משאו וחדלת מעזוב לו עזוב תעזוב עמו (כג,ה) ואמרו
חכמינו ז״ל (בבא מציעא לב) שבאם בעל החמור אומר הואיל והמצוה עליך, טעון בעצמך,
אזי הוא פטור מלעוזרו. וכמו כן הוא תלמיד אצל הרב, שמחויב הוא גם כן לעשות כל
שאפשר לו ולהשתתף עמו, והוא גם כן יסייע לצדיק. כי באם אינו עושה כלל, רק שסומך
עצמו על הצדיק, אזי ח״ו לא יוכל הצדיק לעשות לו פעולה (תולדות אדם ליל ח׳ דחנוכה ע׳
ק)

(28)   היהודי הקדוש מפשיסחה זצ״ל אמר שהי׳ נותן את כל עוה״ז ועוה״ב שלו בעד שערה אחת
של יהדות (אידישקייט), ובאמת מה זה מוסיף לחסידים המבדילים עצמם מעולם הזה בלי
חסידות, כי הלא העיקר הוא לנטוע בעומק הלב ובמקומות הסתר של הלב ששם אין שום
איש יודע מהנעשה רצון לעבודת ה׳ באמת ורק מי לחסיד אז יש נגיעה בעבודת ה׳ אבל אם לא
כן מה יתן ומה יוסיף הלשון גם אם יסעו לצדיקים לזמנים ארוכים לא יצא להם כלום מזה
(חידושי הרי״ם 350)

(32)   סיפר הרה״ק המפורסם ר׳ שמואל דוב שליט״א מבוסקוויטץ, כי לאחר פטירת הרב הקדוש
ונורא ר׳ אורי מסטרעליסק זצוק״ל בא חסיד אחד מאנשי שלומיו להסתופף בצל קדושת
אדמו״ר הרה״ק הרבי בונם ז״צל מפרשיסחא. ושאל הרבי ר׳ בונם זצוק״ל לאותו החסיד : ״
במה היה עיקר דרכו בקודש ללמד אתכם עבודת השי״ת ודרכי החסידות?״ והשיב החסיד :
״ דרכו בקודש היה העיקר ללמד אותנו ולנטוע בנו מדת ענוה ושיפלות. ומנהגו בקודש היה
שכל מי שבא אליו, אפילו רב גדול, או עשיר רב גדול, היה מוכרח להביא מן השוק שני כדים
מים גדולים שקורין ׳קאנין׳ ועוד מלאכות בזויות כאלה, בכדי לשתל ולנטוע בנו מדת ענוה

ושפלותי". ענה הרה"ק חכם הרזים הרבי ר' בונם ואמר לו: " אני אספר לך מעשה. פעם אחת גזר המלך על שלשה אנשים שישבו במאסר בבור חשוך ואפל, ואלו הג' אנשים, שנים היו חכמים ואחד סכל ובער. ובכל יום ויום היו משלשלין להם לאכול ולשתות. והנה השוטה, מחמת שהיה שם חושך ואפלה, לא היה יכול להבין מה שנותנין לו. ולמשל על כף חשב שהוא קערה קרה וכדומה. ולזאת לא היה יודע איך ליטול הכלי אל פיו לאכול ולשתות. והנה אחד מן החכמים למדהו בכל פעם סימנים, לידע בכל הכלים מה הם. והיה צריך ללמדהו בכל פעם, כי בכל פעם היו נותנים כלים ודברים אחרים. והחכם השני היה יושב ושותק ולא למדהו כלום. פעם אחת שאל החכם הראשון להחכם שני: " מפני מה אתה יושב ושותק ולא תלמוד כלום עם השוטה, רק אני צריך בכל פעם לטרוח וללמוד עמו? תלמוד גם אתה עמו איזה פעם". השיב לו החכם השני: " אתה תטריח עצמך ללמוד עמו בכל פעם ולא תבוא עד עולם לידי גבול. כי מה תעשה אם למחר יהא נותן לו כלי אחר, שוב אתה צריך ללמוד אותו. ומה יהיה אם יתנו על זה, לא ידע על זה. אני יושב ומתבונן איך לחתור חתירה בהכותל להיות זורחת אור השמש בפה, ואז יראה הכל". (התגלות הצדיקים עמ' 114-115)

(36) ...והענין בזה כי כמה פעמים ילמוד האדם בתורה דיני המצות והחקים והמשפטים ועסק המדות הישרות, ואחר כל אלה עוד לא ידע ולא יבין איך להתנהג בהם ואיך יפלס משקל עשייתם כמו במדת הצדקה ומדת הענוה וכדומה בעבודה שבלב זו תפילה וכיוצא מהמצות שאינו יודע על איזה אופן יעשה ואיך תהי' אופן עשייתם על צד החסידות. אכן באם יראה עשייתם מאיזה צדיק או חסיד אזי תברר לו ענין עשיית מצוה זאת באיזה התלהבות תשוקה וחפצה והחן אשר נמצא בה... (אהל תורה נט)

(37) ...ברם לא זו הדרך הנכונה של החינוך. הרבי האמיתי צריך לפתוח את לבו של התלמיד ולהביאו לידי כך, שיתעוררו כשרונותיו והשגותיו שלו ויוכל להבין ולהשפיע בעצמו. במובן זה צריך הרבי להיות בבחינה של נקבה, שעושה את התלמיד לבעל השפעה. (שם משמואל הגדה של פסח 74)

(40) ...וסיפר היהודי הקדוש ז"ל לפני הרבי ז"ל שמצא כתוב בעת לומדו ספר רזיאל המלאך אשר צריך להסתלק מזה העולם תיכף אחר ר"ה. ואז אמר הרבי הקדוש אל היהודי הקדוש ז"ל בלשון אשכנז בלייבט בייא אינ'ך ר"ה וועט מען אייך דער האלטין. והיהודי הקדוש לא השגיח על זה רק לקח פרידת שלום מהרבי ז"ל ונסע לביתו. באמצע הדרך סיפר היהודי ז"ל לפני תלמידיו את כל המעשה ואמר בזה הלשון אפשר מיינט עטץ דער רבי האט חי"ל גיזאגט ליגינט ער וואלט מיך טאקי גיקענט דער האלטין נאר ער האט מי גיוואלט ציא נעמין דיא מדריגות אידער אזוי א לעבין וויל איך נישט. (נפלאות היהודי פו)

(44) אם החסידים אינם רוצים גם הצדיקים לא יוכלו לעזור כי העיקר היגיעה שכל אחד יתיגע בעצמו בתו"מ והלא הפסוק מזהיר אל תבטחו בנדיבים וכוונת האזהרה אפי' על מי שהפסוק קוראו נדיב מי שנאמר עליו לבי לחוקקי ישראל המתנדבים בעם והיינו צדיקי הדור וע"ז נאמר אל תבטחו בנדיבים רק אשרי שאל יעקב בעזרו שברו על ה' אלוקיו. ובאמת בפשיסחא הי' הוא מעין הרבה בזה אם לא הי' טוב יותר לבטל את ענין ההנהגה הזאת יען כי העולם סומכים עצמם יותר מדי על הצדיקים ולכן אינם עושים בעצמם... (חידושי הרי"ם שנב)

הביקורת של פרשיסחא על חסידות זמנה

(48) שמעתי מעשה מהרה"ק היהודי זצ"ל. פעם אחת הי' היהודי זצ"ל לן בלילה עם הרה"ק ר' שמחה בונם זצ"ל שהי' תלמידו. והיהודי לא הי' ישן רק הי' חושב וגנח מאוד. ושאל לו ר' שמחה בונם זצ"ל מה מעי"כ גונח? ואמר היהודי זצ"ל אני חשבתי שלאחר משה היו שופטים

ולאחר שופטים נביאים ואח"כ אכנה"ג ואח"כ היו תנאים ואמוראים ופוסקים ואח"כ היו מוכיחים לשם. ואחר כך נתקלקל שנתרבו מוכיחים לשם. ואחר כך נתקלקל שנתרבו מוכיחים שלא לש"ש ואח"כ התחילו רעב"ס. ע"ז אני גונח שאני רואה שגם זה יתקלקל. מה יעשו ישראל?! (ליקוטים חדשים עמ' נו)

(53) במשנה בפאה מי שאינו חיגר או סומא ועושה א"ע כאחד מהם אינו מת מהזקנה עד שיהא כאחד מהם והקשה הרבי ר' בונם אלא מעתה מי שאינו רבי ועושה רבי וכי היושר שיהא נעשה אח"כ רבי נמצא חוטא נשכר, ואמר משל ע"ז שאדון אחד נסע בדרך וראה עני אחד שיכור שוכב בדרך וצוה וצוה למשרתיו שיניחו אותו על העגלה שלו, וכשבא לבית צוה למשרתיו שיקחו השיכור ויניחו אותו בחדר יפה וירחצו אותו ויגלחו אותו וילבישוהו כתונת חדש ויניחו אותו במטה יפה, ויניחו אצלו בגדים של כומרים, וכן עשו כ"ז בהיותו עדיין שיכור והי' ישן במטה, והאדון צוה למשרתיו כשיקיץ השיכור ילכו תיכף אליו וישאלו לו ויקראו אותו בלשון אדוני כומר מה אתה רוצה, וכשהקיץ השיכור העני הזה והמשרתים עשו כאשר נצטוו אדוניהם ויתמה השיכור מאוד מה זאת שהוא זוכר שהוא איש עני ובזוי ועתה שוכב בחדר יפה וקוראים אותו אדוני כומר גם מונח אצלו בגדים של כומרים ע"כ הי' נבוך מאוד ומסופק אפשר מה שהוא זוכר שהי' עני ובזוי הוא רק חלום אבל באמת הוא כומר, או להיפך שבאמת הוא איש עני ובזוי ועתה הוא חלום והמשרתים נותנים כל מה שהוא רוצה וקוראים אותו אדוני כומר והתיישב א"יע לעשות מבחן אם הוא באמת כומר או חלום הוא, היינו שיעיין בהספרים של הכומרים ויראה אם יוכל ללמוד בהם הנה אז וודאי אמת שהוא כומר ומה שזוכר שהי' איש עני בזוי הוא חלום ובאם לא יוכל ללמוד בהם וודאי מה שזוכר שהי' עני זהו האמת. ומה שקוראין לו כעת כומר זהו חלום, ובחן וקרא בהספרים הנ"ל וראה שאין יכול ללמוד בהם ואעפי"כ קוראין לו כומר, חזר ויישב א"יע שלעולם באמת הוא כומר וראי' לזה שקוראין לו כומר, ומה שאינו יכול ללמוד בספרים של הכומרים אין ראי'.שכל הכומרים אינם יכולים ללמוד בספרים של הכומרים, והנמשל מי שיודע מי שאינו רבי ואנשים קוראין לו רבי ג"כ מסופק אם הוא באמת רבי. בתחלה בוחן ולומד ברזין דאורייתא וראה שאין יכול ללמוד בהם ואעפ"יכ קוראין לו רבי מיי שב א"ע שבאמת הוא רבי ומה שאינו יכול ללמוד ברזין דאורייתא נעשה כופר ואומר ששום צדיק אינו יכול ואינו יודע כלל, וזה כמו מי שאינו חיגר ולא סומא ועושה עצמו חיגר העונש שנעשה באמת חיגר כן כאן בתחלה עושה עצמו רבי ומכחש קצת ואח"כ הוא העונש שנעשה כופר ממש ויש לו רח"ל עונש גדול בעוה"ב השי"ת יצילנו ודפ"ח. (מאמרי שמחה נד)

(54) בשם ההי"ק הרר"יב זי"ע שאל תחשב שעשו הי' נראה כאיכר מגושם אלא הי' לבוש לבנים ואמר תורה בג' סעודות, ואיתא במדרשות שלעתיד יבוא עשו וישב בראש כולם ואין מוחה בידו עד שיבוא הקב"ה ובעצמו ישליכהו לחוץ, ואם בעוה"ב שהוא כולו אמת נסתר רשעתו מכש"כ בעוה"ז שהוא כולו מלא שקרים עאכו"כ. (שיח שרפי קודש 10 . 6 . 3)

(59) (ברכות) בשעה שישראל וכו' ועונין יהא שמיה וכו'. סיפר מה ששמע מרבו הרבי ר' בונם מפשיסחא זצ"ל: כאשר נתגלה הבעש"ט זצ"ל והתחילו להתקבץ סביבו חסידים, חרד היצר הרע וזעק לעבר כת דיליה: הבה ונתכס עצה מה נעשה להבעש"ט וחסידיו, הלא עלולים הם לשרוף הבלי העולם בקדושתם. בא היצר להחסידים ואמר להם: אכן מעשיכם יפים וטובים וזכותכם רבה, אבל הלא הינכם רק אחד בעיר ושנים במדינה וצריכים אתם מנין, כדאיתא בגמרא (ג.) בשעה שישראל וכו' ועונים יהא שמיה וכו' הקב"ה מנענע בראשו ואומר אשרי המלך וכו' ואוי להם לבנים וכו', הלך היצר וקיבץ עוד שמונה חסידים מאנשיו ועשאם למנין עשרה. והנה חסרו להם מעות לבנין בית הכנסת וכתיבת ספר תורה, הביא היצר איש עשיר מאנשיו שיתפלל עמהם ויתן כל ההוצאות. ולאחר מכן אמר היצר לכת דיליה: הנה מעתה

אין לי לדאוג כי אנשי רבים מהחסידים של הבעש"ט ואחרי רבים להטות וההלכה כמותם. (חשבה לטובה פד)

(67 ...דהנה יש שני גווני צדיקים: יש צדיקים, שנתקדשו מאבותיהם, שהיו קדושים ויראים ושלמים, והתורה מחזרת על אכסניא שלה. ויש צדיקים הנקראים 'נזירים' על שם פרישותם מעצמם, אף על פי שהם בני עניי הדעת. והצדיקים ההם לא במהרה הם יכולים לפול ממדרגתם הקדושה, כי אין להם על מה שיסמוכו, והם נכנעים בדעתם ומשגיחים על עצמם בעינא פקיחא תמיד, בלי הפסק. אבל הצדיקים הקדושים, שנתקדשו מאבותיהם, אף שהם מלאים תורה ומצות, מחמת זכות אבותם מסייעתם, לפעמים יכולים לבא על ידי- זה פניה וגדלות מזה, ויפלו מהר ממדרגתם. וזהו: אמר אל הכהנים בני אהרן- פרוש: רמז לאותן צדיקים, אשר הם בני צדיקים, והם נקראים 'כהנים'-'בני אהרן'- תזהיר אותם מאוד, שלא יעלה על מחשבתם כלל יחוס אבותיהם, רק ינזרו ויפרשו לעצמם פרישות מחדש ויבחרו להן הדרך הטובה, וזהו: דבר אל אהרן ואל בניו, וינזרו מקדשי בני-ישראל- רוצה לומר, שגם הם יהיו נזירים ופרושים מעצמם וישגיחו גם כן על עצמם מאוד, ולא ישגיחו על זכות אבותם,כדי שלא יבא להם, חלילה, איזה התנשאות מחמת יחוסיהם, ותועבת ה' כל גבה לב. (נעם אלימלך, פרשת אמר)

(83 הרבי מקאצק זצ"ל אמר לי, בעת שחלה היהודי הקדוש מפשיסחא זצ"ל, אמרו העולם תהילים ואני עמדתי אצל התנור ולא רציתי לאמר תהילים, בא אלי הרבי ר' בונם זצ"ל ואמר לי, למה אתה מפציר כל כך, ולא ידעתי מה שרוצה ולאחר שנפטר אמר שוב, " עס איז דאך שוין פארפאלין דער רבי איז נישט דא, יראת שמים האט אינץ איבער גילאזט, יראת שמים איז נישט קיין פישקעלע, ווי עס איז דא אין רעבינס ווערטיר דא איז דער רבי" ולא השבתיו... (חשבה לטובה קכא)

פרק ו

החיפוש אחר האמת

(3 ...אכן נראה שהענין בזה, כי האדם בעת שהוא משוקע בסבך הנגיעה אינו מרגיש כלל נגיעתו וידמה לו שהוא תמים רק בצאתו ממנה אזי מרגיש כי הי' נוגע למפרע... (אהל תורה יג)

(6 צדק לבש וילבישני כלומר גם בענין המצות ועבודה ושלימות לבש דבר המיועד לו וזה וילבישוני (קול שמחה קג)

(9 דהנה פרעה ...חשב בעצמו שהגיע לקצת מדריגת יראת אלהים וכבר הוציא השי"ת מחשבתו אל הפועל. כי זה הוא מדרך הכסילים בהשיגו מעט בדעת וביראה חושב שכבר עלה למדרגה גדולה ולא ידע כי נבער הוא מדעת. (קול שמחה פרשת וארא ס)

(10 שמעתי מהאדמו"ר הק' א"א מפרשיסחא שאמר בשם אביו הקדוש א"א הגאן היהודי ז"ל שברר לקיים שני מצות במס"נ יותר מכל המצות. (נפלאות היהודי נט)

(12 ...ר"ל שיפתח ה' עיניו עיני השכל שלו לראות אל איזה מהצדיקים אשר הוא צריך לדבק בו, אשר הוא משורש נשמתו, ושם ימצא מרגוע לנפשו. (תורת שמחה עב)

(13 רבי אומר איזהו דרך ישרה שיבור וכו' כל שהיא תפארת לעושיה וכו' (אבות פ"ב) היינו שכל נשמה מכאו"א יש לה סגנון אחד בעבודת השי"ת לקיים התורה והמצות בלי שום שינוי. רק בעניני המדות והמצות הם מחולקים שיש צדיק שהנהגות שלו הם בסיגוף גופו ויש צדיק

שאוכל ושותה ואינו מסגף עצמו כלל. והוא ג"כ צדיק גדול וקדוש מאוד נעלה כידוע בט"ז אה"יע סי' כ"ה. וכן בשאר עניינים יש חילוק בין הצדיקים וזה מחמת שהולכים בדרך הישרה ששייך לנשמתו באמת. ע"כ אינו תופס בדרך שאינו מיוחד לו ואף שמשבח מאוד דרך הצדיק בעבודה ויפה בעיניו יותר מדרך שלו אעפ"כ אינו זז ואוחז צדיק דרכו וזהו סימן שהוא דרכו האמתי. וזה פי' המשנה איזהו דרך ישרה שיבור לו האדם כל שהיא תפארת לעושיה. שהדרך שהוא עושה בעצמו ונוח לו מחזיק בו אעפ"כ ותפארת לו מן האדם. היינו שמשובח ומשופר דרך חבירו הצדיק והבן הדברים. כי הוא כלל גדול בעבודת השי"ת שלא לילך בגדולות שאינו בערכו ואפי' בעניני העוה"ז כן. וזה שאמרו חייב אדם לומר מתי יגיעו מעשי למעשה אבותי. היינו שיהיה לו צירוף כנ"ל אבל לא שיחמוד להיות צדיק כאבות עולם. ואמר בזה"ל אם היו שואלים אותי כמה תתן שתתחליף מדתך עם אאע"ה. והוא יהיה כמותך ואתה כמותו. לא הייתי נותן אפי' פרוטה. עד"מ בין כך ובין כך לא יהיה וויתור להשי"ת כלל ודו"ק. (רמתים צופים י, יז)

(18) בחולין פרק כל הבשר אמר מר עוקבא אנא חלא בר חמרא לגבי אבא, שאילו אבא כי הוה אכיל בשרא לא הוה אכיל גבינה עד למחר ואנא בהא סעודתא לא אכילנא, ובסעודתא אחריתא אכלינא והקשה הרבי ר' בונם למה קרא עצמו עבור זה חלא בר חמרא והלא גם הוא יכול להתנהג כמו אביו שלא יאכל גבינה עד למחר, ותירץ שאם אין ברצונו לעשות החומרא רק בשביל שעשה אביו החומרא ורוצה לעשות ג"כ כמו שעשה אביו אינו רשאי והבן. (תורת שמחה מח)

(23) וכל הבארות אשר חפרו וגו' סתמום פלשתים וגו'. נראה (פירושו), דהנה כל דרך שעושין להשם צריך להיות בו חיות פנימי. ואם אין בו חיות פנימי אינו עולה למעלה. והנה הפלשתים רצו ללכת בדרכי אברהם אבינו ע"ה והיו עושין כמו שהיה אברהם אבינו עושה רק שלא היה בו חיות פנימי וזה סתימת הדרך הזה והבן. ויצחק אבינו רצה לחפור הבאר הזה. אף שהיה לו דרכים לה' מצד עצמו, אף על פי כן לא נמנע מלחפור באר אביו כמ"ש. ואח"כ חפר הוא עצמו בארות. דהנה כל איש הישראלי הנגש לעבודת השם ברוך הוא צריך שיחפור בעצמותו באר אשר על (ידו) יוכל להתדבק בבוראו יתברך ויתעלה... (קול שמחה, פרשת תולדות כט)

(26) הרבי מקאצק זצ"ל אמר, אינני יודע מה שהם רוצים ממני, בכל ימות השבוע עושה כל אחד מה שלבו חפץ, וכשבא שבת קודש, הריהו מתעטף בגלימת המשי השחורה, מתהדר באבנט שחור ועוטה את השטריימל והנה הוא כבר מחותן עם לכה דודי, אני אומר כמעשהו בחול כך מעשהו בשבת. (חידושי הריי"ם שח)

(27) ...והיינו עפ"י מה שהגיד כ"ק זקיני האדמו"ר הגדול זצללה"ה מקאצק שנקודת האמת אינה נמצאת בעולם רק בכ"ג בשעה שנכנס לבית קדשי קדשים, עכת"ד. (שם משמואל ב. רט)

(29) אם אני –אני, ואתה –אתה, הרי אני –אני, ואתה –אתה. אבל אם אני –אתה, ואתה –אני, הרי אני לא אני ואתה לא אתה. (דברים נחמדים)

(31) וגם שמעתי עוד מפי אדמו"ר זצוק"ל מפרשיסחא כדברים האלה ע"פ (פ' ואתחנן) ובקשתם משם כו' היינו כל החכמות והחקירות להשיג השם וייחודו נקרא משם היינו ממקום אחר. אבל האמת לאמתו הוא במקומו ממש היינו בלבו. (רמתים צופים ה.צו)

(34) ...והרה"ק מפרשיסחא ז"ל אמר פי' הכתוב אם תבקשנה ככסף וכמטמונים תחפשנה, כי בקשה הוא שאדם מבקש למצוא מציאות, וחיפוש הוא דבר הנאבד ממנו וחופש אחריו. והחילוק הוא כי מי שנאבד לו דבר מצטער ביותר לחפש אחריו, אבל כשמצאו אין השמחה

גדולה כל כך כי כבר הי' לו דבר זה מעולם, ומי שמבקש מציאות הוא להיפך אין הצער גדול, והשמחה גדולה, ולכן אמר הכי בעבודת השי"ת צריך להיות שניהם להיות הצער גדול לייגע עצמו למצוא כדבר הנאבד ממנו, ואח"כ כשזוכה למצוא צריך להיות השמחה גדולה, כמוצא שלל רב עכ"ד. (תורת שמחה צז)

(37) תורת אלהיו בלבו כו' (תהלים ל"ז) . אמר ז"ל שאין חוש מן החושים להרגיש התורה הקדושה כ"א הלב. כי החושים של אדם הוא להרגשה כידוע אבל להתורה הקדושה ואלקותו יתברך אין כאן חוש רק הלב. ובפרט סודות התורה שנקראו תורת אלקים הוא בלבו דייקא ההרגשה. ולכן לא יטעה ח"ו עכדה"ק. (רמתים צופים יא. כט)

(44) אכן שמעתי מאדמו"ר כו' מ"י שמחה בונם מפרשיסחא ז"ל כי מהעת שבטל יצרא דע"ז שהיה בוער כמ"ש בפרק חלק שאמר מנשה מלך ישראל ז"ל אי הוית התם הוית נקיטא בשיפולי גלימך ורהטת אבתראי נצטנן התבערה מעבודת הבורא ב"ה ג"כ ואין חשק כ"כ לקדושה כי זה לעומת זה עשה אלקים. (רמתים צופים ב. סו)

(46) ...וכמו שאמר הרבי הקדוש ר"ב זצללה"ה מפרשיסחא לרבו היהודי הקדוש זצ"ל ששאלוהו מה שמע חדשות בהיותו בדאנציג, ואמר ששמע אבידת ממון אינו כלום, ואבידת " קוראזש" הוא אבידה בכולו, עכ"ד. (שם משמואל יתרו רסח)

(48) ...הרה"ק רש"ב מפרשיסחא זצ"ל אמר איתא הבוחר בשירי זמרה שיש לאחר השירה והזמרה מאיר הפנימיות שבלב שנתמלא חשק ורצון לשורר ולשבח לעולם בלי הפסק וזהו הבוחר בשירי זמרה שהקב"ה בוחר במה שנשאר מהזמרה החשק והדביקות... (חידושי הרי"ם קמד)

(52) ...אמר כי כאשר יתחיל המתחיל בעבודה יתנו לו מן השמים התעוררות ורצון לעבודה, ואם ישכיל על זה וישמור דרכו ולא יעזבנו אזי טוב לו ולנפשו. ואם לא יתבונן בזה להשקיע כל כוחו זה ולהזהר שישאר לו זה הרצון לזמן רב אזי זה התלהבות ה' נתן וה' לקח והוא נשאר ריק כאשר היה מקדם... (קול שמחה קכג)

(54) ועשיתם לכם פסל תמונת כל אשר צוך ד' אלקיך. הפירוש שהאדם לא יעשה במרמה ושוא שיאמר שלומד לשמה ובאמת אינו לומד לשמה וזה הוא תמונה רק יעשה הכל לשם שמים בלי שום פניי' (שיח שרפי קודש 1 .11 .13)

(56) ויאמר אל נא אחי תרעו. בס' צבי עדיו לגאון בפי' תרומה בשם ההי"ק היהודי זצללה"ה מפרשיסחא שהיי מבקש מאנ"ש ואומר להם אל נא אחי תרעו, מלת נא מצינו בתורה על חצי צלוי, גם כאן אמר אל נא אחי תרעו, שלא תהיי חצי אחים, עי"כ. (שיח שרפי קודש החדש וירא 31)

(58) דרשן אחד באשכנז דרש ע"פ מטבע של אש הראה לו, ולמה לא של מתכת, אלא עיקר נתינת המטבע הוא האש, ההתלהבות. ופלא, שחידוש כזה נתחדש באשכנז, והרבי זצ"ל מקאצק אמר, יען שמקפידים במקום הזה על קיום מצות הכנסת אורחים, בזכות זה נתגלה להם תורה כזו. (חידושי הרי"ם קטז)

(61) חותמו של הקב"ה אמת (שבת נה.) . הוא חותם כזה אשר אי אפשר לזייפו, משום שאם יזייפו אותו לא יהיה אמת. (שיח שרפי קודש 3 .25 .124)

צריך להיות רדיפת הצדק בצדק- ולא בשקר, כמאמר הכתוב (דברים טז, כ) צדק צדק תרדוף. (שפת אמת פרשת שופטים שנת תרל"א לד, ב.)

(63) במדת האמת איכא ד' מאות דרכים עד יבלתי להי לבדוי. (ויקהל שלמה טו,ב)

67) פ"א לאחר ר"ה כשפטר מלפניו את העולם אנ"ש לביתם לשלום אמר לכל או"א, אני שואל
ממך דבר אחד להבטיחו שתצייתו לי. ובודאי השיב לו כל אחד שיציית לו. אז אמר לו
שמבקש ממנו שלא יאמר שקר כי אם אמת. ולכ"א אמר הדברים הללו. (רמתים צופים א"ז
כט. פא)

68) פ"א דיבר ההי"ק מפרשיסחא זי"ל אודות השקר הנהוג מאוד אצל המון עם ודבקו מאוד
באמירת שקר ועבירה גדולה היא רח"ל מכל עבירות שבתורה, ואמר בזה"ל באם שאמירת
שקר יהי' חמור אצל המון עם כניאוף ר"ל אזי יבוא הגואל צדק במהרה בימינו ודי"ל. (שיח
שרפי קודש 1 116. 617.)

69) בשם ההי"ק הרר"ב מפרשיסחא זי"ל במדרש רבה בראשית פ"ח בשעה שבא הקב"ה לבראות
את עולם חסד א' יברא וכו' ואמת אמר אל יברא שכולו שקרים וכו' שלום א' אל יברא
שכולו קטטה מה עשה הקב"ה נטל אמת והשליכו לארץ וכו' והק' הלא עדיין נשאר שלום
שאמר אל יברא. אכן יי"ל דאחר שהשליך האמת ארצה לא הי' שלום יכול לקטרג שאם
השקר מתגבר אז בעלי מחלוקת נראים כאוהבים ואין קטטה בעולם עכי"ל. (שיח שרפי
קודש 2 86. 286.)

74) כל העושה מצוה שלא לשמה, - שאנכיות עצמית מעורבת בה, הרי הוא כעובד אלילים, כי אין
הבדל בין עובד אלילים לעובד את עצמו... (ב. מינץ ב'כתובים' משנת תרפ"ז גליון נב.)

75) ...ושמעתי בשם הרבי מקאצק זצ"ל פירוש שילמוד על זה האופן שיבוא על כל פנים לשמה
ומיושב קושיית התוספות. (ויש לפרש, דהיינו שכך יחשוב האדם על למודו שאינו עדיין בגדר
לשמה ומתוך כך יתגבר בעבודתו להגיע לשלימות הלימוד, אבל אם באמת לומד שלא לשמה
אין לו ללימוד זה ערך כלל). (חשבה לטובה פח)

76) צדק צדק תרדוף. להבין מלת צדק בכפל, כי דרך המשקרים באמונה להתראות במלבוש
אמת וצדק ואומרים צדיקים אנחנו ולא חטאנו. ודרכם לחפש אחר ראיות התורה לעשות
סמוכים לדבריהם להצדיק עצמם. ובאמת לא נכון לעשות כן ותועבת ה' כל עושה אלה, אך
לרדוף למצוא תוקף ועוז לדברי צדק באמת. (קול שמחה, פרשת שופטים קט)

78) וכמו ששמעתי מרבינו מפרשיסחא זלה"ה כי כל מה שהאדם מתייגע ומתעורר אפשר שהוא
מחיצוניות שלה כי הלב יש לו חדרי חדרים אבל זה שהוא מן השמים כנ"ל יורד לחיותו
ממש במה שהוא חי ודי"ל. (רמתים צופים ו. כח)

81) ...ואם יטהר האדם עצמו יכיר מתוך התורה אלוקותו ית' וא"צ לחקירות ומופתים רק
התורה בעצמה תאיר עיניו ויראה האמת ושהתורה תורת אמת. (רמתים צופים יז. מז)

87) והי' שם הסדר שבחדר החיצוני שמשמש היו נכנסין אל חדרו של הרבי ר'בונם בקודש פנימה
היו יושבים החברים הק' מתלמידי ההי"ק. וכל חסיד הבא פעם ראשונה לרבם הק' לא
הניחוהו לכנוס עד שבחנו אותו בשבע בחינות אם הריח בירֵאת ה' ואם טעם מה מטעם לשד
החסידות. והנה כאשר באו המה בחדר החיצוני והתמהמהו שם בטרם זכו לכנוס החלו
החברים ההם הידועים לסלסל בם אותם בעניני חסידות ובתוך כך ירו חצים שנונים
בלבם בדברים בוטים כמדקרות לנסותם. (אור שמחה יח)

91) ...פתח ואמר יש חסידים שסוברים שהשיגו מעט יראה בהרגשת הלב וסוברים שזהו פתח
הקדושה כמו שמבואר בזוה"ק במאמר זה השער. תדעו שאינו כן שעדיין יש להם בע"ד
ויכול להיות הוא עצמו בע"ד וכי הבע"ד עצמם אינם יראים וזוחלים ורועדים ממנו ית'
תמיד ואעפ"כ המה מהסט"א וסיים אך זה הוא הענין והאריך בפירוש הדברים הרבה ואיני
זוכה לזכור זה. (רמתים צופים ג.כא)

374

95) ...ואמר הוא ז"ל עוד מה נדבר ומה נצטדק היינו כשהאדם מסתכל בעצמו ורואה עצמו מה שרואה ומר לו מר. וטבע האדם להצדיק את עצמו... (אמונת צדיקים 82)

נגד השגרה

97) לא תעשון כן לה' אלוהיכם (יב,ד) בכל דור ודור מי שהוא צדיק הדור, רואה רצון השי"ת, כמו שכתוב (משלי י,לב) שפתי צדיק ידעון רצון. והיהודי הקדוש זללה"ה בדורו ראה רצון השי"ת באיחור זמן תפלה, ונסמך על מאמר הכתוב ' לא תעשון כן לה' אלוהיכם', 'כן' רומז על קביעות בלי חיים. וכשראה רצון השי"ת בזה, לכן התאחר בתפלתו. ונשמתו מאירה בגן עדן מזה, כי כיון לאור רצון השי"ת, אף כי יכול זאת בשינוי זמנים להשתנות, מכל מקום נאמנה את אל רוחו עד עת קץ. (מי השילוח חלק ב פרשת בהעלותך ע' כט)

98) ...וזה שבח גדול ליודעי דעת שלא היו רוצים לעשות מצות מלומדה בלא טעם אף שהענין בעצם הוא דבר טוב. וזהו מחמת שהיה בהם דעה שיודעים לברר ולהבדיל מן השקר ולא הלכו מן הקצה אל הקצה רק בדרך הממוצע. וזהו מדת אמת מדת יעקב וזהו דרך התורה הקדושה. (קול שמחה פרשת מטות ק)

99) עוד כי הר"ר שלום גערשט הנ"ל בשם קדשו, בפי' שופטים, כי ואתה לא כן נתן לך ה"א, כי ישראל אינו רשאי לקבוע דרכו דייקא כן תמיד, רק פעם כך, ופעם כך, שישנה הרגילות והטבע. (תורת שמחה רנא)

101) אמר רביה"ק הרבי בונים מפרשיסחא זצ"ל: מה יועיל אם נאמר כל ימינו 'ואהבת', כשאיננו מקיימים זאת. משל למה הדבר דומה? למלמד דרדקי המלמד נער כסיל. אומר לו:"אמר אל"ף", והנער אומר:"אמר אל"ף"... (תורת כהן, ליקוטים קכח,ב)

102) ...ואמר הוא ז"ל כי ענין פסל ותמונה הוא ציור ותמונת הדבר שאינו עצם הדבר בפועל. וזאת הזהירה התורה שנשמור עצמינו מלעשות מן "אשר ציוך ה' אלהיך, פסל ותמונה". ודקדק לומר פסל וגו' להעיר באם מי תהי' מעשי עבודת האדם בלתי כוונה הנבחרת היא תיעוב גדול בעיני ה' כמו פסל ותמונה של ע"ז ממש. וגמר אומר אשר ציוך לשלול תמונת אשר ציוך. ודוק כי עמוק הוא. (רמתים צופים יד.ז)

105) ...המה בטלו כל יתרון וחלוקת כבוד בניהם. נער וזקן, גדולים חקרי לב ופרחי תורה,עשירים ואביונים היו כרעים גמורים בני מצב אחד,כשוים בשנים ובדעת. ובתואר נוכח יחיד "אתה" (דוא) פגש עול ימים את איש שיבה. ואם באנשי בריתם כך, מה היו בעיניה זקנים ולומדים, בנים ובעלי בתים אחרים?... (כתר כהונה 128)

112) עוד שמעתי בשמו הק'. שפ"א אמר יש איש רוצה להיות פרוש ולהתבודד בתוך מרחק היערות לעבוד השי"ת, אך בדעתו שאולי ידע שום אדם מהתבודדות שלו. זה האיש גרוע הוא מאוד. (שיח שרפי קודש 1. 54. 255)

115) העולם הי' דוחפין אי"ע לשמוע מה מזה שדוחפין בגופן, ועיקר דחיפה להיות הטוב יהודי בלב, חסידות מפרשיסחא הי', שלא לעשות באברים חיצונים אפי' רשימה אינה עושה רק העיקר לעשות מבפנים ולהמשיך חיות פנימי במעשה וכאשר יעשה מבפנים ממילא יכוף את אברים החיצונים. (שיח שרפי קודש 3 46. 104.)

116) ...בשם רבו היהודי הק' זי"ע כי לאדם צריך להיות שתי (פייגין) וכשמראה מקודם האחד לעצמו (כלומר שאין מחשיב אי"ע) אינו ירא מאחרים ויכול להראותם (הפייג) השני. (תפארת היהודי קעא. עו)

120) ...וכמו שאמר רבייה"ק הרבי רבי בונם מפרשיסחא זצ"ל על מאמרם ז"ל שאין בין גן העדן
לגיהנם אלא כחוט השערה. (זכותא דאברהם.חיהרי"ם עה"ת רלד)

פרק ז

תורת האדם

1) ...בשם הגה"ק הרבי ר' בונם שא', רציתי לחבר ספר עס זאל זיין איין גרויס איין פערטיל
פאפיער. אין איך זאל עס א נאמין געבין אדם. אין עס זאל שטיין אין דערינין דער גאנצער
מענטש. אבל נתייישבתי שלא לחבר הספר הזה. (אור שמחה סד)

8) אמר "היהודי הק' זצללה"ה, שכל הכללים שאדם עושה לעצמו בעבודת השי"ת אינם כלל
וגם זה הכלל עצמו אינו כלל וד"ל. (תפארת היהודי עמ' 176,צג)

24) ...כי שמעתי מאדמו"ר מפרשיסחא זי"ע שאמר כשיש עולם גדול על ש"ק אזי קשה לו לומר
תורה כי צריך תורה בשביל כאו"א ולכלול בתורה כאו"א. וכ"א יקבל שלו. (רמתים צופים
ח. קה)

27) א' שיש שופטים למעלה איזה איש יוושע ע"י צדיק וע"י איזה צדיק והד"ת שאומר בשולחן
הם הם הרפאות להנשמות, ולכן אמר אבטליון (אבות פ"א) חכמים הזהרו בדבריכם שמא
תחובו חובת גלות ותגלו למקום כו'. אב טליון, אב ומורה לתלמידים הקטנים במדריגה
ממנו, טליון לשון קטנים. והוא א' כו' כמו הרופא המומחה ברפאות גשמיות, כן צריך
הרופא הנשמות לשקול דבריו יותר, כי הם סכנה יותר והבן זה, ואמר הוא ז"ל שקשה לו
לומר תורה כשיש עולם גדול אזי צריך לשקול שיהיה לכאו"א רפואה למכאוביו. וע"כ דבר
קשה שהרופא יתן רפואה אחת לכמה חלאים במיניהם ולא יזיק ח"ו לאחד מהם ואדרבה
שיהיה רפואתו רפואה לכאו"א. (תורת שמחה רכז)

טבע

31) בס' "רמזי אש" שעל התדב"א דף ו' ע"ב וז"ל הקדוש מו"ר הר"ר בונם מפרשיסחא זצ"ל
אמר שהעולם נברא בתורה שהיא עולם הטבע... (שיח שרפי קודש 2. 83. 272)

33) עוד שמעתי בשמו הק' זיי"ע. על מחז"ל גדולה הכנסת אורחים יותר מקבלת פני השכינה, מן
אאע"ה שרץ לקראת המלאכים, אף שהי' ד' נצב עליו, והקשו מהיכן הי' אברהם אבינו ע"ה
בעצמו יודע זה. ואמר שרש"י ז"ל פי' בפ' וירא, מהו וירא וירא שני פעמים הראשון לשון
ראיה ושני לשון לשון הבנה וזהו שאאע"ה הבין דבר זה בדעתו, ובודאי כן צריך להיות, משום זה
וירץ לקראתם. והבן. (שיח שרפי קודש 1. 48. 218)

40) הראשונים שלא ניתנה תורה להם והם קיימו אותה מאליהם מצד תמימותם שהלכו
בתמימות אשר להם והורה להם התמימות שיעשו מה שיעשו...והתמימות הגיע להם שיעשו
המעשים אשר עשו. ובלא ידיעה הגיע להם שהלכו בתורת ה'. כך כשנתן הקב"ה התורה
לעמו צוה לנו על מצות אשר נעשו אותן המעשים אשר הורה לנו מצד תמימותו...ומזה נראה
שהגיע השי"ת (אלינו) אותה תמימות בעצמה אשר היה היה לצדיקים הראשונים. אשר גם הם
הורה להם התמימות שיעשו אותן המעשים בעצמן אשר הגיעו מתמימות של השי"ת. וזה
יורה שנתאחדו הצדיקים הראשונים והשי"ת בתמימות כאחד וזה שספר עצמו

והבן...כוונתו להוכיח שעשה אברהם אבינו קרבן עד שלא נצטווה (רק) שהתתמימות הורה לו שיעשה קרבן. (קול שמחה פג)

(47) ...כי פרעה הי' סובר. כי החסיד הוא צריך דווקא-לחלוץ מתענוגי עוה"ז. ולא יחשוב על כבודו ותהלוכתו. וראה שיוסף הצדיק הוא יפה תואר ומסלסל בשערו. אמר הנמצא כזה איש אשר רוח אלקים בו כי' הנמצא איש כזה שילך מלובש נאה ומסלסל בשערו. שיהי' רוח אלקים בו. חוץ מיוסף והי' לפלא בעיניו... (שיח שרפי קודש 1 . 9 . 3.)

(51) ...ושמעתי בשם ההי"ק בעל קול שמחה ז"ל דודאי הן כבר שמענו מאנשים שרוח אלקים נוססה בם כמו חנוך נח אברהם יצחק ויעקב וכדומה אבל רק בתמימי דרך המתבודדים רק בעבודת הש"י לבד, ואין עסק להם עם הבריות הן במסחר או במלאכה, משא"כ יוסף הצדיק שהי' פקיד בבית פוטיפר ומושל בכל אשר לו הן בבית הן בשדה ויודע ומכיר בלשונות שונות ועם כל זה רוח אלקים בו זה לא שמענו ולא ראינו ולא ראינו וזה הנמצא כזה, איש אשר רוח אלקים בו כו' עכ"ל. (שיח שרפי קודש 2 . 85 . 285.)

(55) ...כמו ששמעתי בשם הרה"ק מפרשיסחא זצללה"ה שמי שאומר שמתייגע מדברי תורה אין עבודתו באמת כדכתיב (דברים ל', י"ד) כי קרוב אליך הדבר מאוד וגו' ואיתא(דברים רבה פרשה י"א, ה') חייכם כל החכמה וכל התורה דבר קל הוא, כל מי שמתיירא אותי ועושה דברי תורה כל החכמה וכל התורה בלבו. (פרי צדיק בשלח י"ג)

חטא ורע

(56) ...וכפי ששמעתי בשם כ"ק אדמו"ר הקדוש מו"ה שמחה בונם זי"ע מפרשיסחא הפירוש שגם אחר החטא קראו אדם כמו האשה שאף אחר הגירושין נקראת אשה. (רמתים צופים פרק א)

(58) וזהו פירוש סור מרע, כלומר שלא ישגיח ברע. (קול שמחה צה)

(61) תנו רבנן, מצות נר חנוכה, נר איש וביתו. והמהדרין נר לכל אחד ואחד. והמהדרין מן המהדרין, בית שמאי אומרים יום ראשון מדליק שמונה מכאן ואילך פוחת והולך, ובית הלל אומרים יום ראשון מדליק אחת מכאן ואילך מוסיף והולך (שבת כא). דבית שמאי אומרים פוחת והולך היינו שקודם יתקן מעשיו בבחינת 'סור מרע', ובית הלל אומרים מוסיף והולך היינו שיוסיף בתורה ובמצוות ועל ידי זה ממילא יסור הרע. ונמנו וגמרו שהלכה כבית הלל דמוסיף והולך, כי כאשר ימתין האדם עד שיתקן את הרע יכלו הימים והם לא יכלו. (אילנא דחיי פרשת משפטים ע' כה).

(62) ...ומה עוד אם אדם קלקל ח"ו לדבר חמור ועוסק בסור מרע לראשונה כמו שכתוב, הריהו חושב על הקלקול, ומקום שהמחשבה נמצאת שם האדם, עם כל נפשו, אז הוא בתוך הרע והוא בטח לא ישוב בתשובה כי מוחו יתגשם ויגרום לטמטום הלב ועלול ליפול לתוך עצבות חלילה, ואפילו לא עבר לדבר חמור ומוחו לא יתגשם ולבו לא יטמטם אבל כשיחשוב על סור מרע ועל הבוץ, הפוך בבוץ והוא ישאר בוץ. כן חטא לא חטא מה יש להקב"ה מזה, ובזמן שהוא חושב על זה הריהו יכול להיות נוקב נקב מרגליות, עשה טוב מה יש להקב"ה מזה, ושיהי' משהו מזה למלכות שמים. לכן סור מרע, הפנה עצמך מרע, אל תהרהר ברע, עשה טוב, עשית חבילות עבירות עשה מצות כנגדן, היום, לפני יום כיפורים צריכים להרגיש את עזיבת החטא, עם ישוב הדעת, מעומקא דליבא, לא ע"י התפעלות, רק קבלה בלב על העתיד ולהיות בשמחה, לומר "על חטא" במהירות ולא לשקוע בהם, רק ב י' ותמלוך אתה ה' לבדך" (חידושי הרי"ם רסא.)

(67) ויאמר נעשה אדם בצלמנו וגו' (כי) אדם מגזירת אדמה הכל מפואר ומהודר רצה ה' להראות מעשיו שיראה הכל מכל הנמצא. והמציאות לבד מאדם לא ישיג כי אם כל אחד את עצמו. לכך ברא ה' את האדם שהוא כח כלול מעליונים ותחתונים אשר יוכל לדמות הכל בנפשו. זה מהות אדם שיראה ויבין וידמה לא זולתו. וזהו נעשה אדם בצלמנו כדמותנו בכף הדמיון, כי לא ישער אלא הדומה קצת בדומה. (קול שמחה ח)

(70) ההה"ק הרר"ב מפרשיסחא ראה פ"א כפרי אחד בונה בית ושני נסרים באליעס אינם יכולים להשתוות יחד כי היה בא באחד סנעק ועמד וראה מה הכפרי יעשה וחצב ונקב בהצד כדי שיכנוס הסנעק בתוך הנקב ואמר להחסידים ראו איך שיכולים לעשות שלום בין הצדדים לא שיכופו דוקא להשתוות הסנעק מהעקשן רק לכוף את השני שיכנוס בתוכו הסנעק ועי"ז יתחזק יותר הבנין כמו כן האחדות יהי' יותר מקודם כי הכניע אי"ע לפני השני. (שיח שרפי קודש 5. 114)

(74) עוד שמעתי בשמו. שאמר שכל אוי"א צריך להיות לו שני קעשינעס. להשתמש בו בעת צרכו. בקעשינע אחד בשבילי נברא העולם.(סנהדרין דל"ז. תדא"ר פכ"ה) ובהקעשינע השני אנכי עפר ואפר. (פ' וירא). והבן.(שיח שרפי קודש 1. 50 . 232)

(79) בס' הזכרון דף קע"ג הובא עוד בשם הרבי ר' בונם זי"ע שהי' אומר החכם, הוא אפיקורס, בעל לב טוב, הוא איש תענוג, נוטה לתאות הבשר, והאדוק ומרבה תפלה, הוא רע לבריות. וישאלוהו, אם כל אלה לא יזכו, מה טוב לאדם, להיות שלשתם יחד, היתה התשובה, חכם, לב טוב, ואדוק. עכ"ל. (שיח שרפי קודש 3 . 6 . 14)

(82) שמעתי מתלמידיו שסמוך לפטירתו ז"ל שמע שאשתו היתה בוכה. אמר לה למה אתה בוכה הלא כל ימי חיי היה רק כדי שאלמד אי"ע למות עכד"ק. (רמתים צופים, לא. קד)

(85) הרבי רב בונם זצ"ל אמר : מאוד היה היש ישר בעיני, להיות סאלע גדולה עם מטות וקנאפעס, ושלחנות עם יין וצלי ואינדיקעס, ולומר מעט תורה, ומי שמבקש לישן ישן קצת, ויאכל צלי וויין, ולומר עוד דברי תורה מעט, באמת הוא טוב כך, כי כשלוקחין הכל למקום הצריך הוא טוב מאוד, ואין צריך להיות סגור, רק יוכל להתפשט גם בכל הדברים וללוקחם לפה, ולמשה רבינו ע"ה אמר הקב"ה של נעלך, הסר מסגרותך, רק להיות מתפשט בכל, ולהעלות למקום הראוי. (חשבה לטובה צט)

פרק ח

ניתוח עצמי

(2) ששמעתי מרבנו זלה"ה מפרשיסחא כי כל מה שהאדם מתייגע ומתעורר אפשר שהוא מחיצוניות הלב כי יש לו חדרי חדרים אבל זה שהוא מן השמים כנ"ל יורד לחיותו ממש במה שהוא חי ודו"ל. (רמתיים צופים,ו. כח)

(8) ...כי כשמתקבצים חסידים ביחד, זה רואה מעלתו של זה, ומתחרט בעצמו על מעשיו הרעים, אבל כשאינו הולך אין לו חרטה על מעשיו הרעים ודפח"ח עי"ש. (שיח שרפי קודש 4. 43)

(10) ...שנה תמימה רצה מדי פעם לכנוס פנימה לרבו הרבי ר' בונם זצ"ל לדבר עמו, ובכל פעם שבא לבית לא מצא את עצמו ראוי לזה. פעם אחת הלכתי בשדה ובכיתי הרבה ורצתי להרבי ר' בונם זצ"ל, ושאל מה אתה בוכה, אמרתי, הלא אני בריאה בעולם, ונבראתי בעינים ולב

וכל האיברים, ואיני יודע למה נבראתי, ומה אני מועיל בעולם. והשיב לו הרבי ר' בונם צז"ל,
גם אני מתהלך באותה מחשבה, " פארעל איך גייא אויך ארים מיט דעם, דיא וועסט מיט
מיר עסין וויעטשערי" (חשבה לטובה רכב)

(12) ...ועל דרך מה שאמר לי הרב האיש היהודי נ"ע על הכתוב צדק צדק תרדף למען תחיה וגו'
והתמצית הוא על דרך מ"ש בס"ק שכל חיותו של האדם הוא שיתקן מה שצריך לתקן ועד
כלות תיקונו נמשך ימי חיותו.וזה שאומר הכתוב צדק. פירוש הגם שכבר צדקת את מעשיך
על כל זה צדק. פירוש תראה עוד יותר להצדיק מעשיך בתוספת קדושה יתירה. (נפלאות
היהודי 56)

(13) אמר אא"ז היהודי הקדוש זצ"ל שיש ג' בחינות בעבודה. א' מי שהוא עוסק במצות ומע"ט
כל היום ונדמה לו שעדן לא פעל מאומה וזהו מעלה גבוה שאין למעלה הימנה, ב' מי שהוא
פעל עדיין כלום אך שיודע שלא תיקן שום דבר שהוא ג"כ טוב כי יש לו תקוה שיקח
א"ע לתשובה. אבל מישהו שהוא יודע שהוא צדיק הוא מאנה א"ע כל ימיו והתו"מ ילך
לאבדון ר"ל וכו' ע"כ. (תפארת היהודי קעט, קא)

עצבות

(19) ...כמו שאמר כ"ק אדמו"ר זי"ע ע"פ (תהלים קמ"ז) הרופא לשבורי לב. ולב נשבר הוא טוב
מאוד והרפואה הוא שמנקים אותו מן העצבת ונשאר לב נשבר בלא שום עצבות כלל רק
בשמחה. וזהו מדריגת הצדיקים הגדולים שהם בלא חטא כלל והבע"ת צריך כל ימיו לקוות
לזה אולי יראה השם בעניו ויקבל אותו ויתן לו לב טהור בלי שום עצבות. וכמאמר אדמו"ר
מפרשיסחא זי"ע בשם כ"ק אדמו"ר ז"ל מק"ק לענטשני בהיותם אצל הרב הקדוש היהודי
זלה"ה. שצריך בודאי לב נשבר אך שצריך להיות שלם ג"כ ושניהם יהיו יחדיו תואמים
שבור ושלם עכדה"ק ז"ל. (רמתים צופים ה. יא)

(23) והיה אם שכוח תשכח את ה' אלהיך (דברים ח, יט). יש לדקדק על כפל הלשון דכתיב "
שכוח תשכח". ויש לומר, לפי דאמרינן (ויקרא רבא יא, ז) דכל 'ויהיי' לשון שמחה,וזהו והיה
אם שכוח, היינו אם שכוח את שמחה, אז תשכח את ה' אלקיך, כי מתוך עצבות אין יכולים
לעבוד את ה'.(שושנים לדוד על תהלים פרק קמז ע' שלד)

(25) עוד שמעתי "בשם היהודי הקדוש" זצללה"ה על מאמר חז"ל כל השערים ננעלים חוץ
משערי דמעות, אמר בשם הי' שערי דמעות ננעלו ח"ו לא הי' יכולים לכנוס ח"ו הדמעות
משום זה אין ננעלין. כי הדמעות המה בבחי' עצבות וקשה לכנוס דרך שער הננעל. אבל עם
השמחה קען מען לעכערין דיא פר שלאסינע טויערין. והבן. (תפארת היהודי קפ. קז)

(26) ...כי זקיני היהודי הק' זצללה"ה אמר בבחי' עצבות למנעו מעבודת ד' וכל ימיו הי'
עבודתו לבא לשמחה ולולי זאת הי' עוד גדול יותר במדריגתו... (תפארת היהודי קע. סט)

(30) ...ובכלל התמרמר נגד עשיית המצוות בלי פנימיות מחשבה ויגנה את המענים את נפשם
ואינם חפצים ליהנות מטוב החלד וממנעם התענוגים החושיים, ובלבד שלא יתנגדו לדתנו
ולחוקי המוסר והצניעות. ע"כ ראינו את חסידי פשוסחא יוצאים יום יום לשמוע זמרות
המנצחים בנגינות לפני אנשי החיל הולכים לשוח בגנים ופרדסים, או לשבת באחו, בהר
ובשפלה על נאות דשא ושיח. עצבון לא ידעו, היום היה היה לרובם, העוסקים במסחר וקנין-
לעבודה, והלילה לחברה, להשתעשע בנעימים, ללמוד גפ"ת בעיון וגם ספרי מחקר ומוסר
ולפלפל בסברה. בחלה נפשם ברפיון יתר כתות החסידים ולא הלכו ברחוב בבלויי סחבות
ופאות עבותות מלאות נוצות ולא במנעלים קרועים חשופי עקב, וכפתור ערום לא נראה
כגרונם יוצא מצואר פרוע, רק לבשו מכלול ועל בגדיהם לא נמצא שמץ דבר, רביד על צוארם

ושער ראשם מסולסל במסרק, ברגליהם מנעלים ארוכים (שטיפפעל) וכל צלמו כלו אומר
כבוד... (כתר כהונה 129)

שמחה

33) ...עצבות אינה עבירה, אבל טמטום הלב שבעצבות יכולה להביא, אין העבירה החמורה
ביותר יכולה להביא. מה שאנו אומרים תמיד שמחה,אין מובנה שמחה של מצוה, זוהי
מדריגה לחוד. שמחה אנו מתכוונים רק שלא להיות בעצבות. פשוט, יהודי המהלך ואינו
בשמחה הריהו כפוי טובה לשמים, וסימן הוא, שמעולם לא הבין מובנה של הברכה שלא
עשני גוי. ממשש את עצמו אם חסיד אני או לא, זהו גאות. מה זה חסיד, העיקר יהודי אני.
עצבות הרי היא שאול תחתית. מהי עצבות בעצם, מגיע לי, חסר לי, הן בגשמיות והן
ברוחניות, הכל אני. מרירות זו היא שבירת הלב, משום שבאמת איש נאמן לא יתכן ללא
מסירות נפש. לא עשיתי מאומה ומכל מקום אני חי בעולם, שואף אויר, אם כן זוהי שמחה.
והוא היפך מעצבות. אלא שבין עצבות ומרירות כחוט השערה. כל התורה כחוט השערה,
נשחט רובו כשר מחצה טרפה וכו'. הגם שנודעים מעבדות נכון.משום שבשכל העצמי האדם
רק מאנה את עצמו. אלא שזהו החילוק וההבדל שבין עצבות ומרירות, שמעצבות הגוף כבד
ונשכב לישון, אינו סובל עצמו ואינו סובל אחרים, חזק בעצמו. אבל מרירות מונעת השינה,
הרי לא התחלתי לעשות כלום, חוטפים תפילה, לימוד, מצוה, מרגישים יהודי, נהנים
ממראיתו. אף על פי כן המרירות העדינה ביותר, מכל מקום יש בה נגיעה עם עצבות. אבל
השמחה, אף שאינה מזוקקת, צומחת מן הקדושה. (חשבה לטובה 202)

34) בספר נפלאות חדשות בליקוטים משמו שאמר שיותר יכולים לפעול בתפלה ובשמחה ממה
שיכולים לפעול בבכיה ומעשה שהי' בעת שהי' בדאנציג שראה שנפל אחד להם ונטבע שם
ואמר לו הרב בלשון אשכנז גריס מיר דעם לויתן, ואח"כ עזר לו הש"י שאחז בדף אחד
ונצול, וסיפר הרה"ק המעשה הנ"ל ואמר שלא הי' יכול לעזור לו מחמת שהי' לו צער גדול
מאוד עד שאמר לו מלתא דבדיחותא והי' לו קצת שמחה מזה אז הי' יכול לעזור להנטבע.
(מאמרי שמחה מט)

35) ...הרבי ר' בונם זצ"ל אמר בשם הרבי ר' משה לייב מסאסוב זצ"ל ששאל פי' הכתוב תחת
אשר לא עבדת את ה' אלקיך בשמחה וגו', האם בשביל זה יבואו כל הקללות, ואמר שכל
הרע נובע מזה אשר אינו עובד את ה' בשמחה. (חידושי הרי"ם קצא)

38) שמעתי בשם ההי"ר הרי"ר שמחה בונם ז"ל מפרשיסחא שאמר : שהקלים, טוב להם בעולם
הזה, משום שהם בשמחה תמיד...אבל היראים, על ידי זה שהם בדאגה ועצבות רוב
הזמנים, על ידי זה ממשיכים על עצמם דינים, והם מחוסרי פרנסה ר"ל. (דרך צדיקים אות
כ"ג)

42) ...וגם צחקו שמה במשחק הקוַארטעַן. קלא דלא פסיק יצא במחנה העברים, כי בארגז אשר
לרגלי ארון הקודש נמצא השופר ויתר הכלים לתשמישי קודש, ובצדם בקבוק עם יי"ש
ולוחות הקוַארטעַן, וכאשר שאלום מה זאת? השיבו בהלצה : אלה המלכים היוצאים מן
השופר" (כתר כהונה 129-130)

44) ...כמו שאמר הרבי ר' בונים זצ"ל : דהעצבות היותר טוב- מלובש בגיאות. והשמחה היותר
קטנה- מלובש בעניוות. (יכהן פאר, קדושים דף קי"ז)

ענוה

(51 ויברכם ביום ההוא לאמר.נראה פרושו, דהנה האדם כאשר עובד ה' בבהירות גדול אף על פי
כן נדמה בעיניו שעדיין לא השיג שום דבר... (קול שמחה 50)

(53 וירא אליו ה' באלוני ממרא (יח,א). שנראה ונדמה לאברהם אבינו שהשראת השכינה
והאלוהות הוא באלוני ממרא, (שמרוב ענוה היה נראה לו שה' ית' שוכן אצל ההמון עם
הנראים בעיני כל לרשעים וממרים בה'). כדרך כל הצדיקים שרואים תמיד מעלת חבירם
ושפלות עצמו,(ובדעתם כי המפורסמים לרשעים יוצאים ידי שמים יותר ממנו). והוא יושב
פתח האהל, שהוא אברהם עוד לא השיג כלל. (הרישא במשרת איתמר פרשת וירא פ' ח)

(54 ויאמר..דהנה האדם המביט בגדולת השם יתעלה צריך להביט בכל (חלקי) הנפש. והבחינה
על זה היא שבשעת הבינה ההיא אינו יודע אם רואה אם לאו, כי כל חלקי הנפש מלובש
בראיה זו וזה בשביל שהסתיר פניו, היינו שהפשיט את עצמו מכל וכל. בשכר הזה זכה
לראות ודו"ק. (קול שמחה 54)

(55 אשירה.. כי ג' 'גאים הם וכו'.. והנה אי אפשר לשורר להקב"ה אם לא שנסתלק (מדת)
הגאוה מהאדם ומכיר שכל הגאות הוא לה' ברוך הוא. (קול שמחה 66)

(56 הרבי ר' בונם זצ"ל אמר, כח בטחון הוא מגזירת בטח, כי מי שבוטח וברור בעיניו בלי שום
ספק שיהי' לו, זהו הבוטח ומקיים תמיד בטחונו ומהו באמת הבטחון ולמה מובטח, הרי
אין מגיע לאדם כלום מהבורא יתברך שמו, אך בהיפוך הוא שמי שבדעתו שהוא קצת ראוי
ירא שמא לא יתנו לו כלום מכפי הראוי, אבל מי שיודע שאינו ראוי לכלום, א"כ רק מתנת
חנם,שנותנין לו בחסד גמור, אם כן מובטח על הכל כי מהו החילוק בין מעט לרב. (חידושי
הריי"ם 374)

(62 הרבי ר' בונם זצ"ל התנצל לפני הרבי מלובלין זצ"ל, הלא הוא אין, והשיב לו, זאת טוב הוא,
התחיל פעם שניה הלא באמת אני אין, והשיב לו, ראוי לאדם להיות אין מאין, מלהיות יש
מיש. התחיל הרבי ר' בונם זצ"ל לשאוג, אוי מה אני, הלא באמת אני אין " גאר נישט",
השיב לו, על כל פנים יש לך מדה של הקב"ה, כי איתא בגמרא(שבת נה.) חותמו של הקב"ה
הוא אמת, ובאם האדם חושב שיש לו כלום הוא שקר, כי אלמלא הקב"ה עוזרו לא היה
יכול לו כמאמר הגמרא. (קידושין ל:) (חשבה לטובה 121)

(63 עוד אמר לי שזקיני הקדוש היהודי זי"ע בעודו באבו הופיע עליו רוח קדושתו שהרה"ק
היהודי זצללה"ה אמר כד הוי טליא מיקרי דדרדקי בעת שהי' לומד אלי"ף בי"ת מלמד
למד לעצמו לימוד גדול באם שיושבים יחד לשתות כוס משקה וכל אחד ואחד מבטל א"ע
לגבי חבירו ואין רואה מעלות עצמו גבוה ממעלות חבירו אז השי"ת יסלח להם עונותיהם.
כי בעת שהי' לומד אצל מלמדו אלי"ף בי"ת שואל אותו מה זו נקודה אחת. השיבו
המלמד נקודה אחת זו יו"ד . ואח"כ שאל ותו של שני נקודות. והשיבו שהוא שני יודי"ן
הוי' ב"ה. ואח"כ כשראה שני נקודות באורך בין פסוק לפסוק הי' סבור ג"כ למיקרי שם הוי'
ב"ה. ואמר לו המלמד כלל זה יהי' בידך אם נמצא כתוב שני יודי"ן בשוה ולא אחד על גבי
חבירו הוא שם הוי' ב"ה. אבל שני יודי"ן באורך זה על גב זה אינו שם הוי'. ומזה שלמד אם
שני אנשים באים ביחד ומבטלים כל אחד לגבי חבירו ואינו מחזיק א"ע במעלה גבוה נגד
חבירו הוא שם הוי' ב"ה. (נפלאות היהודי פה)

(70 בפי' ויעש כן אהרן וכו' וברש"י להגיד שבחו של אהרן שלא שינה, לכאו' מה הרבותא והפי'
שלא נתפעל מזה מאומה, ולא נשתנה ולא עלה בלבו שום גבהות, שבא לגדולה כזאת. (תורת
שמחה קט)

381

73) ולתתך עליון על כל הגוים גו'. הרבי ר' בונם זצ"ל אמר כמו שמגבי' קופסה מלמטה למעלה, היינו שלא ירגיש שום נדנוד של התנשאות, כי בעיני ה' יקר נמוכי רוח מכל מדות טובות. (חידושי הרי"ם רמט)

79) פעם אחת נטל רבנו הק' את כל המדרגות וההשגות של תלמידו הרה"ק רבי שמחה בונם מפרשיסחא, עד שהיה כאיש פשוט. והיה מתפלל ומביט בתוך הסידור כאיש פשוט, ושם בה' מבטחו שיהיה בעזרתו. וזכה על ידי זה להשיג כל ההשגות בשלימות כבראשונה. (ישמח ישראל, שמחת תורה ע' צ.)

81) באחד מימי חג השבועות אמר רבנו הק' 'תורה' על שולחנו, והיה ווי א קאכדיגער קעסיל-בוער ממש כאש כיורה רותחת). ואחרי היראה והרעדה באמירת התורה סיים את דבריו, סוף דבר הכל נשמע את האלהים ירא ואת מצוותיו שמור כי זה כל האדם (קהלת יב, יג) כי אחרי כל ההשגות ואחרי כל המדריגות, מיז מען ערשט אויין הייבען צי ווערין איין פשוטער איד(-צריך להתחיל מחדש, להיות יהודי פשוט). (אהל שלמה חלק ב' ע' יז)

82) פעם אחת בא לפניו איש אחד מפשוטי העם שלמד בילדותו יחד עם רבינו זצ"ל ובבואו לפניו הגיד בזה"ל בטח כ"ק זוכר שלמדנו יחד וכ"ץ נעשה רבי ואני הנני איש פשוט. והשיבו ע"ז אתה פשוט? אתה עקום ואני פשוט. (אמת ואמונה 845)

84) פעם אחת בא הגה"ק רבי ברוך פרנקיל-תאומים מלייפניק בעל " ברוך טעם" אל אחיו הגאון הגביר הצדיק רבי לייביש שהיה דר בזאויכוואסט, ופגש ברבנו הק', שהיה באותם הימים משמש כמלמד בביתו. שאלו, למה אתה מסתופף בצל הרבי מלובלין, הלא יכול אתה ללמוד יותר הימינו, ומה לומדת אתה מרבך. השיבו ר' הק', למדתי מרבי, שכאשר אך אני מניח את עצמי לישן, אז תיכף ומיד כרגע הנני נרדם בשינה. (נפלאות היהודי עמ' 65)

86) אמר הן אמת שהחסידים יש להם שפלות ונעשים כאין. אך צריך לקבל את אלוהותו ואחדותו יתברך במקום שבטל את עצמו ונשאר המקום פנוי שם יקבל את אלהותו ואדנותו. כי מה מועיל שפלותו וביטולו אם לא לשרות בו אדנותו יתברך במקום הנ"ל עכ"ד... (קול שמחה קכד)

87) וכזה כתוב בשם אדמו"ר א"א קדוש הרב ר' בונם זלה"ה, כי אף אם מואס האדם בתאות עוה"ז, עדיין אין זה שלמות כי העיקר הוא שיכניס האדם א"ע בעול תו"ע וכו' ע"ש. (תורת שמחה 91)

פרק 9

4) ...כי אין קדושה הנמצא אצל האדם בעצם אך בהתקדש אדם עצמו כפי הכנתו כן לקדושה כן יושפע עליו מלמעלה... (קול שמחה מז)

5) פעם אמר רביה"ק הרבי בונים מפרשיסחא זצ"ל: " קדושים תהיו- בהויתכם תהיו". והסבירו דבריו, ששנינו: "ולדי קדושים, בהויתן הן קדושים" (זבחים קיד ע"ב) ולא ממעי אמן. אף הקדושה אינה נקנית לאדם ממעי אמו, ואינו 'קדוש מרחם', אלא חיב לעמל עליה בעצמו מיום צאתו לאויר העולם... (משרתיו אש לוהט, רכח)

6) הכנה למצוה כמצוה עצמה. וראיה לכך מגמרא (בבא מציעא פג:) דפועל, בכניסתו משלו, ביציאתו משל בעל הבית... (שם משמואל פרשת חיי שרה ע' רלח)

7) ...הכנה לתפלה, שהיה בבחינת ' כל עצמותי תאמרנה'... (תפארת היהודי 29. 161.)

(10) ...שכך הוא האמת שהאדם צריך להכין את עצמו לתפלה ביראה ואהבה וקדושה רבה בכל יכולתו וזה הוא הכלים שיכין לסעודת המלך... (קול שמחה פז)

(12) ...כי באם האדם ממתין ומישב עצמו זמן מה קודם עשיית מצוה ותורה ועבודה, אזי יוכל לקיים כמו שצוה השי"ת... (תורת שמחה יט)

(13) ...ונראה לבאר דאף שכל בנין העולם ותיקונו תלוי במעשי עם בני ישראל, אף על פי כן אין הסברא נותנת שמעשי בני אדם יהיו נאים ונבחרים יותר ממעשי המלאכים, כי בודאי מעשי המלאך זך ונקי יותר ממעשי בן אדם אשר הרכבתו מוכן לכח הרע, אך לענין ההכנה שיגיע לשלימת אמיתת המעשה שעל ידה יבא האדם להתדבק בו יתברך, בזאת מעשי בני אדם יותר מעולים, כי האדם מסובך בסך המניעות העצומות הסובבים אותו בכל עת אשר הוא קרוץ מחומר, לא כן מלאכי עליון אשר המה קדושים וטהורים בעצם ואינם גשם כלל ולא יפול בהם שום השתנות... (אהל תורה נב)

(15) ויקח מן הבא בידו, ההיי"ק מקאצק זיי"ע פי' כך, מי שיקח מכל מה שבא בידו לעשות אותם, ואינו מיישב עצמו אם טובה הוא אם לאו, זה אינו כלום, אפי' הוא סבר שהוא מצוה, אינו כן אלא הוא מנחה לעשיו, שסטי"א מתגבר ח"ו. (שיח שרפי החדש 1. מג)

(16) ...ונראה כי רק ההכנה למצוה נצרך להיות במתינות, אבל המצוה עצמה יותר טוב שתהי' במהירות. (אהל תורה צח)

(18) שמעתי מחסיד ישיש שהרר"ב זיי"ע אמר ליישב קו' הרשב"א ז"ל מ"ט לא מברכין על מצי"ע דנתינת צדקה. ואמר ז"ל דאם נעשה ברכה כמו על כל מצוה ומצוה צריך הכנה בנקיות וטבילה ולשם יחוד, וכדומה ובין כך ימות עני ברעב לזאת לא הוצרכה התורה שום ברכה והכנה כדי שלא יהי' להאדם שום תי' אשר אינו מוכן עוד לעשות ברכה ודפח"ח. (שיח שרפי קודש 130)

(20) אמר בחז"ל שערי דמעות לא ננעלו, ולכאורה אם כן למה נעשו השערים, רק שאם יבוא שוטה ויבכה, אז נועלים השערים. (מאמרי שמחה עט)

(21) פ"א אמר אדמו"ר ז"ל. מעשה באחד שהיה מתפלל לפני התיבה ביוה"כ. והיה בוכה הרבה מאוד. ומתוך לא היה יכול להביט בתוך המחזור והיה אומר הרבה טעויות. ואמר לו הלא יותר טוב היה שלא תבכה ותביט במחזור ותאמר עברי כראוי. (רמתים צופים 31. 95)

(26) איש אחד קיבל על עצמו את ניסיון השתיקה ולא דיבר כלום במשך שלוש שנים חוץ מדברי תורה ותפילה. שלח 'היהודי' לקרוא לו: " אברך", אמר לו, " מה זה שאיני שומע שום דיבור ממך בעולם האמת?". "רבי ", הצטדק האיש, " למה לי לדבר דברי הבל, האם לא נאות יותר ללמוד ולהתפלל בלבד?". "ובכן,, אמר 'היהודי', " הרי ממך עצמך אין שום דיבור בא בעולם האמת. מי שלומד ומתפלל בלבד, ממית את דיבורו של עצמו. מה משמע: לדבר דברי הבל? אפשר לומר כל- דבר- שהוא כדבר הבל, אפשר לומר כל- דבר-שהוא כדבר אמת... (אור הגנוז 398)

(27) כאשר ספרו לפניו בשבח איש אחד שמסיים בכל יום ספר תהלים, העיר, אם בחצי הספר נאמר ויפתוהו בפיהם ובלשונם יכזבו לו (תהילים ע"ח) מי שגומר כל התהלים על אחת כמה וכמה ע"כ... (שיח שרפי קודש 2. 13 .14)

(28) ...כמו שמצינו בתורה בעניני נזיר אם ימות מת עליו בפתע פתאום, סותר הנזירות ויספור פעם שנית, אף שכבר סיפר כ"ט יום אם ימות מת עליו בפתע פתאום סותר כל כ"ט יום וצריך לספור מחדש, ולמה לא הזכיר התוה"ק ענין הטומאת כהנים, שהכהן ג"כ צריך ליזהר מטומאה. אך הכהן הוא חכם, ולא תאונה לו שום רעה, אבל הנזיר שקבל עליו

פרישות, ואסר עליו דברים שמותרים לו, מחמת פרימקייט קרה לו טומאה פתאומית. (שיח שרפי קודש 2. 13. 14)

(29) שמעתי ממורי מפרשיסחא ז"ל. שמג"ע לגיהנם הוא כחוט השערה... (תורת שמחה סח)

(30) סיפר לי מר אבי ז"ל שפעם אחת הלך הרבי מלובלין לקריאת מגילה בליל פורים לבית המדרש. ופתאום ייבשו רגליו ולא יכול להלוך. וכן הי' כ"פ. אבל הי' נושאים אותו. ועתה נעשה כבד ולא יכלו לנשאו בשום אופן. גם הגבורים היהודי הק' וחבריו לא יכלו לנושאו ממקומו. לא יאומן כי יסופר מה שהי' מפורסם בזמנו. וציום הרבי אשר החכם בונם ישאהו. והוא לקחו בשתי זרועותיו ונשאו לבית המדרש. ושמעתי מהה"ק ר' בנימין מלובלין ז"ל כי היהודי שאל להרבי ר' בונם איזו כוונה הי' לו אז. במה שזכה יותר מחבריו. השיב. היה בדעתי אז כי מצווים לי לישא קורה עץ בעלמא... (אור שמחה פג)

(31) בשם הרב מהרש"ב זלל"ה..כי אם שאין אדם בשלימות ביראת ד' אזי צריך גדרים הרבה ולכן נתוסף עלינו חומרות וגדרים הרבה אבל מי שלבו שלם ביראת ד' אזי אין צריך לזה... (שיח שרפי קודש 5. 70)

(34) הרב שלי הרבי ר' בונם זצ"ל, "האט אלע מאל אונטער גערירקט לחסידים, האבין זיי גערידערט", זאת היה היה טוב לפי שעה. אני רוצה, אז זיי זאלין זיך אליין מוטשע"ן שיעמלו בעצמם, בזה יהיה קיום ביותר. " מען ווערט געפלאטטשט פין דעם, אז מען מיטשעט זיך אליין, און מען הארט אמאל, גייט עס געכער אריין." (חשבה לטובה קכד)

(37) ...וכמו ששמעתי ממו"ר מפרשיסחא ז"ל שמי שמבקש מהשי"ת על יראה ואינו מבקש על פרנסה. זה סימן שגם זה שמתפלל על יר"ש אינו מאמתת לבו שאי אפשר זה בלא זה ע"כ. (רמתיים צופים 5. 111)

(38) ...ואז הי' חל חג השבועות ביום א' ב'. ואמר המגיד בש"ק להמשיך קדושת שבת להכנת קבלת תורה שלא לדבר שיחת חולין עד אחר קריאת היו"ד דברות. וכולם לא דיברו. והרבי ר' בונם קרא לאחד ורמזו עליו בכעס מדוע עובר מצות המגיד ואמר. שוטים אם אצטרך לצלוחות קאווי לא אדבר להמשרת ליתן לי... (אור שמחה 15)

תענית

(40) עוד כתב לי הרב הנ"ל כי פעם אחת בא אחד לפני הרבי ר' בונם ושאל אותו היות דאיתא בספה"ק שהיושב בתענית כל כך ימים זוכה לגילוי אליהו ז"ל, והוא ישב כ"כ תעניתים ולא זכה לזה. והשיב לו. כי הבעש"ט הקדוש הי' נצרך לנסוע דרך רחוקה, ושכר עגלה וסוסים, אך לפנים, אבל אמר שם הק' מקפיצת הדרך, ובאופן זה בא למחוז חפצו, והנה הסוסים אשר היו אסורים להעגלה, ידעו והי' מורגלים כי נותנים להם אכילה ושתי' בכל תחנה ותחנה, ועתה בנסיעה על ידי קפיצת הדרך לא עמדו לנוח. ולא ניתן להם אכילה ושתי' בתחנה ראשונה, וכן לא בתחנה שני', רק כמו כשבאו בליל לנוח באיזה עיר אשר אינם כלל סוסים, רק המה בני אדם, ולכן כשבאו בלילה לנוח באיזה עיר אשר המנהג הי' שכל בני אדם נוסעים בדרך זה אוכלים שמה אז גם להם יתנו לאכול, אבל בראותם שגם במקומות שבני אדם אוכלים אינם עומדים לנוח ולא נותן להם לאכול רק פרחו הלאה מעיר לעיר. שוב נגמר בדעתם שאינם גם בני אדם רק מלאכים ממש. ולכן אינם בני אכילה ושתיה. אבל כשבא הבעש"ט ז"ל למחוז חפצו והעמידו את הסוסים ברפת ונתנו לפניהם לאכול. האבין זיי זיך צו גיחאפט צום עסיין אזוי ווי די א פערד. כן הדבר היושב בתענית וחושב שכבר זכה להיות כמלאך הוא כבר לזכות לגילוי אליהו. אבל העיקר הוא שאחר שגומר מספר התעניתים. וכשנותנים לו לאכול ער זיך נישט צו חאפין צום עסין אזוי ווי א

פערד. דאל"כ אז נשאר סוס כמקדם והבן. וכ"כ לי הגאבד"ק פלונסק שיחי'. (מאמרי שמחה
לו)

(43) ...עינינו ראו לא אחת, איך ישבו באגודה על הספסלים וצחוק מלא פיהם ועתר ענן הקטורת
יצא מגרונם, בעת ישבו האבלים ע חורבן מקדשנו בט"ב ודמעתם על לחם. על התעניותים
אמרו : כי כלם אבדו זכותם במשפט, מלבד יוה"כ, וט"ב עודנו תלוי ועומד ולא נודע איך
יחרץ משפטו. לכן אכלו בכל שנה ושנה בצום גדליה בבקר, בעוד הרבה הקהל בסליחות או
בתפלה- מאפה חורי(בייגעל) חם. (כתר כהונה 129)

(44) הרבי רבי בונם זי"ע אמר פעם אחת : אילו היה בכחי, הייתי מבטל כל התעניות, מלבד יום
הכיפורים ותשעה באב. כי ביום כיפור מי צריך לאכול, ובתשעה באב מי יכול לאכול. (כתבי
חסידים)

השפעתו של ר' בונים

(47) "דבר בהתלהבות ובאמונה פנימית כל כך, עד שהאמין שיש ביכלתו להחזיר בתשובה את כל
הכופרים" (יצחק מיזס)

(48) ...כה זוכרים אנחנו בשחרות נעורינו, את המסלה החדשה אשר סלל הרב הפלוסופי זה
לנגררים אחריו. את חיל צבאו לקח רק מבני עליה- לומדים מופלגי תורה ובעלי בינה יתירה.
(כתר כהונה 128)

(49) אחד מגדולי אנשי הרוח שבזמנו בכל אירופה... (ר' אהרן מרכוס "חסידיזמוס" עמ' 167)

(50) החסידים מספרים, שפעם ישב רבי שמחה בונם עם תלמידיו ועסקו בעניני תשובה. התלהב
רש"ב, קם ממקומו ואמר : הרמב"ם אומר :"ומה היא התשובה?-שיעזוב החוטא חטאו
ויסירו ממחשבתו ויגמור בלבו שלא יעשהו עוד, ויעיד עליו יודע תעלומות, שלא ישוב לזה
החטא מעולם" מי שאינו עושה תשובה כזאת, אין לו מקום אצלי!...נבהלו התלמידים
מאימת רבם וברחו כולם. נשאר רק רבי מנדל מקוצק שאמר : אין לי כח לברוח...
(רבינוביץ, ר' בונים 75)

(51) ...כשלקח הרר"ב את יד תלמידו לידו, אף מאיש פשוט, תו"מ נתלהב, עם האט עהם אן
גהובען צו ברענען יודישקייט, עד שכ"א רצה לנשק להשם יתברך, ורץ ללמוד, וכלל א"ע עם
התורה ואותיותיה באהבה עצומה, ונשק כל האותיות, ובדמעות שליש מסר א"ע על מזבח
קדושת השיי"ת, והי' מוכן לזה בתשוקה נפלאה ובכל כחותיו וחיותו... (אהל יצחק 19)

(52) ...וכך שמעתי מפי חותנו ז"ל : הלשינו על המתחסדים שהם שכורים זוללים וסובאים בעלי
מדות רעות, ושר ההשכלה בימים היה איש נאור מבעלי דעה הגדולים, נוסע בכל המדינה
לדרוש ולחקור על כל הענינים, ובדרך נסיעתו בקר גם את ר' בונם ז"ל בפרשיסחא, וכמה
השתומם למצוא בהרבי הנ"ל שהלשינו עליו לבעל הזיה מה שלא מצא בכל הרבנים בזמנו,
איש פלוסופי וחוקר. ומה שהשתומם ביותר לראות לפניו חכם גדול המדבר צחות בשפת
אשכנז, פולניה ורומית. באיש הזה מצא אחד מבעלי האשכלות, איש שהכל בו, שהאיר לו
את הדרך והמסלה החדשה, שכל דרכם של הכת לקדש ולצרף את המחשבה והמצות
המעשיות. (חליפת מכתבים בין רא"י וייצנפלד ובן חביריו,עמ'81)

(53) אדמו"ר זצ"ל מאלכסנדר דיבר בקדשו אודת התדבקותם ברבם הקדוש הרר"ב זצ"ל,
ובישבו בש"ק על שלחנו הטהור השפיע התלהבות רשפי אש קודש על כל העומדים שם,
ובעת ישבו על השלחן בסעודה שלישית הגיעה אז דבקותם עד למעלה, והרר"ב זצ"ל הי'
אומר דסעודה ג' הוא מעין ימי הסליחות שאין אוכלין ואין שותין והם ימי עלי, והמקורבים

385

ביתר אל רבם הרר"ב זצ"ל הי' זרם של דמעות שוטף מעיניהם אז, ולא הי' ביכולתם
להתאפק מלבכות, והי' זה לסימן ולאות אצלם לידע מי מי המה אשר דבקה שם בדיבוק
והתקשרות אמתית בהרר"ב זצ"ל, וסיפר אדמו"ר הנ"ל זצ"ל כי כאשר הי' כבר רבינו זצ"ל
איזה פעמים בפרשיסחא, רצה הוא לעמוד על דעתו זצ"ל עד כמה הנהו מקושר ודבוק כבר
ברבם זצ"ל, ובש"ק קודם סעודה ג' העמיד עצמו אחורי רבינו זצ"ל ובתוך הסעודה כשהי'
בבהמ"ד חושך אפלה משש את מצח קדשו של רבינו זצ"ל והנה כל פניו מלאות דמעות, אז
ידע והבין כי כולו שלהם הוא עכל"ק. (מאיר עיני הגולה קיד)

(56) בן אחד הי' לרבינו זצ"ל אשר בהיותו כבן ד' שנים הראה נפלאות ברב חריפותו וחריצות
שכלו, ורבינו זצ"ל הגיד עליו גדולות ונוראות אודת נשמתו הגבוהה, ופ"א כשהכין רבינו
א"ע ליסע לפרשיסחא הרבתה אשתו הרבנית ז"ל לבכות רב בכי והתחננה לפניו שלא ישים
בסכנה את נפש בנם הילד החביב עליהם כבבת עינם. אבל רבינו זצ"ל לא השגיח ע"ז והילד
הי' אז כבן ז' שנים ולוה אותו את רבינו זצ"ל בדרכו לפרשיסחא עד חוץ לעיר וווארשא, וכאשר שב
רבינו זצ"ל מפרשיסחא, מצא את בנו הנ"ל מושכב במטה, ובמשך איזה ימים נפטר לבית
עולמו תנצב"ה. (מאיר עיני הגולה קכד)

(57) וכאשר פתר רבינו כן הי' כי אח"ז נתגברה עליו ההקפדה מאת הצדיקים על התדבקו
במסנ"פ כ"כ ברבו הקדוש מפרשיסחא, והי"ל סבות רבות רח"ל מפטירת בניו היקרים,
ופ"א סיפר רבינו זצ"ל בעצמו בזה"ל יי"ז נסיעות נסעתי לפרשיסחא וי"ז סיבות הי' לי
מהעדר בנים רח"ל וידעתי בטח שהעונש הי' מהקפדתם של הרבנים הקדושים מקאזיניץ
ומאפטא זצ"ל, אבל אין לי שום חרטה על מעשי. (מאיר עיני הגולה קכב)

(58) במשך הזמן שלא נסע רבינו זצ"ל לקאזניץ, התאמצו חסידי פרשיסחא שבווארשא ידידי
רבינו מכבר לפעול אצלו ליסע לפרשיסחא ורבינו זצ"ל אמר להם שטוב בעיניו הדבר אבל
הנהו חושש מאוד מהקפדתו של הרה"ק ר"מ מקאזיניץ לאשר יש לו שנאה מיוחדת על
חסידי פרשיסחא ורבם הרבי ר"ב זצ"ל ומכש"כ לאשר הוא נתגדל אצל המגיד זצ"ל וחיבבו כבנו
יש יותר מקום לחוש להקפדה, וגם גילה להם הצער מאשתו שהיא בוכה ומיללת עליו שלא
יסכן נפשות זרעם חייו מפאת הקפדת הרה"ק מקאזיניץ ואמר להם כי אמת הדבר שבמה
שנוגע לעבודת הש"י לא ישגיח על שום דבר אבל לא הוחלט עדיין אצלו אם דייקא זהו הדרך
האמתי לעבודת הש"י. (מאיר עיני הגולה צד)

(59) ...וכן אמר אדמו"ר זצ"ל מקאצק כי רבו הרבי ר' בונם מפשיסחא זצ"ל הרים ועזר לכל
הבאים לחסות בצלו, ואני רוצה שיקח לו כל אחד בעצמו...(חשבה לטובה כ)

פרק י

תפילה

(4) ואתחנן אל ה' וגו'. אין כתיב ואחנן, רק בת"ו לשון התפעל, כמו שאמר הרבי ר' בונם זצ"ל
על הפסוק (תהלים קט, ד), ואני תפלה, שנעשה הוא בעצמו תפלה, כן אמר ואתחנן, " אין בין
געווארען בעהטיוודיג" (נעשיתי תחינה) (חשבה לטובה ס)

איחור זמן תפילה

(9) בכל דור ודור מי שהוא צדיק הדור, רואה רצון השי"ת, כמו שכתוב (משלי י, לב) שפתי צדיק ידעון רצון. והיהודי הקדוש זללה"ה בדורו ראה רצון השי"ת באיחור זמן תפלה, ונסמך על מאמר הכתוב (דברים יב,ד) ' לא תעשון כן לה' אלהיכם', 'כן' רומז על קביעות בלי חיים. וכשראה רצון השי"ת בזה, לכן התאחר בתפלתו. ונשמתו מאירה בגן עדן מזה, כי כיון לאור רצון השי"ת, אף כי יכול זאת בשינוי זמנים להשתנות, מכל מקום נאמנה את אל רוחו עד עת קץ. (מי שילוח חלק ב' פרשת בהעלותך ע' כט)

(10) ידוע מזקני הקדוש והנורא היהודי זצלה"ה שהתפלל אחר זמן התפלה, באמרו, כי הוא עושה זמן תפלה לבדו בעבורו. ותפלתו היתה במסירות נפש כידוע. (ארן עדת, מאמרי חג השבועות ע' כד)

(13) ...אכן נראה, דהתפלה היא מקובלת דוקא אם היא מעומק הלב ובעצמות הנפש הוא מתפלל אז התפלה הזאת רצויה... (קול שמחה מט, פרשת ויגש)

(15) ועשו לי מקדש ושכנתי בתוכם. הרבי ר' בונם זצ"ל אמר : כשמתפללין צריכה רק הנפש לבד להתפלל, והגוף יהיה כמו שנגרר אחריו אלומה של תבן, " אייז סנאף שטרוי שלעפט זיך נאך", ואז ושכנתי בתוכם, בתוכם ממש. וזה ועשו לי מקדש, שאם לא כן, הרי הוא עץ בעלמא, "אייז שטיק האלץ". (חשבה לטובה כח)

(16) כשהייתי פעם ראשון לפני אדמו"ר הרה"ק מפרשיסחא קבלתי אי"ע לפניו שכואב ראשי אלי בעת התפלה שדחקתי אותי מאוד להתפלל בכוונה. ובלימוד לא כאב ראשי. ואמר כי מה לראש אצל התפלה העיקר היא עבודת הלב כמ"ש (תענית ב'.) ולעבדו בכל לבבכם... (רמתים צופים ג .יט)

(17) אמר שהתפלה צריך שיהיה מוחו ולבו שוין ונובעת מלבו ונפשו כחץ מכל חושיו בלא שום עבודה ודחק, וכל העבודה הוא רק קודם התפלה, ואם אינו במדרגה זאת ועם כ"ז דוחק את עצמו בכל מאמצי כוחות נפשו ואינו מגיע למדריגה זו, ידע שבכל תיבה ותיבה פודה את נפשו ממיתה בידי שמים אחת עכד"ק. (תורת שמחה רקו)

(18) ...והי' אומר שהיהודי הקדוש זצללה"ה אשר הוא הי' משהה זמן כביר בתפלתו. הי' שוהה רק בעבודתו הגדולה במקום אחד עד אשר הי' (מכוון) וכשהי'(מכוון) הי' מתפלל אח"ז כל התפלה בזמן קצר מאוד. (תפארת היהודי קסה)

סגנון התפילה

(19) עבודת היהודי הק' זי"ע בכל כחו הי' במסה"נ. הרה"צ החסיד מ"ו משהלי"י מראזוווידוב בקיר"ה אמר כמעט כר' יהודה דהוי מצלי בכל תלתין יומן (רי"ה לי"ה) לא הי' יכול להשלים כל תפלתו כשהגיע לויברך דוד ראו כמעט יציאת נשמתו מאהבה ודבקות. (תפארת היהודי קעא. עד)

(24) סיפר היהודי הקדוש זי"ע שהי' רואה פי"א את הקדוש ר' נטעילי חעלעמער זצללה"ה שלא הי' מתפלל בר"ה לא בלילה ולא ביום א' (אך הי' עומד על רגליו בלי שום תנועה עיין בס' רמי"ץ) אמר היהודי הק' זי"ע שזה הוא מחמת יראה ופחד. (תפארת היהודי קסו. נה)

(26) ובאזנינו שמענו שהקדוש הרבי ר' בונם מפרשיסחא זצללה"ה, היה מתפלל בלי שום תנועה, אלא היה עומד כמו עמוד של אבן, ורק עיניו זולגות דמעות ושופעות ללא הפוגות. (שם משמואל פ' ואתחנן, שנת תרע"ה)

(27) ...שסיפר כ"ק אבי אדמו"ר זצללה"ה שבאשר היותו בנעוריו חלש ורוקק דם רח"ל לקחהו זקיני אדומו"ר הגדול זצללה"ה מקאצק להיות מתפלל ברי"ה עמו בחדרו שעל יד בהמ"ד הגדול וראה אותו מתפלל שמ"ע ברי"ה ברכות ותקיעות בלי שום תנועה והתפעלות אלא שהיו פניו בוערות כלפידים... (שם משמואל פרשת קרח, רסז)

(30) סיפר הרה"צ הר' הירש טאמאשאוער זצ"ל כי בפעמים הראשונים שבא רבינו זצ"ל לפרשיסחא הי' הוא ביחד עמו בבהמ"ד וכו', והנה רבינו זצ"ל הי' רגיל כ"פ לעשות תנועות משונות הן בהכנה לתפלתו הן בעת עיונו העמוק, והיו אז איזה חסידים שהביטו בתמהון על תנועותיו המשונות כי לא הורגלו בזה, והי' הדבר מוזר מאוד אצלם, ובעת שהכין א"ע להתפלל, נגש להשלחן א' מחשובי החסידים וחטף את התפילין שלו, ואדמו"ר הק' מקאצק זצ"ל עמד בקצה האחר של הבהמ"ד וראה זאת מרחוק ותיכף רץ לשם במהירות ונתן קולו בגערה על החסיד ההוא " צריך להיות לך דרך ארץ" (מאיר עיני הגולה קיג)

(31) פ"א אמר במוצאי יוה"כ שהיה לו יוה"כ טוב ושהיה עומד במדריגה אחת משעה שנכנס יום הכפורים עד מוצאי יוה"כ בלי נטייה כלל וכלל ואפילו רגע אחד עכד"יק. (רמתים צופים לא. ק)

(39) ...ואגב סיפר ההגה"ק שליט"א מביאלעברזיג שפ"א בא איש לפני צדיק אחד שהי' צריך לישועה בעת צרתו. וביקש מהצדיק הנ"ל שיתפלל בעדו. ושאל אותו הצדיק לאיזה רב הוא נוסע. והשיב להרה"ק היהודי זיי"ע. ואמר לו אם יקבל עליו מהיום והלאה שלא יתנהג בהתנהגות היהודי הק' זיי"ע ולאחר זמן תפלה בטח יושע במהרה. והאיש הנ"ל מחמת שהי' בעת צרה ר"ל קיבל עליו את דברי הצדיק הנ"ל. (נפלאות היהודי פג)

(43) ...היא הרגיז חומות המחזיקים בנושנות בהורותו, כי לא יוכל בן אנוש להיות כמכונה זו ערוכה בכל ושמורה לעשות ככל אשר יגיעה מסובב אופניה בקרבה, וכי פחתה היא ביקרת כבוד הבורא לחשוב אותו כעומד ובידו מורה שעות לראות אם מלא היהודי בזמן וברגע קבוע ככל אשר נטל עליו, ומראה פנים נזעמים לכל אשר יאחר להביא לו קרבן תודתו לבקש רחמיו... (כתר כהונה 128)

(44) ...עפ"י רוב ישבו בבתי המדרש של המתנגדים, למרות עיניהם, וכלי מקטרת בידם בעת התפלה, ולא שעו גם בהגיע הש"ץ לקדושה וברכו, באמרם: אי רבנו אדומ"ר מיתרים אחוזים בעקבות הש"ץ, אשר אם יתנועע הוא לנתר ולדלג, נקפץ גם אנחנו לחפצו. המה התפללו תפלת שחרית על הרוב אחר חצות היום, ורק רגעים אחדים עמדו בטלית ותפילין ברגש קודש ...ואם היה להם מקום תא מיוחד, לא התפללו בו בצבור, רק באו שמה להתבודד במועדם. (כתר כהונה 129)

(46) (שמיני עצרת) הרבי ר' בונם זצ"ל הזהיר את החסידים שביום שמיני עצרת יתפללו כולם בציבור ובזה יתוקנו כל התפלות שהתפללו ביחידות במשך כל השנה. (חידושי הרי"ם רסח)

(55) ...ששמעתי ממורי ז"ל מפרשיסחא, שפעם אחת שמע דרך הכותל שאיש א' מתפלל בכוחות גדולות, הבין והשכיל שמייגע את עצמו להעביר המחשבות זרות. המתין לו עד אחר התפלה, ושאל אותו מה זה שהרעשת בכוחות גדולות בהתפלה, ושתק ולא ענהו לו. ומורי ז"ל מחמת שהבין שזה היה מחמת מחשבות זרות, אמר לו איעצך בני שמע בקולי וטוב לך. כאשר יבא לך איזה מחשבה זרה, כגון סוס או כדומה, אל תדחה אותה. רק תעמוד מעט במחשבתך,

388

ותאמת שיש כאן סוס וכדומה. ובאמת הרי אין כאן שום דבר, ובזה יבוטלו המחשבות. (בית יעקב אלכסנדר פ׳ נח)

פרק יא

הביקורת נגד פרשיסחא

(3) בתשעה באב אחרי חצות היום, בשנת תק״פ ביום ההילולא של החוזה מלובלין התכנסו רבים מאדמו״רי פולין, אמרו לטכס עצה נגד בית פשיסחה ״הסוטה״ מהדרך המקובלת לדעתם של רבים מהמשתתפים. עדים שנראו בעיני הבאים כנאמנים הפליגו בסיפורי זוועה על התנהגותם של תלמידי פשיסחה המגיעה להתפרקות מכל מוסר ודרך ארץ, מיראת שמים ויראת חטא, מהם והעידו על חסידי פשיסחה המקילים בהנחת תפילים ומהם שהעידו על מעשים הגובלים בחילול שבת, מהם ודרשו להתיר דם, לראות בהם פורקי עול שיש להתנהג כלפיהם לפי העקרון של מורידין ואין מעלין ומהם ודרשו להטיל נגדם חרם חמור, לא באו המשתתפים לידי הסכמה כללית, החליטו לזמן אסיפה נוספת. (ספר אלכסנדר 21)

(10) כאשר ראו מתנגדי הרר״יב זצ״ל הכבוד שנתכבדו רבינו זצ״ל וחביריו מאת הרה״ק מאפטא זצ״ל הרע הדבר מאד בעיניהם, והחליטו לעורר טענותיהם בגלוי לפני כל וראש המדברים הי׳ הרה״ק ר׳ יוסילי יארטשובער הנ״ל כי הבינו שדבריו יתקבלו יותר יען הנהו ספון וחשוב אצל הרה״ק מאפטא זצ״ל והוא עורר את כל הנאספים כי עת לעשות לה׳ ולעמוד בפרץ ולנדות ולהחרים ח״ו את הרר״יב מפרשיסחא ואת כל ההולכים בעקבותיו ונמשכים אחריו כי הנם סרים ממש מדרכי החסידות, מדברים תועה ומבזים את כל הצדייקים ותלמידיהם, מקילים בכמה מיני איסורים, ומאחרים את זמן התפלה עד אחר חצות היום, וכמעט שפסק לגמרי אצלם לימוד תורה הנגלית, עושים כל ימיהם כחגים, אוכלים ושותים ומזמרים ומרקדים, ועי״ז נעשים כל החסידים לקלס ולשמצה בעיני העם ונצמח מזה חילול השם. (מאיר עיני הגולה קן)

(11) ...והיו אז כמה מהולכי רכיל שהוציאו דבה על חסידי פרשיסחא שאינם נזהרים לקיים דינים המפורשים בש״ע ושמקילים בפירסום שלא לצום בד׳ תעניות ושלא להמתין שיעור הזמן הקבוע בין אכילת בשר לחלב וכדומה... (מאיר עיני הגולה פו)

(12) ...ה׳ יש לאל ידו, וזרוע מושלה לו, להושיע לתורתנו הקדושה! ובודאי רצונו בכל לב לעשות כן! ...להכנע מפני תלמידי חכמים, למען יינקו משדי תורת הויות דאביי ורבא, על פיהם ילכו. ולא יטו מחוקי המסורה מחכמינו ז״ל, עוד קטן לגדול יבזה, ולכנות שם גנאי- למצוה רבה תחשב להם...עוברים על דיני ׳שולחן ערוך׳ בשאט נפש, לשלוח חצי גבור שנונים, לבזות תלמידי חכמים, כי כל חכמי הגמרא כאין נגדם! בי״ז בתמוז אכלו לאור היום, ואבל תשעה באב- לשמחה הפכו ...למען קדושת שמו יתברך ותוה״ק, אחלי יכונו דברי באזניו, ואת הטוב יקבל ואת הרע לא יקבל, כי מרוב שיחי וכעסי על עלבון התורה ולומדיה כתבתי, ובפרט, שלא אותו והנמשכים אחריו, נשאתי חרפה למען בושת פניהם, אפס, על אותם אשר יחפו דברים! לא כן עליו, אשר לא עלה על לבו, ולא יעלה על אחד מקטני עמנו, האחוזים בתורתנו הקדושה באמת״!... (מהמכתב של הרב חרל״פ לר׳ בונים)

15) את קולו, קול עוז חוצב להבות אש, בין אבני אש יתהלך, אזני שמעה ותבן לה, תוכחת מגולה וגו'. ונאמנים פצעי אוהב ה' ותוה"ק, יהלמני צדיק חרפה כהנא וכהנה. ידעתי כי לא משנאה וקנאה ידבר, רק מתוך רשפי אש ה' אשר בקרבו, ואהבת תמים דעים בשלהבת ה'. חכמתו יראתו וגדולת למודו, שמעה אזני מפי כבוד אוצר בלום בנסתר ונגלה וגו' מו"ה יצחק מלובלין זלה"ה, ומה גם מכבוד מרן הרב הגאון מו"ה יעקב יצחק היהודי זלה"ה, כמעט לא זז מחבבו, ותמיד תהלתו בפי הי'. על כן, פקודתו שמרה רוחי. ואולי אוכל רבות עשות, ואעשה למען קדושת שמו יתברך ואהבתו כלבי, ועל כל פשעים תכסה אהבה ושלום למר ולתורתו. (מכתב של ר' בונים)

16) ...יש דרך פשוטה בעבודת הבורא.. לעשות כל המצוות לאמיתן, להתפלל בציבור ובזמנה ולהתרחק מכל מיני שחוק וטיול לבטלה, וזה נקרא דרך צדיקים. ויש עוד דרך אחרת, דהיינו שלא להתפלל לפעמים עם הציבור, ופעמים לאחר זמן התפילה, בכדי להתפלל בכוונה יתירה ושאר עניינים בדומה לזה, וזה נקרא מעשיהם של רשעים לשמה. (לקוטי מהרי"ל, פ' בראשית, ד"ה במדרש)

18) ...אומרים על הרבי ר' בונים מפרשיסחא שהוא בעל מוחין ומדרגות, תאמר לרבך בשמי שאני מבקש מהשי"ת הבקשה הכתובה בתורה ממשה רבינו ע"ה שאמר מחני נא מספרך אשר כתבת, וכוונתי לבקש מהשי"י מחני נא, תן לי מוחין והשגות אבל רק מספרך אשר כתבת, שהשגות והמדרגות יבואו לי מן לימוד התורה, אמנם לא מן מסחרם ותיאטראות בדאנציג... (מאיר עיני הגולה 99)

20) סיפר חסיד ישיש מעיר וורשא שנסע פ"א ביחד עם רבינו זצ"ל לקאזניץ לרבם הרה"ק ר"מ זצ"ל ועמדו להנפש באמצע הדרך בכפר א' באכסניא, וכשרצו ליסע הלאה באה מרכבה א' לאותו כפר וירד מהמרכבה הרבי ר"ב זצ"ל מפרשיסחא וכשראה את רבינו זצ"ל שאלו בזה"ל אברך מאין אתה ומה שמך והגיד לו שמו ושהנהו מעיר וורשא ושאלו למה אינך בא אלי לפרשיסחא, והשיב לו אני נוסע לקאזניץ והחסידים בקאזניץ אומרים שצריכים לברך בכל יום שלא עשני פרשיסחער חסיד. אמר לו הרבי ר"ב זצ"ל תדע כי עוד תבוא אלי בפוזמקאות של רגליך. (מאיר עיני הגולה פט)

21) ...תלמיד הרוצה להתלמד, לא יאבה להתנהג במנהג העוקר איזה הלכה מדברי תורתנו הקדושה, כגון לבטל עונת קריאת שמע ועונת תפילה בזמנים שקבעו חז"ל. הגם שיפתוך כמה אנשים מתחכמים לדעתם, באומרים שמן הצורך להמתין עד ירגישו יפעת שפעת מוחין דגדלות, תדע ידידי שזו עצת היצר הרע" (דרך פיקודיך, מצוות לא תעשה, טז)

30) עוד מהני"ל בעת שהמשיך עדה אחרי פטירת רבו הק' היהודי זצ"ל התקרבו אליו אנ"ש בהתלהבות עד שהפקירו עצמם. ולא דאגו על לפרנסה ומזונות ב"ב כלל. וע"ז נפל החן שלו בעיני הבעלי" המתנגדים יותר משאר צדיקי דורו. וכל מה שרדפוהו יותר התקרבו אליו יותר. ופי"א בא אליו אברך מופלג מופלא להסתופף בצילו ונסע אחריו חותנו. ובא לפניו הרבי ר' בונם בחוצפא לאמר הלא אתם מקלקלים אנשים בעלי צורה, לישב אצליכם ולהשליך הכל, ואתם אומרים שמלמדים אתם יראת שמים הלא אתנו הס' ראשית חכמה ורוקח ועוד שכתוב בהם יותר ממה שאתם בעצמיכם...(אור שמחה לו)

ההבדלים בין ר' בונים ליהודי ומנחם מנדל

48) פעם אחת סעד ר' הקדוש אחר התפלה לחם עם בארשט(- חמיצת סלק), והיה נדמה לו שהיתה לו הנאה מהמאכל, וקיבל על עצמו עונש עבור שנהנה מהעולם הזה. (אור הנר ע' יב)

49) הרה"ק רבי ישראל מרוזין אמר להרב הקדוש רבי נחמיה יחיאל מביחאווע, כי שמע שאביו, רבנו הק', הדריך מאוד את בניו הקדושים ויסרם לילך בדרך ה'. על כך השיבו, אמת. וסיפר לו שפעם אחת בימי חורף נסע אביו הק' אל הרה"ק רבי מנחם מענדיל מרימנוב, ולקח עמו את בנו הרב הקדוש רבי ירחמיאל. בנסיעתם תעו בדרך ונסעו כל הלילה, ובבוקר כשהאיר היום עלו על דרך המלך, וקרוב לחצות באו לכפר אחד, ושם היה ליהודי אחד קרעטשמי (אכסניה). ויהי כאשר נכנסו אליו, הכין עצמו רבנו הק' לתפלת שחרית, ובנו הק' התפלל בחדר אחר. לאחר התפלה, יען כי חלש לבו למאד, לקח הרב הקדוש רבי ירחמיאל תפוח אדמה וזרקו אל התנור, ונטלו במהירות לאכלו. תוך כדי כך פתח רבנו הק' את דלת חדרו וקראו אליו ואמר לו, כל הלילה תעינו ונסענו כל העת וחצי היום בדרך, וכעת אשר תודה לה' כי באנו לישוב, הזהו ישוב הדעת' שלך לאכול בתאוה ובמהירות. וקנס אותו עבור זה שעד רימנוב לא לקחו אל תוך מרכבתו, והוכרח לעמוד בחוץ על הדרגש, אף כי היה קר מאוד. (תפארת היהודי 148 .9)

50) הרבי רב בונם זצ"ל אמר: מאוד היה ישר בעיני, להיות סאלע גדולה עם מטות וקנאפעס, ושלחנות עם יין וצלי ואינדיקעס, ולומר מעט תורה, ומי שמבקש לישן ישן קצת, ויאכל צלי ויין, ולומר עוד דברי תורה מעט, באמת הוא טוב כך, כי כשלוקחין הכל למקום הצריך הוא טוב מאוד, ואין צריך להיות סגור, רק יוכל להתפשט גם בכל הדברים וללוקחם לפה, ולמשה רבינו ע"ה אמר הקב"ה נעל מסגרותך, הסר להיות מתפשט בכל, ולהעלות למקום הראוי... (חשבה לטובה צט)

53) ...שיש צדיק שהנהגות שלו הם בסיגוף גופו ויש צדיק שאוכל ושותה ואינו מסגף עצמו כלל, והוא ג"כ צדיק גדול וקדוש מאוד נעלה בטו"ז אה"ע סי' כ"ה... (תורת שמחה רפט)

54) ...כדרכו בימי עשרון כי הי' מפונק גדול. ואכל ושתה שם איזה שבועות עד שעלה לסך חמישה ועשרים רו"כ ... (אור שמחה נו)

55) שמעתי בשם הרה"ק ר' שמחה בונם מפרשיסחא זצ"ל שהי' רואה בג' איך שרב צדוק התענה מ' שנים והיה תנא, והי' רואה איך שתנא א' היה אוכל עגלים פטומים אמר כיוון שיכול להיות תנא אפילו אוכל עגלים פטומים מוטב שאוכל ואהיה תנא מלהתענות עי"ש. (תורת שמחה שיח)

68) ...וקשה איך היו רגליו מתנגדות לדעתו ורצונו אך באמת היו רגליו מוליכים אותו למקום שהיה חפץ רק שע"י שהלך בעסקים הגשמים ג"כ בחשבון עי"ז נתוסף בו כח להשתוקק לתוה"ק וזה חשבתי דרכי בכל הדרכים עי"ז ואשיבה רגלי אל עדותיך. (אמת ואמונה תמה)

76) שמעתי בשם הרה"ק רבי שמחה בונם מפרשיסחא זצ"ל זיי"ע שאמר על המשנה באבות (פרק ו' משנה ד'): כך היא דרכה של תורה, פת במלח תאכל, ומים במשורה תשתה, ועל הארץ תישן, וחיי צער תחיה, ובתורה אתה עמל וכו'...גם הקשה, מהו לשון וחיי צער 'תחיה'. ואמר, אף שחייך הם לי"ע חיי צער, אעפ"כ- 'תחיה', ולא יהא לך שום עצבות, רק תהיה בשמחה ובחיות. (נפלאות חדשות דף ד' ע"ב)

79) ...מה שאמר כ"ק זקיני זצללה"ה מקאצק על ספר בחינות עולם וז"ל מה ענינו שהוא מהביל העולם מי יתן שגם הגוף יהי' כן. (שם משמואל פרשת אמור ש)

85) ...פ"א נתן על ידו סוחר אחד את בנו להשגיח עליו. והוא ימכור העצים שלו בלילה הלך עמו. ופתאום נעלם מאתו ויחפש אחריו ולבו ניבא לו על בן הסוחר שהלך לבית זונות. ונכנס לשם ובבית החצון עמד שם עוגב (פורטיפייאנע) ומשוררת אחת ישבה שם ושילם לה שתשיר מאתו הנומר הידוע לו. שבכח זה הניגון להוציא איש ממקומו עד שיצא מהחדר הפנימי. וכראותו אותו עשה א"ע כלא ידע. ואמר לו הלא בא א' סוחר א' אתה כאן. הלא בא סוחר א' עבור הסחורה.

ומהרה הלך אתו. ומחמת הבושה אולי מרגיש הרר״ב. עד דאזיל סומקא ואתי חוורא. הראה
לו הרבי ר׳ בונם כאילו אינו כ״כ מקפיד. ושחק עמו בקלפי הקארטין. עד שהחזירו לדעת
הישרה, ולמחרת הלך עמו על הטיאטר. אבל הרבי ר׳ בונם שכב שם בחדרו בפישוט ידים
ורגלים באמירת תהלים בהתלהבות עד שהוציא את האברך מכוחותיו החומרים ונעשה
בע״ת גמור... (אור שמחה מב)

(86) 'משכיל' למדן אחד היה בקראקא, שהיה נוטה למינות רח״ל, והחסידים חסו על תורתו
ובקשו לעורר בקרבו יראת שמים, ואמר לו אחד מהם שיואל לנסוע עמו לתייר בעולם,
והסכים לכך, ובתום נסיעתם באו לפרשיסחא, ושם הפציר בו הלה שיכנס עמו אל רבנו הק׳,
בתואנה כי יהיה לו ממה להתלוצץ, ואף לכך הסכים. כשבאו אל רבנו הק׳, קירב את
ה'משכיל' למאוד, ולקח הכובע שלו והלביש וכיסה את ראש ה'משכיל' ושוב לקחו בחזרה
אליו. מני אז חזר ה'משכיל' בתשובה ונעשה אדם גדול. (תפארת היהודי 174 . 86)

(87) ...שמעתי בשם הרבי ר׳ בונם מפרשיסחא זצוק״ל שאמר,שלא נחשוב שאאע״ה היה נוהג
כמו האדמורי״ם בזמננו, שהם יושבים בביתם והחסידים נוסעים אליהם, הוא לא היה נוהג
כך, אלא היה מסתובב בחוצות וקורא בקול גדול : שיש בורא עולמים אחד ומיוחד, שמשגיח
על כל אחד ואחד. (שפתי צדיקים, לך לך עומר השכחה, דף ל״ז)

פרק יב

סוף המרד הקדוש

חידושי הרי״ם

(7) סיפר ששמע כמ״פ ממרן החי' הרי״ם זצוקללה״ה שאמר בשם הגה״ק הר״ב מפשיסחא
זצוקללה״ה שאמר שמה שהעולם רצים ודבקים עתה בהרביי״ם בזמננו הוא עונש
עמ״ש השכם ושלוח ביד עבדיו הנביאים וכו' היינו שלא רצו לשמוע אל הנביאים אשר נשלח
להם. ואולם בחורף האחרון סיפר ג״כ כזה בשם הגה״ק מפשיסחא זצוק״ל וסיים בזה״ל
וכמדומה לי שאינו עונש אלא תיקון שמפני שהעולם סוברים עתה על הצדיק שהוא איש
כשר ואמת לזה רצים אחריו ודבקים בו, עכלה״ק זיי״ע אמן. (שיח שרפי קודש 5 . 9)

(8) עוד בשמו הק׳. משל למלך שהי' לו בן יחיד והי' אוהב אותו מאוד והי' מפונק מאוד כבן
יחיד. פ״א סרח על המלך והגלהו למדינה רחוקה והי' נע ונד. פ״א עלה בדעת המלך אודות
בנו יחידו ושלח איפרכס אחד לבקשו הלך וביקש אותו ומצאו בכפר אחד בין החקלאים
בבית הקרעטשמי ומשתכר ומרקד עמהם והלך יחף ובלא מלבוש ושאל אותו האפרכוס מה
טובך ושאל בשלומו. והשיב לו אילו הי' לו בתי רגלים ומלבוש חם מי דומה לו אין בנמצא
אדם שיהי' לו טוב יותר ממנו כי מחמת שנתגשם מאוד לא הי' מרגיש שום דבר עבודה
וחסרון. והבן זה המשל על הגלות. וע״ז אמר הרה״ק וכו' הררי״ים זצ״ל מגור. שאפשר שזה
הי' טובה שמסתמא נתעורר מזה רחמנות יותר... (שיח שרפי קודש 5. 244)

(10) והוצאתי אתכם מתחת סבלות מצרים. והקשה על זה האדמו״ר מקראנעוויץ זצ״ל בשם
הגה״ק מוהרש״ב זצלה״ה מפרשיסחא זצ״ל מדוע לא נכתב עבדות או לשון רק מלשון
סבלות, ועל זה השיב כי בתחלת השעבוד היה אצליהם קשה הדבר ואחר כך גם כן הרגלו
אצליהם והיה אליהם כהרגילות כי הרגל נעשה טבע ואחר כך כאשר השי״ת ראה שהם
רגילים לעבדות פרעה ומשוקעים היו בחומר ובלבנים ולא הרגישו ואמר והוצאתי אתכם

392

מתחת סבלות מצרים בלשון עטץ קאנט שוין סובל זיין די מצרים טויג ניכט וועל איך ענק
אויס לייעזען" עכל"ק ודפח"ח והמב"י. (שיח שרפי קודש החדש פרשת וארא 63)

(11) בפסוק (שמות ו,ו) והוצאתי אתכם מתחת סבלות מצרים כו'. אמו"ז ז"ל פירש שבני ישראל
עצמם לא יוכלו לסבול תאות מצרים. וזה קצת גאולה... (שפת אמת וארא עמ' 55)

(12) וכל הבארות אשר חפרו וגו' סתמום פלשתים וגו'. נראה (פירושו), דהנה כל דרך שעושין
להשם צריך להיות בו חיות פנימי. ואם אין בו חיות פנימי אינו עולה למעלה. והנה
הפלשתים רצו ללכת בדרכי אברהם אבינו ע"ה והי' עושין כמו שהיה אברהם אבינו עושה
רק שלא היה בו חיות פנימי וזה סתימת הדרך הזה והבן. ויצחק אבינו רצה לחפור הבאר
הזה. אף שהיה לו דרכים לה' מצד עצמו, אף על פי כן לא נמנע מלחפור באר אביו כמ"ש.
ואח"כ חפר הוא עצמו בארות. דהנה כל איש הישראלי הנגש לעבודת השם ברוך הוא צריך
שיחפור בעצמותו באר על אשר על (ידו) יוכל להתדבק בבוראו יתברך ויתעלה... (קול שמחה,
פרשת תולדות כט)

(13) הבארות אשר חפרו בימי אברהם סתמו הפלשתים, איתא בזוה"ק שהיום הוא הבארות
במצות ציצית ותפילין ופשוט, רק שצריך לייגע א"ע להבין בלשון הזוה"ק והי' אומר
שהפלשתים מסתמים את זה וממלאים עפר והי' אומר, שאין לנו מקום ליגע בהעבודה רק
מהאבות בבארות שלהם. והי' אומר, הא אומרים בכל יום אבל אנחנו עמך בני בריתך בני
אברהם אוהבך בני יצחק שנעקד על גב המזבח בני יעקב בכורך, שנכתוב בכאן כל אחד
מהאבות עם מדה שלו, ואיך לא יהי' בושה לאמר זאת ולא יגע במעשיהם, העיקר הרצון
והמבוקש הוצרך כבוד שמים ולא לחשוב בעצמו... (שיח שרפי קודש 3. 48. 116)

(15) ...ושאל מה נעשה בנותר היינו מה לעשות מהתנדבות זה אשר המה מתנדבים עוד בלי
הפסק, יותר ויותר, ואמר לו הקב"ה לך ועשה בהם משכן לעדות היינו שזה עיקר המעשה
משכן אשר עדות לישראל שהקב"ה שוכן בתוכם בלי הפסק. (חידושי הרי"ם 144)

(16) ...ושמעתי מאא"ז מו"ר ז"ל פירוש הפסוק (שה"ש ז,ב) מה יפו פעמיך בנעלים בת נדיב
ופירש כי נדיבות הרצון צריך מנעל ושמירה שלא יתפשט הרצון והחשק לדברים אחרים כו'.
(שפת אמת ויקהל עמ' 339)

(24) בבוא ההי"ק הרי"מ מווארשא מסאדגורי' והודיעו מההתנגדות דשם עליו, אמר לההי"ק
הרי"מ, ומה יעשו אם יהי' משיח מאנשי קאצק. (שיח שרפי קודש 3. 13)

(25) ...תראו להתמיד בלימוד ולהיות החפץ והרצון אמת לעשות רצון השי"ת אשר הודיענו
בתורתו, והי' מסייע להולכי בתום, וזולת זאת הכל הבל, ומה שאדם פועל אצלו איזה נטי'
לטוב ע"י ישוב הדעת הדבר טוב הרבה יותר מע"י כוחות התפלה, כי בזה יש הרבה דמיונות
שוא ע"י הרתיחות התפלה, ואינו דבר של קיימא כלל, לא כן ע"י ישוב הדעת שמברר אצלו
הטוב לטוב, הגם שאינו מרגיש בעצמו כ"כ, יש לו לשמוח אשר אינו מביא לידי גסות
כי זה העיקר, טוב ארוחת ירק וכו', וה' יתן לכם ברכה ושלום וכי"ט. (מאיר עיני הגולה 2.
(109

(30) בשם ההי"ק הרבי מקאצק זצ"ל...החילוק שבין חסיד למתנגד, החסיד יש לו פחד ומורא
מהשי"ת, ומתנגד יש לו מורא מ"השלחן ערוך". (שיח שרפי קודש 5. 44)

(32) סיפר הר' בונים משמש ע"ה שבתחלת ימי בואו לעיר גור הלך עמו פ"א בחודש אלול בבוקר
לטבול במקוה וכאשר יצא מחדרו שמע שמתפללים בציבור בבהמ"ד תפלת שחרית וכאשר
בא חזרה לא נשמע עוד קול המתפללים ואמר להר"ב כנראה כבר סיימו תפלתם וקול שופר
לא נשמע אחר התפלה וא"ל שילך להתודע אם לא שכחו לתקוע בשופר והלך ר"ב ונתודע

שלא תקעו ובא בחזרה ולא הגיד כלל לרבינו שום תשובה רק כמו שחוק קל ניכר על פניו ביודעו כי עד עתה לא היו נזהרים חסידי קאצק בזה והבין רבינו שלא תקעו בשופר ונתלהבו פניו הקדושים ואמר לר"ב שילך לביהמ"ד לצוות שיתקעו בשופר ואמר בזה"ל הלא צריכים להבין באם הי' גם על להלאה הרצון בשמים להההנהגה הקודמת א"כ מדוע לקחו את המנהיג. (מאיר עיני הגולה 343)

(37 האדמו"ר רבי ירוחם ליינער זצ"ל, בנו של ה"בית יעקב" נכד של ה"מי שילוח", כותב ("תפארת ירוחם", דף קמט, ד"ה "למען האמת") : " העירוני לקרוא את 'הדאר' גליון כז, ג' סיון תשי"א, שנדפס שם מאמר בשם " הרבי מקוצק" (תמונות ממחזה על הרבי מקוצק) ובמחזה מדובר על איזו " מאורע בליל שבת הידוע" ועל איזה רופא-שינים ד"ר קוך, שהיה מקורב להרבי. ושהמאורע הזה לא פסק מלהסעיר את הרוחות בחסידות הפולנית ונתפרש בכמה פנים ונשמר בסוד בין זקני החסידים, ובמחזה זה הואר המאורע באור המסורת החסידות שנשתלשלה איש מפי איש עדי ראייה של המאורע, ושהמאורע הזה גרם למחלוקת בין הרבי מקוצק ז"ל ובין אדוני אבי-זקני הרבי מאיזביצא ז"ל. ויען כי אנכי מבני-בניו, מצאתי לחוב קדוש לכתוב שורותי אלו להעמיד את האמת על תלה ולהצדיק הצדיק. והריני להעיד באמונה על פי מסורת אבותי הקדושים ז"ל, שכל זה הוא שקר מוחלט, ולא היו דברים מעולם, לא היה שום "מאורע ליל שבת".

BIBLIOGRAPHY

I. Primary Sources

The Yehudi (R. Yaakov Yitzhak of Przysucha)

Kedushat ha-Yehudi. H.S. Ilanberg. Bene Berak: 1997.

Keter ha-Yehudi. R. Yehezkel of Kozienice. Jerusalem: Aryeh Mordecai Rabinowitz, 1929 (Jerusalem: 1992).

Nifla'ot ha-Yehudi. Yo'etz Kim Kadesh Rakatz. Piotrkow: 1909 (Jerusalem: 1992).

R. Ya'akov Yitzhak of Pryzsucha. Zvi Meir Rabinowitz. Piotrkow: 1932.

Tiferet ha-Yehudi. Yo'etz Kim Kadesh Rakatz. Jerusalem: 1987.

Torat ha-Yehudi ha-Kadosh. Yosef Yeruham Fishel Hager. Jerusalem: 1997.

Torat ha-Yehudi. R. Yaakov Oren. Bilgoria: 1911 (Jerusalem: 1992).

R. Simhah Bunim of Przysucha

Hashavah le-Tovah. R. Hanoch Heinich of Alexander. Piotrkow: 1929 (Jerusalem: 1990).

Hiddushei ha-Rim. R. Yitzhak Meir of Gur. Jerusalem: 1987.

Kol Mevaser. Yehuda Menahem Boem. 4 vols. Raanana: 1992.

Kol Simhah. R. Aharon Walden. Breslau: 1859 (rpr. 1903; Jerusalem: 1997).

Likkutei Kol Simhah, M. Nirenberg. New York: 1955.

Meir Einei ha-Golah. Abraham Yissachar Benyamin Eliyahu Alter. Piotrkow: 1928–1932 (rpr. Brooklyn: 1970).

R. Bunim. Yehuda Menahem Boem. 2 vols. B'nai Berak: 1997.

R. Simhah Bunim of Pryzsucha. Zvi Meir Rabinowitz. Tel Aviv: 1955.

Ramatayim Zofim. R. Shmuel of Sieniawa. Warsaw: 1882 (rpr. Jerusalem: 1963).

Sefer Alexander. Yehuda Leib Levin. Jerusalem: 1969.

Shem mi-Shmuel. R. Avraham Bornstein. Jerusalem: 1992.

Siach Sarfei Kodesh. Yoetz Kim Kadesh Rakatz. 5 vols. Lodz-Piotrkow: 1923–1932.

Siah Sarfei Kodesh he-Hadash. Yoetz Kim Kadesh Rakatz. 4 vols. Bene Berak: 1989.

Simhat Yisrael (Or Simhah, Ma'amarei Simhah, Torat Simhah). R. Yisrael Berger. Piotrkow: 1910 (rpr. Israel: 1958).

R. Menahem Mendel of Kotzk

Amud ha-Emet. M. Feller. Tel Aviv: 1956.

Emet ve-Emunah. Y.Y. Artun. Jerusalem: 1948 (with numbered sections; the latter editions have only page numbers).

Ohel Torah. R. Eliezer Zvi Zeligman. Lublin: 1909.

R. Yitzhak of Vorki

Ohel Yitzhak. R. Aharon Walden. Piotrkow (rpr. Israel: 1968).

Other Hasidic Sources

Abir ha-Ro'im. R. Zvi Yehudah of Amalak.Piotrkow: 1935.

Aron ha-Edut. R. Shraga Yair of Bialobrzegi. Piotrkow: 1922.

Ateret le-Rosh Zaddik. R. Yaakov Zvi of Parisov. Tel Aviv: 1965.

Avodat Yisrael ha-Shalem. R. Yisrael of Koznitz. Munkacz: 1928.

Bet Yaakov. R. Yaakov Aaron Yanovski of Alexander. Piotrkow: 1900.

Bet Yisrael. R. Yisrael of Gur. Jerusalem: 1978.

Bikkurei Aviv. R. Yaacov Ariyeh of Radzymin. London: 1947.

Degel Mahaneh Efrayim. R. Moshe Hayyim Ephraim of Sudylkov. Jerusalem: 1963.

Derekh Zaddikim. R. Abraham Yellin. Piotrkow: 1912.

Eretz Zvi. R. Aryeh Zvi Frumer of Koziglov. Bene Brak: 2000.

Eser Atarot. R. Yisrael ben R. Yizhak Simhah Berger. Piotrkow: 1913.

Eser Nifla'ot. R. Azriel Hayim Zamlung. Piotrkow: 1932.

Eser Orot. R. Yisrael ben R. Yizhak Simhah Berger. Piotrkow: 1907.

Eser Tzahtzahot. R. Yisrael Berger of Bucharest. Piotrkow: 1910.

Esh Dat. R. Moshe Yehiel of Ozrov. Tel Aviv: 1955.

Hasidim Mesaprim. R. Yehudah Leib Lewin. Jerusalem: 1992.

Hasidismus. R. Aaron Marcus. Tel Aviv: 1954.

Hekhal ha-Berakhah. R. Yitzhak Yehudah Yehiel of Komarna. Lemberg: 1864–1874.

Hemdat Zvi. R. Zvi David Glazer. Jerusalem: 1933.

*Hitgalut ha-*Zaddikim. Shlomo Gavriel Rosenthal. Warsaw: 1927.

Ilana de-Hayyei. R Yitzhak Mordechai Padova of Oputshana. Piotrkow: 1908.

Imrei Emet. R. Abraham Mordechai of Gur. Jerusalem: 1980.

Imrei Kodesh ha-Shalem. R. Uri of Strelisk. Jerusalem: 1961.

Knesset Yisrael. Reuven Zak of Austila. Warsaw: 1906.

Likkutei Maharam Shick. R. Yosef Pinchas ha-Kohen Singer. Munkacz: 1903.

Likkutei Maharil. R. Yehudah Leib of Zekelekov. Lublin: 1899.

Likkutim Hadashim. R. Yehiel Moshe of Yadimof. Warsaw: 1899.

Maggid Devarav le-Ya'aqov. R. Dov Berish of Biale. Jerusalem: 1994.

Maggid Yesharim. R. Yisrael of Koznitz. Bilgoraj: 1937.

Ma'or va-Shemesh. R. Kalonimus Kalman Epstein. Warsaw: 1902.

Mareh Deshe. R. Aaron Israel Bornstein. Jerusalem: 2004.

Mei Shiloah. R. Mordechai Yosel of Izbica. Jerusalem: 1976.

Mikhtevei Torah. R. Abraham Mordechai of Gur. Tel Aviv: 1967.

Migdal David. R. Moshe David Leida of Virslitz. Piotrkow: 1893.

Milin Haditin. R. Abraham Yitzhak of Zubas. Piotrkow: 1901.

Mishmeret Itamar. R. Itamar of Konskivali. Warsaw: 1869.

Neot Deshe. R. Avraham of Sochaczew. 2 volumes. Edited by Aaron Israel Bornstein, Tel Aviv, 1974–1978.

Nifla'ot Hadashot. R. Yehiel Moshe of Yadimova. Piotrkow: 1897 (though the published approbations are dated 1886).

No'am Elimelekh. R. Elimelekh of Lyzhansk. Jerusalem: 1960.

No'am Siah. R. Shalom Meir Valach. Bene Berak: 2004.

Ohel Shlomo. R. Yitzchak Mordechai Rabinowitz of Palavna. Piotrkow: 1924.

Ohel Yitzhak. R. Moshe Menahem Walden. Piotrkow: 1914.

Or ha-Me'ir. R. Zeev of Zhitomir. Jerusalem: 1998.

Or ha-Ner. R. Yitzchak Mordechai Padova of Opotshana. Piotrkow: 1908.

Or ha-Nifla'ot. R. Moshe Mendel Walden. Piotrkow: 1913.

Or la-Shamayim. R. Meir ha-Levi of Apta. Lublin: 1909.

Orhot Hayyim. Gershon Henokh Leiner. Warsaw: 1890.

Pri Zaddik. R. Zaddok of Lublin. 5 vols. Jerusalem: 1972.

Sefat Emet. R. Yehudah Aryeh Leib Alter of Gur. 5 vols. Piotrkow: 1905.

Sefer Ba'al Shem Tov. R. Shimeon Menahem Mendel Vodnik of Gavardshaw. Lodz: 1938.

Sefer ha-Berit. R. Pinhas Eliyahu Horowitz. Vilna: 1897.

Sha'arei Aryeh. R. Arye Mordechai Rabinowitz. Bene Berak-Jerusalem: 1958.

She'erit Yitzchak. R. Yisrael Yitzchak Beidis of Balzitsh. Warsaw: 1910.

Shoshanim le-David. R. Shlomo Yosef Hershtok of Yozeipof. Piotrkow: 1897.

Siftei Zaddik. R. Pinhas Menahem Alter of Peltz. Jerusalem: 1970.

Tanya: Likkutei Amarim. R. Shneur Zalman of Liady. Brooklyn: 1966.

Tiferet Shlomoh. R. Shlomoh of Radomsk. Brooklyn: 1976.

To'afot Re'em. R. Aaron Menahem Mendel of Radzimin. Warsaw: 1936.

Toldot Adam. R. Yehoshua of Ostrova. Jerusalem: 1975.

Toldot Ya'akov Yosef. R. Jacob Joseph of Polonoyye. Jerusalem: 1962.

Torat Emet. R. Leibel Eiger of Lublin. 1890.

Torat Kohen. R. Alexander Zusha ha-Kohen of Plotzk. Warsaw: 1939.

Vayakhel Shlomo. R. Shlomo Zalman Rapaport. Piotrkow: 1919.

Yekhahen Pe'er. R. Hanoh Zvi Lewin of Bendin. Jerusalem: 1964.

Yekhabed Av. R. Moshe Menahem Walden. Piotrkow: 1923.

Yismah Yisrael. R. Yerahmiel Yisrael Yitzhak Danziger. Lodz: 1911.

Zekhuta de-Avraham. R. Aryeh Mordechai Rabinowitz. Bene Brak: 1949.

Zikhron Shmuel. R. Shmuel Shmaryahu of Ostovatza. Warsaw: 1917.

II. Secondary Literature

Aescoly, Aaron Ze'ev. *Hasidut be-Folin.* Edited by David Assaf. Jerusalem: Magnes, 1999.

Abrams, Meyer H., *The Mirror and the Lamp: Romantic Theory and the Critical Tradition.* New York: 1958.

Alfasi, Yitzhak. *Gur.* Tel Aviv: Sinai, 1954.

Idem. *Ha-Hasidut.* Tel Aviv: 1969.

Idem. *Ha-Hozeh mi-Lublin.* Jerusalem: Mossad Ha-Rav Kook, 1969.

Idem. *Bi-Sedeh ha-Hasidut.* Tel Aviv: 1986.

Idem. "Supernatural Apprehensions and Miracles in Hasidism" (Hebrew). In *Sefer ha-Besht,* edited by Y.L. Maimon, 12–28. Jerusalem: 1960.

Idem. "Galut u-geulah be-mishnat ha-Hozeh mi-Lublin." In *Sefer Aviad.* Jerusalem: Mossad ha-Rav Kook, 1986, 85–88.

Idem. "The Great Wedding in Austila" (Hebrew). *Shanah be-Shanah* (1988): 325–331.

Assaf, David. *Derekh ha-malkhut: R. Yisrael mi-Ruzhin* (The Regal Way: The Life and Times of R. Israel of Ruzhin). Jerusalem: Merkaz Zalman Shazar, 1997.

Idem. "Polish Hasidism in the Nineteenth Century: The State of Scholarship and Bibliographic Analysis" (Hebrew). In *Hasidism in Poland,* 357–379.

Idem. "The Expansion of Hasidism: The Case of Rabbi Nehemia Yehiel of Bychawa" (Hebrew). In *Studies in Honor of Chone Shmeruk,* edited by I. Bartal, E. Mendelsohn and C. Turniansky, 269–298. Jerusalem, 1993.

Idem. "One Event, Two Interpretations: The Fall of the Seer of Lublin in Hasidic Memory and Maskilic Satire" (Hebrew). In *Within Hasidic Circles: Studies in Memory of Mordechai Wilensky.* Jerusalem: Mossad Bialik, 1999, 161–208.

Bacon, Gershon. "Prolonged Erosion, Organization and Reinforcement: Reflections on Orthodox Jewry in Congress Poland (up to 1914)." In *Major Changes within the Jewish People.* Jerusalem: 1996, 71–91.

Bartal, Israel. *The Jews of Eastern Europe, 1772–1881.* Philadelphia: PennPress, 2002.

Idem, Rachel Elior and Chone Shmeruk (eds.). *Hasidism in Poland* (Hebrew). Jerusalem: Mossad Bialik, 1994.

Bloom, Harold. *The Ringers in the Tower: Studies in Romantic Tradition.* Chicago: University of Chicago Press, 1971.

Brill, Alan. *Thinking of God: The Mysticism of Rabbi Tzadok of Lublin.* New York: Yeshiva University Press. 2002.

Idem. "Grandeur and Humility in the Writings of R. Simhah Bunim of Przysucha." In *Hazon Nahum.* New York: Yeshiva University Press, 1997, 419–448.

Buber, Martin, *For the Sake of Heaven* (Hebrew title: *Gog u-Magog*). Philadelphia: Jewish Publication Society, 1953.

Idem. *Or ha-Ganuz.* Tel Aviv: 1977.

Idem. *Tales of the Hasidim.* 2 vols: *Early Masters; Later Masters.* Translated by Olga Marx. New York: Schocken, 1947–1948 (1961).

Idem. *The Origin and Meaning of Hasidism.* Translated and edited by Maurice Friedman. New York: Harper, 1960.

Calmanson, Jacques. *Uwagi nad niniejzzym stanem Zydow Polskich y ich wydoskonaliem.* Warsaw: 1797.

Cohen, Aviezer. *"Al ketivah ve-hoser ketivah le-bet Przysucha." Dimui* (2005).

Dan, Joseph. *Gershon Scholem and the Mystical Dimension of Jewish History.* New York: New York University Press, 1997.

Dubnow, Simon. *Toldot ha-Hasidut.* Tel Aviv: 1975.

Douglas, Mary. *Natural Symbols.* Second edition. London: Routledge, 1996.

Dynner, Glenn. "Men of Silk: The Hasidic Conquest of Polish Jewry, 1754–1830." Ph.D. diss., Brandeis University, 2002. (This work was recently published in book form with the title *Men of Silk: The Hasidic Conquest of Polish Jewish Society*, New York: Oxford Univeristy Press, 2006.)

Edinger, Edward. *Ego and Archtype: Individuation and the Religious Function of the Psyche.* New York: G.P. Putnam's Sons, 1972.

Eisen, Arnold. *Rethinking Modern Judaism: Ritual, Commandment, Community.* Chicago: University of Chicago Press, 1998.

Eisenbach, Artur. *The Emancipation of the Jews in Poland, 1780–1870.* Edited by A. Polonsky; translated by J. Dorosz. Oxford: Basil Blackwell in association with the Institute for Polish-Jewish Studies, 1991.

Eliach, Yaffa. "Jewish Chasidism, Russian Sectarians: Non-Conformists in the Ukraine, 1700–1760." Ph.D. diss., 1973.

Elior, Rachel. "The Argument over the Heritage of Habad" (Hebrew). *Tarbiz* 49 (1980): 166–186.

Idem. "Between *Yesh* and *Ayin*: The Doctrine of the Zaddik in the Works of Jacob Isaac, the Seer of Lublin." In *Jewish History: Essays in Honor of Chimen Abramsky.* London, 1988.

Idem. "Bein yirah ve-ahavah, be-omek ve-gavan." *Tarbiz* 62–63 (1993): 381–432.

399

Idem. "*Yesh* and *Ayin* as Fundamental Paradigms in Hasidic Thought" (Hebrew). In *Masuot: Professor Efraim Gottlieb Memorial Volume,* edited by A. Goldreich and M. Oron, 53–76. Jerusalem: 1994.

Encyclopaedia Judaica. 16 vols. New York: Macmillan, 1971.

Ermarth, Elizabeth. *The Premise of Realism: Realism and Consensus in the English Novel.* Princeton: Princeton University Press, 1983.

Etkes, Immanuel. *Rabbi Israel Salanter and the Beginnings of the Mussar Movement: Seeking the Torah of Truth.* Philadelphia-Jerusalem: JPS, 1993 (Hebrew: Jerusalem, 1982).

Faierstein, Moshe. *All Is in the Hands of Heaven: The Teachings of Rabbi Mordechai Joseph of Izbica.* New York: 1989.

Idem. "Gershom Scholem and Hasidism." *Journal of Jewish Studies* 38 (1987): 221–233.

Idem. "Personal Redemption in Hasidism." In *Hasidism Reappraised,* edited by Rapoport-Albert, 214–224.

Fox, Joseph. *Rabbi Menahem Mendel mi-Kotzk.* Jerusalem: Mossad ha-Rav Kook, 1967.

Frank, Nathan. *Yehudei Polin bi-yemei mlhamot Napoleon.* Warsaw: 1913.

Gellman, Yehuda. *The Fear, the Trembling, the Fire.* New York: University Press of America, 1994.

Glicksburg, S.Y. *Ha-Derashah bi-Yisrael.* Tel Aviv: 1940.

Green, Arthur, trans. and ed. *The Language of Truth: The Torah Commentary of the Sefat Emet, R. Yehudah Leib Alter of Ger.* Philadelphia: JPS, 1998.

Gries, Zeev. "The Hasidic Managing Editor as an Agent of Culture." In *Hasidism Reappraised,* 141–155.

Heschel, Abraham Joshua. *Passion for Truth: Reflections on the Founder of Hasidism, the Kotzker and Kierkegaard.* New York: Farrar, Straus and Giroux, 1973.

Idem. *Kotzk: Ein Gerangel far Emesdikeit* (Yiddish). 2 vols. Tel Aviv: 1973.

Idem. *The Circle of the Baal Shem Tov: Studies in Hasidism.* Edited by Samuel H. Dresner. Chicago: University of Chicago Press, 1985.

Hillman, D.Z. *Iggerot Ba'al ha-Tanya uv'nei Doro.* Jerusalem: 1953.

Hundert, Gershon David (ed.). *Essential Papers on Hasidism.* New York: New York University Press, 1991.

Idel, Moshe. *Kabbalah: New Perspectives.* New Haven: Yale University Press, 1988.

Idem. *Hasidism, Between Ecstasy and Magic.* Albany: SUNY Press, 1995.

Idem. *Messianic Mystics.* New Haven, Connecticut: Yale University Press, 1998.

Idem. "'Unio Mystica' as Criterion: Observations on 'Hegelian' Phenomenologies of Mysticism." *JSRI* 1 (Spring 2002): 305–333.

James, J.T. *Journal of a Tour: 1813–1814.* London: 1827.

Jacobs, Louis. *Hasidic Prayer.* New York, 1978.

Johnston, Robert. *Travels through Part of the Russian Empire and the Country of Poland.* New York, 1816.

Kallus, Menahem. "An Examination of the Term 'Thought' in the Teachings of the Besht and his Thought Transformation Practices." Paper delivered at AJS Conference, 2001.

Katz, Jacob. *Tradition and Crisis.* ed. B.D. Cooperman. New York: Schocken, 1993.

Idem. "Jewish History through the Prism of a Marxist-Zionist" (Hebrew). In his work, *Leumiyyut Yehudit: Massot u-Mehkarim* (Jerusalem: Mossad Ha-Rav Kook, 1979), 243–251.

Lederhendler, Eli. "The Decline of the Polish Lithuanian Kahal." *Polin* 2 (1987): 150–162.

Leslie, R.F. *Polish Politics and the Revolution of November 1830.* Westport, CT: Greenwood, 1969.

Levin, Yehudah Leib. *Sefer Alexander: Ha-Admor R. Hanoch Heinich ha-Kohen.* Jerusalem: 1949.

Levinger, Yaacov. "The Torah of the Rebbe from Kotzk in Light of the Statements Attributed to Him by his Grandson, R. Shmuel of Sochaczew" (Hebrew). *Tarbiz* 55 (1986): 413–431.

Idem. "The Authentic Statements of the Rebbe of Kotzk" (Hebrew), *Tarbiz* 56 (1987), 109–129.

Mahler, Raphael. *Hasidism and the Jewish Enlightenment: Their Confrontation in Galicia and Poland in the First Half of the Nineteenth Century.* Trans. E. Orenstein, A. Klein and Maachlowitz-Klein. Philadelphia: JPS, 1985.

Maimon, Solomon. "On a Secret Society." In Hundert (ed.), *Essential Papers on Hasidism,* 20:11–24.

Maimon, J.L. (ed.). *Sifrei ha-Besht.* Jerusalem: 1960.

Marcus, A. *Der Chasidismus.* Hamburg an Elbe: S. Marcus, 1927.

Morgenstern, Aryeh. *Messianism and the Settlement of Eretz Israel in the First Half of the Nineteenth Century* (Hebrew). Jerusalem: 1985.

Piekarz, Mendel. *The Beginnings of Hasidism, Ideological Trends, Midrash and Mussar Literature* (Hebrew). Jerusalem: 1978.

Idem. *Ideological Trends of Hasidism in Poland During the Interwar Period and the Holocaust* (Hebrew). Jerusalem: 1990.

Idem. "Devekuth as Reflecting the Socio-Religious Character of the Hasidic Movement" (Hebrew). *Da'at* 241 (1990): 127–144.

Idem. "Ha-Hasidut be-Aspaklariat *Tiferet Shlomo* shel R. Shlomo mi-Radomsk" (Hebrew). *Gal-Ed* 14 (1995): 37–58.

Idem. "Hasidism as a Socio-Religious Movement on the Evidence of 'Devekut.'" In *Hasidism Reappraised,* edited by Ada Rappoport-Albert, 225–248.

Polonsky, Antony, et al. *The Jews in Old Poland, 1000–1795.* London: Taurus, 1993.

Rabinowitz, Zvi Meir. "Mekorot u-te'udot le-toldot ha-Hasidut be-Folin" (Hebrew). *Sinai* 82 (1978): 82–86.

Idem. *Bein Pshyskha le-Lublin* From Przysucha to Lublin). Israel: 1997.

Rapoport-Albert, Ada, ed. *Hasidism Reappraised.* London: Vallentine Mitchell, 1996.

Idem. "The Problem of Succession in the Hasidic Leadership, With Special Reference to the Circle of Nahman of Bratslav." Unpublished doctoral dissertation, University College of London, 1970.

Idem. "God and the Zaddik as the Two Focal Points of Chasidic Worship." *History of Religions* 18:4 (1979), 296–325.

Idem. "Hasidism after 1772: Structure, Continuity and Change." In Rapoport-Albert (ed.), *Hasidism Reappraised,* 76–140.

Rosen, Kopul. *Rabbi Israel Salanter and the Mussar Movement.* London: 1945.

Idem. "The Concept of Mitzvah." Ph.D. diss., University College of London: London, 1960.

Rosman, Moshe, *Founder of Hasidism: A Quest for the Historical Baal Shem Tov.* Berkeley: University of California Press, 1996.

Idem. "Meidzyboz and Rabbi Israel Baal Shem Tov." In Hundert (ed.), *Essential Papers on Hasidism,* 209–225.

Sadeh, Pinchas. *Ish be-Heder Sagur.* Jerusalem: 1993.

Schatz-Uffenheimer, Rivka. *Hasidism as Mysticism.* Jerusalem: Magnes and Princeton: Princeton University Press, 1993. (Hebrew: Jerusalem, 1968; third expanded edition: 1988).

Idem. "Le-mahuto shel ha-zaddik be-hasidut: iyunim be-torat ha-zaddik shel R. Elimelekh mi-Lyzansk" (Hebrew). *Molad* 18 (1960): 365–370.

Idem. "Contemplative Prayer in Hasidism." In *Studies in Mysticism and Religion Presented to Gershom G. Scholem.* Jerusalem: 1967, 209–226.

Schiper, Yitzhak. "The History of Hasidism in Central Poland" (Hebrew). In *Hasidism in Poland,* 23–57.

Scholem, Gershom. *Major Trends in Jewish Mysticism.* New York: Schocken, 1967.

Idem. *The Messianic Idea in Judaism and Other Essays.* New York: Schocken, 1972.

Idem. *On the Kabbalah and Its Symbolism.* New York: Schocken, 1969.

Idem. *On the Mystical Shape of the Godhead: Basic Concepts in the Kabbalah.* New York: Schocken, 1991.

Idem. *Origins of the Kabbalah.* Philadelphia: JPS, 1987.

Idem. "Devekut, or Communion with God." In *The Messianic Idea in Judaism,* 203–227; reprinted in Hundert (ed.), *Essential Papers on Hasidism,* 275–298.

Sharot, Stephen. *Messianism, Mysticism, and Magic: A Sociological Analysis of Jewish Religious Movements.* Chapel Hill, N.C.: University of North Carolina Press, 1982.

Sherwin, Byron. *The Mystical Theology and Social Dissent: The Life and Works of Judah Loew of Prague.* Rutherford, NJ: Fairleigh Dickinson University Press, 1982.

Shmeruk, Chone. "Yitshak Schiper's Study of Hasidism in Poland." In *Hasidism Reappraised,* edited by Ada Rapoport-Albert, 404–414.

Shragai, Shlomoh Zalman. "The Hasidism of the Baal Shem Tov According to Izbica-Radzin" (Hebrew). *Sefer ha-Besht.* Jerusalem: Mossad Ha-Rav Kook, 1960.

Smolenski, Wladysla. *Mieszcanstwo warszawskie w kosncu wieku XVIII.* Warsaw: 1976.

Taylor, Charles. *Sources of the Self: The Making of the Modern Identity.* Cambridge, MA: Harvard University Press, 1989.

Teitelbaum, Mordechai. *Ha-rebbe mi-Liady u-mifleget Habad.* 2 vols. Warsaw: 1910–1913; Jerusalem: 1970.

Weiss, Joseph. *Studies in Bratslav Hasidism* (Hebrew). Jerusalem: 1974.

Idem. *Studies in Eastern European Jewish Mysticism.* Edited by D. Goldstein. Oxford: 1985.

Idem. "The Religious Determinism of Rabbi Joseph Mordechai Leiner of Iscbize" (Hebrew). *Sefer yovel le-Yitzhak Baer.* Jerusalem: 1961.

Weissenfeld, Avraham Yaacob. *Exchange of Letters between Weissenfeld Avraham Yaacob and His Friends.* Cracow: 1900.

Werses, Shmuel. "Ha-hasidut be-aspaklaria belletristit: Iyunim be-Gog u-Magog shel Martin Buber." In *Hasidism in Poland,* 317–356.

Wilensky, Mordechai. *Hasidism and mitnaggedim: A Study of the Controversy between Them in the Years 1772–1815* (Hebrew). 2 vols. Jerusalem: 1970.

Idem. "The Polemic of Rabbi David of Makov against Hasidism." *PAAJR* 25 (New York, 1956): 137–156.

Idem. "Some Notes on Rabbi Israel Loebel's *Polemic against Hasidism.*" *PAAJR* 30 (New York, 1962): 141–151.

Idem. "Hasidic–Mitnaggedic Polemics in the Jewish Communities of Eastern Europe: The Hostile Phase." *Essential Papers,* edited by Hundert, 244–275.

Wodzin, Marcin. *Oswiecenie zydowsl w Krolestwie Polsk wobec chasydyzi.* Warsaw: 2003.

Ysander, Torsten. *Studien zum Bestschen Hasidismus in Seiner Religious geschichtlichen Sonderart.* Uppsala: 1933.

Zak, Bracha. "Iyun be-torato shel ha-Hozeh mi-Lublin." In *Hasidism in Poland,* 219–239.

Zederbaum, Alexander (Erez). *Keter Kehunnah.* Odessa: 1866.

GLOSSARY

Amidah (lit.: "standing"): core of the Jewish prayer service, recited standing three times daily

Ayin: nothingness

Baal Davar: the devil

Baal Shem Tov (lit.: "Master of the Good Name"): the popular name given to R. Israel b. Eliezer, the founder of Hasidism

Besht: acronym formed from the name Baal Shem Tov

Bet midrash: house of study and prayer

Devekut: attachment to God, a goal of Jewish mysticism

Ehad: (lit.: "one") the last word of the first line of the Shema

Emet: "truth"; said by the rabbis to be the seal of God

Enlightenment (Haskalah): the movement of Westernization and modernization among Jews in Europe, beginning in the late eighteenth century

Frumkeit: Yiddish for the religious pose

Gartel: a belt worn during prayer

Gemara: rabbinical discussion of law world based on the Mishnah

Galut: exile, denoting the geographical, political and metaphysical condition of Israel

Habad: lit.: acronym of *hokhmah* (wisdom), *binah* (understanding), and *da'at* (awareness). A type of Hasidism associated primarily with the Belorussian Lubavitch dynasty, beginning with R. Shneur Zalman of Liady (1745–1813)

Ha-Kadosh Baruch Hu (lit. "the Holy One, blessed be He"): God

Hakham: lit.: wise person

Halakhah: lit. "the way"; Jewish religious law

Hasid (-im): lit. "devotee." In the context of Hasidism, a follower of one of the hassidic rebbes

Humash: printed Bible

Ilui: child prodigy

Kabbalah (lit. "that which is received; tradition"): the speculative and theosophical aspects of Jewish mysticism, based on texts dating from the twelfth century

Kavanah: inner devotion during the performance of a religious act

Kedushah (lit. "holiness"): sanctification

Keter (lit. "crown"): the introductory word of the doxology according to the Ari, which became typical of the Hasidic rite.

Kishke: Yiddish for guts

Kodshim: a section of the Mishnah dealing with the Temple

Lekha Dodi: a poem sung on Friday night when greeting the Shabbat

Maharal: R. Judah Lowe of Prague (1525–1609), influential preacher and exegete

Maariv: the evening service

Maggid: preacher

Maskil (-im): an "enlightened" one, meaning a Westernized or modernized Jew, opposed to Hasidism

Midrash: the non-legal exegesis of the Rabbis

Mikveh: ritual bath

Minhah: afternoon prayer

Mishnah: the oldest code of post-biblical Jewish law, comprising the teaching of the Tannaim, edited around the beginning of the third century CE

Mintnaggedim: opponents of the Hasidim

Mitzvah: divine commandment; by extension, a good deed

Moreh derech: guide, teacher

Mussar: the Mussar movement, a revival of ethical pietism among mitnaggedic Jews in the late nineteenth century founded by R. Israel Salanter

Ninth of Av: anniversary of the destruction of the First Temple by Nebuchadnezzar and of the Second Temple by Titus

Parashah: section of the Torah

Peshat: the literal meaning of the text

Prayer book (Heb. Seder ha-tefillot, i.e., Order of Prayers; also called in short: Siddur, i.e., "Order"): compilation of the daily prayers in their prescribed order

Rav: rabbi; legal authority

Rebbe: Hasidic leader or master

Reshimu: (lit.: impression) and by extension "what remains"

Rosh Hashanah: Jewish New Year

Ruah ha-kodesh: holy spirit

Sefirah: hypostasis of a divine attribute emanating and contracting from the Godhead and constituting part of the world emanation

Segulah: talisman

Se'udah shelishit (lit. "third meal"): The concluding meal of the Sabbath, generally held communally among Hasidim, a time of special communal intensity

Shabbat: Shabbat is observed from sundown on Friday till darkness on Saturday evening.

Shaharit: morning service

Sheliah zibbur: leader of the prayer service

Shekhinah: indwelling presence of God on earth; in the Kabbalah described in female terms

Shema Yisrael: the declaration of faith in God derived from Deuteronomy 6:4 and recited twice daily

Shofar: ram's horn, blown as part of the Rosh Hashanah service

Shtibl: Hasidic prayer house

Shulhan Arukh: code of Jewish law written by R. Joseph Karo, sixteenth century

Simhah: joy

Sukkah: the frail outdoor booth in which Jews are commanded to dwell during the fall harvest festival of Sukkot

Talmid hakham: a scholar intellectual

Talmud (learning, teaching): Canonical collection of the oral teachings of the Rebbes that were compiled during the first centuries of the Common Era

Tallit: prayer shawl

Tanya: a Hasidic work written by R. Shneur Zalman of Liady

Tefillah: prayer

Tefillin: phylacteries

Teshuvah: lit. "return"; repentance, the return to God of those who have strayed; hence also, for the mystic, the longing of all things to return to their single Source

Tisha be-Av: see Ninth of Av

Tikkun (lit. "fixing"): the redemptive process, the restoration of cosmic wholeness

Tish: (lit.: table): communal meal at the rebbe's table

Torah:: as a book, "Torah" refers to the Pentateuch

Tosafot: exegesis of the Gemarah by twelfth- and thirteenth-century rabbis of northern France and Germany

Vort: lit. "word" (Yiddish): an aphorism or pithy Hasidic teaching

Yeshivah: academy for higher-level Torah study

Yetzer hara: evil inclination

Yom Kippur: Day of Atonement

Zaddik: (lit.: righteous one) master of a Hasidic sect; holy man

Zohar: kabbalistic classic, first published in Spain in the thirteenth century

Index of Biblical and Rabbinic Sources

General Index*

General Index

General Index

General Index

Index of Names: Rabbis and Modern Scholars

Index of Names: Rabbis and Modern Scholars

Index of Names: Rabbis and Modern Scholars

Michael Rosen is the founder of Yakar (Jewish Center for Tradition and Creativity) in London, Jerusalem and Tel Aviv. He received his rabbinical ordination from Yeshivat Beer Yakov and from Chief Rabbi Unterman (Israel). Rabbi Dr. Michael (Mickey) Rosen received his Ph.D. from University College in London for his thesis entitled "A Commentary of *Job* Attributed to Rashbam."